Boston

"All you've got to do is decide to go
and the hardest part is over.

So go!"

TONY WHEELER, COFOUNDER – LONELY PLANET

THIS EDITION WRITTEN AND RESEARCHED BY

Mara Vorhees

Contents

Welcome to Boston

Boston's history recalls revolution and transformation, and it is still among the country's most forward-thinking, barrier-breaking cities.

Art & Music

The arts have thrived in Boston ever since the 19th century, when this cultural capital was dubbed the Athens of America. Certainly, the intellectual elite enjoyed their fine paintings and classical music, but they were also dedicated to spreading the cultural wealth, establishing museums, libraries and symphony orchestras. Today, the lucky residents of (and visitors to) Boston benefit from their largesse. These venerable institutions play an integral role on Boston's cultural stage, which has significantly expanded to include dynamic contemporary art and music scenes.

Sports

'Fanatic' is no idle word here. Boston fans are passionate about sports. With the four-time world-champion Patriots, the long-overdue World Series–winning Red Sox, the winningest basketball team in history, the Celtics, and the highly successful hockey team, the Bruins, there is a lot to be passionate about. Boston's college teams also inspire fierce loyalties and staunch rivalries. No less spirited are the country's oldest and most celebrated running event, the world-famous Boston Marathon, and the world's largest two-day rowing event, the Head of the Charles Regatta.

Food

A word of advice: when in Boston, eat as much seafood as possible. Local specialties include the 'sacred cod,' fresh steamed lobster, oysters on the half-shell and thick, creamy chowder. You can eat seafood around the city, but especially in the fish-centered Seaport District, where it's accompanied by spectacular harbor views. The creatures of the sea are your top priority, but don't miss the chance to devour delicious servings of pasta in the North End and to sample spicy Asian dishes in Chinatown. Trendy fusion restaurants draw on all of these eclectic influences to present contemporary cuisine that is uniquely Boston.

History

For all intents and purposes, Boston is the oldest city in the USA, and you can hardly walk a step over its cobblestone streets without running into some historic site. The Freedom Trail winds its way around the city, connecting 16 significant Revolutionary sites. These are the places where history unfolded: from the first public school in America to Boston's first church building to sites linked to America's fight for independence from Britain – Boston is, in effect, one enormous outdoor history museum.

Why I Love Boston

By Mara Vorhees, Author

Boston is wicked *smaaht*. I love that Boston is motivated not by money or politics, but by learning. The academic institutions are a source of innovative art, architecture and ideas that we all benefit from. The students provide a renewable source of energy and vibrancy that permeate the city. Yet for all the fancy buildings and big ideas, Boston is still a city of neighborhoods and local people. The students may or may not be here in four years, but my neighbors are here for the long haul. They are the cogs that keep the city running, moving, growing, remembering the past and creating the future.

For more about our author, see p256.

Above: Public Garden (p69)

Boston's
Top 10

Freedom Trail (p26)

1 For a sampler of Boston's famous revolutionary sights, follow the red-brick road. It leads 2.5 miles through the center of Boston, from Boston Common to the Bunker Hill Monument, and traces the events leading up to and following the War for Independence. The Freedom Trail is well marked and easy to follow on your own – an ideal strategy if you actually wish to enter some of the historic buildings and museums. Otherwise, there are plenty of tours that follow the trail, including the National Park Service's free option.

BELOW LEFT: GEORGE WASHINGTON STATUE, PUBLIC GARDEN (P69)

🏃 *Freedom Trail*

Fenway Park (p119)

2 There might as well be signs on I-90 reading 'Now entering Red Sox Nation.' The intensity of baseball fans has only grown since the Boston Red Sox broke their agonizing 86-year losing streak and won the 2004 World Series. The home-town team repeated its feat in 2007 and again in 2013, which means it continues to sell out every game. Catch the boys at Fenway Park, the iconic old-style ball park that has hosted the Sox for over a century.

🏃 *Kenmore Square & Fenway*

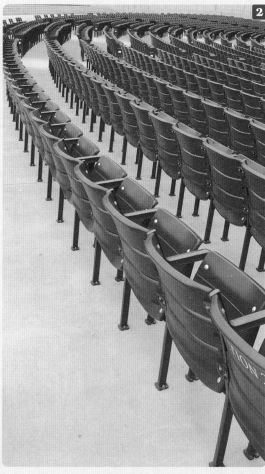

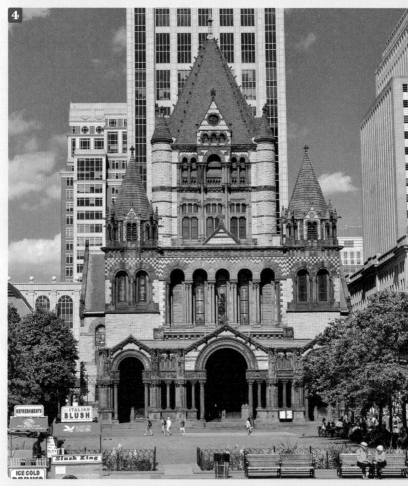

Harvard Square *(p142)*

3 Harvard Sq is overflowing with bookstores and boutiques, coffee shops and record shops, street performers and street dwellers. Many Cantabridgians rightly complain that the square has lost its edge – once-independently-owned shops are continually gobbled up by national chains – but Harvard Sq is still a vibrant, exciting place to hang out. The university is the centerpiece of the square, with ivy-covered architecture and excellent museums. Harvard Sq is also a hotbed of colonial and revolutionary history, from the Cambridge Common to Mt Auburn Cemetery.

⊙ *Cambridge*

Copley Square *(p110)*

4 Boston's most exquisite architecture is clustered around this stately Back Bay plaza. The square's centerpiece is Henry Hobson Richardson's celebrated Romanesque masterpiece, Trinity Church. It's lovely in reality and even lovelier as reflected in the mirrored facade of the modern John Hancock Tower. This assemblage faces off against the elegant neo-Renaissance facade of the Boston Public Library. The plaza itself is peppered with whimsical and serious pieces commemorating the city's biggest sporting event, the Boston Marathon, for which Copley Sq is the finish line.

LEFT: TRINITY CHURCH (P107)

⊙ *Back Bay*

Charles River Esplanade *(p110)*

5 When we talk about the 'waterfront,' we're usually talking about the Boston Harbor. But there's a second, equally appealing waterfront along Charles River. The Esplanade is a long and narrow riverside park that offers endless opportunities for outdoor recreation, from playgrounds and picnic areas to bike trails and ball parks. There's no swimming in the river, but there is sunbathing, sailing, kayaking and canoeing. The Hatch Memorial Shell is a venue for (free) outdoor entertainment, including the annual July 4 concert by the Boston Pops.

🏃 *Back Bay*

Boston Harbor Islands *(p164)*

6 If you're dreaming of an island vacation, you've come to the right place. The Boston Harbor Islands consist of 34 islands, many of which are open for trailwalking, birdwatching, camping, kayaking and swimming. Explore a 19th-century fort at Georges Island; walk the trails and lounge on the beach at Spectacle Island; or climb Boston's iconic oldest lighthouse at Little Brewster. Mostly operated by the National Park Service, the Harbor Islands offer a unique opportunity for outdoor adventure – and they're just a quick boat ride from downtown Boston. BELOW: BOSTON LIGHT, LITTLE BREWSTER ISLAND (P165)

🏃 *Day Trips from Boston*

Art Museums *(p201)*

7 Boston's museums are famed for their collections of Asian, American and European art from days gone by. But this is the 21st century, and Boston artists and curators still have something to say about it – as indicated by the city's flourishing contemporary scene. All of Boston's major art institutions have undergone massive upgrades in recent years, demonstrating that this city is at the forefront of artistic endeavor. The only disappointment is that there is never enough time to see them all.

RIGHT: INSTITUTE OF CONTEMPORARY ART (P131)

👁 *Arts & Architecture*

6

North End *(p62)*

8 What's so special about eating in the North End? For starters, it actually feels like you're in Italy. As one of Boston's oldest neighborhoods, the narrow streets and brick buildings exude an Old World ambience that is only enhanced by its Italian-American population. It sounds like Italy, too, with local residents carrying on lively conversations in the mother tongue. Most importantly, it tastes like Italy. Packed with romantic restaurants, cozy cafes and aromatic bakeries, the North End will delight the senses and the stomach.

✖ *West End & North End*

Walden Pond (p168)

9 In 1854, Henry David Thoreau left the comforts of Concord and built himself a rustic cabin on the shores of Walden Pond, where he lived for two years. From this retreat, he wrote his famous treatise on nature, *Walden; or, Life in the Woods*. Surrounded by acres of forest, the glacial pond remains a respite for children and swimmers who frolic in its cool waters, birdwatchers and walkers who stroll along the pleasant footpath, and nature lovers of all sorts. RIGHT: REPLICA OF HENRY DAVID THOREAU'S CABIN, WALDEN POND (P168)

🏃 Day Trips from Boston

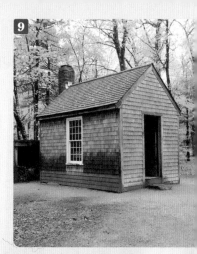

Beacon Hill (p67)

10 With an intriguing history, distinctive architecture and unparalleled neighborhood charm, Beacon Hill is Boston's most prestigious address. It's hard to beat the utter loveliness of the place: the narrow cobblestone streets lit with gas lanterns; the distinguished brick town houses decked with purple windowpanes and blooming flower boxes; and streets such as stately Louisburg Sq that capture the neighborhood's grandeur. The commercial street that traverses the flat of the hill – Charles St – is Boston's most enchanting spot for browsing boutiques and haggling over antiques.

🏠 Beacon Hill & Boston Common

What's New

Harvard Art Museums

The university's expanded and renovated art museum – designed by architect Renzo Piano – brings three distinct collections to coexist under one exquisite roof. (p142)

Edward M Kennedy Institute for the US Senate

Complementing the JFK Presidential Library at Columbia Point, the new EMK Institute contains high-tech, interactive exhibits exploring the inner workings of the US Senate, past and present. (p134)

Design Museum Boston

Design is all around you, which is why this new pop-up museum (www.designmuseum boston.org) hosts exhibits and events in public spaces all around town.

Boston Public Market

The long-awaited market on the Greenway is open every day from May to November, showcasing seasonal produce, local meats and fresh fish from New England. (p87)

New England Aquarium

The centerpiece Giant Ocean Tank has a brand new coral reef, an expanded stock of sea creatures and new windows and lighting by which to see them. (p81)

Museum of Science

The intriguing and interactive exhibits in the new Hall of Human Life encourage visitors to ask and explore how their own bodies and brains work. (p57)

Verb Hotel

Located behind Fenway Park, Boston's newest spot to sleep is a mid-century motel, renovated into a hip tribute to the city's rock-and-roll roots. (p186)

Frost Ice Bar

As if it wasn't cold enough outside, we're now invited to don parkas and perch on ice blocks, while sipping frozen cocktails and admiring Boston-themed ice sculptures. (p88)

Stage Nightclub

Boston's nightlife just got more interesting, with the opening of this Vaudevillian nightclub: acrobats, aerialists, comedians and clowns perform while folks drink, dance and gawk. (p102)

Late-night Transportation

Late-night revelers no longer need to head home two hours before last call. Now the T runs until 2am on Friday and Saturday nights.

For more recommendations and reviews, see **lonelyplanet. com/usa/boston**

Need to Know

For more information, see Survival Guide (p207)

Currency
US dollar ($)

Language
English

Visas
Citizens of many countries are eligible for the Visa Waiver Program, which requires prior approval via the Electronic System for Travel Authorization (ESTA).

Money
ATMs widely available. Credit cards accepted at most hotels, restaurants and shops.

Cell Phones
Most US cell-phone systems are incompatible with the GSM 900/1800 standard used throughout Europe and Asia.

Time
Eastern Standard Time (GMT/UTC minus five hours)

Tourist Information
Boston Common Information Kiosk (GBCVB Visitors Center; Map p234; www.bostonusa.com; Boston Common; ☺8:30am-5pm; Ⓣ Park St) is a good starting place.

Daily Costs

Budget:
Less than $100
➡ Dorm bed: $50
➡ Pizza or dumplings: $5–10
➡ Certain museum nights and walking tours: free
➡ Ride on the T: $2.10–2.65

Midrange:
$100–$250
➡ Double room in a midrange hotel: $100–250
➡ Meal at a midrange restaurant: $15–25
➡ Museum admission: $15–25
➡ Short taxi ride: $15–20

Top End:
more than $250
➡ Double room in a top-end hotel: from $250
➡ Meal at a top-end restaurant: from $30
➡ Concerts, events and other activities: from $50

Advance Planning

One month before Reserve a place to stay. Budget travelers, this means you! Buy your tickets for the Boston Symphony Orchestra, the Boston Red Sox or your favorite Boston band.

One week before Make reservations for weekend dinners.

One day before Buy tickets for tours and museums with timed entrances. Check the weather forecast.

Useful Websites

Lonely Planet (www.lonely planet.com/usa/boston) Destination information, hotel bookings, traveler forum and more.

My Secret Boston (www. mysecretboston.com) Not *that* secret restaurants, nightlife, cultural and family events.

Blue Mass Group (www.blue-massgroup.com) Left-leaning political junkies report on State House goings-on.

Universal Hub (www.universal hub.com) Round-up of local news, with rich local commentary.

Greater Boston Convention & Visitors Bureau (www.boston usa.com) The official guide to what to do and where to stay.

WHEN TO GO

Peak travel times are autumn and spring, with lovely weather and many events. Summer is humid but also busy.

Boston

Arriving in Boston

Boston Logan International Airport Take the subway (blue line) or bus (silver line) to central Boston from 5:30am to 12:30am ($2.10 to $2.65); or catch a taxi for $25 to $30.

South Station Located in central Boston on the red line.

Manchester Airport Catch the shuttle bus to Logan ($72); should be booked in advance.

TF Green Airport Take the commuter rail to South Station ($11).

For much more on **arrival** see p208

Getting Around

➡ **T (Subway)** The quickest and easiest way to get to most destinations. Runs from 5:30am or 6am until 12:30am (Sunday to Thursday) or 2am (Friday and Saturday).

➡ **Hubway** Boston's new bike-share program, with more than a thousand bikes available for travelers to borrow.

➡ **MBTA bus** Supplements the subway system.

For much more on **getting around** see p209

Sleeping

Boston is a relatively expensive place to stay, due to its busy conference and academic calendars and popular tourist appeal. Book in advance online for the best prices. Budget travelers, especially, will find there is a shortage of affordable options, so book your beds as early as possible. A few welcoming guesthouses and smaller hotels welcome midrange travelers, while many hotels of all sizes cater to high-enders. Prices increase dramatically during peak travel times.

Useful Websites

➡ **Boston Green Tourism** (www.bostongreentourism.org) Includes up-to-date listings of ecofriendly hotels.

➡ **Boston Luxury Hotels** (www.bostonluxuryhotels.com) Individualized service for upscale travelers.

➡ **University Hotels** (www.universityhotels.net) Perfect for finding accommodations near a particular university.

➡ **Lonely Planet** (lonelyplanet.com/usa/boston/hotels) Scores of properties from budget hostels to luxury apartments.

For much more on **sleeping** see p178

GOING GREEN IN BOSTON

➡ Get around town by walking, biking or taking the T.

➡ Patronize hotels and restaurants that are making efforts to reduce their environmental impact. Look for the 🌿 icon in the listings.

➡ Check out the environmental education exhibits at the Harvard Museum of Natural History, the Museum of Science and the New England Aquarium.

Top Itineraries

Day One

Downtown & Waterfront (p79)

 Spend your first day in Boston following the **Freedom Trail**, which starts on the Boston Common and continues through Downtown. There's not time to go inside every museum, but you can admire the architecture and learn the history. Highlights include the **Old South Meeting House**, the **Old State House** and **Faneuil Hall**.

 Lunch Grab a bite from one of the many outlets in Quincy Market (p86).

West End & North End (p55)

In the afternoon, the Freedom Trail continues into the North End, where you can visit the historic **Paul Revere House**, **Old North Church** and **Copp's Hill Burying Ground**.

Dinner You are perfectly poised for an Italian feast along Hanover St (p61).

West End & North End (p55)

Move on to the exquisite **Liberty Hotel**, former site of the Charles St Jail. After admiring the impressive architectural transformation in the lobby, head downstairs for a drink in the former drunk tank, which now houses the ultracool club and cocktail bar, **Alibi**.

Day Two

Back Bay (p105)

 Spend the morning admiring Boston's most architecturally significant collection of buildings, clustered around **Copley Sq**. Admire the art and books at the **Boston Public Library**, ogle the magnificent stained-glass windows at **Trinity Church** and gaze at the clean lines on the **John Hancock Tower**.

 Lunch Treat yourself to some smart fine dining at the Courtyard (p112).

Kenmore Square & Fenway (p117)

Your afternoon is reserved for one of Boston's magnificent art museums. Unfortunately, you'll have to choose between the excellent, encyclopaedic collection at the **Museum of Fine Arts** and the smaller but no less extraordinary exhibits at the **Isabella Stewart Gardner Museum**. Either way, you won't be disappointed.

Dinner Eat oysters and drink craft beer at Island Creek Oyster Bar (p125).

Kenmore Square & Fenway (p117)

There is music in the air this evening. It might be emanating from the acoustically perfect **Symphony Hall**, where you can hear the world-renowned Boston Symphony Orchestra (procure tickets in advance).

For lower-brow entertainment, catch a baseball game at **Fenway Park** or go barhopping on **Lansdowne St**.

Day Three

Cambridge (p138)

 Rent a bicycle and spend the morning cycling along the **Charles River**. Feel free to stop for scenic views of scullers and sailboats on the Charles, with the Boston city skyline as the backdrop.

 Lunch Grab a vegetarian bite at Clover Food Lab (p143).

Cambridge (p138)

While away an afternoon in **Harvard Sq**, browsing the bookstores and cruising the cafes. Catch a free campus tour (try the unofficial **Hahvahd Tour**). If you're in the mood for a museum, the university offers several excellent options.

Dinner Go casual at Night Market (p145) or classy at Alden & Harlow (p146).

Cambridge (p138)

See whatever brilliant or bizarre production is playing at the **American Repertory Theater** or at the company's second venue, **Club Oberon**. If that doesn't take your fancy, catch a band at **Lizard Lounge** or **Sinclair**.

Day Four

Downtown & Waterfront (p79)

 Spend the morning on the water. In the best-case scenario, the weather is fine and you book yourself on a **whale-watching tour** to Stellwagen Bank. Alternatively, get a closer view of the marine life inside the **New England Aquarium**. Afterwards, stroll along the **HarborWalk** and across the Old North Bridge, admiring the harbor views along the way.

Lunch Dine (with a view) at Legal Harborside (p133) or Yankee Lobster Co (p133).

Seaport District & South Boston (p129)

 Continue along the HarborWalk to the **Institute of Contemporary Art** for an afternoon of provocative contemporary art. Don't miss the amazing view from the Founders' Gallery.

Dinner Choose from colourful Chinatown (p99) or trendy South End (p96).

South End & Chinatown (p129)

Get fancied up and go out for a night on the town in the **Theater District**. Attend a show at one of the newly renovated theaters, then dance the night away at **Whisky Saigon** or **Tunnel**, or sip cocktails with the sophisticates at **Beehive**.

If You Like...

Revolutionary History

Freedom Trail The 2.5-mile walking trail includes Boston's most important revolutionary sites. (p26)

Lexington & Concord These towns are the sites of the first battles in the War for Independence. (p166)

Boston Tea Party Ships & Museum Includes replicas of the merchant ships that hosted the historic tea party. (p132)

Patriots' Day A day of re-enactments and parades commemorating the first battles of the American Revolutionary War. (p20)

Cambridge Common The city green is where George Washington took command of his army in 1775. (p142)

Contemporary Art

Institute of Contemporary Art Boston's pre-eminent venue for contemporary art boasts a dramatic waterside setting. (p131)

Museum of Fine Arts The Linde Family Wing for Contemporary Art tripled the exhibition space for its growing collection. (p120)

Isabella Stewart Gardner Museum A dynamic artist-in-residency program ensures a rich rotation of innovative exhibits and performances. (p122)

SoWa Artists Guild Visit on the first Friday of the month, when artists open their studios. (p96)

Harvard Art Museum Often shows off contemporary art from its collections in its top-floor temporary exhibit space. (p142)

JEFF MORSE/GETTY IMAGES ©

The Lexington Minuteman Statue on Battle Green, Lexington (p167)

JFK

John F Kennedy National Historic Site See where the 35th US president was born and raised. (p157)

John F Kennedy Library & Museum Learn about Kennedy's political legacy at the official presidential library. (p134)

Union Oyster House Request the JFK booth and order the lobster bisque. (p86)

Edward Kennedy Institute for the US Senate Check out the newest Kennedy venue, a tribute to JFK's brother. (p134)

Rose Kennedy Greenway Pay your respects to the matriarch of the Kennedy clan. (p84)

Literature

Concord (p167) Tour the homes and visit the gravesites of Concord's literary masters; and to Walden Pond to experience *Life in the Woods*. (p168)

Longfellow House See where the Fireside Poet composed the *Song of Hiawatha* and *Paul Revere's Ride*. (p143)

Public Garden Don't miss *Make Way for Ducklings*, a whimsical statue based on Robert McCloskey's children's book. (p69)

Boston Athenaeum Since its founding in 1807, this esteemed institution has counted many noteworthy writers and thinkers among its members. (p73)

Brookline Booksmith (p161) or **Harvard Bookstore** (p152), Boston's best bookstores host regular author talks.

Architecture

Copley Square Some of Boston's most stunning signature buildings are clustered around this plaza. (p110)

Harvard Yard Features the best of all eras, including buildings by Henry Hobson Richardson, Walter Gropius and Le Corbusier. (p140)

Massachusetts Institute of Technology The campus contains masterful examples of 20th-century modernism and 21st-century mayhem. (p141)

Design Museum Boston This pop-up museum hosts exhibits and talks all around town. (p13)

Animals

New England Aquarium Explore the most exotic of nature's marine environments. (p81)

New England Aquarium Whale Watch Sightings of whales, dolphins and other marine life are practically guaranteed. (p91)

Franklin Park Zoo Visit the Serengeti, the Australian outback and the Amazonian rainforest in one afternoon. (p158)

Harvard Museum of Natural History Hundreds of (stuffed) animals peer out of glass showcases, representing all classes and continents. (p142)

Gardens

Public Garden The Victorian-era Public Garden is an island of loveliness, always awash in blooms and breezes. (p69)

Arnold Arboretum Flowering trees galore, with collections of bonsai, lilacs, conifers, roses and fruit-laden *malus*. (p157)

Rose Kennedy Greenway The Fort Point Channel Parks show gardens by the Massachusetts Horticultural Society. (p84)

Back Bay Fens At the end of June, the Kelleher Rose Garden explodes in fireworks of colors and scents. (p124)

For more top Boston spots, see the following:
- Eating (p30)
- Drinking & Nightlife (p33)
- Entertainment (p35)
- Shopping (p37)
- Sports & Activities (p39)

Old North Church Boston's oldest church is surrounded by delightfully secluded gardens, including an 18th-century garden featuring blooms from the days of yore. (p58)

Free Stuff

Freedom Trail The National Park Service offers a free walking tour; several sites along the route do not charge admission. (p216)

Black Heritage Trail Another free NPS walking tour that explores the history of African American settlement in Beacon Hill. (p70)

Free Museum Nights The **MFA** (p120) is free on Wednesday evenings, while the **ICA** (p131) is free on Thursday evenings.

Boston Public Library See the BPL's impressive art and architecture on daily free guided tours. (p108)

Universities Both **MIT** (p141) and **Harvard** (p140) offer free campus tours.

JFK National Historic Site See the birthplace of the 35th president – for free. (p157)

Hatch Memorial Shell The Esplanade stage is the place for free summertime entertainment. (p114)

Samuel Adams Brewery Free tours of the brewery and free samples. (p161)

Month by Month

January

January represents the deepest, darkest part of winter. Expect snow and cold – great weather for sledding and skating.

⛄ Chinese New Year

In January or February, Chinatown lights up with a colorful parade, firecrackers and lots of food.

February

Still cold, but the days are getting longer. Tourists are few and far between, so prices are cheap.

🏃 Beanpot

Local college hockey teams face off in the hotly contested Beanpot Tournament (www.beanpothockey.com).

March

On March 17 the city celebrates Evacuation Day, when the British pulled out of Boston Harbor in 1776.

⛄ St Patrick's Day

The large and vocal South Boston Irish community hosts a parade (www.southbostonparade. org) on West Broadway. After 20 years of contention, the parade allowed participation by gay and lesbian groups for the first time in 2015.

🍴 Dine Out Boston

For the first two weeks of March, scores of restaurants offer prix-fixe menus (www.dineoutboston.com).

April

Emerging crocuses and forsythias signal the arrival of spring; baseball fans await opening day at Fenway Park.

⛄ Patriots' Day

On the third Monday in April, history buffs commemorate the start of the American Revolution (www.battleroad.org), with a re-enactment of the battle on Lexington Green and a commemoration ceremony at the North Bridge in Concord.

🏃 Boston Marathon

The world's oldest marathon (www.bostonmarathon.org) attracts tens of thousands of ambitious runners to pound the pavement for 26.2 miles. Held on Patriots' Day.

☆ Independent Film Festival of Boston

During the last week in April, venues around the city host screenings of independent films (www.iffboston.org).

May

This is one of Boston's most beautiful months. Memorial Day, on the last Monday in May, officially kicks off the summer season.

🔒 Mayfair

When the sun comes out, so do the good folks in Harvard Sq, for Mayfair (www.harvardsquare.org). On the first or second Sunday in May, artists, merchants and restaurants set up booths on the streets.

Lilac Sunday

On the third Sunday in May, the Arnold Arboretum celebrates the arrival of spring on Lilac Sunday (www.arboretum.harvard.edu), when more than 400 varieties of fragrant lilac are in bloom.

Boston Calling

Music lovers take over City Hall Plaza for three days of all-out, rock-out music. The festival (www.bostoncalling.com) occurs during the last weekend in May, and again during the first weekend in September.

June

June brings temperatures ranging from 55°F to 70°F, and lots of rain. Student calendars are packed with events and graduation ceremonies.

Boston Pride Festival

The week-long GLBT festival (www.bostonpride.org) kicks off with the raising of a rainbow flag on City Hall Plaza. On the second Saturday the Pride Parade attracts tens of thousands of participants.

Bunker Hill Day

Charlestown historians remember the crucial Battle of Bunker Hill. The city celebrates with a road race, followed by a parade.

July

By July the city has emptied out, as the students vacate for the summer and Bostonians head to their summerhouses. It's also Boston's hottest month.

Harborfest

The week-long Independence Day festival (www.bostonharborfest.com) starts on the last weekend in June. It includes Children's Day and Chowderfest.

Independence Day

On July 4, Boston hosts a line-up of free performances (www.july4th.org) that culminates with the Boston Pops playing Tchaikovsky's *1812 Overture*. Half a million people watch it live.

August

Summer in the city continues; only at the end of the month will you begin to feel fall coming.

Boston Carnival

Boston's Caribbean community re-creates Carnival (www.bostoncarnival.org), with spectacular costumes, sultry music and spicy cooking. Includes a Kiddies Carnival Celebration and an all-out 'Trini-style' Carnival parade.

Italian Festivals

Throughout July and August, the North End's religious societies sponsor feasts and processions honoring their patron saints. Major celebrations include the Fisherman's Feast (www.fishermansfeast.com) and St Anthony's Feast (www.stanthonysfeast.com).

September

By September the humidity disappears, the students return and the streets are filled with U-Hauls during the first week. The first Monday in September is Labor Day, the official end of the summer season.

Boston Comedy Festival

The second week in September is dedicated to funny guys and gals, who cut up at venues all around town as a part of the Boston Comedy Festival (www.bostoncomedyfest.com).

Boston Film Festival

For four days in mid-September, all Bostonians become film critics at the Boston Film Festival (www.bostonfilmfestival.org).

Beantown Jazz Festival

The Berklee College of Music sponsors this free festival (www.beantownjazz.org) in the South End.

Hub on Wheels

On the third Sunday in September, the bicycle ride, Hub on Wheels (www.bostoncyclingcelebration.com), starts at City Hall Plaza.

October

October is Boston's best month. The academic year is rolling, the weather is crisp and cool, and the trees take on shades of red, gold and amber.

Oktoberfest

On the first or second Sunday in October, Harvard Sq artisans and entertainers take to the streets. The street fair (www.harvardsquare.com) coincides with the crazy-fun Honk! parade (www.honkfest.org).

Head of the Charles Regatta

Spectators line the banks of the Charles River on a weekend in mid-October to watch the world's largest rowing event, the Head of the Charles (www.hocr.org).

✰ Haunted Happenings

Salem goes all out for Halloween at this festival (www.hauntedhappenings. org). The city celebrates for much of October.

November

In November, you can feel winter in the air. You may even see snow flurries. Thanksgiving Day kicks off the holiday season.

✰ America's Hometown Thanksgiving Celebration

Plymouth is the birthplace of Thanksgiving (www. usathanksgiving.com), so it's appropriate that the town celebrates this heritage with a parade, concerts, crafts and food.

December

In early December, the huge festive Christmas trees at the Prudential Center and the Boston Common are lit.

✰ Boston Tea Party Reenactment

On the Sunday prior to December 16, costumed actors march from Old South Meeting House to the waterfront and toss crates of tea into the harbor. The event (www.bostonteapartyship.com) takes place on Griffin's Wharf, where the Tea Party ships are docked .

✰ First Night

New Year celebrations (www.firstnight.org) begin early and continue past midnight, culminating in fireworks over the harbor.

(Top) Boston Marathon finish line

(Bottom) Haunted Happenings Halloween festival, Salem

JIM ROGASH/GETTY IMAGES ©

BOSTON GLOBE/GETTY IMAGES ©

With Kids

Boston is one giant history museum, the setting for many lively and informative field trips. Cobblestone streets and costume-clad tour guides can bring to life the events that kids read about in history books, while hands-on experimentation and interactive exhibits fuse education and entertainment.

MARY KNOX MERRILL/GETTY IMAGES ©

Museum of Science (p57)

Kids' History

USS Constitution & Museum
Aside from exploring the warship, kids can swing in hammocks and experience life as a sailor. (p50)

Massachusetts State House
Check out the Kids' Zone on the website (www.sec.state.ma.us). It features word games, trivia quizzes and the priceless Ladybug Story. (p72)

Old South Meeting House
Scavenger hunts and activity kits direct children at this historic building. (p85).

Old State House
Most of the exhibits are not particularly kid friendly, but the 'Hands-on History' exhibition allows children to build with blocks and peek behind the hidden doors of the State House facade. (p82)

Prudential Center Skywalk Observatory
Assuming your kids are not acrophobes, they will be thrilled to see Boston from above. An audio tour caters to kids. (p111)

Kids' Art

Museum of Fine Arts
The museum offers loads of programs for kids, including Family Place (Tuesday and Thursday), which teaches children over age four to use art, music and poetry to explore the gallery's collections. (p120)

Institute of Contemporary Art
ICA (p131) offers innovative programs for families including Sunday afternoon art classes and monthly 'play dates,' as well as a supercool program (www.icateens.org) organized by teens for teens. (p57)

Kids' Science

Museum of Science
More opportunities to combine fun and learning than anywhere in the city. The Discovery Center is specially designed for kids under eight. (p57)

New England Aquarium

Kids can see eye-to-eye with thousands of species in the Giant Ocean Tank. (p81)

Boston Children's Museum

Hours of fun climbing, constructing and creating. The museum is especially good for kids aged three to eight years. (p132)

Franklin Park Zoo

In addition to the many animal exhibits, the zoo has a wild and wonderful 10,000-sq-ft playground. (p158)

Harvard Museum of Natural History

It's almost as good as the zoo. Sure, the stuffed animals don't move, but they let the kids get really close and look them in the eye. (p142)

MIT Museum

It's too complicated for small kids, but teenagers will get a kick out of the robots, holograms and other science stuff. (p141)

Kids' Outdoor Adventures

Boston Harbor Islands

Spectacle Island (p165) has family-friendly facilities (and beach), while Georges Island (p165) has Fort Warren. Check the website (www.bostonharborislands.org) for lots of kid-oriented activities on weekends.

Castle Island & Fort Independence

Lots of space and a fort to explore, plus beaches and a playground, make this an excellent adventurous outing for kids. (p132)

New England Aquarium Whale Watch

The boat ride can be a thrill, and whale sightings are practically guaranteed. (p91)

Kids' Tours

Boston by Foot

'Boston by Little Feet' is the only Freedom Trail walking tour designed especially for children age six to 12. (p212)

Boston Duck Tours

Kids are invited to drive the duck on the raging waters of the Charles River. Bonus: quacking loudly is encouraged. (p211)

Freedom Trail Foundation

Older kids will appreciate the guides in costume. Download a scavenger hunt or reading list (www.thefreedomtrail.org).

Urban AdvenTours

This bike tour is great for all ages. Kids' bikes and helmets are available for rent, as are bike trailers for toddlers. (p211)

Kids' Entertainment

Quincy Market

There are always jugglers, puppeteers, break-dancers and acrobats performing on weekends at Quincy Market. (p86)

Boston Symphony Orchestra

The BSO has a rich 'Youth & Family' program, with weekend concerts designed specifically to introduce young people to classical music. (p127)

Improv Boston

Improv Boston presents *The Family Show* on Saturdays at 6pm. (p151)

Coolidge Corner Theatre

Sunday morning movies especially for little people. (p161)

NEED TO KNOW

➡ Boston Central (www.bostoncentral.com) is a fantastic resource for families, with listings for activities, outings, shops and playgrounds that are good for kids.

➡ Look for the 🔟 icon in listings indicating family-friendly sights, activities and shops.

➡ Kids under 11 ride the T for free, while junior-high and high-school students pay half-price. Most taxi companies can provide a child seat if you reserve in advance.

➡ Most upscale hotels offer babysitting services or referrals, or try Boston's Best Babysitters (www.bbbabysitters.com) and Nanny Poppins (www.nannypoppins.com).

Like a Local

For all its worldliness, Boston is a city of neighborhoods, home to local people doing their local things. Here are some of the city dwellers' favorite places to go and things to do.

Sights & Activities

Charles River

Bostonians love that dirty water (and the Standells even sang about it). You'll know why if you go for a run or ride a bicycle along the Charles River Bike Path (p154) or just relax and catch some rays on the Esplanade (p110).

Boston Public Library

This is a high-minded city, so it should come as no surprise that Bostonians patronize their public library. You too can plug in your laptop at the BPL (p108). Or, here's a novel concept, read a book there.

Candlepin Bowling

New England's fast disappearing favorite pastime. You can still bowl with the little balls at Sacco's Bowl Haven (p154).

Language

Aside from the notorious local accent, visitors may need some help deciphering the local lingo:

How ah yah?

Boston's standard friendly greeting.

Wicked

A modifier meaning 'extremely.' So something might be 'wicked expensive' or it could be 'wicked cold' outside. The best compliment a Bostonian can give is to say something is 'wicked pisser' (usually pronounced 'wicked pissah').

Coffee

If you order a 'regular' coffee, you'll get cream and sugar.

Sweets

A soda is a 'tonic.' A milkshake is a 'frappe.' A glazed doughnut is 'honey-dipped.' And if you want sprinkles on your ice cream, ask for 'jimmies.'

Food & Drink

Some local specialties (besides seafood):

Food Trucks

Boston's best weekday lunch comes from a truck. Find the good ones on the Rose Kennedy Greenway at Dewey Sq, in front of the Science Center at Harvard Sq, on the Boston Common, and elsewhere around town (p31).

Pizza

Every Bostonian has a favorite neighborhood pizza joint. It might be Galleria Umberto (p61) in the North End, Picco (p96) in the South End, Emma's Pizza (p146) in Cambridge, or – the ultimate local joint – Santarpio's (p64) in East Boston.

Dive Bars

The friendliest locals drink at dive bars, such as Sevens (p76) in Beacon Hill, Biddy Early's Pub (p89) downtown or the Southie original Croke Park Whitey's (p135).

Markets

Bostonian's love to buy produce and other yummies from their neighborhood farmers markets, but they know to head to Haymarket (p87) for the best bargains on fresh fruit, veggies and fish.

Walk the Freedom Trail

Summon your inner Paul Revere and follow the red-brick road from the Boston Common to the Bunker Hill Monument. This 2.5-mile walking trail is the best introduction to revolutionary Boston, tracing the locations of the events that earned this town its status as the 'Cradle of Liberty.'

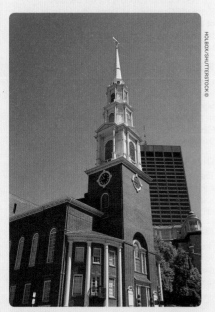

Park Street Church (p73)

1. Boston Common

The Freedom Trail kicks off at the Boston Common (p70), America's oldest public park and the centerpiece of the city. The 50-acre green is criss-crossed with walking paths. Don't miss the powerful monument to the victims of the Boston Massacre, erected in 1888.

2. Massachusetts State House

Overlooking the Boston Common from the northeast corner, the Massachusetts State House (p72) occupies a proud spot atop the city's last remaining hill – land that was previously part of John Hancock's cow pasture. Other Sons of Liberty also had their hands in building the new capitol, literally: Samuel Adams and Paul Revere laid the cornerstones on July 4, 1795.

3. Park Street Church

Just south of the State House, the soaring spire of Park Street Church (p73) has been an unmistakable landmark since 1809. The church earned the moniker 'Brimstone Corner' both for its usage as a gunpowder storage place during the War of 1812 and for its fiery preaching.

4. Granary Burying Ground

Walk north on Tremont St, where you will pass the Egyptian Revival gates of the Granary Burying Ground (p73). Steeped in history, the serene cemetery is the final resting place of many of the Sons of Liberty, as well as the victims of the Boston Massacre and other historical figures.

5. King's Chapel & Burying Ground

Continue north to School St, where the Georgian King's Chapel (p84) overlooks its adjacent burying ground. It is perhaps an odd choice for inclusion on the Freedom Trail, since it was founded as an Anglican Church in 1688. It does, however, contain a large bell crafted by Paul Revere, and the prestigious Governor's pew, once occupied by George Washington.

6. Site of the First Public School

Turn east on School St, and take note of the bronze statue of Benjamin Franklin outside Old City Hall (p84). A plaque commemorates this spot as the site of the country's first public school. Enter the courtyard to discover some of the school's distinguished alumni and quirky artwork.

7. Old Corner Bookstore

Continue down School St to Washington St, where the little brick building is known as the Old Corner Bookstore (p85), a literary and intellectual hotspot for 75 years. Strangely, it is now an option for lunch if you're in the mood for Mexican fast food.

8. Old South Meeting House

Diagonally opposite across Washington St, the Old South Meeting House (p85) saw the beginnings of one of the American Revolution's most vociferous protests, the Boston Tea Party. Come off the street and listen to a reenactment of what went down that day.

9. Old State House

Before the revolution, the seat of the Massachusetts government was the Old State House (p82), a red-brick colonial building that is now surrounded by modern buildings and busy streets. Inside, you can peruse the historic artifacts and listen to firsthand accounts of the revolutionary events. Outside, gaze up at the balcony, where the Declaration of Independence was first read to Bostonians in 1776.

10. Boston Massacre Site

In front of the Old State House, the cobblestone circle marks the site of the Boston Massacre (p82), the revolution's first violent conflict in 1770. On March 5, an angry crowd of protesters was throwing snowballs and rocks at the British soldiers, who eventually fired into the crowd, killing five.

11. Faneuil Hall

Nearly every visitor to Boston stops at Quincy Market to grab a beer or shop for souvenirs, but most bypass historic Faneuil Hall (p83), the original market and public meeting place that was built in 1740. Pause to admire the bronze statue of Samuel Adams, who sits astride his horse in Dock Sq. Then ascend to the 2nd-floor hall, where Adams was one of the many orators to speak out against British rule.

12. Paul Revere House

From Faneuil Hall, cross the Rose Kennedy Greenway and head into the heart of the North End. Turn southeast on Richmond St and you will find yourself in charming North Sq, once home to Paul Revere. The weathered clapboard house here – Paul Revere House (p60) – is the oldest example in Boston, as most other wooden construction was destroyed by the fires that ravaged the city. This is likely where Paul Revere commenced his famous midnight ride.

13. Old North Church

Back on Hanover St, walk two blocks north to Paul Revere Mall. Besides a dramatic statue of the patriot himself, this park also provides a lovely vantage point to view your next destination, the Old North Church (p58). In addition to playing a crucial revolutionary role, the 1723 church is also Boston's oldest house of worship. Take a breather in the delightful gardens behind the church.

NEED TO KNOW

➡ **Start** Boston Common (TPark St)

➡ **Finish** Bunker Hill (TCommunity College)

➡ **Distance** 2.5 miles

➡ **Freedom Trail Foundation** (www.thefreedomtrail.org) Includes extensive information about all 16 sites.

➡ **Freedom Trail Ticket** (adult/child $13/2) covers admission to all paid sites on the trail.

Freedom Trail

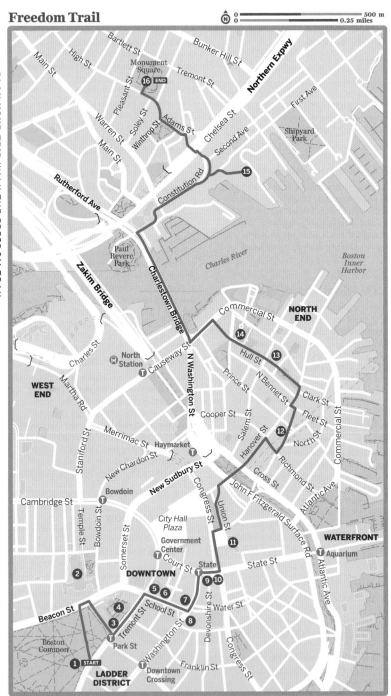

JIAWANGKUN/SHUTTERSTOCK ©

Bunker Hill Monument (p52)

14. Copp's Hill Burying Ground

From the church, head west on Hull St to Copp's Hill Burying Ground (p60). This quiet corner contains some of the city's oldest gravestones and offers grand views across the river to Charlestown. Look for the headstone of Daniel Malcolm, which is littered with bullet holes from British troops who apparently took offense at his epitaph. Incidentally, little is known about Malcolm's actual role in protests or revolution; historical records only show that he was arrested for failing to pay duty on 60 casks of wine.

15. USS Constitution

Continue west on Hull St to its end. Turn left on Commercial St and walk across the Charlestown Bridge. Turning right on Constitution Rd brings you to the Charlestown Navy Yard, home of the world's oldest commissioned warship, the USS *Constitution* (p50). Board the ship for a tour of the upper decks, where you will learn about its exploits in America's earliest naval battles.

TRAIL TIMELINE

➡ **1635** The Puritans establish the first public school in the home of the schoolmaster. Now the Boston Latin School, it still operates in Fenway.

➡ **1688** Amid much wrangling with the local leadership, King's Chapel is founded as an Anglican congregation in Puritan Boston.

➡ **March 5, 1770** The Boston Massacre is the first violent conflict leading up to the War for Independence.

➡ **December 16, 1773** Angry protesters have a Tea Party, storming out of the Old South Meeting House, raiding a merchant ship docked nearby and dumping crates of tea overboard.

➡ **April 18, 1775** The sexton hangs two lanterns in the Old North Church to signal the Redcoats' route to Concord. Paul Revere rides from his home on North Sq to warn the patriots of the Redcoats' approach.

➡ **June 17, 1775** The Battle of Bunker Hill inflicts significant damage on British troops, physically and psychologically.

➡ **July 18, 1776** The Declaration of Independence is read for the first time in Boston, from the balcony of the Old State House.

➡ **October 21, 1797** The USS *Constitution* is launched from a Boston shipyard, just in time for victorious battles in the new nation's first naval wars.

➡ **1798** Symbolic of the new state, the new Massachusetts State House becomes the seat of government for the Commonwealth.

16. Bunker Hill Monument

Walk through the winding cobblestone streets up to the 220ft granite obelisk that is the Bunker Hill Monument (p52). Check out the dioramas in the museum to better understand what transpired on that fateful day in June 1775, when the Battle of Bunker Hill took place. Then climb 295 steps to the top of the monument to enjoy the panorama of the city, the harbor and the North Shore.

Café on Newbury St, Back Bay

Eating

The Boston area is the home of the first Thanksgiving and of bountiful autumnal harvests. It is also America's seafood capital. And in this era of creative culinary discovery, more and more Bostonians are reclaiming their roots in one crucial way: through their appreciation of local, seasonal and organic products. This thriving 'locavore' movement highlights the bounty of local waters and rich New England farms.

Beantown

With a nickname like Beantown, you know that Boston is into food. Culinary historians believe that Native American's cooked beans with fatty bear meat and molasses in earthenware pots. Early settlers likely adapted this recipe by substituting pork for bear meat, resulting in the famed Boston baked beans. Despite the name, you'll have some trouble finding baked beans on a menu in Boston today. Look for it at restaurants specializing in old-fashioned fare, such as Kitchen (p99), Durgin Park (p86) and Union Oyster House (p86).

Seafood

Thanks to its environment, Boston cuisine has always featured plenty of seafood, especially the 'sacred cod,' halibut and various shellfish. Lobster – once so plentiful that it was served to prisoners – is now a recognized delicacy that appears on most local menus. The most traditional preparations are boiled and fried, but nowadays creative chefs are calling on new techniques and all kinds of international influences to present the seafood in even more delicious ways.

Italian & International Influences

The international influence on Boston cuisine cannot be underestimated. A tight-knit immigrant enclave, the North End upholds old-fashioned Italian American cooking, with tomato sauces simmering and pasta boiling on every stove. This neighborhood is still packed with *ristoranti* (restaurants), *enoteche* (wine bars) and *pasticcerie* (bakeries) – making it the city's best eating destination.

In the 20th century, a new wave of immigrants arrived from South America and Asia, bringing the flavors of Brazil, China, India, Korea and Vietnam.

Food Trucks

Boston has dozens of food trucks cruising its streets, serving up cheap, filling fare to hungry patrons who are short on time and/or money. There's a full range of meals on offer, from chicken teriyaki, noodles and tacos to burgers, hotdogs, lobster rolls and vegetarian food.

In Boston, you'll find food trucks on the Rose Kennedy Greenway and on the Boston Common, among other places. In Cambridge, look for trucks on the plaza in front of the Harvard Science Center or on Carleton St across from the Kendall Sq T station. Find out more at the Boston Food Truck Blog (www.bostonfoodtruckblog.com) or Hub Food Trucks (www.hubfoodtrucks.com).

Eating by Neighborhood

➡ **Charlestown** A small selection of welcoming restaurants on Main St and City Sq. (p53)

➡ **West End & North End** Harkening back to Italy, the North End is Boston's most authentic Old World eating destination. (p60)

➡ **Beacon Hill & Boston Common** A mix of cute cafés, business lunches and gourmet delis, with no shortage of swanky spots. (p74)

➡ **Downtown & Waterfront** Sandwich shops and lunch spots catering to a workaday world. (p86)

➡ **South End & Chinatown** Boston's best eating, overflowing with Asian eateries, trendy restaurants and neighborhood cafés. (p96)

NEED TO KNOW

Opening Hours

Breakfast is usually 7am to 10am; lunch 11:30am to 2:30pm or 3pm; and dinner starts around 5pm with last service 9pm or 10pm. Exceptions are noted in reviews.

Price Guide

Prices listed are for main courses.

$ under $15

$$ $15 to $25

$$$ more than $25

Booking Tables

Reservations are recommended for most top-end restaurants, especially on Friday and Saturday evenings. Make reservations at www.opentable.com.

Tipping

In restaurants with sit-down service, customers should leave a 15% tip for acceptable service and a 20% tip for good service; tipping at a lower level reflects dissatisfaction with the service.

Food Blogs

➡ *Urban Spoon* (www.urbanspoon.com)

➡ *Edible Boston* (www.edibleboston.net)

➡ *Boston Foodie* (thebostonfoodie.blogspot.com)

➡ *Boston Vegetarian Society* (www.bostonveg.org)

➡ *Boston Burger Blog* (www.bostonburgerblog.com)

➡ **Back Bay** Classy grills and cozy cafés lined up along Newbury St and Boylston St. (p111)

➡ **Kenmore Square & Fenway** Cheap eats and burger joints, with a few excellent upscale options. (p125)

➡ **Seaport District & South Boston** Seafood, seafood and more seafood, with a few arty cafés and restaurants thrown in. (p133)

➡ **Cambridge** Coffeehouses, sandwich shops, noodle houses, taquerias and upscale restaurants to suit every taste. (p143)

➡ **Streetcar Suburbs** An eclectic assortment of dining options, including kosher delis and other international eats. (p158)

PLAN YOUR TRIP EATING

Lonely Planet's Top Choices

Pomodoro (p61) The quintessential romantic North End hideaway with great Italian food.

El Pelon (p125) Cheap and delicious tacos galore.

Row 34 (p133) A casual but classy seafood restaurant with a well-stocked raw bar.

Courtyard (p112) Exquisite, artistic food, served amid the grandeur of the Boston Public Library.

Alden & Harlow (p146) Small plates with big taste, with creative drink choices to complement.

Best By Budget

$

El Pelon (p125) Fish tacos. Cheap. Delicious.

Casa Razdora (p86) Fresh, housemade pasta topped with fresh, housemade sauces. Like your nonna made.

Clover Food Lab (p143) Original, affordable and animal free.

$$

Gourmet Dumpling House (p99) Our favorite Chinatown haunt.

Coda (p112) A South End gastropub that won't bust your budget.

Lolita Cocina (p112) Modern Mexican fare with a twist.

$$$

Ten Tables (p160) Original preparations of local, seasonal fare.

Island Creek Oyster Bar (p125) The luscious oysters are only the beginning.

O Ya (p101) You've never had sushi like this before.

Best by Cuisine

Seafood

Yankee Lobster Co (p133) It doesn't get any fresher than this retail fish market.

Row 34 (p133) Eight kinds of oysters, five kinds of fish, seafood galore.

Daily Catch (p62) It's not fancy, but it sure is fresh.

Italian

Pomodoro (p61) The most romantic hole-in-the-wall on Hanover St.

Carmen Trattoria (p62) A special-occasion destination with only a handful of tables.

Scampo (p61) Italian food, as done by celeb-chef Lydia Shire.

Chinese

Gourmet Dumpling House (p99) Often packed, but always worth the wait for soup dumplings.

Winsor Dim Sum Café (p100) Dim sum – it's not just for breakfast anymore.

Taiwan Café (p99) Quickly becoming Chinatown's hottest spot for *xiao long bao*.

Best for Vegetarians

Veggie Galaxy (p146) Your favorite diner fare – all animal free.

Sweetgreen (p111) Caters to every kind of special diet, as well as people who enjoy fresh, delicious food.

Life Alive (p146) Smoothies, salads and sandwiches that are good for body and soul.

Clover Food Lab (p143) Clover's chickpea fritter is a thing of beauty.

Best for Kids

Friendly Toast (p146) No need for a kids' menu, because the regular menu has everything that kids love.

Flatbread Co (p154) Pizza, bowling and plenty of love for the little ones.

Life Alive (p146) Smoothies (and other deceptively healthful food) – plus a dedicated play area.

Tasty Burger (p126) Burgers on the menu and billiards in the house.

Best Late-Night Grub

BarLola (p112) Packed with hungry diners until after midnight. *Muy auténtico.*

Kaze Shabu Shabu (p100) One of many late-night options in Chinatown.

Franklin Café (p97) Delicious full menu every night until 1:30am.

jm Curley (p87) Irresistible snacky snacks and hefty sandwiches round out the late-night menu.

South Street Diner (p101) Open around the clock for your noshing needs.

Best Brunch

Beehive (p101) Listen to jazz and feast on eggs *shakshuka*.

Paramount (p74) An old-fashioned family place where they still call it breakfast.

Mike & Patty's (p100) Out-of-this-world breakfast sandwiches, every day until 2:30pm.

West End Johnnies (p65) JC's corned-beef hash and eggs plus live reggae music equals happiness.

Drinking & Nightlife

Despite the city's Puritan roots, modern-day Bostonians like to get their drink on. While the city has more than its fair share of Irish pubs, it also has a dynamic craft-beer movement, with a few homegrown microbreweries; a knowledgeable population of wine drinkers (and pourers); and a red-hot cocktail scene, thanks to some talented local bartenders. So pick your poison...and drink up!

Where to Drink

ALCOHOL

Boston's drinking scene is dominated by four categories: dive bars, Irish bars, sports bars and a new breed of truly hip cocktail bars. Any of these types might cater to discerning beer drinkers, with local craft brews on tap or a wide selection of imported bottles. Some also morph into dance clubs as the night wears on. Boston also boasts a few sophisticated and semi-swanky wine bars, which are delightful for a glass of Pinot Noir (and usually accompanying food).

COFFEE

Aside from Dunkin' Donuts on every corner, there are scores of cute cafés and cool coffeehouses, many of which serve dynamite sandwiches and pastries. Many coffee shops also offer wireless internet access (sometimes free, sometimes for a fee), which is basically an invitation to stay all day.

Where to Dance

There's really only one neighborhood in Boston where the dancing goes down: the Theater District. Boylston St is the main drag, but there are venues all over this groovy 'hood. There are also clubs in Back Bay, Cambridge and Downtown. Most clubs organize thematic dance parties, often centered on a particular type of music, clientele or DJ. As such, the atmosphere can vary greatly from night to night.

Drinking & Nightlife by Neighborhood

➡ **Charlestown** An eclectic mix of drinking options, ranging from historic to exotic. (p54)

➡ **West End & North End** Drink beer (West End) or Campari (North End) with your sports on the tube. (p64)

➡ **Beacon Hill & Boston Common** There are only a few local watering holes in the bastion of Brahmins. (p76)

➡ **Downtown & Waterfront** Some perennial favorites are embedded in the streets away from the Freedom Trail. (p88)

➡ **South End & Chinatown** Gay-friendly and ubertrendy places to drink, plus the city's hottest clubbing scene. (p101)

➡ **Back Bay** Divey student haunts at one end, trendy yuppy bars at the other, with plenty in between. (p113)

➡ **Kenmore Square & Fenway** Overflowing with drinking joints for students and sports-lovers. (p126)

➡ **Seaport District & South Boston** Salty treats in Seaport for the diligent drinker, but head into Southie for a Boston Irish experience. (p135)

➡ **Cambridge** Students and scholars congregate at creative cafés and beloved dives. (p147)

➡ **Streetcar Suburbs** Some of Boston's best pubs and clubs are in these outlying areas. (p160)

NEED TO KNOW

Opening Hours

➡ Most drinking venues are open until midnight during the week, and until 1am or 2am on Friday and Saturday.

➡ Clubs open 10pm to 2am, but most of the action is after midnight.

➡ Remember that the T runs until 2am on Friday and Saturday, but only until about 12:30am from Sunday to Thursday.

Tipping

➡ Tip your bartender 15% to 20% of the tab, or leave a dollar or two per drink if you are paying as you go.

Clubbing

➡ Expect to pay a cover charge of $10 to $20.

➡ Most clubs enforce a dress code.

Lonely Planet's Top Choices

Café Pamplona (p147) Quintessentially Cambridge Euro-style café.

Bleacher Bar (p126) Sneak a peek inside Fenway Park at this sweet sports bar.

Drink (p135) Sets the standard for Boston cocktail bars.

Best for Beer

Publick House (p160) Thirty-plus drafts, including the good stuff from Belgium.

Bukowski Tavern (p113) Many kinds of beer, served with sass.

Cambridge Brewing Co (p149) Ambers, porters, ales and stouts, brewed right here in Cambridge, Mass.

Tip Tap Room (p76) Classy gastropub with 40 kinds of cool craft beers.

Best for Cocktails

Drink (p135) Let the mixologists create something that suits.

Highball Lounge (p88) Gets creative with drinks and games.

Hawthorne (p126) Custom cocktails served in a sophisticated setting.

Ward 8 (p64) West End bar serving up the namesake cocktail and many others.

Best Cafés

Voltage Coffee & Art (p148) Calling all coffee drinkers and art lovers.

Pavement Coffeehouse (p127) Boho hangout for coffee-drinking students, musicians and other hipsters.

Thinking Cup (p88) Delectable coffee and irresistible pastries – right across from the Boston Common.

Best Irish Pubs

Plough & Stars (p148) Tiny pub serving cold beer, folk music and Irish breakfast.

Brendan Behan Pub (p160) A dark and inviting pub, fit also for poets and dogs.

Mr Dooley's Boston Tavern (p88) Downtown classic, with live music and good craic.

Best Sports Bars

Bleacher Bar (p126) Big sandwiches and Boston beers, with a view into Fenway Park.

West End Johnnies (p65) Upscale sports bar near the TD Garden.

Caffé dello Sport (p65) Here's how they do sports bars in Italy.

Four's (p64) The classic fanatic's Boston sports bar.

Best Hidden Haunts

Café Pamplona (p147) Much-loved but hard-to-find Harvard Sq institution.

Lucky's Lounge (p135) You must be in-the-know to find this place with no sign.

Alley Bar (p89) Down an alley and through an unmarked door.

Corner Tavern (p113) Back Bay local, tucked into a corner brownstone basement.

Best Dance Scene

Ryles Jazz Club (p150) Non-stop Latin dance party.

Middlesex (p148) Small but sexy Cambridge dance club.

Whisky Saigon (p102) The hottest spot to shimmy on Boylston St.

Best Gay & Lesbian Scene

Midway Café (p161) Thursday night is dyke night, but queers are cool at any time.

Alley Bar (p89) A friendly bear bar that welcomes all.

Club Café (p114) The fun never stops with dinner, dancing, karaoke and gay cabaret.

Best Views

Barking Crab (p133) Cold beers and breezy harbor views.

Pier Six (p54) Watch the sun drop behind the Boston city skyline.

Top of the Hub (p114) See the whole city from the top floor of the Pru.

Entertainment

Welcome to the Athens of America, a city rich with artistic and cultural offerings. With the world-class Boston Symphony Orchestra, two opera companies, a ballet company and several nationally ranked music schools, Boston is a true musical mecca. The Theater District is packed with venues showcasing the city's opera, dance and dramatic prowess, while more innovative experimental theaters are in Cambridge and the South End.

Music

CLASSICAL MUSIC

Home to the Boston Symphony Orchestra and the New England Conservatory of Music, Boston boasts some of the country's oldest and most prestigious houses for symphonic experiences.

ROCK, HIP-HOP & INDIE

Boston's modern music scene is centered in the student areas of Cambridge and Allston/Brighton. To figure out who's playing where, take a look at the clubs' websites or listings in the *Phoenix* or *Weekly Dig*. Most shows are for those aged 21 and over.

JAZZ

Since jazz is the music of intellectuals, it comes as no surprise that Boston has a thriving scene. It starts with the students and faculty of the music institutes, and ends with intimate venues that attract big names.

Comedy

Boston is a funny place, and we mean funny ha-ha. To cite some famous examples, Conan O'Brien, Jay Leno and Denis Leary are all from Boston. The Wilbur Theater is Boston's largest comedy venue, but there are smaller funny outlets all around town.

Theater

In the Theater District, several big-ticket venues consistently book top shows, produce premieres and serve as testing grounds for many plays that eventually become hits on Broadway. The Theater District is also home to two professional opera companies and the Boston Ballet. For innovative, independent and sometimes wacky theater, check out the smaller venues in Cambridge and the South End.

Entertainment by Neighborhood

→ **Charlestown** The closest thing to 'cultcha' is trivia night at the Warren Tavern. (p54)

→ **West End & North End** Big-name concerts at the Garden, and one comedy venue. (p65)

→ **Beacon Hill & Boston Common** Shakespeare on the Common, but nothing on the hill. (p77)

→ **Downtown & Waterfront** The spillover from the Theater District includes several Downtown venues. (p89)

→ **South End & Chinatown** The epicenter of Boston's cultural life; dozens of theaters. (p102)

→ **Back Bay** Home to music venues associated with the Berklee College of Music. (p114)

→ **Kenmore Square & Fenway** Avenue of the Arts includes Symphony Hall and other venues. (p127)

→ **Seaport District & South Boston** Outdoor concert venue; performances at the ICA. (p135)

→ **Cambridge** Huge selection of innovative music, theater, dance and comedy. (p149)

→ **Streetcar Suburbs** Quiet for entertainment, but Boston's best indie music scene is up the street in Allston/Brighton. (p161)

NEED TO KNOW

Tickets

➡ Tickets for opera, theater and dance are available online or at individual theater box offices.

➡ Most music venues offer advance online ticket sales.

Opening Hours

Classical music, theater and dance performances usually start at 7pm or 8pm, and there may be weekend matinees. Club concerts often start at 9pm or 10pm, though venues might offer an early show at 7pm or 8pm.

BosTix

BosTix (www.bostix.org) offers discounted tickets to theater productions (up to 25% off for advance purchases online). Discounts up to 50% are available for same-day, in-person purchase.

Internet Resources

➡ **Boston Music Intelligencer** (www.classical-scene.com)

➡ **World Music** (www.worldmusic.org)

➡ **Unscene Comedy** (www.unscenecomedy.com)

Lonely Planet's Top Choices

Wally's (p102) Low-down blues bar with funky live music.

Café 939 (p114) Berklee-student-run venue with up-and-coming stars in an intimate setting.

Lizard Lounge (p149) The Boston area's best small music

venue, for diversity of music and coolness of club.

Club Passim (p149) Legendary club that constitutes the folk scene in Boston.

Comedy Studio (p149) Cutting-edge comedy, every night of the week.

Best for Indie Rock

Lizard Lounge (p149) Dark basement club with groovable local music.

Sinclair (p149) Long overdue in Harvard Sq, this newish venue books awesome indie bands.

Great Scott (p162) Gritty Allston club; one of the city's best places to hear cool music.

Toad (p149) A closet-sized Cambridge club with free local music every night.

Best for Jazz & Blues

Wally's Café (p102) You won't have the blues for long at this legendary club.

Red Room @ Cafe 939 (p114) Not only jazz, but all kinds of experimental and innovative music.

Ryles Jazz Club (p150) Where local jazz artists show their stuff.

Scullers Jazz Club (p162) A soulless club showcasing soulful music.

Best for Classical Music

Boston Symphony Orchestra (p127) Boston's world-class philharmonic plays at Symphony Hall.

New England Conservatory (p128) Look for free recitals in the impressive Jordan Hall.

Longy School of Music (p150) Up-and-coming talent is often on display at this Cambridge music school.

Best for Theater

American Repertory Theater (p149) Racking up Tony awards for its artistic interpretations of classic musicals.

Huntington Theatre Company (p128) Winner of the 2013 Regional Tony.

Boston Center for the Arts (p102) Home to a slew of independent theater companies, including the radical Company One.

Club Oberon (p150) Fun and funky black box theater, where the ART lets loose.

Opera House (p89) Lavish venue for musicals on tour after Broadway.

Citi Performing Arts Center (p103) Including the Wang and the Shubert Theaters.

Best for Comedy

Comedy Studio (p149) Nothing but funny stuff at this Harvard Sq noodle house.

Dick's Beantown Comedy (p89) Dick Doherty and other funny guys keep the laughs coming.

Great Scott (p162) It's a Gas on Friday nights.

Improv Asylum (p65) A new show every night of the week.

Best for Poetry

Lizard Lounge (p149) The Sunday night poetry slam is an unforgettable event melding music and minds.

Grolier Poetry Bookshop (p144) Check the store calendar for poetry readings and other events.

Cantab Lounge (p151) Poets descend on Wednesday nights.

Shopping

Boston is known for its intellect and its arts, so you can bet it's good for bookstores, art galleries and music shops. These days, the streets are also sprinkled with offbeat boutiques – some carrying vintage treasures and local designers. Besides to-die-for duds, indie shops hawk handmade jewelry, exotic household decorations and arty, quirky gifts. Fun to browse, even if you don't intend to buy.

Fashion

Fashionistas continue to take their cues from New York, but a few local designers are trying hard to make Boston *à la mode*. Recognizing Boston's conservative tastes in clothes, the styles tend to be relatively down to earth and decidedly wearable compared to what you might see in *Vogue* magazine. That Boston's most famous names in the fashion industry are Bert and John Jacobs (Life is Good) proves the point.

Recycled Goods

Vintage is very hot in Boston. Sure, you can buy 'vintage-inspired' clothing, or you can go for the real deal at one of Boston's many second-hand clothing stores. Other popular recyclables include books, records, jewelry and wicked nice furniture.

Locally Made

Boston's vibrant art scene makes its presence known in local shops, galleries and markets that are dedicated to arts and crafts. High-quality handmade items run the gamut from designer clothes and jewelry to colorful ceramics and housewares. Sometimes quirky and clever, sometimes sophisticated and stylish, these handmade, locally made items are hard to classify, but easy to appreciate.

Food & Drink

Some of Boston's best souvenirs are consumables. Stock up on standard New England favorites like maple syrup, artisanal cheeses and chocolates, and cranberry anything. (Cardullo's Gourmet Shop (p152) has a whole section dedicated to tantalizing local products.) Browse North End specialty shops for all things Italian, or explore Chinatown for hard-to-find Asian ingredients and medicinal herbs. If all else fails, you can always take home a lobster package from Legal Seafoods.

Shopping by Neighborhood

➡ **West End & North End** Get some gourmet treats from the Italian grocers in the North End. (p65)

➡ **Beacon Hill & Boston Common** Cutesy boutiques and scads of antiques. (p77)

➡ **Downtown & Waterfront** One large department store and smaller practical retail outlets cater to workaday Boston. (p90)

➡ **South End & Chinatown** Fast becoming Boston's best shopping destination, with trendy boutiques and excellent galleries. (p103)

➡ **Back Bay** The traditional 'shopping and lunch' destination. (p114)

➡ **Kenmore Square & Fenway** Not much appeal, unless you're in the market for used records. (p128)

➡ **Seaport District & South Boston** One iconic fashion center and one art gallery. Period. (p135)

➡ **Cambridge** Long famous for its used bookstores and secondhand record shops. (p151)

➡ **Streetcar Suburbs** Sweet shopping strips with eclectic collections of interesting shops. (p157)

NEED TO KNOW

Opening Hours

Stores are generally open Monday through Saturday from 10am or 11am until 6pm or 7pm. Most are also open on Sunday from noon to 5pm.

Sales Tax – Not!

There is no sales tax in Massachusetts on clothing up to $175 because – get this – it's a necessity! Now, if we could only convince our frugal partner of the *necessity* of those designer jeans...

Lonely Planet's Top Choices

Ward Maps (p151) Awesome antique and reproduction maps; get one printed on a T-shirt.

Weirdo Records (p153) A tiny shop packed with music you never knew you loved.

Sikara & Co (p114) Exotic jewelry designs inspired by international locales.

Salmagundi (p161) Hip hats for everyone's heads.

SoWa Open Market (p103) A weekly outdoor extravaganza of arts and crafts.

Best for Women's Fashion

Crush Boutique (p77) Basement boutique packed with unexpected fashion finds.

Lunarik Fashions (p115) Eclectic selection of handbags, many by local designers.

In-Jean-ius (p66) Denim to fit every body, plus cute shirts and sweaters.

Lucy's League (p90) Fashionable duds for sports fans.

Best for Men's Fashion

Bobby From Boston (p103) Vintage clothing from Boston's hippest cat.

Sault New England (p104) Cool clothing and unusual gifts from South End style mavens.

Uniform (p104) Find affordable duds by the biggest names in men's fashion.

Ball & Buck (p115) All-American jeans and plaid for urban hipsters.

Best for Locally Made

SoWa Open Market (p103) or **Greenway Open Market** (p90) The city's biggest and best artist markets.

Made in Fort Point (p135) Store selling art and handicrafts made by Fort Point artists.

Cambridge Artists' Cooperative (p152) Three floors of exquisite, hand-crafted pieces.

North Bennet Street School (p66) Woodwork, jewelry and journals crafted.

Best for Sportswear

Ibex (p115) Warm, merino wool outerwear, straight from Vermont.

New Balance Factory Store (p153) A great selection of discount shoes and sportswear.

Core de Vie (p77) Yoga gear and other casual everyday-wear.

Best for Kids

Red Wagon (p78) Cute clothes for kids.

Boing! (p161) Where shopping equals playing.

Eureka Puzzles (p161) Best selection of puzzles, games and other mind-bending fun.

Best Bookstores

Brookline Booksmith (p161) The city's most beloved bookstore.

Harvard Bookstore (p152) Excellent bookstore with a schedule of lectures and talks.

Brattle Book Shop (p90) Treasure trove of used books, strong on local history.

Best for Gifts

Blackstone's of Beacon Hill (p77) Tiny shop crammed with quirky and clever gifts.

On Centre (p161) Jewelry and other inventive items – much of it made by local creatives.

Black Ink (p78) Packed floor to ceiling with stuff you never knew you needed.

Fairy Shop (p115) Add a little magic to your life.

Best for Antiques

Cambridge Antique Market (p152) Old warehouse crowded with trash and treasures.

SoWa Vintage Market (p104) Intriguing indoor flea market, open on Sundays.

Marika's Antique Shop (p78) Beacon Hill classic, hawking antiques for more than 50 years.

Eugene Galleries (p77) Maps, magazines and other old printed matter.

Best for Jewelry

Sikara & Co (p114) 'Modern fusion jewelry' from around the world.

Twentieth Century Ltd (p78) Boston's best selection of vintage costume jewelry.

Ruby Door (p77) Vintage inspired, locally designed, beautifully crafted.

College hockey action in the Beanpot Tournament (p20)

Sports & Activities

Considering Boston's large student population and extensive green spaces, it's no surprise to see urban outdoorsy people running along the Esplanade and cycling the Emerald Necklace. For seafaring types, the Charles River and the Boston Harbor offer opportunities for kayaking, sailing and even swimming. Meanwhile, the keenest of sports fans are planted in front of their televisions watching the Red Sox (or the Patriots, or the Bruins).

Spectator Sports

FOOTBALL

Super Bowl champions in 2002, 2004 and 2005, then again in 2015, the New England Patriots (www.patriots.com) are considered a football dynasty. They play in the state-of-the-art Gillette Stadium, 32 miles south of Boston in Foxborough. The season runs from late August to late December.

Now part of the competitive Atlantic Coast Conference (ACC), the Boston College Eagles football team (www.bceagles.com) plays in the new Alumni Stadium every second Saturday from September to November. Staunch Ivy League rivalries bring out alumni and fans to see the Harvard Crimson (www.gocrimson.com) play at Harvard Stadium, across the river from Harvard Sq.

BASEBALL

The intensity of baseball fans has only grown since the Boston Red Sox broke their agonizing 86-year losing streak and won the 2004 World Series. The Red Sox play from April to September at Fenway Park (p128), the

PLAN YOUR TRIP SPORTS & ACTIVITIES

nation's oldest and most storied (and most expensive) ball park.

BASKETBALL

The Boston Celtics have won more basketball championships than any other NBA team, most recently in 2008. From October to April, they play at TD Garden (p65).

The Boston College Eagles basketball team (www.bceagles.com) is competitive in the Atlantic Coast Conference (ACC) and is usually still standing for March Madness. The Eagles play at Conte Forum.

HOCKEY

Stanley Cup winners in 2011, the Boston Bruins (www.bostonbruins.com) play ice hockey at the TD Garden from mid-October to mid-April. College hockey is also huge in Boston, as Harvard, Boston College and Boston University teams earn the devotion of spirited fans. The local rivalries come out in full force during the annual Beanpot tournament (www.beanpothockey.com), which occurs the first two weeks in February.

Cruises & Whale-Watching

If you're not up for commandeering your own boat, there are also tours that will allow you to experience Boston from the water. Tour boats cruise the Inner Harbor and the Charles River, as well as journey out to the Harbor Islands. These tours generally run from April to October, though the season is shorter for the Harbor Islands.

The most rewarding boat trip from Boston is a whale-watching tour, which cruises out to Stellwagen Bank, a rich feeding ground for marine life. Eagle-eyed passengers usually see several species of whales, including humpback, fin and minke, as well as white-sided dolphins and many kinds of sea birds. There are naturalists on board to answer questions and help spot. Whale-watch cruises run from April to October.

Cycling

Boston is becoming an excellent cycling city, as each year sees more bicycle lanes, more bicycle parking and more bicycle safety awareness. For those not comfortable riding on the crowded city streets, there are several scenic off-road cycling trails.

Water Sports

Boston is a city by the sea, and on a river. These two waterfronts offer lots of chances for watery fun, including canoeing, kayaking, sailing and swimming. The season is relatively short (April to October; July to September for swimming) and the water is cold (average 68°F in summer), but the air is salty and the breeze is sweet.

Winter Sports

In Boston, there's plenty of winter to go around. Outdoor ice skating rinks offer an easy way to embrace winter in the city, and there are also ski facilities (downhill and cross-country) just a few miles from the city center, including the Blue Hills Ski Area (www.ski-bluehills.com) and the Weston Cross-Country Ski Track (www.skiboston.com).

Sports & Activities by Neighborhood

➡ **Charlestown** Set sail on the harbor. (p54)

➡ **West End & North End** Home of TD Garden, the venue for the Bruins and the Celtics. (p66)

➡ **Beacon Hill & Boston Common** Outdoor fun on the Common and the Charles River. (p78)

➡ **Downtown & Waterfront** The waterfront offers many boating adventures. (p91)

➡ **South End & Chinatown** Take a tour or take a class. (p104)

➡ **Back Bay** The Charles River Esplanade is prime for running, cycling, sunning and funning. (p116)

➡ **Kenmore Square & Fenway** Baseball at Fenway Park and loads more opportunities for fun in the Back Bay Fens. (p128)

➡ **Seaport District & South Boston** Boston's best city beaches. (p135)

➡ **Cambridge** Easy access to the city's best cycling and kayaking routes. (p153)

➡ **Streetcar Suburbs** The Emerald Necklace traverses these leafy suburbs. (p162)

Lonely Planet's Top Choices

New England Aquarium Whale Watch (p91) Journey out to Stellwagen Bank, a feeding ground for ample marine life.

Urban AdvenTours (p211) The best way to see the city is on two wheels.

Fenway Park (p128) See the Red Sox battle it out at America's oldest ball park.

Frog Pond (p78) Ice skating on the Boston Common is the quintessential Boston winter activity.

Best Sporting Events

Boston Marathon (p20) The longest-running marathon, occurring on Patriots' Day since 1897.

Head of the Charles Regatta (p21) The world's largest two-day rowing regatta, held in Cambridge.

Beanpot Tournament (p20) Boston's rabidly competitive college hockey tournament.

Hub on Wheels (p21) A city-wide bicycle race for cyclists of all capabilities.

Best for Cycling

Charles River Bike Path (p154) A 17-mile circuit that runs on both sides of the Charles River between Boston and Watertown.

Minuteman Bikeway (p153) A 10-mile rails-to-trails bikeway that runs from Cambridge to Bedford, MA.

Emerald Necklace (p158) Frederick Law Olmsted's ribbon of green that cuts across Boston, from the Common to Franklin Park.

Southwest Corridor (p116) An urban bike route, running five miles from Back Bay to Jamaica Plain.

Best for Swimming

Walden Pond (p168) Famous from literature, this scenic kettle pond is a delightful place for a cooling dip.

Boston Harbor Islands (p164) Ferry out to the islands to lounge on deserted beaches and swim in frigid water.

Carson Beach (p135) Boston's best city beach gets crowded on weekends.

Castle Island (p132) The small swimming beach is only the beginning of the fun.

Best for Sailing & Kayaking

Charles River Canoe & Kayak Center (p153) With two convenient locations, you can paddle on the Charles or in the Harbor.

Community Boating (p78) Experienced sailors can take a fixed-keel, four-seat sailboat out on the Charles River Basin.

Courageous Sailing (p54) Sailing rental and instruction available out of Charlestown.

Jamaica Pond (p162) Rent a sailboat or rowboat to explore ultracalm waters.

Best Boat Rides

New England Aquarium Whale Watch (p91) A boat ride and wildlife-watching all in one.

Little Brewster (p165) Cruise out to this distant Harbor Island and tour historic Boston Light.

Codzilla (p91) A wild ride on the Boston Harbor.

Liberty Clipper (p91) Set sail on a schooner for a two-hour scenic adventure.

Swan Boats (p69) These charming boats on the lagoon in the Public Garden are a Boston institution.

Best for Winter Sports

Frog Pond (p78) The outdoor rink on the Boston Common gets crowded, but you can't beat it for atmosphere.

Community Ice Skating @ Kendall Square (p154) Off the beaten track in Kendall Sq, this outdoor rink is a great find.

Rink at the Charles (p154) Ice skating and people watching in Harvard Sq.

Best for Golf

Brookline Golf Club at Putterham (p162) A public golf course in Brookline, right next door to the famous country club.

Fresh Pond Golf Course (p154) Nine holes of golf wrapping around an idyllic reservoir.

Explore Boston

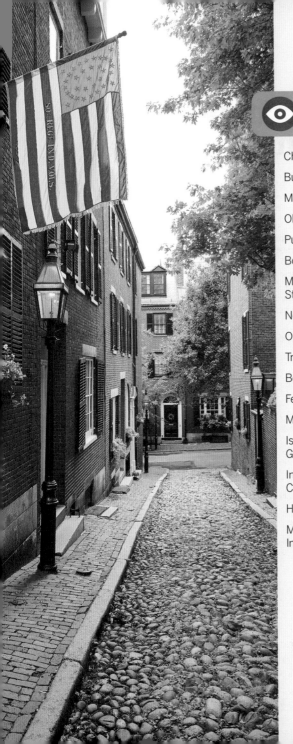

BOSTON'S TOP SIGHTS

Neighborhoods at a Glance

① Charlestown p48

The site of the original settlement of the Massachusetts Bay Colony, Charlestown is the terminus for the Freedom Trail. Many tourists tromp across these historic cobblestone sidewalks to admire the USS *Constitution* and climb to the top of the Bunker Hill Monument, which towers above the neighborhood.

② West End & North End p55

Although the West End and North End are physically adjacent, they are atmospherically worlds apart. The West End is an institutional area without much zest. By contrast, the North End is delightfully spicy, thanks to the many Italian *ristoranti* and *salumerie* that line the streets.

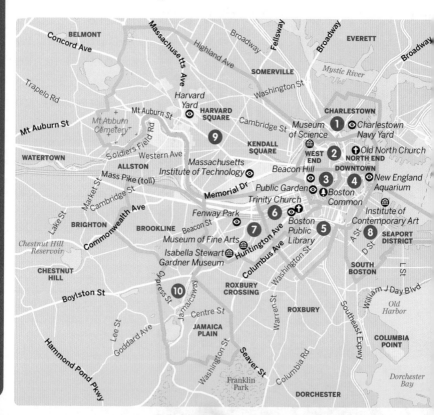

❸ Beacon Hill & Boston Common p67

Abutted by the Boston Common and topped with the gold-domed Massachusetts State House, Beacon Hill is the neighborhood most often featured on Boston postcards. The retail and residential streets on Beacon Hill are quintessentially Boston.

❹ Downtown & Waterfront p79

Much of Boston's business and tourist activity takes place in this central neighborhood. Downtown is a bustling district crammed with modern complexes and colonial buildings, including Faneuil Hall and Quincy Market. The Waterfront is home to the HarborWalk, the Harbor Island ferries and the New England Aquarium.

❺ South End & Chinatown p94

Chinatown, the Theater District and the Leather District are overlapping areas, filled with glitzy theaters and the remnants of Boston's shoe and leather industry. Nearby, the Victorian manses in the South End have been reclaimed by artists and gays, in a vibrant restaurant and gallery scene.

❻ Back Bay p105

Back Bay includes the city's most fashionable latte-drinking and people-watching area, on Newbury St, as well as its most elegant architecture around Copley Sq.

❼ Kenmore Square & Fenway p117

Kenmore Sq and Fenway attract club-goers and baseball fans to the streets surrounding Fenway Park, as well as art lovers and culture vultures to the institutions along the Avenue of the Arts (Huntington Ave).

❽ Seaport District & South Boston p129

The Seaport District is a section of South Boston that is fast developing as an attractive waterside destination, thanks to the dynamic art museum and new dining options. Travel deeper into Southie for seaside breezes, a little history and a lot of beer.

❾ Cambridge p138

Stretched out along the north shore of the Charles River, Cambridge is a separate city that boasts two distinguished universities, a host of historic sites, and artistic and cultural attractions galore.

❿ Streetcar Suburbs p155

A chain of parks known as the Emerald Necklace leads south to the Streetcar Suburbs. Brookline was the birthplace of John F Kennedy, while Jamaica Plain is a progressive residential community with gracious Victorian architecture and a cutting-edge music scene.

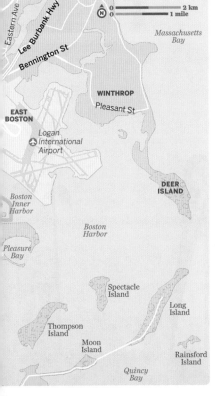

NEIGHBOURHOODS AT A GLANCE

JOHN F. WENCESLAO, MD/GETTY IMAGES ©

1. Boston skyline by night **2.** House of Blues (p128), Lansdowne St
3. Washington St, Theater District

Top Neighborhoods at Night

As with all things, Boston's nightlife is richer thanks to the huge population of students who keep it real. In Cambridge, Allston and Kenmore Square, you'll find them – cool and casual – drinking, dancing, and rocking out to awesome indie music. The scene goes upscale in the city center, especially in the Theater District.

Theater District

Put on your fancy pants before heading out to the Theater District (p102). This is where you'll find the glamorous set attending a show behind a neon marquee or getting their groove on at a glitzy nightclub like Whisky Saigon or Stage. After hours, drinkers and dancers go to Chinatown for late-night noshing.

Central Square, Cambridge

Gritty Central Square (p148 and p150) is the focal point of the Cambridge music scene, with the Middle East and other venues lined up along Mass Ave. Before or after the show, you can grab a drink at low-key bars such as Brick & Mortar and Green Street Grill.

Lansdowne Street

Three words: beer, music and baseball. Fenway Park occupies one side of the street, and the opposite side is lined with fun-filled nighttime venues (p126) such as House of Blues, Bill's Bar and Lansdowne Pub. No matter where you spend the evening, there *will* be a TV showing how the Sox are faring across the street.

Harvard Ave, Allston

West of downtown Boston, Allston (p162) is fondly known as the student ghetto, so it's no surprise that it's home to Boston's best venues for live indie music. See what's on the docket at Great Scott or Brighton Music Hall.

Charlestown

Neighborhood Top Five

1 Counting the 294 steps as you climb to the top of the **Bunker Hill Monument** (p52), then catching your breath while you admire the 360-degree view of Boston, Cambridge and beyond.

2 Sipping an ale at the same bar that propped up the founding fathers in the **Warren Tavern** (p54).

3 Learning about the long and storied history of the **USS Constitution** (p50) from US Navy sailors.

4 Watching the sun set behind the city skyline from **Pier Six** (p54).

5 Taking your kids to the **USS Constitution Museum** (p51) to experience the life of a sailor.

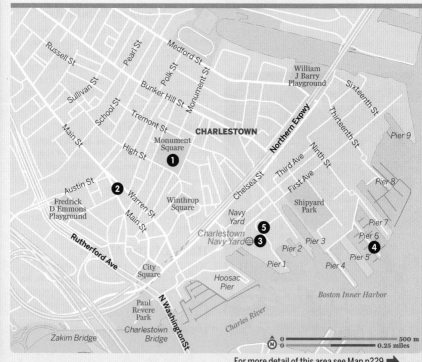

For more detail of this area see Map p229 ➡

Explore Charlestown

Spend a day following the Freedom Trail and you will end up in Charlestown, as the final two sites are located here. Besides seeing the historic USS *Constitution* and the commemorative Bunker Hill Monument, strolling inland from the Charlestown waterfront provides an opportunity to explore the neighborhood's aged narrow streets, lined with 19th-century Federal and colonial houses. Afterwards, there are a handful of restaurants and cafés surrounding City Sq and lining Main St.

Despite the historic significance, Charlestown retains the distinctive atmosphere of a local neighborhood, with real people (known as 'Townies') inhabiting the restored town houses and working in the granite buildings. Even the eateries – however recommended – are places to patronize if you happen to be in the area, not normally meriting a special trip.

Charlestown was incorporated into Boston in 1873; but this neighborhood remains apart, both geographically and atmospherically. On the north shore of the Charles River, it is connected to the rest of the city by the Old Charlestown Bridge. So even though C-town sees its fair share of tourists trudging along the Freedom Trail, the sights and streets will not be as crowded as those in downtown Boston.

Local Life

→ **Coffee with Kids** Townies of all ages love the coffee and doughnuts at Zume's Coffee House (p54); but it's especially popular among the mommy set, who bring their kids to play with puzzles and eat grilled cheese sandwiches.

→ **Sundowners** Little known outside of Charlestown, Pier Six (p54) attracts the local after-work crowd with its informal atmosphere and unbeatable city view.

→ **Historic Hang-out** Even though the Warren Tavern (p54) is a historic site of sorts, it's still a favorite place for Townies to drink beers and eat burgers.

Getting There & Away

→ **Metro** The closest T stations are Community College (orange line) and North Station (junction of orange and green lines), both a 20-minute walk from the Charlestown sights.

→ **Boat** The MBTA runs the **Inner Harbor Ferry** (www.mbta.com; $3.25; ⊙6:30am-8:30pm Mon-Fri, 10am-6:30pm Sat & Sun; TAquarium) every 15 to 30 minutes between Charlestown Navy Yard and Long Wharf on the Boston waterfront.

Lonely Planet's Top Tip

For a unique perspective on Charlestown and Boston, walk northeast from the Navy Yard, following the shoreline from pier to pier. Crowded with boats, this working waterfront boasts one of the best views of the Boston Harbor and skyline.

 CHARLESTOWN

Best Places to Eat

→ Navy Yard Bistro & Wine Bar (p53)
→ Figs (p53)
→ Brewer's Fork (p53)

For reviews, see p53 ➡

Best Places to Drink

→ Warren Tavern (p54)
→ Pier Six (p54)
→ Zume's Coffee House (p54)

For reviews, see p54 ➡

Best Boats

→ USS *Constitution* (p50)
→ USS *Cassin Young* (p51)
→ Green Turtle (p181)
→ Inner Harbor Ferry (p49)

For reviews, see p50 ➡

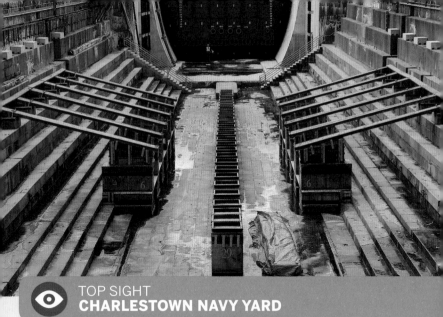
BOSTON GLOBE/GETTY IMAGES ©

◉ TOP SIGHT
CHARLESTOWN NAVY YARD

No longer operational, the Charlestown Navy Yard stands as an architectural and historical monument to the US Navy and its vessels. The oldest commissioned US Navy ship, the USS *Constitution*, has been moored here since 1897. Another formidable warship, the USS *Cassin Young*, also docks here, inviting visitors to learn about its feats during WWII. There is an excellent museum dedicated to the USS *Constitution* and more general naval history, while the rest of the shipyard remembers the history of the shipbuilding industry.

USS Constitution

'Her sides are made of iron!' So cried a crewman as he watched a shot bounce off the thick oak hull of the USS *Constitution* during the War of 1812. This earned the legendary ship her nickname, 'Old Ironsides.' Indeed, she won no fewer than three battles during that war, and she never went down in a battle. On her last mission in 1853 she seized an American slave ship off the coast of Africa.

The **USS Constitution** (www.oldironsides.com; Charlestown Navy Yard; ⊙2-6pm Tue-Fri, 10am-6pm Sat & Sun; ⚓; 🚌93 from Haymarket, ⛴Inner Harbor Ferry from Long Wharf, Ⓣ North Station) **FREE** is still the oldest commissioned US Navy ship, dating to 1797, and she is normally taken out onto Boston Harbor every July 4 in order to maintain her commissioned status.

Currently undergoing restoration, the USS *Constitution* is now in dry dock until approximately 2018. She is still open to the public, but tours (given by Navy personnel) are limited to the top deck. You'll still learn lots of fun facts, though, like how the captain's son died on her maiden voyage (an inauspicious start). Make sure you bring photo ID to go aboard.

DON'T MISS

➡ Guided tour of the USS *Constitution*

➡ Exhibit on the Barbary War and birth of the US Navy at the USS *Constitution* Museum

➡ Model Shipwright Guild workshop

PRACTICALITIES

➡ www.nps.gov/bost

➡ ⊙visitor center 9am-6pm Jul-Sep, to 5pm Oct-Jun

➡ 🚌93 from Haymarket, ⛴Inner Harbor Ferry from Long Wharf, Ⓣ North Station

USS Constitution Museum

For a play-by-play account of the various battles of the USS *Constitution,* as well as her current role as the flagship of the US Navy, head to the **USS Constitution Museum** (www.ussconstitutionmuseum.org; First Ave, Charlestown Navy Yard; donation adult/child from $5/3; ⊙9am-6pm Apr-Oct, 10am-5pm Nov-Mar; ⊕; ⬜93 from Haymarket, ⬛Inner Harbor Ferry from Long Wharf, ⬤North Station). Most interesting is the exhibit on the Barbary War, which explains the birth of the US Navy during this relatively unknown conflict – America's first war at sea.

On the ground floor, the Model Shipwright Guild operates a workshop, where visitors can see volunteer modelers working on fantastically detailed miniatures of the USS *Constitution* and other ships.

Upstairs, kids can experience what it was like to be a sailor on the USS *Constitution* in 1812. The interactive exhibit *All Hands on Deck* showcases the swashbuckling lifestyle.

USS Cassin Young

This formidable vessel is an example of a Fletcher-class destroyer – a W W II craft that was the Navy's fastest, most versatile ship at the time. This 376ft destroyer was designed as an all-purpose ship, able to fight off attacks on all fronts. Able to refuel at sea, the destroyer could travel further and operate more effectively in the vastness of the Pacific.

USS *Cassin Young* (Charlestown Navy Yard; ⊙10am-5pm Tue-Sun Jul & Aug, to 4pm Apr-Jun & Sep-Nov; ⬜93 from Haymarket, ⬛Inner Harbor Ferry from Long Wharf, ⬤North Station) FREE participated in the 1944 Battle of Leyte Gulf, as well as the 1945 invasion of Okinawa. Here, the ship sustained two kamikaze hits, leaving 23 crew members dead and many more wounded. These days she has been completely refurbished, as you can see during a free 45-minute tour, or if you choose to wander around the main deck.

Charlestown Navy Yard

Besides the historic ships docked here and the museum dedicated to them, the Charlestown Navy Yard is a living monument to its own history of shipbuilding and naval command. It was a thriving shipbuilding center throughout the 19th century, but finally closed in 1974, ushering in a new era for the neighborhood. (Nowadays, it's tourists instead of sailors who come ashore here.) Most of the buildings are not open to the public, but you can wander around the dry docks and see how the ships were repaired while resting on wooden blocks. The oldest building in the yard is the imposing Federal-style Commandant's House, dating to 1805.

FREE FILM

Don't miss the free 10-minute introductory film about the history of the Charlestown Navy Yard, shown throughout the day at the NPS visitor center.

The copper fastenings for the interior of the USS *Constitution* were made in Paul Revere's metalworks shop.

USS CONSTITUTION MUSEUM

The USS *Constitution* Museum is a private, nonprofit organization dedicated to preserving the memory of, and promoting education about, the historic ship, so your admission donation goes to a good cause.

A former commanding officer of the USS *Constitution*, Tyron Martin, spent 30 years compiling a database of some 15,000 sailors who served on the ship over the years, including the 1182 individuals who served during the War of 1812.

TOP SIGHT
BUNKER HILL MONUMENT

'Don't fire until you see the whites of their eyes!' came the order from Colonel Prescott to revolutionary troops on June 17, 1775. Considering the ill-preparedness of the revolutionary soldiers, the bloody battle that followed resulted in a surprising number of British casualties. Ultimately, the Redcoats prevailed, but the victory was bittersweet. The British lost more than one third of their deployed forces, while the colonists suffered relatively few casualties. Equally importantly, the battle demonstrated the gumption of the upstart revolutionaries.

Bunker Hill Monument

Climb the 294 steps of the Bunker Hill Monument to enjoy the panorama of the city. From April to June, you'll need a climbing pass, which is available at the museum across the street.

The 220ft granite obelisk monument was built between 1827 and 1843, overseen by a design team that included such local luminaries as orator Daniel Webster and artist Gilbert Stuart. Long on ideas but short on cash, the team had to sell off most of the battleground to fund the monument, retaining only the land at the summit. By the way, the name of the Battle of Bunker Hill is misleading, as most of the fighting took place on Breed's Hill, where the monument stands today.

DON'T MISS

➡ The view from the top!

➡ Bunker Hill Day road race and parade

➡ Diorama of the Battle of Bunker Hill

PRACTICALITIES

➡ www.nps.gov/bost

➡ Monument Sq

➡ admission free

➡ ⊘9am-5:30pm Jul & Aug, to 4:15pm Sep-Jun

➡ ♿

➡ 🚌93 from Haymarket, Ⓣ Community College

Bunker Hill Museum

Opposite the monument, the **Bunker Hill Museum** (43 Monument Sq; ⊘9am-5pm; ♿; 🚌93 from Haymarket, Ⓣ Community College) `FREE` contains two floors of exhibits, including historical dioramas, a few artifacts and an impressive 360-degree mural depicting the battle. If you can find where the artist signed his masterpiece, you win a prize.

LENNY ZAKIM & BUNKER HILL

Driving north from Boston on the Central Artery, your car emerges from the Tip O'Neill Tunnel into the open air, where you are surrounded on all sides by the Boston city skyline and the crisp white cables of the Leonard Zakim Bunker Hill Bridge. Capped with obelisks that mirror its namesake monument, it is the widest cable-stayed bridge in the world. And against the clear blue sky or dark night, it is stunning.

Lenny Zakim was a local human-rights activist who spent years railing against racism. Bunker Hill was the battle where the patriots first proved their potency in the War for Independence. As Mayor Menino said at the dedication: 'The Leonard P Zakim Bunker Hill Bridge will showcase the diversity and the unity of race, religion and personal background that exist in Boston today, because of the work of community leaders like Lenny Zakim and because patriots fought long ago in Charlestown to make our country independent.' It's a stretch, but he managed to merge these disparate dedicatees.

SIGHTS

CHARLESTOWN NAVY YARD HISTORIC SITE
See p50.

BUNKER HILL MONUMENT MONUMENT
See p52.

GREAT HOUSE SITE ARCHAEOLOGICAL SITE
(City Sq; ⊙dawn-dusk; ⚓Inner Harbor Ferry from Long Wharf, ⊤North Station) FREE Besides being an urban plaza, the aptly named City Sq is also an archaeological site. Big Dig construction unearthed the foundation of a structure called the Great House, widely believed to be John Winthrop's house and the seat of government in 1630.

JOHN HARVARD MALL SQUARE
(btw Main & Harvard Sts; ⊙dawn-dusk; ⚓F4 from Long Wharf, ⊤North Station) North of City Sq, a shady, brick plaza leads up Town Hill. Back in the days of the earliest European settlements, a fort crowned Town Hill, which you can read about on the bronze plaques along the mall.

EATING

★BREWER'S FORK PIZZA $$
(www.brewersfork.com; 7 Moulton St; small plates $8-14, pizza $14-18; ⊙5-11:30pm; ⊒93 from Haymarket, ⚓Inner Harbor Ferry from Long Wharf, ⊤North Station) This casual hipster hangout – a Charlestown newcomer – has quickly become a local favorite, thanks to its enticing menu of small plates and pizzas, not to mention the excellent, oft-changing selection of about 30 craft beers. The wood-fired

oven is the star of the show, but this place also does amazing things with its cheese and charcuterie boards.

★NAVY YARD BISTRO & WINE BAR FRENCH $$
(www.navyyardbistro.com; cnr Second Ave & Sixth St; mains $18-28; ⊙5-10pm; ⊒93 from Haymarket, ⚓Inner Harbor Ferry from Long Wharf, ⊤North Station) Dark and romantic, this hideaway is tucked into an off-street pedestrian walkway, allowing for comfortable outdoor seating in summer months. Inside, the cozy, carved-wood interior is an ideal date destination – perfect for roasted quail or braised short ribs.

★FIGS ITALIAN $$
(www.toddenglishfigs.com; 67 Main St; mains $15-20; ⊙11:30am-10pm; ⚐⚐; ⊤Community College) This creative pizzeria – which also has an outlet in Beacon Hill – is the brainchild of celebrity chef Todd English, who tops whisper-thin crusts with interesting, exotic toppings. Case in point: the namesake fig and prosciutto with gorgonzola cheese. The menu also includes sandwiches and fresh pasta.

LEGAL OYSTERIA SEAFOOD $$
(☎617-712-1988; www.legalseafoods.com; 10 City Sq; mains $17-25; ⊙4pm-1am Mon-Fri, 10am-1am Sat & Sun; ⊒93 from Haymarket, ⊤North Station) Not an *osteria,* but an 'Oysteria.' Get it? This is seafood with an Italian twist, so you'll find dishes like Ligurian fish stew, swordfish *salmoriglio* and even roasted clam pizza. The seafood is a welcome addition to the limited dining options in Charlestown.

LOCAL KNOWLEDGE

WARREN TAVERN

Eliphelet Newell was an ardent supporter of the revolutionary cause and a supposed participant in the Boston Tea Party. When the War for Independence was over, he opened a tavern and named it after his dear friend General Joseph Warren. Although Warren had died in the Battle of Bunker Hill, he had been an active member of the Sons of Liberty and a respected leader of the revolution.

So when the Warren Tavern was opened in 1780 it quickly became a popular meeting place, especially among admirers of General Warren. Over the years Paul Revere was a regular and even George Washington stopped by for a visit when he was in town. Nowadays locals still love to gather here to drink a few pints and engage in debates.

TANGIERINO   MOROCCAN **$$$**
(🍴617-242-6009; www.tangierino.com; 83 Main St; tapas $9-15, mains $25-36; ⊘5pm-1am; 🚗; ⊤Community College) This unexpected gem transports guests from a colonial town house in historic Charlestown to a sultan's palace in the Moroccan desert. North African specialties include *harira* (a traditional tomato and lentil soup), couscous and tajine, all with a modern flair.

🍷 DRINKING & NIGHTLIFE

★WARREN TAVERN   PUB
(www.warrentavern.com; 2 Pleasant St; ⊘11am-1am Mon-Fri, 10am-1am Sat & Sun; ⊤Community College) One of the oldest pubs in Boston, the Warren Tavern has been pouring pints for its customers since George Washington and Paul Revere drank here. It is named for General Joseph Warren, a fallen hero of the Battle of Bunker Hill.

PIER SIX   BAR
(www.pier6boston.com; 1 Eighth St, Pier 6; ⊘11am-1am; 🚌93 from Haymarket, 🚢Inner Harbor Ferry from Long Wharf, ⊤North Station) Set at the end of the pier behind the Navy Yard, this understated tavern offers one of the loveliest views of the Boston Harbor and city skyline.

ZUME'S COFFEE HOUSE   CAFÉ
(www.zumescoffeehouse.com; 223 Main St; ⊘6am-6pm Mon-Fri, 7am-5pm Sat & Sun, reduced hours in winter; 📶🚻; ⊤Community College) This is slightly off the beaten path (aka the Freedom Trail), but locals love it for the comfy leather chairs, homemade English muffins and decadent doughnuts.

KOULLSHI   LOUNGE
(www.koullshi.com; 83 Main St; ⊘5pm-1:30am; ⊤Community College) First and foremost, it's a hookah lounge, with plush furniture, ornately carved woodwork, nightly belly-dancing shows and sophisticated flavors of tobacco. A little bit exotic, a little bit erotic (a little bit expensive). Since people are smoking anyway, they added a cigar bar with a walk-in humidor. Perhaps exotic, but not so erotic.

FIREHOUSE
VENDING MACHINE   VENDING MACHINE
(34 Winthrop St; ⊤Community College) The kind firefighters at Engine Company 50 work in a sweet 19th-century firehouse with the Freedom Trail passing close by. On most summer days, they open up one of the bays so that hot walkers have access to a vending machine that sells cold drinks, embedded in some old wooden lockers covered in departmental patches.

🏃 SPORTS & ACTIVITIES

COURAGEOUS SAILING   SAILING
(🍴617-242-3821; www.courageoussailing.org; Pier 4; per hour sailboat rental/lesson $15/45; ⊘noon-sunset Mon-Fri, 10am-sunset Sat & Sun Jun-Oct; 🚼; 🚌93 from Haymarket, 🚢Inner Harbor Ferry from Long Wharf, ⊤North Station) Named after a two-time America's Cup winner, Courageous Sailing offers instruction and boat rental for sailors and would-be sailors. Kayaks are also available. A unique public-private partnership, this outfit was established by the City of Boston with the support of private individuals, with the aim of making sailing accessible to kids and adults of all ages, incomes and abilities.

West End & North End

Neighborhood Top Five

❶ Strolling the cobblestone streets, browsing the boutiques and soaking up the Old World atmosphere in the North End, then squeezing into one of the candlelit tables at **Pomodoro** (p61) for amazing Italian food and service.

❷ Gawking at the architecture and appreciating the irony at the **Liberty Hotel** (p181).

❸ Gazing at the steeple of the **Old North Church** (p58) and imagining the lanterns signalling the Redcoats' approach.

❹ Discovering how fun science can be at the **Museum of Science** (p57).

❺ Exploring the quaint, cramped quarters at the **Paul Revere House** (p60), Boston's oldest home.

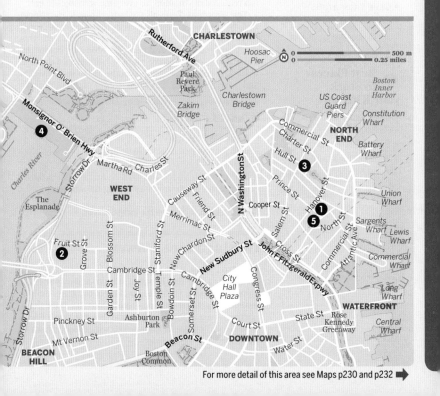

For more detail of this area see Maps p230 and p232 ➡

Lonely Planet's Top Tip

Bad news: it's impossible to park in the North End. Good news: **Parcel-7 parking garage** (136 Blackstone St) offers three hours of parking for $3 if you get your ticket validated by a North End establishment.

Best Places to Eat

➤ Pomodoro (p61)

➤ Neptune Oyster (p62)

➤ Scampo (p61)

➤ Galleria Umberto (p61)

For reviews, see p60 ➡

Best Places to Drink

➤ Ward 8 (p64)

➤ Caffè Vittoria (p65)

➤ Boston Beer Works (p64)

For reviews, see p64 ➡

Best Places to Stock your Kitchen

➤ Salumeria Italiana (p108)

➤ Polcari's Coffee (p108)

➤ Bricco Salumeria (p65)

➤ Wine Bottega (p66)

For reviews, see p65 ➡

Explore West End & North End

These side-by-side neighborhoods could not be more different from each other. The West End – formerly a multicultural, working class neighborhood – was virtually razed by 'urban renewal' in the 1950s. Now its streets are dominated by concrete monoliths and institutional buildings, including the extensive facilities of Mass General Hospital and many government buildings. Most visitors to Boston bypass this bleak district, unless they are catching a train at North Station or attending an event at the Garden.

That said, the West End borders Beacon Hill and downtown Boston, putting many historic and cultural sites within walking distance. The West End is actually a convenient and comfortable place to stay, and there are a few fine hotels that offer excellent value for the location.

By contrast, the North End feels like an Old World enclave that has hardly changed in the last century. Italian immigrants and their descendants have held court in this warren of narrow streets and alleys since the 1920s. Old-timers still carry on passionate discussions in Italian and play bocce in the park. The neighborhood's main streets are packed with *ristoranti* and *salumerie* (Italian delis), not to mention bakeries, pizzerias, coffee shops, wine shops and cheese mongers. The North End is a required destination for everyone who likes to eat.

The Freedom Trail also winds through the North End, with stops at the Paul Revere House, the Old North Church and Copp's Hill Burying Ground. Indeed, this peninsula was an integral part of Boston long before the Italians arrived, and some of these landmarks date back to the 17th century. Come during the day to see the sights and learn the history, but come back at night for dinner.

Local Life

➤ **Drinks** Watch *futbol,* drink Campari and speak Italian (or just listen) at Caffè dello Sport (p65) or Caffè Paradiso (p65).

➤ **Saints** North Enders get lively in August, when they celebrate their favorite saints during the weekend Italian Festivals. If you can't come in August, visit All Saints Way (p109) to see the locals' fervor.

Getting There & Away

➤ **Metro** For the West End, use the red-line Charles/MGH or the blue-line Bowdoin station to access sites along Cambridge St. At the junction of the green and orange lines, North Station is more convenient for the northern part of the neighborhood. For the North End, the closest T station is Haymarket, which lies on both the green and orange lines.

This educational playground has more than 600 interactive exhibits. Favorites include the world's largest lightning-bolt generator, a full-scale space capsule, a world population meter and a butterfly house. The amazing array of exhibits and presentations explores computers and technology, maps and models, the human body and human evolution, and the birds and the bees (both literally and figuratively).

Dinosaurs

One of the museum's main attractions is its excellent collection of dinosaur fossils and life-size models, including the rare 23ft-long triceratops known as Cliff. The centerpiece of the exhibit is the impressive *Tyrannosaurus rex* model, which has evolved significantly from the original model that was built in the 1960s. The exhibit demonstrates how paleontologists use fossils to learn about extinct animals and their evolutionary predecessors.

Hall of Human Life

This fascinating new biology exhibit examines the intricacies of the human body, posing and answering questions like: 'What keeps you awake?' and 'How efficiently do you walk?' In some 70 different interactive displays, visitors can measure their own bodily functions and track their own data. Don't miss the incubator full of hatching chicks.

Alternative Energy

There are excellent exhibits on alternative sources of energy, including a detailed look at how energy is generated from wind turbines and solar power. *Catch the Wind* allows visitors to monitor the electricity being produced by turbines on the museum's roof. *Energized!* follows the path of energy as it travels from sunlight to rooftop panels to the 'Theater of Electricity.'

Green Wing

The Green Wing contains the museum's old-fashioned exhibits, including dioramas of New England habitats and taxidermied animals. *A Bird's World* contains a stuffed specimen of every single bird found in the region.

Discovery Center

This hands-on play area and educational center is specifically designed for children under the age of eight. Museum staff oversee science experiments, engineering projects and live-animal presentations. Costumes and oversized climbing structures invite little ones to imagine life inside a beehive or a bird's nest.

Charles Hayden Planetarium & Mugar Omni Theater

The museum also houses the **Charles Hayden Planetarium** (adult/child $10/9) and Mugar Omni Theater (p65). The planetarium boasts a state-of-the-art projection system that casts a heavenly star show, and offers programs about black holes and other astronomical mysteries, and evening laser light shows with rock music.

DON'T MISS

➡ *Tyrannosaurus rex*
➡ Full-size model of the *Apollo* command module that landed on the moon
➡ Hall of Human Life

PRACTICALITIES

➡ Map p230
➡ www.mos.org
➡ Charles River Dam
➡ adult/child $23/20
➡ ⊘9am-7pm Sat-Thu Jul & Aug, to 5pm Sep-Jun, to 9pm Fri year-round
➡ P ♿
➡ ⊤Science Park/ West End

WEST END & NORTH END MUSEUM OF SCIENCE

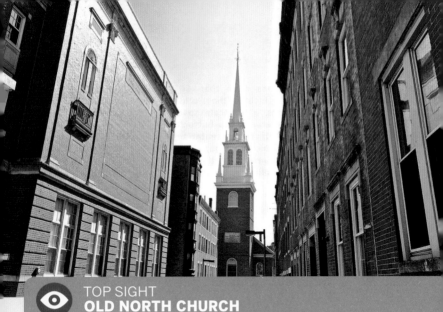

HONRG/SHUTTERSTOCK ©

TOP SIGHT
OLD NORTH CHURCH

'Hang a lantern aloft in the belfry arch/Of the North Church tower as a signal light/One if by land, two if by sea/And I on the opposite shore will be...' Longfellow's poem, 'Paul Revere's Ride,' has immortalized this graceful church. It was here, on the night of April 18, 1775, that the sexton hung two lanterns from the steeple, as a signal that the British would advance on Lexington and Concord via the sea route.

Also called Christ Church, this 1723 place of worship is Boston's oldest church. Many of the tall pew boxes bear the brass nameplates of early parishioners who had to purchase their pews. The brass chandeliers used today were first lit on Christmas in 1724. Note the candles – there is no electric lighting in the church. This remains an active church; the grand organ is played at the 11am Sunday service.

The 175ft **steeple** houses the oldest bells (1744) still rung in the US. Restored in 1975, the eight bells are normally rung on Saturday mornings. Today's steeple is a 1954 replica, since severe weather toppled two prior ones, but the 1740 weather vane is original.

All visitors are invited to enjoy a free 10-minute presentation about the history of the Old North Church. For more detailed information, a 30-minute **Behind the Scenes tour** (hourly July to October) takes visitors up into the belfry and down into the crypt.

Behind the church, several hidden brick courtyards offer quiet respite for a moment of peaceful meditation. Heading down the hill, shady **Paul Revere Mall** perfectly frames the Old North Church. Often called 'the Prado' by locals, it is a lively meeting place for North Enders of all generations.

DON'T MISS

➡ Elaborate brass chandeliers lit with candles

➡ The decorated Bay Pew

➡ Behind the Scenes tour into the belfry and crypt

➡ Lovely 18th-century gardens behind the church

PRACTICALITIES

➡ Map p232

➡ www.oldnorth.com

➡ 193 Salem St

➡ requested donation $3, tour adult/child $6/4

➡ ⊙9am-5pm Mar-Oct, 10am-4pm Tue-Sun Nov-Feb

➡ Ⓣ Haymarket or North Station

⊙ SIGHTS

⊙ West End

MUSEUM OF SCIENCE   MUSEUM
See p57.

WEST END MUSEUM   MUSEUM
Map p230 (www.thewestendmuseum.org; 150 Staniford St; ⊙noon-5pm Tue-Fri, 11am-4pm Sat; Ⓣ North Station) **FREE** This gem of a neighborhood museum is dedicated to preserving the memory of the West End and educating the public about the ramifications of unchecked urban development. The main exhibit *The Last Tenement* traces the history of the neighborhood from 1850 to 1958, highlighting its immigrant populations, economic evolution and eventual destruction.

Additional space is devoted to temporary exhibits that highlight former residents, neighborhood architecture and broader issues of historic preservation. The museum also hosts occasional concerts, book talks and guided tours.

OTIS HOUSE   HISTORIC SITE
Map p230 (www.historicnewengland.org; 141 Cambridge St; adult/child $10/5; ⊙11am-5pm Wed-Sun; Ⓣ Charles/MGH) This stern, Federal brick building was the first of three houses designed by Charles Bulfinch for Mr Harrison Gray Otis at the end of the 18th century. Preservationists have recreated the interior of Otis' day, complete with flashy wallpaper and exquisite period furnishings. Tours take place every half-hour.

A real-estate developer, congressman and mayor of Boston, Otis and his wife Sally were renowned entertainers who hosted many lavish parties here. Since then the house has had quite a history, serving as a women's bath and rooming house. These days it is the headquarters of the preservationist society Historic New England.

NEW ENGLAND SPORTS MUSEUM   MUSEUM
Map p230 (www.sportsmuseum.org; TD Garden; adult/child $12/6; ⊙10am-4pm except event days; Ⓣ North Station) Nobody can say that Bostonians are not passionate about their sports teams. The New England Sports Museum is not the best place to witness this deep-rooted devotion (try Fenway Park for that), but sports fans will enjoy the photographs, jerseys and other items from Boston sports history. The highlight is the Boston Garden Theater, complete with boards, glass and the hard wooden seats from the storied old Boston Garden.

Also on display are Larry Bird's locker, Adam Vinatieri's shoes and Tony Conigliaro's baseball (yes, the one that landed on his left eye and derailed his career). Other interesting exhibits showcase the development of women's basketball, the history of football before the Patriots and – of course – a century in Red Sox nation.

This museum is actually in the concourse area of the Garden's box seats. The good news is that if you go on a game day, you may see the Celtics or the Bruins warming up. The bad news is that it often closes for special events at the Garden; closing days are posted in advance on the website.

ETHER DOME   HISTORIC SITE
Map p230 (www.massgeneral.org; Mass General Hospital, 4th fl; ⊙9am-5pm; Ⓟ; Ⓣ Charles/MGH) **FREE** On October 16, 1846, Thomas WG Morton administered ether to the patient Gilbert Abbott, while Dr John Collins Warren cut a tumor from his neck. It was the first use of anesthesia in a surgical

WEST END & NORTH END SIGHTS

GREAT MOLASSES FLOOD OF 1919

For years Boston was a leader in the production and export of rum, made from West Indian sugar cane. Near the water's edge in the North End stood a storage tank for the Purity Distilling Company. On a January morning in 1919, the large tank, filled to the brim with brown molasses, suddenly began shuddering and rumbling as its bindings came undone.

The pressure caused the tank to explode, spewing 2 million gallons of molasses into the city like a volcano. The sweet explosion leveled surrounding tenements, knocked buildings off their foundations and wiped out a loaded freight train. Panic-stricken, people and animals fled the deadly ooze. The Great Molasses Flood killed a dozen horses and 21 people, and injured more than 100. The clean-up lasted nearly six months. *Dark Tide*, by journalist Stephen Puleo, provides a fascinating account of the causes and controversy surrounding this devastating explosion.

procedure and it happened in this domed operating room in Mass General Hospital. The dome is still used today for meetings and lectures, so it is sometimes closed.

The dome looks like a typical, old-fashioned hall used for lectures and medical demonstrations, up to and including the skeleton hanging in the corner. There are a few other items to see, including a painting of the first anesthetized surgery.

⊙ North End

OLD NORTH CHURCH CHURCH
See p58.

PAUL REVERE HOUSE HISTORIC SITE
Map p232 (www.paulreverehouse.org; 19 North Sq; adult/child $3.50/1; ⊙9:30am-5:15pm mid-Apr–Oct, to 4:15pm Nov–mid-Apr, closed Mon Jan-Mar; ♿; ⊤Haymarket) When silversmith Paul Revere rode to warn patriots of the British march to Lexington and Concord, he set out from his home on North Sq. This small clapboard house was built in 1680, making it the oldest house in Boston. A self-guided tour through the house and courtyard gives a glimpse of what life was like for the Revere family (which included 16 children!).

Also on display are some examples of his silversmithing and engraving talents, as well as an impressive bell that was forged

---

LOCAL KNOWLEDGE

ITALIAN FESTIVALS

In July and August, the North End takes on a celebratory air, as old-timer Italians host festivals to honor their patron saints. The streets fill with local residents listening to music, playing games and eating. The highlight is the saint's parade, where the life-size likeness of the saint is hoisted onto a wooden platform and carried through the streets, while residents cheer and toss confetti. Banners stream behind the statue so that believers can pin on their dollar bills, thus earning the protection of the saint's watchful eye. While the saints' festivals occur throughout the summer, the biggest events are the **Fisherman's Feast** (www.fishermansfeast.com) and **St Anthony's Feast** (www.stanthonysfeast.com), both in late August.

---

in his foundry. The Freedom Trail ticket (which includes entry to the Paul Revere House, the Old State House and the Old South Meeting House) is $13.

The adjacent Pierce-Hichborn House, built in 1710, is a fine example of an English Renaissance brick house. Also maintained by the Paul Revere Memorial Association, you can visit it by guided tour.

COPP'S HILL BURYING GROUND CEMETERY
Map p232 (Hull St; ⊙dawn-dusk; ⊤North Station) The city's second-oldest cemetery – dating to 1660 – is the final resting place for an estimated 10,000 souls. It is named for William Copp, who originally owned this land. While the oldest graves belong to Copp's children, there are several other noteworthy residents.

Near the Charter St gate you'll find the graves of the Mather family – Increase, Cotton and Samuel – all of whom were politically powerful religious leaders in the colonial community. Front and center is the grave of Daniel Malcolm, whose headstone commemorates his rebel activism. British soldiers apparently took offense and used the headstone for target practice.

NARROWEST HOUSE HISTORIC SITE
Map p232 (44 Hull St; ⊤North Station) Across the street from Copp's Hill Burying Ground, this is Boston's narrowest house, measuring a whopping 9½ft wide. Sometimes called a 'spite house,' the four-story, c 1800 edifice was reportedly built to block light from the neighbor's house and to obliterate the view of the house behind it.

EATING

✕ West End

After the massive redevelopment of the 1950s and more recent construction related to the Big Dig, the West End is suffering from a shortage of eating options.

CAFE RUSTICO ITALIAN $
Map p230 (www.caferusticoboston.com; 85 Canal St; mains $7-10; ⊙7am-4pm Mon-Sat; 🔊✏♿; ⊤North Station) This family-run Italian joint is one of Boston's best-kept secrets. But those in the know keep coming back for more – staff seem to know everyone by name, or at least by favorite sandwich. The gnocchi is the hands-down favorite.

SCAMPO
ITALIAN $$$

Map p230 (617-536-2100; www.scampoboston. com; 215 Charles St; mains lunch $10-18, dinner $25-38; 11:30am-10pm Sun-Wed, to 11pm Thu-Sat; ; Charles/MGH) Celeb chef Lydia Shire is the brains and brawn behind this trendy restaurant on the ground floor of the Liberty Hotel. Scampo offers handmade pasta and irresistible thin-crust pizza, as well as a full mozzarella bar.

✖ North End

The streets of the North End are lined with *salumerie* and *pasticcerie* (pastry stores) and more *ristoranti* per block than anywhere else in Boston. Hanover St is the main drag, but the southern end of Salem St is loaded, too. Many places do not take reservations, so arrive early.

MARIA'S PASTRY
BAKERY $

Map p232 (www.mariaspastry.com; 46 Cross St; pastries $3-5; 7am-7pm Mon-Sat, to 5pm Sun; ; Haymarket) Three generations of Merola women are now working to bring you Boston's most authentic Italian pastries. Many claim that Maria makes the best cannoli in the North End, but you'll also find more elaborate concoctions like *sfogliatelle* (layered, shell-shaped pastry filled with ricotta) and *aragosta* (cream-filled 'lobster tail' pastry). Note the early closing time.

GALLERIA UMBERTO
PIZZA $

Map p232 (289 Hanover St; mains $2-6; 11am-2:30pm Mon-Sat; ; Haymarket) Paper plates, cans of soda, Sicilian pizza: can't beat it. This lunchtime legend closes as soon as the slices are gone. And considering their thick and chewy goodness, that's often before the official 2:30pm closing time.

PIZZERIA REGINA
PIZZA $

Map p232 (www.pizzeriaregina.com; 11½ Thacher St; pizzas $14-21; 11am-11:30pm; ; Haymarket) The queen of North End pizzerias is the legendary Pizzeria Regina, famous for brusque but endearing waitresses and crispy, thin-crust pizza. Thanks to the slightly spicy sauce (flavored with aged romano), Regina repeatedly wins accolades for its pies and pitchers of beer.

PAULI'S
SANDWICHES $

Map p232 (www.paulisnorthend.com; 65 Salem St; sandwiches $7-9, lobster rolls $16; 8am-

MIKE'S VS MODERN

Only slightly less tempestuous than the rivalry between the Red Sox and the Yankees, is the rivalry between **Mike's Pastry** (Map p232; www.mikes-pastry.com; 300 Hanover St; pastries $3-5; 8am-10pm Sun-Thu, to 11:30pm Fri & Sat; Haymarket) and **Modern Pastry** (Map p232; www.modernpastry.com; 257 Hanover St; sweets $2-4; 8am-10pm Sun-Thu, to 11pm Fri, to midnight Sat; Haymarket), only a block apart on Hanover St. If you have time to wait in line, you might as well sample both and decide for yourself. If you don't have time to wait in line, go to **Maria's**.

9pm Mon-Sat, 9am-5pm Sun; ; Haymarket) If you're in the mood for a 'lobsta roll,' head directly to Pauli's to be served up 7oz of pink succulent goodness, stuffed into a lightly grilled hot dog roll.

LULU'S SWEET SHOPPE
DESSERTS $

Map p232 (www.lulussweetshoppeboston.com; 57 Salem St; sweets $2.50-5; 11:30am-9pm; ; Haymarket) If you ever wondered what constitutes a 'shoppe' with a double-p-e, this is it. Come to Lulu's for old-fashioned, high-end sweet treats like fancy cupcakes and homemade ice cream (but no cannoli). There's also a selection of fun retro candy that you haven't seen since the olden days.

★ POMODORO
ITALIAN $$

Map p232 (617-367-4348; 351 Hanover St; mains brunch $12, dinner $23-24; 5-11pm Mon-Fri, noon-11pm Sat & Sun; Haymarket) Pomodoro has a new (slightly larger) location, but it's still one of the North End's most romantic settings for delectable Italian. The food is simple but perfectly prepared: fresh pasta, spicy tomato sauce, grilled fish and meats, and wine by the glass. Cash only.

PARLA
ITALIAN $$

Map p232 (617-367-2824; www.parlaboston. com; 230 Hanover St; mains brunch $12-16, dinner $22-27; 4pm-midnight Mon-Sat, 11am-midnight Sun; ; Haymarket) If you have a hankering for something a little different, duck into this tiny hole-in-the-wall with a retro, Prohibition-era theme. The food is Italian, but the chef does not shy away from international influences and modern cooking techniques, resulting in quite original (and mostly delicious) dishes. Cocktails are inventive, as you would expect from a speakeasy.

DAILY CATCH SEAFOOD $$

Map p232 (www.dailycatch.com; 323 Hanover St; mains $18-23; ⊘11am-10pm; ⊤Haymarket) Although owner Paul Freddura long ago added a few tables and an open kitchen, this shoebox fish joint still retains the atmosphere of a retail fish market (complete with wine served in plastic cups). Fortunately, it also retains the freshness of the fish..

GIACOMO'S RISTORANTE ITALIAN $$

Map p232 (www.giacomosblog-boston.blogspot.com; 355 Hanover St; mains $14-19; ⊘4:30-10:30pm Mon-Sat, 4-9:30pm Sun; ⊿; ⊤Haymarket) Customers line up before the doors open so they can guarantee themselves a spot in the first round of seating at this North End favorite. Enthusiastic and entertaining waiters plus cramped quarters ensure that you get to know your neighbors. The cuisine is no-frills southern Italian fare, served in unbelievable portions. Cash only.

CARMELINA'S ITALIAN $$

Map p232 (www.carmelinasboston.com; 307 Hanover St; mains $16-24; ⊘noon-10:30pm; ⊿; ⊤Haymarket) There's a lot to look at when you sit down at Carmelina's, whether you face the busy, open kitchen or the massive windows overlooking Hanover St. This understated, contemporary space serves up truly drool-worthy Sicilian dishes.

★NEPTUNE OYSTER SEAFOOD $$$

Map p232 (⊿617-742-3474; www.neptuneoyster.com; 63 Salem St; mains $19-35; ⊘11:30am-10pm Sun-Thu, to 11pm Fri & Sat; ⊤Haymarket) Neptune's menu hints at Italian, but you'll also find elements of Mexican, French and old-fashioned New England. The daily seafood specials and raw bar confirm that this is not your traditional North End eatery.

CARMEN TRATTORIA ITALIAN $$$

Map p232 (⊿617-742-6421; www.carmenboston.com; 33 North Sq; mains lunch $14-21, dinner $23-36; ⊘noon-3pm Thu-Sat & 5:30-9pm Tue-Sun; ⊤Haymarket) Exposed brick walls and candlelit tables are good for romance; interesting and exotic menu combinations are good for culinary indulgence. The innovative menu offers a selection of small plates providing a fresh take on traditional fare; mains such as pork roast and seared tuna sit alongside classic pasta dishes.

⚡ Local Life
Italian Culture in the North End

The North End's warren of alleyways retains the old-world flavor brought by Italian immigrants, ever since they started settling here in the early 20th century. And when we say 'flavor,' we're not being metaphorical. We mean garlic, basil and oregano, sauteed in extra-virgin olive oil, rich tomato sauces that have simmered for hours, amaretto and anise, and delicious, creamy gelato.

❶ North End Park

Grab a snack from Maria's Pastry (p61), then cross the street to sit in the shade under grape vines in **North End Park** (Map p232; www.rosekennedygreenway.org; ⊤Haymarket), designed as the neighborhood's 'front porch.'

❷ Polcari's Coffee

Since 1932, **Polcari's Coffee** (Map p232; www.polcariscoffee.com; 105 Salem St; ⊘9:30am-6pm Mon-Sat; ⊤Haymarket) is where North Enders have stocked up on their beans. Look for 27 kinds of imported coffee, over 150 spices and an impressive selection of legumes, grains and loose teas.

❸ North End Branch Library

The **local library** (Map p232; 25 Parmenter St; ⊘10am-6pm Mon-Sat; ⊤Haymarket) FREE contains an impressive plaster model of the Palazzo Ducale in Venice, built in the early 20th century by a local artist and school teacher, Miss Henrietta Macy, who moved to Venice but never forgot her students back in Boston. Figurines of 16th-century Venetians show off the fashions of the era.

❹ Gigi Gelateria

Gelato is a denser, softer version of American ice cream. It's made with milk instead of cream, giving it a lower fat content, but it's no less satisfying on a hot day – stop by **Gigi Gelateria** (Map p232; www.gelateriacorp.com; 272 Hanover St; gelato $3-5; ⊘10am-midnight; ⊕; ⊤Haymarket) to sample one of their dozens of flavors.

LOU JONES/GETTY IMAGES ©

Polcari's Coffee

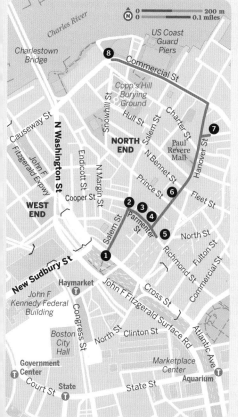

❺ Salumeria Italiana

Shelves stocked with extra-virgin olive oil and aged balsamic vinegar; cases crammed with cured meats, hard cheeses and olives of all shapes and sizes; boxes of pasta; jars of sauce – the **Salumeria Italiana** (Map p232; www.salumeriaitaliana.com; 151 Richmond St; ⊗8am-7pm Mon-Sat, 10am-4pm Sun; ⊤Haymarket) is the archetype of North End specialty shops.

❻ St Leonard's Church

Founded in 1873, **St Leonard's** (Map p232; www.saintleonardchurchboston. org; 320 Hanover St; ⊗9:30am-2:30pm; ⊤Haymarket) was the first church in New England built by Italian immigrants. If the church is open, peek inside to see the city's oldest shrine to St Anthony, most beloved of Italian saints. The attached Peace Garden is always open for a moment of serenity.

❼ All Saints Way

'Mock all and sundry things, but leave the saints alone' – so goes an old Italian saying posted on the wall of this tiny **alleyway** (Map p232; 4 Battery St; ⊤Haymarket) and surrounded by thousands of images of saints. The shrine is the pet project of local resident Peter Baldassari, who has been collecting holy cards since his childhood.

❽ Langone Park

Designed by Frederick Law Olmsted, this peaceful waterside **park** (Map p232; Commercial St; ⊤North Station) belies the history of this site: in 1919, a huge distillery tank burst, sending forth a flood of molasses that destroyed homes, killed 21 people and injured 150 more. Nowadays, you'll see North Enders speaking Italian and playing bocce. Take in the harbor views and enjoy!

WORTH A DETOUR

PIZZA IN EASTIE

People are passionate about pizza in the North End, home to Boston's oldest and most beloved pizzerias. But if you are serious about sampling the city's best slices, wander far away from the Freedom Trail to edgy East Boston, fondly known as Eastie.

East Boston is a blue-collar, rough-and-tumble part of town. It's the site of Logan Airport, and also the setting for much of the Academy Award–winning movie *Mystic River*. Most importantly, Eastie is the home of the pizza place that constantly tops the lists of Boston's best pizza pies:

Santarpio's (www.santarpiospizza.com; 111 Chelsea St, East Boston; pizza $10-15; ⊙11:30am-11pm; ⊘⊞; ⓣAirport) Boston Bruins posters and neon beer signs constitute the decor here. A gruff waitress might offer a menu, but you come here for the thin-crust pizza – unique for its extra crispy, crunchy texture. This well-done crust is topped with slightly sweet sauce, plenty of pepperoni and not too much cheese.

TARANTA
FUSION $$$

Map p232 (☑617-720-0052; www.tarantarist.com; 210 Hanover St; mains $25-35; ⊙5:30-10pm; ⓣHaymarket) ⊘ Europe meets South America at this Italian restaurant with a Peruvian twist. So, for example, gnocchi is made from cassava root and served with a spicy lamb ragout, salmon fillet is encrusted with macadamia nuts, and beef tenderloin with crushed espresso beans. There's an incredible selection of Italian, Chilean and Argentinean wines.

◍ DRINKING & NIGHTLIFE

♥ West End

When the city fathers bulldozed and rebuilt this area in the 1950s and 1960s, one casualty that never recovered was nightlife. However, several of the city's most popular rowdy sports bars are clustered near TD Garden, home of the Bruins and Celtics.

WARD 8
COCKTAIL BAR

Map p230 (www.ward8.com; 90 N Washington St; ⊙4:30pm-1am Mon-Fri, 10am-1am Sat & Sun; ⓣNorth Station) The bartenders at this throwback know their stuff, mixing up a slew of specialty cocktails (including the namesake Ward 8) and serving them in clever thematic containers.

EQUAL EXCHANGE CAFE
CAFÉ

Map p230 (www.equalexchangecafe.com; 226 Causeway St; ⊙7am-7pm Mon-Fri, 8am-5pm Sat, 9am-4pm Sun; ⓢ; ⓣNorth Station) ⊘ Just by drinking rich delicious coffee and eating sweet dark chocolate, you are doing a good deed. All the coffees and cocoas are organically grown, fairly traded and locally roasted. The café has also received the city's green business award, thanks to its comprehensive recycling program.

BOSTON BEER WORKS
BREWERY

Map p230 (www.beerworks.net; 112 Canal St; ⊙11am-midnight; ⓐ; ⓣNorth Station) Boston Beer Works is a solid option for beer lovers and sports lovers (conveniently located near the city's major sporting venues). The excellent selection of microbrews offers something for everyone, including plenty of seasonal specialties. Fruity brews like blueberry ale get rave reviews, with tasty sweet-potato fries as the perfect accompaniment.

ALIBI
COCKTAIL BAR

Map p230 (www.alibiboston.com; Liberty Hotel, 215 Charles St; ⊙5pm-2am; ⓣCharles/MGH) Housed in the former Charles St Jail, this hot-to-trot drinking venue is set in the old 'drunk tank' (holding cell for the intoxicated). The prison theme is played up, with mugshots hanging on the brick walls and iron bars on the doors and windows. Upstairs, the Lobby Bar is set under the soaring ceiling in the hotel atrium. Both places are absurdly popular. Dress sharp.

FOUR'S
SPORTS BAR

Map p230 (www.thefours.com; 166 Canal St; ⊙11am-1am; ⓐ; ⓣNorth Station) Boasting all sports, all the time, the Four's makes a great place to appreciate Boston's near-fanatical obsession with sporting events. The large two-level bar was established in

1976 and retains a dash of character from that period. In addition to the game of your choice, admire a jersey collection and loads of pictures depicting legendary events in Boston's sporting past.

WEST END JOHNNIES SPORTS BAR

Map p230 (www.westendjohnnies.com; 138 Portland St; ⊙4pm-2am Tue-Sat, 11am-4pm Sun; ⊤North Station) West End Johnnies is a grown-up sports bar, with black leather furniture and retro sports paraphernalia adorning the walls. On weekend nights, it's also a dance club. And most importantly, on Sundays it's a brunch destination. No matter where you spent Saturday night, JC's corned-beef hash and eggs and live reggae music make for an excellent way to recover.

North End

Despite the vibrancy of Hanover St, the colorful North End is devoid of proper bars. If you weave your way through all the late-night bakeries and restaurants, you'll find a handful of cafés where you can drink in Italian American style.

CAFFÉ VITTORIA CAFÉ

Map p232 (www.vittoriacaffe.com; 290-296 Hanover St; ⊙7am-midnight; 🔊; ⊤Haymarket) A delightful destination for dessert or aperitifs. The frilly parlor displays antique espresso machines and black-and-white photos, with a pressed-tin ceiling reminiscent of the Victorian era. Grab a marble-topped table, order a cappuccino and enjoy the romantic setting. Cash only, just like the olden days.

CAFFÉ DELLO SPORT SPORTS BAR, CAFÉ

Map p232 (www.caffedellosport.us; 308 Hanover St; ⊙6am-midnight; 🔊; ⊤Haymarket) An informal crowd of thick-accented guys from the 'hood sit at glass-topped tables and drink coffee and Campari. This is a great place to watch a football game (and yes, we mean soccer). Cash only.

CAFFÉ PARADISO BAR, CAFÉ

Map p232 (www.caffeparadiso.com; 255 Hanover St; ⊙7am-11pm; 🔊; ⊤Haymarket) Some regulars are so dedicated that they organize their business calendars so they don't miss their spot at the counter. The bartender masterfully attends to the espresso machine and pours neat cognacs with efficient

and understated finesse. It's a great place to watch Premier League and Series A football matches. Cannoli and cappuccini get raves.

☆ ENTERTAINMENT

TD GARDEN BASKETBALL, ICE HOCKEY

Map p230 (ℹinformation 617-523-3030, tickets 617-931-2000; www.tdgarden.com; 150 Causeway St; ⊤North Station) The TD Garden is home to the Bruins, who play hockey here from September to June, and the Celtics, who play basketball from October to April.

MUGAR OMNI THEATER CINEMA

Map p230 (www.mos.org; Science Museum, Charles River Dam; adult/child $10/9; ♿; ⊤Science Park) For total IMAX immersion, check out the space-themed and natural science–oriented flicks at the Museum of Science's theater.

IMPROV ASYLUM COMEDY

Map p232 (www.improvasylum.com; 216 Hanover St; tickets $15-25; ⊙shows 8pm Sun-Thu, 7:30pm, 10pm & midnight Fri & Sat; ⊤Haymarket) A basement theater is somehow the perfect setting for the dark humor spewing from the mouths of this offbeat crew. No topic is too touchy, no politics too correct. While the shows vary from night to night, the standard Mainstage Show mixes up the improv with comedy sketches.

🛍 SHOPPING

Every visitor to Boston goes to the North End to savor the flavors of Italian cooking. These old streets are packed with specialty markets selling imported food products, wine, spices, fresh produce, meats and seafood. The flow of foot traffic has started to attract funky boutiques and galleries, too. There's not much in the way of shopping in the West End.

BRICCO SALUMERIA FOOD & DRINK

Map p232 (www.briccosalumeria.com; 241 Hanover St; ⊙10am-8pm Mon-Fri, 9am-8pm Sat & Sun; ⊤Haymarket) Duck down Board Alley and into this sense-piquing specialty shop. Sausages and cured meats hang from the ceiling, while the cases are stocked with fresh cheeses, handmade pastas, rich olive oils and spicy sauces. Follow your nose to the lower-level bakery for fresh *ciabatta* and other Italian breads.

NORTH BENNET STREET SCHOOL
HANDICRAFTS

Map p232 (www.nbss.org; 150 North St; ⊙9am-3pm Mon-Fri; T Haymarket) The North Bennet Street School has been training craftspeople for over 100 years. Established in 1885, the school offers programs in traditional skills like bookbinding, woodworking and locksmithing. The school's on-site gallery sells incredible hand-crafted pieces made by students and alumni. Look for unique jewelry, handmade journals and exquisite wooden furniture and musical instruments.

WILLIAM CARLTON WORKSHOP
ACCESSORIES

Map p232 (148a Salem St; ⊙vary; T Haymarket) Like something out of another era, this old-timey hat shop is littered with artifacts and antiques (including a sewing machine that is actually used to make the hats). The headgear – all custom-made – includes stylish but simple flat caps, baseball caps and work caps, all with retro flare.

IN-JEAN-IUS
CLOTHING

Map p232 (www.injeanius.com; 441 Hanover St; ⊙11am-7pm Mon-Sat, noon-6pm Sun; T Haymarket) You know what you're getting when you waltz into this denim haven. Offerings from over 30 designers include tried-and-true favorites and little-known gems, and staff are on hand to help you find the perfect pair. Warning: the surgeon general has determined that it is not healthy to try on jeans after a gigantic plate of pasta.

SEDURRE
CLOTHING

Map p232 (www.sedurreboston.com; 28½ Prince St; ⊙11am-8pm Mon-Sat, to 6pm Sun; T Haymarket) If you speak Italian, you'll know that Sedurre's thing is sexy and stylish. (It means 'seduce.') The shop started with fine lingerie – beautiful lacy nightgowns and underthings for special occasions. Sisters Robyn and Daria were so good at that, they created an additional space next door for dresses and evening wear.

TWILIGHT
CLOTHING

Map p232 (www.twilightboutique.com; 12 Fleet St; ⊙11am-7pm Mon-Sat, noon-6pm Sun; T Haymarket) Alison Barnard proved that she could do jeans when she opened In-Jean-ius on Hanover St. She then proceeded to get her girls dressed up, opening a slick dress shop around the corner. The purple velvet drapes and black chandeliers create an elegant atmosphere to browse the racks of fancy wear.

SHAKE THE TREE
ACCESSORIES, GIFTS

Map p232 (www.shakethetreeboston.com; 67 Salem St; ⊙11am-7pm Mon-Sat, noon-5pm Sun; T Haymarket) You never know what you will find at this sweet boutique, but it's bound to be good. The little shop carries a wonderful, eclectic assortment of jewelry by local artisans, alongside stationery, designer handbags and clothing, and unique housewares.

WINE BOTTEGA
FOOD & DRINK

Map p232 (www.thewinebottega.com; 341 Hanover St; ⊙11am-9pm Tue-Sat, noon-8pm Sun & Mon; T Haymarket) With a large choice of wines packed into a small space, this is a delightful place to browse. The ownership is enthusiastic about educating their customers, so they will love to help you find something you love, too.

V CIRACE & SON, INC
FOOD & DRINK

Map p232 (www.vcirace.com; 127 North St; ⊙9am-7pm Mon-Thu, to 8pm Fri & Sat; T Haymarket) It's the third generation of the Cirace family that runs this North End institution. Established in 1906, V Cirace & Son carries an impressive selection of Italian wines, grappa and spirits. Other specialties include artisanal pasta and olive oil, Italian sweets and honey, and imported ceramics.

LIT BOUTIQUE
CLOTHING

Map p232 (www.litboutique.com; 236 Hanover St; ⊙11am-8pm; T Haymarket) One more sharp, fashion-forward boutique on Hanover St, this one crowded with sexy city-wear. The clothing here is eclectic, featuring lace and leather, flowy skirts and shorty shorts.

🏃 SPORTS & ACTIVITIES

NORTH END MARKET TOUR
WALKING TOUR

(📞617-523-6032; www.bostonfoodtours.com; tours $54; ⊙tours 10am & 2pm Wed & Sat, 10am & 3pm Fri) A three-hour tour around the North End that includes shopping in a *salumeria,* sampling pastries at the local *pasticceria,* smelling the herbs and spices that flavor Italian cooking, and sampling spirits at an *enoteca* (wine bar).

OLD BOSTON TOURS
WALKING TOUR

Map p232 (📞800-979-3370; www.oldbostontours.com; 11 North Sq; tours $18) Spend two hours on the Original Secret Tour and learn all about the sordid past of the North End, one of Boston's oldest and most enigmatic neighborhoods.

Beacon Hill & Boston Common

Neighborhood Top Five

1 Breathing in the sweet smell of flowering trees and blooming beds as you admire the seasonal display in the **Public Garden** (p69). A ride in a swan boat on the lagoon completes an idyllic outing.

2 Exploring the **Massachusetts State House** (p72) in search of the Sacred Cod and the Holy Mackerel.

3 Packing a picnic for an evening of **Shakespeare on the Common** (p77).

4 Browsing for trash and treasure in the antique shops that line **Charles Street** (p77).

5 Following the **Black Heritage Trail** (p75) to learn about the early African American settlement on Beacon Hill.

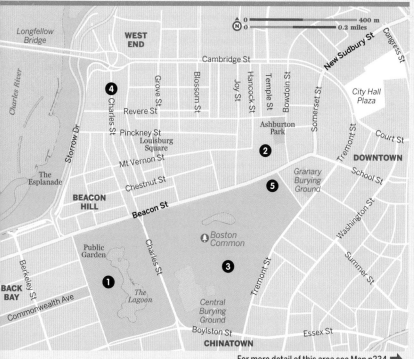

For more detail of this area see Map p234 ➡

Lonely Planet's Top Tip

Get a great view of Boston's skyline from the Longfellow Bridge, also known as the 'salt and pepper bridge,' which crosses the river at the top of Charles St.

✖ Best Places to Eat

➡ Paramount (p74)
➡ Grotto (p74)
➡ 75 Chestnut (p74)
➡ No 9 Park (p76)

For reviews, see p74 ➡

🍷 Best Places to Drink

➡ Tip Tap Room (p76)
➡ 21st Amendment (p76)
➡ Bin 26 Enoteca (p76)

For reviews, see p76 ➡

👁 Best Boutiques & Antiques

➡ Crush Boutique (p77)
➡ Ruby Door (p77)
➡ Eugene Galleries (p77)
➡ Marika's Antique Shop (p78)
➡ Moxie (p78)

For reviews, see p77 ➡

Explore Beacon Hill & Boston Common

The Boston Common is the starting point for the Freedom Trail and, as such, the starting point for many visitors' exploration of Boston. Whether or not it is the first place you visit in Boston, it is a central meeting point, a jumping-off point for several neighborhoods and an always-enjoyable place for a picnic lunch. You'll likely find yourself passing through more than once.

Besides the Common, several other Freedom Trail sights lie within the borders of Beacon Hill, including the impressive gold-domed Massachusetts State House. This is the focal point of politics in the Commonwealth – the building famously dubbed 'the hub of the solar system' – and the neighborhood buzzes with the business of local politicos and State House staffers.

But the appeal of this neighborhood lies behind the landmarks, along the narrow cobblestone streets that crisscross the hill. Lined with brick town houses and lit by gas lanterns, these streets are a delightful setting to spend an afternoon – whether browsing boutiques and haggling for antiques, or just sipping a cappuccino and admiring the quintessentially Bostonian landscape.

Local Life

➡ **Book Nook** Local writers and bibliophiles enjoy the artistic atmosphere and historic setting at the Boston Athenaeum (p73).

➡ **Local Politics** State House staffers hang out across the street at the 21st Amendment (p76) when their working day is through.

➡ **Secret Spot** Escape the crowds on Charles St and retreat to 75 Chestnut (p74) to hobnob with the locals.

Getting There & Away

➡ **Metro** At the junction of the red and green lines, Park St T station services the Boston Common and sights in the southeastern part of Beacon Hill. Also on the red line, Charles/MGH T station is convenient to Beacon Hill's Charles and Cambridge Sts, as well as the Charles River Esplanade. The blue-line Bowdoin T station is a less-used stop convenient to the eastern end of Cambridge St.

TIM MAINIERO/GETTY IMAGES ©

◉ TOP SIGHT
PUBLIC GARDEN

The Public Garden is a 24-acre botanical oasis of Victorian flowerbeds, verdant grass and weeping willow trees shading a tranquil lagoon. Until it was filled in the early 19th century, it was (like Back Bay) a tidal salt marsh. Now, at any time of the year, it is an island of loveliness, awash with seasonal blooms, gold-toned leaves or untrammeled snow.

Monuments
At the main entrance, visitors are greeted by a **statue of George Washington** (Map p234; ⊤Arlington), looking stately atop his horse. Other pieces of public art are more whimsical; the most endearing is **Make Way for Ducklings** (Map p234; ⊤Arlington), always a favorite with tiny tots who can climb and sit on the bronze ducks. The sculpture depicts Mrs Mallard and her eight ducklings, the main characters in the beloved book by Robert McCloskey. As the story goes, Mrs Mallard and her ducklings are stuck at a busy street until a friendly Boston policeman helps them across.
On the northwest side of the lagoon, the **Ether Monument** (Map p234; ⊤Arlington) commemorates the first use of anesthesia for medical purposes, which took place in Boston.

Swan Boats
The story of the **swan boats** (Map p234; www.swanboats.com; Public Garden; adult/child $3/1.50; ⊙10am-5pm Jun-Aug, to 4pm mid-Apr–May, noon-4pm Sep; ⊤Arlington) goes back to 1877, when Robert Paget developed a catamaran with a pedal-powered paddlewheel. Inspired by the opera *Lohengrin,* in which a heroic knight rides across a river in a swan-drawn boat, Paget designed a graceful swan to hide the boat captain. While today's swan boats are larger than the 1877 original, they still utilize the same technology and they are still managed by Paget's descendants.

DON'T MISS

➡ *Make Way for Ducklings* statue
➡ Swan Boats
➡ Rose Gardens

PRACTICALITIES

➡ Map p234
➡ www.friendsofthe publicgarden.org
➡ Arlington St
➡ ⊙6am-midnight
➡ 🚻
➡ ⊤Arlington

FLIPHOTO/SHUTTERSTOCK ©

TOP SIGHT
BOSTON COMMON

The 50-acre Boston Common is the country's oldest public park. If you have any doubt, refer to the plaque emblazoned with the words of the treaty between Governor Winthrop and William Blaxton, who sold the land for £30 in 1634. The Common has served many purposes over the years, including as a campground for British troops during the Revolutionary War and as green grass for cattle grazing until the 1830s. Although there is still a grazing ordinance on the books, the Common today serves picnickers, sunbathers and people-watchers.

Bostonians hustle to and from the nearby T stations; others stroll leisurely, enjoying the fresh air or engaging in any number of Common activities, from free concerts to political rallies to seasonal festivities. In winter, the Frog Pond (p78) attracts ice-skaters, while summer draws theater-lovers for Shakespeare on the Common (p77). This is the first link in the Emerald Necklace (p158) and the starting point for the Freedom Trail.

DON'T MISS
➡ Blaxton Plaque
➡ Robert Gould Shaw Memorial
➡ Boston Massacre Monument

PRACTICALITIES
➡ Map p234
➡ btwn Tremont, Charles, Beacon & Park Sts
➡ ⏱6am-midnight
➡ P ♿
➡ T Park St

Robert Gould Shaw Memorial
The magnificent **bas-relief memorial** (Map p234; cnr Beacon & Park Sts; T Park St), sculpted by Augustus Saint-Gaudens, honors the 54th Massachusetts Regiment of the Union Army, the nation's first all-black Civil War regiment (depicted in the 1989 film *Glory*). These soldiers steadfastly refused their monthly stipend for nearly two years, until Congress increased it to match the amount that white regiments received. Shaw and half his men were killed in a battle at Fort Wagner, South Carolina. The National Park Service (NPS) tour of the **Black Heritage Trail** (Map p234; www.nps.gov/boaf; ⏱tours 2pm Mon-Sat Apr-Oct, plus 10am & noon Jun-Aug; T Park St) FREE departs from here.

Brewer Fountain

This bronze beauty dates to 1868, when it was gifted to the city of Boston by the wealthy merchant Gardner Brewer. After a recent restoration, the **fountain** (Map p234; TPark St) is looking lovely with its four aquatic deities from antiquity. The design won a gold medal at the 1855 World's Fair.

Boston Massacre Monument

This 25ft **monument** (Map p234; Boston Common; TPark St) pays tribute to the five victims of the Boston Massacre. It replicates Paul Revere's famous engraving of this tragic event. Revere's effective propaganda depicts soldiers shooting down defenseless colonists in cold blood, when in reality they were reacting to the aggressive crowd in self-defense.

Soldiers & Sailors Monument

Dedicated in 1877, this massive **monument** (Map p234; Boston Common; TPark St) atop Flagstaff Hill pays tribute to the soldiers and sailors who died in the Civil War. The four bronze statues represent: Peace, the female figure looking to the South; the Sailor, the seaman looking toward the ocean; History, the Greek figure looking to heaven; and the Soldier, an infantryman standing at ease.

Great Elm Site

A plaque marks the **site of the Old Elm** (Map p234; Boston Common; TPark St) that stood here for more than 200 years. History has it that Ann Hibbens was hanged on a branch of the elm tree for witchcraft in 1656, and Mary Dyer for religious heresy in 1660. On a happier note, the Sons of Liberty hung lanterns on its branches as a symbol of unity. Boston's 'oldest inhabitant' was damaged in 1869 in a brutal storm and destroyed for good by another storm in 1876.

Central Burying Ground

Dating to 1756, the **Central Burying Ground** (Map p234; Boylston St; ⊘9am-5pm; TBoylston) is the least celebrated of the old cemeteries, as it was the burial ground of the down-and-out (according to an account in Edwin Bacon's *Boston Illustrated,* it was used for 'Roman Catholics and strangers dying in the town'). Some reports indicate that it contains an unmarked mass grave for British soldiers who died in the Battle of Bunker Hill. The most recognized name here is the portrait artist Gilbert Stuart.

Parkman Bandstand

The site of concerts, rallies and other rabble-rousing, **Parkman Bandstand** (Map p234; Boston Common; TPark St) has been a landmark on the Boston Common since its construction in 1912.

AFFORDABLE PARKING

After 4pm on weekdays and all day on weekends, you can park in the lot under the Common for up to three hours for $14. Enter from Charles St.

The Boston Common is often called 'the Common' in local parlance, but never 'the Commons.' Use the singular or risk ridicule by locals!

THE BARD

Every summer the Commonwealth Shakespeare Company hosts the free Shakespeare on the Common (p77) for picnic-packing theater-lovers.

The Boston Common is one of many places in the city that offers Wicked Free Wi-fi for all comers.

WALKING TOURS

Both the Freedom Trail (p26) and the Black Heritage Trail (p75) begin at the Boston Common.

Dating to 1897, Park St station is the oldest subway station in America.

TOP SIGHT
MASSACHUSETTS STATE HOUSE

High atop Beacon Hill, Massachusetts' leaders and legislators attempt to turn their ideas into concrete policies and practices within the State House. John Hancock provided the land, Charles Bulfinch designed the commanding state capitol, but it was Oliver Wendell Holmes who called it 'the hub of the solar system' (thus earning Boston the nickname 'the Hub').

Free 40-minute tours cover the history, artwork, architecture and political personalities of the State House.

Second Floor Halls

Tours start in the **Doric Hall**, the columned reception area directly below the dome. Once the main entryway to the State House, these front doors are now used only by a visiting US president or by a departing governor.

The nearby **Nurses Hall** is named for the moving statue of a Civil War nurse tending to a fallen soldier. The circular **Memorial Hall**, known as the Hall of Flags, honors Massachusetts soldiers by displaying some of the tattered flags that have been carried to battle over the years. Finally, the impressive marble **Great Hall** is hung with 351 flags, representing all the cities and towns in Massachusetts.

Legislative & Executive Chambers

Upstairs, visitors can see both legislative chambers: the House of Representatives, also home of the famous Sacred Cod; and the Senate Chamber, residence of the Holy Mackerel. The Governor's office is here, though it's not open to the public.

State House Lawn

On the front lawn (closed to the public), statues honor important Massachusetts figures, among them orator Daniel Webster, religious martyrs Anne Hutchinson and Mary Dyer, and President John F Kennedy.

DON'T MISS

➡ Women's Memorial, just outside Doric Hall

➡ Robert Reid's murals in the Nurses Hall

➡ The clock in the Great Hall

➡ The Sacred Cod and the Holy Mackerel

PRACTICALITIES

➡ Map p234

➡ www.sec.state. ma.us

➡ cnr Beacon & Bowdoin Sts

➡ ⏱9am-5pm, tours 10am-3:30pm Mon-Fri

➡ Ⓣ Park St

 **SIGHTS**

PUBLIC GARDEN GARDENS
See p69.

BOSTON COMMON PARK
See p70.

**MASSACHUSETTS STATE
HOUSE** NOTABLE BUILDING
See p72.

PARK STREET CHURCH CHURCH
Map p234 (www.parkstreet.org; 1 Park St; ☻9am-4pm Tue-Sat mid-Jun–Aug; ⊤Park St) Shortly after the construction of Park St Church, gunpowder for the War of 1812 was stored in the basement, earning this location the moniker 'Brimstone Corner.' But that was hardly the most inflammatory event that took place here. Noted for its graceful, 217ft steeple, this Boston landmark has been hosting historic lectures and musical performances since its founding.

In 1829 William Lloyd Garrison railed against slavery from the church's pulpit. And on Independence Day in 1831, Samuel Francis Smith's hymn 'America' ('My Country 'Tis of Thee') was first sung.

GRANARY BURYING GROUND CEMETERY
Map p234 (Tremont St; ☻9am-5pm; ⊤Park St) Dating to 1660, this atmospheric atoll is crammed with historic headstones, many with evocative (and creepy) carvings. This is the final resting place of all your favorite revolutionary heroes including Paul Revere, Samuel Adams, John Hancock and James Otis. Benjamin Franklin is buried in Philadelphia, but the Franklin family plot contains his parents.

The five victims of the Boston Massacre share a common grave, though the only name you are likely to recognize is that of Crispus Attucks, the freed slave who is considered the first person to lose his life in the struggle for American independence. Other noteworthy permanent residents include Peter Faneuil, of Faneuil Hall fame, and Judge Sewall, the only magistrate to denounce the hanging of the so-called Salem witches. The location of Park St Church was once the site of the town granary; as the burying ground predates the church, it is named after the grain storage facility instead. While it is sometimes called the Old Granary Burying Ground, it's not the oldest in Boston; King's Chapel and Copp's Hill date back further.

BOSTON ATHENAEUM LIBRARY
Map p234 (☎617-227-0270; www.bostonathenaeum.org; 10½ Beacon St; donation $5; ☻9am-8pm Mon-Thu, to 5.30pm Fri, to 4pm Sat, noon-4pm Sun; ⊤Park St) Founded in 1807, the Boston Athenaeum is an old and distinguished private library, having hosted the likes of Ralph Waldo Emerson and Nathaniel Hawthorne. Its collection has half a million volumes, including an impressive selection of art, which is showcased in the on-site gallery. The library itself is open to members only, but tourists can visit the gallery. Tours of the whole library are conducted at 3pm on Tuesday and Thursday; reserve your spot in advance.

**JOHN ADAMS
COURTHOUSE** NOTABLE BUILDING
Map p234 (www.mass.gov/sjc; 1 Pemberton Sq; ☻8:30am-5pm Mon-Fri; ⊤Government Center) **FREE** Peek inside the impressive courthouse on Pemberton Sq, which is home of the Massachusetts Supreme Judicial Court (the oldest appellate court in the country), as well as the Appeals Court and the Social Law Library. You can't enter the courtrooms, but you can admire the barrel-vaulted ceiling in the Great Hall and peruse the small exhibits – one on John Adams and the other on the Sacco and Vanzetti trial.

**MUSEUM OF AFRICAN
AMERICAN HISTORY** MUSEUM
Map p234 (www.afroammuseum.org; 46 Joy St; adult/child $5/free; ☻10am-4pm Mon-Sat; ⊤Park St or Bowdoin) The Museum of African American History occupies two adjacent historic buildings: the African Meeting House, the country's oldest black church and meeting house; and Abiel Smith School, the country's first school for blacks. The museum offers rotating exhibits about the historic events that took place here, and is also a source of information about – and the final destination of – the Black Heritage Trail.

Within these walls William Lloyd Garrison began the New England Anti-Slavery Society, which later expanded to become the American Anti-Slavery Society. Here, Maria Stewart became the first American woman – a black woman, no less – to speak before a mixed-gender audience. Frederick Douglass delivered stirring calls to action within this hall, and Robert Gould Shaw recruited black soldiers for the Civil War effort.

LOCAL KNOWLEDGE

HIDDEN BEACON HILL

Take a detour away from Charles St to discover a few Beacon Hill gems.

Louisburg Square (Map p234; ⊤Charles/MGH) There is no more prestigious address than this lane, a cluster of stately brick row houses facing a private park.

After she gained literary success, Louisa May Alcott's home was at No 10; at the northern corner of the square is the home of Senator John Kerry and his wife Teresa Heinz.

Acorn Street (Map p234; ⊤Charles/MGH) Boston's narrowest street. This cobblestone alleyway was once home to artisans and to the service people who worked for the adjacent mansion dwellers. The brick walls on the north side of the street enclose examples of Beacon Hill's hidden gardens.

NICHOLS HOUSE MUSEUM   MUSEUM

Map p234 (www.nicholshousemuseum.org; 55 Mt Vernon St; adult/child $10/free; ⊕11am-4pm Tue-Sat Apr-Oct, Thu-Sat Nov-Mar; ⊤Park St) This 1804 town house offers the rare opportunity to peek inside one of these classic Beacon Hill beauties. Attributed to Charles Bulfinch, it is unique in its merger of Federal and Greek Revival architectural styles. Equally impressive is the story told inside the museum – that of the day-to-day life of author, pacifist and suffragette Miss Rose Standish Nichols, who lived here from 1885 to 1960.

EATING

PIPERI MEDITERRANEAN
GRILL   MIDDLE EASTERN $

(www.piperi.com; 1 Beacon St; mains $6-8; ⊕7am-6pm Mon-Fri, 11am-3pm Sat; 🍴🚻; ⊤Government Center) The concept is simple. Decide whether you want a flatbread sandwich, salad or mezze plate. Choose chicken, steak or veggies as a main ingredient. Then add fresh toppings such as hummus, tabouleh, slaw, cheese, etc. Hungry Boston workers line up out the door for this quick, healthy, fresh and affordable lunch.

★PARAMOUNT   CAFETERIA $$

Map p234 (www.paramountboston.com; 44 Charles St; mains breakfast & lunch $6-12, dinner $15-23; ⊕7am-10pm Mon-Thu, to 11pm Fri, 8am-11pm Sat, to 10pm Sun; 🍴🚻; ⊤Charles/MGH) This old-fashioned cafeteria is a neighborhood favorite. A-plus diner fare includes pancakes, homefries, burgers and sandwiches, and big, hearty salads. Banana and caramel French toast is an obvious go-to for the brunch crowd. Don't sit down until you get your food! At dinner, add table service and candlelight, and the place goes upscale without losing its down-home charm.

GROTTO   ITALIAN $$

Map p234 (☎617-227-3434; www.grottorestaurant.com; 37 Bowdoin St; mains $21, 3-course prix-fixe dinner $38; ⊕11:30am-3pm Mon-Fri & 5-10pm daily; ⊤Bowdoin) In a word: romantic. Tucked into a basement on the back side of Beacon Hill, this cozy, cavelike place lives up to its name. The funky decor – exposed brick walls decked with rotating art exhibits – reflects the innovative menu. Reservations recommended, as the place is tiny.

75 CHESTNUT   AMERICAN $$

Map p234 (www.75chestnut.com; 75 Chestnut St; mains $18-27; ⊕10:30am-2:30pm Sat, 11:30am-3:30pm Sun, 5-11pm daily; 🚻; ⊤Charles/MGH) You might not think to take a peek around the corner, away from the well-trod sidewalks of Charles St. But locals know that Chestnut St is the place to go for tried-and-true steaks and seafood and a genuine warm welcome. It's a perfect place to stop for a drink, complemented by cheese and crackers served at the bar.

SCOLLAY SQUARE   AMERICAN $$

Map p234 (www.scollaysquare.com; 21 Beacon St; sandwiches & small plates $11-13, dinner mains $17-23; ⊕11:30am-10pm Mon-Fri, 10am-10pm Sat & Sun; ⊤Park St) Down the road from the former Scollay Sq, this retro restaurant harks back to the glory days of its namesake. Old photos and memorabilia adorn the walls, while suits sip martinis to big-band music. The classic American fare is reliably good, with lobster mac 'n' cheese the perennial favorite.

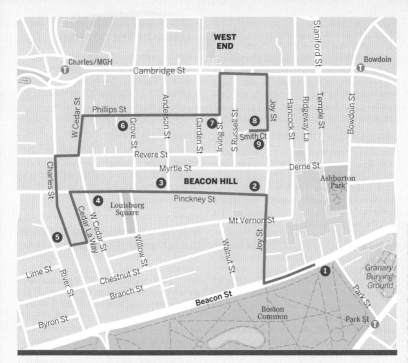

Neighborhood Walk
Black Heritage Trail

START BOSTON COMMON
END MUSEUM OF AFRICAN AMERICAN
HISTORY
LENGTH 1.2 MILES; 90 MINUTES

Beacon Hill was never the exclusive domain of blue-blooded Brahmins. In the 19th century, freed African Americans settled on the back side of the hill and the neighborhood became a hive of activity focused on improving housing, establishing schools and creating opportunities for black residents. NPS rangers lead free tours of the Black Heritage Trail (www.nps.gov/boaf).

If you are heading out solo, start at the **1 Robert Gould Shaw Memorial** (p70) on the Boston Common. Walk north to the **2 George Middleton House**, the oldest existing house that was built by an African American. Middleton was an honorary colonel who led an all-black regiment in the American Revolution. Further west, the **3 Phillips School** became one of Boston's first interracial schools in 1855.

John J Smith lived in the house at **4 86 Pinckney St** after the Civil War. He had been a barber, an impassioned abolitionist and a harborer of fugitive slaves. After the war, he became a representative to the Massachusetts State Legislature.

Further west, then south down Charles St, the **5 Charles St Meeting House** formerly housed the African Methodist Episcopal Church.

Walk north on Charles St, then cut up to Phillips St. The house at **6 No 66** – which was a station on the Underground Railroad – belonged to Lewis Hayden, an escaped slave and tireless abolitionist. Further east lies the **7 John Coburn House**. An active member of the New England Freedom Association and the Boston Vigilance Committee, Coburn purportedly harbored fugitives and established a gaming house here.

Heading south on Joy St, the cluster of **8 residential buildings** on Smith Ct is representative of the homes where black Bostonians lived in the 19th century. The tour ends at the **9 Museum of African American History** (p73).

FIGS
PIZZA $$

Map p234 (www.toddenglishfigs.com; 42 Charles St; mains $16-21; ⏱11:30am-11pm; 🅿🚇; ⓣCharles/MGH) The brainchild of celebrity chef Todd English, Figs rakes them in with its innovative whisper-thin pizzas. For a real treat, order the signature fig and prosciutto pizza with gorgonzola. Equally delish are the sandwiches, salads and pastas.

ZEN SUSHI BAR & GRILL
JAPANESE $$

Map p234 (www.zensushibar.com; 21a Beacon St; sushi $5-12, lunch specials $10-15, dinner mains $17-22; ⏱11:30am-10pm Mon-Thu, noon-11pm Fri & Sat, 2:30-10pm Sun; ⓣPark St) The minimalist decor and extensive menu are typical sushi-bar stuff, but the place is immaculate and the sushi and rolls are spot on.

NO 9 PARK
EUROPEAN $$$

Map p234 (☎617-742-9991; www.no9park.com; 9 Park St; mains $39, 3-course prix-fixe dinner $69; ⏱5:30-9pm Sun & Mon, to 10pm Tue-Sat; ⓣPark St) Set in a 19th-century mansion opposite the State House, this swanky place tops many fine-dining lists. Chef-owner Barbara Lynch has been lauded by food and wine magazines for her delectable French and Italian culinary masterpieces and her first-rate wine list. She has now cast her celebrity-chef spell all around town, but this is the place that made her famous.

MOOO...
STEAK $$$

Map p234 (☎617-670-2515; www.mooorestaurant.com; 15 Beacon St; 3-course prix-fixe lunch/dinner $25/45; ⏱7am-10:30pm Mon-Fri, 8am-11pm Sat, 10am-10pm Sun; ⓣPark St) This super-cool, modern steakhouse presents a challenge: don't fill up on the irresistible rolls before your food arrives. You'll be glad you saved room for the meaty specialties such as steak tartare and Kobe beef dumplings. For an extra decadent, carnivorous touch, steaks are served with bone-marrow butter. You can order a la carte, but the prix-fixe is an unbeatable deal.

🍷 DRINKING & 🍸 NIGHTLIFE

TIP TAP ROOM
BAR

Map p230 (www.thetiptaproom.com; 138 Cambridge St; ⏱11:30am-2am Mon-Sat, 10:30am-2am Sun; 📶; ⓣCharles/MGH or Bowdoin) The 'tips' are steak, lamb, turkey, chicken or swordfish. The 'taps' are nearly 40 kinds of beer,

---

LOCAL KNOWLEDGE

LUNCH ON THE COMMON

Various food trucks park on the Boston Common, near the entrance to the Park St T station. Our favorites are Clover Food Lab (www.cloverfoodlab.com) and the Chicken & Rice Guys (www.chickenriceguys.com).

---

ranging from local craft brews to international ales of some renown. The food is good and the beer is even better. There's no other place on Beacon Hill with this trendy but friendly vibe.

21ST AMENDMENT
PUB

Map p234 (www.21stboston.com; 150 Bowdoin St; ⏱11:30am-2am; ⓣPark St) Named for one of the US Constitution's most important amendments – the one repealing Prohibition – this quintessential tavern has been an ever-popular haunt for overeducated and underpaid statehouse workers. It feels especially cozy in the winter, when you'll feel pretty good about yourself as you drink a stout near the copper-hooded fireplace.

BIN 26 ENOTECA
WINE BAR

Map p234 (☎617-723-5939; www.bin26.com; 26 Charles St; ⏱noon-11pm Mon-Fri, 11am-11pm Sat, to 10pm Sun; ⓣCharles/MGH) If you are into your wine, you'll be into the Bin. Big windows overlook Charles St and wine bottles line the walls. The 60-page wine list spans the globe, including a moderately priced house wine that is bottled in Italy just for the restaurant. Staff will insist you order food (due to licensing requirements), but you won't regret sampling the simple, seasonal menu.

SEVENS
DIVE BAR

Map p234 (www.sevensalehouse.com; 77 Charles St; ⏱11:30am-1am; ⓣCharles/MGH) Beacon Hill's long-standing neighborhood dive bar looks old school, with its wooden bar placed under hanging glasses, and a few comfortable booths. Service is brusque but endearing. The place serves only wine and beer, including a house brew from Harpoon.

6B LOUNGE
COCKTAIL BAR, CLUB

Map p234 (www.6bloungeandrestaurant.com; 6 Beacon St; cover after 9:30pm Fri $5; ⏱11am-2am; ⓣPark St) Most nights of the week, this is a pleasant but innocuous cocktail bar with forgettable food. But come Friday night, the bar morphs into a wildly popular 1990s dance party (from 10pm), featuring the local spinning legend DJ T-Rex. Saturday nights are fun, too (and free), with all your favorite pop tunes from Madonna, Rick James, Michael Jackson and Wham!

CHEERS   PUB

Map p234 (www.cheersboston.com; 84 Beacon St; ⊙11am-1am; TArlington) We understand that this is a mandatory pilgrimage place for fans of the TV show. But be aware that the bar doesn't really look like its famous TV alter ego, unless you sit in the 'set bar,' which is a replica of the set. It's also not really charming or local or 'Boston' in any way. In short, nobody knows your name.

ENTERTAINMENT

★SHAKESPEARE ON THE COMMON   THEATER

Map p234 (www.commshakes.org; Boston Common; ⊙8pm Tue-Sat, 7pm Sun Jul & Aug; TPark St) Each summer, the Commonwealth Shakespeare Company stages a major production on the Boston Common, drawing crowds for (free) Shakespeare under the stars. Productions often appeal to the masses with a populist twist. Thus *The Taming of the Shrew,* set in a North End restaurant.

SHOPPING

There was a time when Charles St was lined with antique shops and nothing else: some historians claim that the country's antique trade began right here on Beacon Hill. You'll also find plenty of contemporary galleries, preppy boutiques and practical shops to go along with all that old stuff.

★RUBY DOOR   JEWELRY

Map p234 (www.therubydoor.com; 15 Charles St; ⊙11am-6pm Mon-Sat; TCharles/MGH) What will you find behind the ruby door? Gorgeous, hand-crafted jewelry, much of it featuring intriguing gemstones and unique vintage elements. Designer and owner Tracy Chareas reworks antique and vintage jewels into thoroughly modern pieces of art. There is also plenty of more affordable jewelry for bauble lovers. Great for browsing, with no pressure to buy.

CRUSH BOUTIQUE   CLOTHING

Map p234 (www.shopcrushboutique.com; 131 Charles St; ⊙10am-7pm Mon-Sat, 11am-6pm Sun; TCharles/MGH) Fashion mavens rave about this cozy basement boutique on Charles St, which features both well-loved designers and up-and-coming talents. The selection of clothing is excellent, but it's the expert advice that makes this place so popular.

BLACKSTONE'S OF BEACON HILL   GIFTS, ACCESSORIES

Map p234 (www.blackstonesbeaconhill.com; 46 Charles St; ⊙10am-6:30pm Mon-Sat, 11am-5pm Sun; TCharles/MGH) Here's a guarantee: you will find the perfect gift for that certain someone at Blackstone's. This little place is crammed with classy, clever and otherwise unusual items. Highlights include the custom-designed stationery, locally made handicrafts and quirky Boston-themed souvenirs like clocks and coasters.

GOOD   JEWELRY, GIFTS

Map p234 (www.shopatgood.com; 133 Charles St; ⊙10am-7pm Tue-Fri, to 6pm Sat; TCharles/MGH) So many lovely things to look at, from exquisite custom-designed jewelry and attractive housewares to quirky baby gifts, chic scarves and handbags. It's hard to ascertain the common theme here, except the items are unique, stylish and supremely classy. Browsing is encouraged.

BEACON HILL CHOCOLATES   FOOD & DRINK

Map p234 (www.beaconhillchocolates.com; 91 Charles St; ⊙11am-7pm Mon-Sat, noon-5:30pm Sun; TCharles/MGH) This artisanal chocolatier puts equal effort into selecting fine chocolates from around the world and designing beautiful keepsake boxes to contain them.

CORE DE VIE   CLOTHING

Map p234 (www.coredevie.com; 40 Charles St; TCharles/MGH) Work that thang in the on-site studio, then reward yourself with a new outfit to show off your fit self. The main attraction is the excellent, ever-renewing selection of active wear, but there's also versatile, comfortable clothing that you can wear in your everyday life.

EUGENE GALLERIES   ANTIQUES

Map p234 (www.eugenegalleries.com; 76 Charles St; ⊙11am-6pm Mon-Sat, noon-6pm Sun; TCharles/MGH) This tiny shop has a remarkable selection of antique prints and maps, especially focusing on old Boston. Follow the history of the city's development by examining 18th- and 19th-century maps and witness the filling-in of Back Bay and the greening of the city.

HELEN'S LEATHER
SHOES, ACCESSORIES

Map p234 (www.helensleather.com; 110 Charles St; ⊙10am-6pm Mon-Sat, noon-6pm Sun; ⊤Charles/MGH) You probably didn't realize that you would need your cowboy boots in Boston. Never fear, you can pick up a slick pair right here on Beacon Hill. (Indeed, this is the number-one distributor of cowboy boots in New England.)

MARIKA'S ANTIQUE SHOP
ANTIQUES

Map p234 (130 Charles St; ⊙10am-5pm Tue-Sat; ⊤Charles/MGH) More than 50 years ago, a Hungarian immigrant opened this treasure trove in Boston's antique central. Today, it is run by her grandson, who is extremely knowledgeable about his inventory.

TWENTIETH CENTURY LTD
JEWELRY

Map p234 (www.boston-vintagejewelry.com; 73 Charles St; ⊙11am-6pm Mon-Sat, noon-5pm Sun; ⊤Charles/MGH) Not just jewelry, but vintage jewelry, especially Bakelite, silver and art-deco designs – costume jewelry made by the great designers of yesteryear. The selection is overwhelming, with something to fit everybody's price range.

BLACK INK
GIFTS

Map p234 (www.blackinkboston.com; 101 Charles St; ⊙11am-7pm Mon-Sat, noon-6pm Sun; ⊤Charles/MGH) Black Ink started as a shop for stationery and rubber stamps (thus, the name), but it has developed into something so much more fun. The tagline – 'unexpected necessities' – conveys the fact that most of this stuff is functional, as well as quirky and clever (if not exactly necessary).

MOXIE
SHOES, ACCESSORIES

Map p234 (www.moxieboston.com; 51 Charles St; ⊙10am-7pm Mon-Fri, 11am-6pm Sat & Sun; ⊤Charles/MGH) 'No outfit is complete without that perfect pair of shoes.' And, 'Why have one bag when you can have a collection?' These bits of wisdom are what inspired avid shopper Karen Fabbri to open a store dedicated to shoes, handbags and other accessories.

RED WAGON
CHILDREN

Map p234 (www.theredwagon.com; 69 Charles St; ⊙10am-7pm Mon-Sat, 11am-6pm Sun; ⛹; ⊤Charles/MGH) The Red Wagon carries adorable, unusual outfits for small tykes, as well as books and toys. Upstairs, you'll find sweet and sassy fashions for 'tweens.

WISH
CLOTHING

Map p234 (www.wishboston.com; 49 Charles St; ⊙10am-7pm Mon-Fri, 11am-6pm Sat & Sun; ⊤Charles/MGH) Some skeptics complain about the more-fashionable-than-thou attitude, but others argue that it does not detract from the way-cool women's wear at Wish. Snazzy suits and sweaters by top-end designers have price tags to match; the dress selection is superb, so it's a nice place to splurge on a special-occasion gown.

🏃 SPORTS & ACTIVITIES

BOSTON COMMON FROG POND
SKATING

Map p234 (www.bostonfrogpond.com; Boston Common; admission adult/child $5/free, rental $10/5; ⊙10am-4pm Mon, to 9pm Tue-Sun mid-Nov–mid-Mar; ⛹; ⊤Park St) When temperatures drop, the Boston Common becomes an urban winter wonderland, with slipping and sliding, swirling and twirling on the Frog Pond. Weekends are often crowded, as are weekdays around noon, as local skate fiends spend their lunch break on the ice. In warmer weather, the Frog Pond becomes a wet and wild spray pool where kids can cool off.

The nearby **Tadpole Playground** (Map p234; ⊤Park) is another fun place for the kids to expend some extra energy.

COMMUNITY BOATING
WATER SPORTS

Map p234 (www.community-boating.org; Charles River Esplanade; kayak/sailboat per day $40/79; ⊙1pm-dusk Mon-Fri, 9am-dusk Sat & Sun Apr-Oct; ⊤Charles/MGH) Offers experienced sailors unlimited use of sailboats and kayaks on the Charles River, but you'll have to take a test to demonstrate your ability. A 30-day 'learn to sail' package is $99, while a 60-day boating pass is $219.

GONDOLA DI VENEZIA
CRUISE

Map p234 (☑617-876-2800; www.bostongondolas.com; Community Boating, Charles River Esplanade; tours per couple $99-229; ⊙2-11pm Fri-Sun Jun-Oct; ⊤Charles/MGH) Make no mistake about it – the Charles River is not the Grand Canal. However, the gondolier's technique and the craftsmanship of the boat make these private gondola rides a romantic treat. Advanced reservations required.

Downtown & Waterfront

FANEUIL HALL | QUINCY MARKET | DOWNTOWN CROSSING | FINANCIAL DISTRICT | WATERFRONT

Neighborhood Top Five

1 Frolicking in the Ring Fountain, riding the carousel and walking the labyrinth in the **Rose Kennedy Greenway** (p84).

2 Taking a **whale-watching boat** (p91) out to Stellwagen Bank to spy on whales, dolphins and other sea life.

3 Remembering the first violent confrontation of the American Revolution at the **site of the Boston Massacre** (p82).

4 Seeing eye-to-eye with multicolored fish, toothy sharks and massive sea turtles at the **New England Aquarium** (p81).

5 Eating, drinking, shopping and general merrymaking at **Faneuil Hall** and **Quincy Market** (p83), Boston's oldest marketplace.

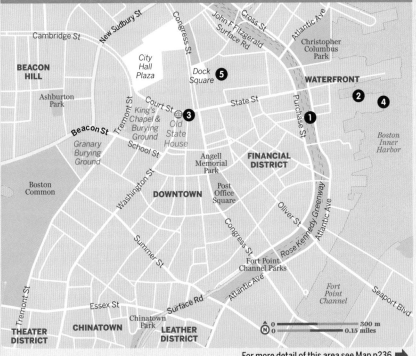

For more detail of this area see Map p236 ➡

Lonely Planet's Top Tip

If you are following the red-brick road, consider purchasing the Freedom Trail Ticket (adult/child $13/2), which includes admission to the Old State House, the Old South Meeting House and the Paul Revere House.

✕ Best Places to Eat

➡ Koy (p86)

➡ Casa Razdora (p86)

➡ Pedro's Tacos (p86)

➡ jm Curley (p87)

➡ Marliave (p87)

For reviews, see p86 ➡

☕ Best Places to Drink

➡ Highball Lounge (p88)

➡ Silvertone (p88)

➡ Thinking Cup (p88)

➡ Caffe Nero (p88)

For reviews, see p88 ➡

◉ Best Historic Buildings

➡ Old State House (p82)

➡ Faneuil Hall (p83)

➡ Custom House (p86)

For reviews, see p83 ➡

Explore Downtown & Waterfront

Almost every visitor will traipse through this neighborhood while following the Freedom Trail to Faneuil Hall and Quincy Market. Indeed, the marketplace is one of the most visited tourist sites in the country. Even though it's basically a shopping mall (but a *historic* shopping mall!), it's a fun stop to admire the public art, cheer on the street performers and soak up the festive atmosphere.

The marketplace is a stark contrast to the neighborhood's interior streets around Downtown Crossing and the Financial District. This is the Boston of the work-a-day world – a bustling place, but after hours the streets are eerily empty.

Along the waterfront, the dismantling of the Central Artery has meant that the call of seagulls and the lapping of waves no longer compete with the roar of cars. Instead, pedestrians can stroll across the Rose Kennedy Greenway parks to the harbor, enjoying the greenery and admiring the Rings Fountain along the way. The focal point of the waterfront is the excellent New England Aquarium. From Long Wharf, you can catch the ferry out to the Boston Harbor Islands. Harbor cruises and trolley tours also depart from these docks, while seafood restaurants and outdoor cafés line the shore.

It's tourist central, and with good reason. With the sun sparkling off the water and the boats bobbing at their moorings, it's hard to resist this city by the sea.

Local Life

➡ **Block Party** On Thursday evenings in summer, the Greenway hosts a block party on **Dewey Sq** (Map p236; www.rosekennedygreenway.org; Atlantic Ave & Summer St; Ⓣ South Station), where local workers gather for drinks and music.

➡ **Happy Hour** Mr Dooley's Boston Tavern (p88) is the rare downtown bar that feels like a neighborhood bar.

Getting There & Away

➡ **Metro** To reach Faneuil Hall and Quincy Market, take the green, orange or blue line to Haymarket, Government Center or State. The blue-line Aquarium stop offers access to the waterfront, as does State (orange or blue). Downtown Crossing sits at the junction of the red and orange lines. Just west of here, Park St station is on the red and green lines.

➡ **Boat** City Water Taxi stops at Long Wharf on the waterfront, while the MBTA water shuttle runs from Long Wharf to Charlestown Navy Yard.

 TOP SIGHT
NEW ENGLAND AQUARIUM

Teeming with sea creatures of all sizes, shapes and colors, this giant fishbowl is the centerpiece of downtown Boston's waterfront. The main attraction is the newly renovated, three-story Giant Ocean Tank, which swirls with thousands of creatures great and small, including turtles, sharks and eels. Countless side exhibits explore the habitats of other underwater oddities, as well as penguins and marine mammals.

Harbor seals hang out in an observation tank near the aquarium entrance, while the open-air **Marine Mammal Center** is home to northern fur seals and California sea lions. Visitors can watch training sessions where the pinnipeds show off their intelligence and athleticism. Note that some animal rights groups make a strong case that marine mammals should not be kept in captivity, no matter how classy their quarters.

The **Shark and Ray Touch Tank** recreates a mangrove swamp teeming with Atlantic rays, cownose rays, bonnethead sharks and epaulette sharks. Descend to the lower level to discover a room full of ethereal **sea jellies**. Despite having no bones, brains or hearts, these captivating species have somehow managed to survive for millions of years.

Most of the aquarium's first floor is occupied by an enormous **penguin exhibit**, home to more than 80 birds representing three different species. Throughout the day, visitors can see live demonstrations and feedings. Six different tanks showcase the flora and fauna of the **Amazon rainforest**, including piranhas, anacondas, electric eels and poison dart frogs.

The 3-D Simons IMAX Theatre (p89) features films with aquatic themes. The aquarium also organizes whale-watching cruises (p91). Combination tickets are available.

DON'T MISS

➡ The magical Leafy Sea Dragon
➡ The ethereal Moon Jelly
➡ The three-story Giant Ocean Tank
➡ Myrtle the green sea turtle

PRACTICALITIES

➡ Map p236
➡ www.neaq.org
➡ Central Wharf
➡ adult/child $25/18
➡ ⊙9am-5pm Mon-Fri, to 6pm Sat & Sun, opens 1hr later Jul & Aug
➡ P ♿
➡ T Aquarium

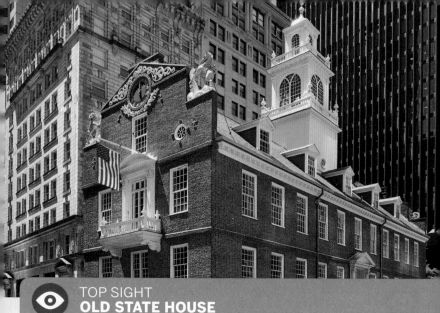

TOP SIGHT
OLD STATE HOUSE

Dating to 1713, making it Boston's oldest surviving public building, the Old State House is where the Massachusetts Assembly used to debate the issues of the day before the revolution. It occupies a once prominent spot on State St (then known as King St), which was Boston's main thoroughfare. The building is best known for its balcony, from where the Declaration of Independence was first read to Bostonians in 1776.

Museum

Inside, the Old State House contains a small museum of revolutionary memorabilia, with videos and multimedia presentations about the Boston Massacre. An informative exhibit *From Colony to Commonwealth* utilizes audio presentations and items from the Bostonian Society's collection to trace important events of the independence movement.

Boston Massacre Site

Directly in front of the Old State House, encircled by cobblestones, a **bronze plaque** (Map p236; cnr State & Devonshire Sts; T State) marks the spot where the first blood was shed for the American independence movement. On March 5, 1770, an angry mob of colonists swarmed the British soldiers guarding the State House. Sam Adams, John Hancock and about 40 other protesters hurled snowballs, rocks and insults. Thus provoked, the soldiers fired into the crowd and killed five townspeople, including Crispus Attucks, a former slave. The incident sparked enormous anti-British sentiment. Paul Revere helped fan the flames by widely disseminating an engraving that depicted the scene as an unmitigated slaughter. Interestingly, John Adams and Josiah Quincy – both of whom opposed the heavy-handed authoritarian British rule – defended the accused soldiers in court, and seven of the nine were acquitted.

DON'T MISS

➡ *From Colony to Commonwealth* audio tour
➡ Paul Revere's engraving of the Boston Massacre
➡ Boston Massacre Site

PRACTICALITIES

➡ Map p236
➡ www.revolutionary boston.org
➡ 206 Washington St
➡ adult/child $10/free
➡ ⊘9am-6pm Jun-Aug, to 5pm Sep-May
➡ T State

SIGHTS

⊙ Faneuil Hall, Quincy Market & Around

Historic Faneuil Hall, along with the three long granite buildings that make up Quincy Market, served as the center of the city's produce and meat industry for almost 150 years. In the 1970s the old buildings were redeveloped into today's touristy, festive shopping and eating center, so it still serves its original purpose, albeit with all the modern trappings.

OLD STATE HOUSE HISTORIC BUILDING
See p82.

FANEUIL HALL HISTORIC BUILDING
Map p236 (www.nps.gov/bost; Congress St; ⊙9am-5pm; ⊤Haymarket or Government Center) FREE 'Those who cannot bear free speech had best go home,' said Wendell Phillips. 'Faneuil Hall is no place for slavish hearts.' Indeed, this public meeting place was the site of so much rabble-rousing that it earned the nickname the 'Cradle of Liberty.' After the revolution, Faneuil Hall was a forum for meetings about abolition, women's suffrage and war. The historic hall is normally open to the public, who can hear about the building's history from NPS rangers.

The brick colonial building – topped with the beloved grasshopper weather vane – was constructed in 1740 at the urging of Boston benefactor and merchant Peter Faneuil. In 1805 Charles Bulfinch enlarged the building, enclosing the 1st-floor market and designing the 2nd-floor meeting space, where public ceremonies are still held today. On the 3rd floor the Ancient & Honorable Artillery Co of Massachusetts, which was chartered in 1638, maintains a peculiar collection of antique firearms, political mementos and curious artifacts.

BLACKSTONE BLOCK HISTORIC SITE
Map p236 (cnr Union & Hanover Sts; ⊤Haymarket) Named after Boston's first settler, this tiny warren of streets dates to the 17th and 18th centuries. Established in 1826, Union Oyster House (p86) is Boston's oldest restaurant. Around the corner in Creek Sq, the c 1767 Ebenezer Hancock House was the home of John Hancock's brother. At the base of the shop next door, the 1737 **Boston Stone** (Map p236; Creek Sq; ⊤Haymarket) served as the terminus for measuring distances to and from 'the Hub.' (The State House dome now serves this purpose.)

NEW ENGLAND HOLOCAUST MEMORIAL MEMORIAL
Map p236 (www.nehm.org; btwn Union & Congress Sts; ⊤Haymarket) Constructed in 1995, the six luminescent glass columns of the New England Holocaust Memorial are engraved with six million numbers, representing those killed in the Holocaust. Each tower – with smoldering coals sending plumes of steam up through the glass corridors – represents a different Nazi death camp. The memorial sits along the Freedom Trail, a sobering reminder of its larger meaning.

CITY HALL PLAZA SQUARE
Map p236 (⊤Government Center) City Hall Plaza is a cold, windy, 56-acre concrete plaza, surrounded by government office buildings. Occupying the site of the former Scollay Sq, the plaza was supposed to be a model of innovation and modernization when it was built in the 1960s. But it has been much maligned, topping at least one list of the world's ugliest buildings. The plaza hosts food trucks, public gatherings and occasional summertime performances.

LOCAL KNOWLEDGE

STEAMING TEA KETTLE

The **Steaming Kettle** (Map p236; 63-65 Court St) on Sears Crescent has been a Boston landmark since 1873, when it was hung over the door of the Oriental Tea Co at 57 Court St. The teashop held a contest to determine how much tea the giant kettle might hold. The answer – awarded with a chest of premium tea – was 227 gallons, two quarts, one pint and three gills.

The tea kettle was relocated to its current location on the western tip of the Sears Crescent building in 1967, when 'urban renewal' swept this neighborhood. Tea drinkers are grateful that this icon of old Boston was saved, although many are miffed that it now marks the spot of a Starbucks.

Designed by IM Pei, City Hall Plaza is home to the fortress-like Boston City Hall and the twin towers of the John F Kennedy Federal Building. The plaza's high points are the gracefully curved brick **Sears Crescent** (Map p236; cnr Court & Tremont Sts), one of the few buildings that remains from the Scollay Sq days, and the sweeping curve of the modern **Center Plaza** (Map p236; Cambridge St; TGovernment Center), which mirrors Sears Crescent.

⊙ Downtown Crossing & Financial District

KING'S CHAPEL & BURYING GROUND   CHURCH, CEMETERY

Map p236 (www.kings-chapel.org; 58 Tremont St; self-guided tour donation $2, Bells & Bones tour $8; ⊙10am-5pm Mon-Sat, 1:30-5pm Sun; TState) Puritan Bostonians were not pleased when the original Anglican church was erected on this site in 1688. The gran-

ite chapel standing today – built in 1754 – houses the largest bell ever made by Paul Revere, as well as a historic organ. The adjacent burying ground is the oldest in the city. Besides the bi-weekly services, recitals are held here every week (12:15pm Tuesday).

The church was built on a corner of the city cemetery because the Puritans refused to allow the Anglicans to use any other land. As a result, these are some of the city's oldest headstones, including one that dates to 1623. Famous graves include John Winthrop, the first governor of the fledgling Massachusetts Bay Colony; William Dawes, who rode with Paul Revere; and Mary Chilton, the first European woman to set foot in Plymouth.

In addition to the self-guided tour, visitors are invited on the **Bells & Bones tour**, which ascends the bell tower to admire Paul Revere's work and descends into the crypt to wander among 250-year-old remains.

OLD CITY HALL   HISTORIC SITE

Map p236 (www.oldcityhall.com; 45 School St; TState) This monumental French Second

---

WORTH A DETOUR

ROSE KENNEDY GREENWAY

The gateway to the newly revitalized waterfront is the **Rose Kennedy Greenway** (Map p236; www.rosekennedygreenway.org; ⊞; TAquarium or Haymarket). Where once was a hulking overhead highway, now winds a 27-acre strip of landscaped gardens and fountain-lined greens, with an artist market for Saturday shoppers, and food trucks for weekday lunchers.

Walking the Greenway from North to South, here's what you'll find along the way:

➡ **North End Park** Designed as the North End neighborhood's front yard, the wide lawn is a perfect place for a picnic.

➡ **Labyrinth** Calm your mind and contemplate the moment as you follow the granite path, winding its way along a serpentine route. The **labyrinth** (Map p236; www.rosekennedygreenway.org; Rose Kennedy Greenway; ⊞; THaymarket) represents the journey of life. (The destination is beside the point.)

➡ **Greenway Carousel** Take a ride on the backs of local sea and woodland creatures, such as American lobsters, harbor seals, monarch butterflies and red-tailed hawks. This one-of-a-kind **carousel** (Map p236; $3; ⊙11am-7pm Apr-Dec; ⊞; THaymarket) was designed by local artist Jeff Briggs with help from local school children.

➡ **Boston Harbor Islands Pavilion** Want more information about the Boston Harbor Islands? Stop by this seasonal **information center** (p216). Don't miss the nearby Harbor Fog Sculpture, which immerses passers-by in the sounds and sensations of the harbor.

➡ **Rings Fountain** This playful **fountain** (Map p236; TAquarium) is unpredictable and irresistible, especially on a hot day.

➡ **Dewey Sq Parks** With food vendors and farmers markets, this is a popular lunch spot for the working world. Dewey Sq is also the site of Boston's most prominent street art – usually a mural by an artist of some renown.

➡ **Chinatown Park** Asian gardens, Chinese chessboards and Falun Gong practitioners populate this plaza, which serves as the gateway to Chinatown.

MILLENNIUM TOWER

For nearly 100 years, Filene's Department Store was the cornerstone of Downtown Crossing. But when city dwellers started moving out to the suburbs and shopping at malls, fortunes changed for the department store and for this downtown shopping area. By the late 20th century, many storefronts were empty and Filene's was struggling. In 2006, the retail chain was sold to Macy's, and the flagship store was eventually shuttered.

Much to the dismay of Bostonians, the building was demolished in 2008 (though the historic facade was preserved). There were grand plans for the site, but they didn't get too far before the developer ran out of money. Downtown Crossing was left with a massive hole in its core.

Five years later, Bostonians were relieved when work started anew on this site. Filene's successor will be **Millennium Tower** (Map p236; www.millenniumtowerboston. com; Washington St; TDowntown Crossing) – a high-rise residential tower, and the tallest skyscraper outside the Back Bay. It's been a long time in coming, but the city has high hopes that this endeavor will pump some new life into this declining district.

Empire building occupies a historic spot. Out front, a plaque commemorates the site of the country's first public school, Boston Latin, founded in 1635 and still operational in Fenway. The hopscotch sidewalk mosaic, *City Carpet,* marks the spot where Benjamin Franklin, Ralph Waldo Emerson and Charles Bulfinch were educated.

Statues of Benjamin Franklin, founding father, and Josiah Quincy, second mayor of Boston, stand inside the courtyard. They are accompanied by a life-size replica of a donkey, symbol of the Democratic Party. ('Why the donkey?' you wonder. Read the plaque to find out.) Two bronze footprints 'stand in opposition.'

OLD CORNER BOOKSTORE
HISTORIC BUILDING

Map p236 (cnr School & Washington Sts; TDowntown Crossing) In the 19th century, this historic house was leased to a bookseller, Carter & Hendlee. This was the first of nine bookstores and publishing companies that would occupy the spot, making it a breeding ground for literary and philosophical ideas. The most illustrious was Ticknor & Fields, publisher of books by Thoreau, Emerson, Hawthorne, Longfellow and Harriet Beecher Stowe.

In the earliest days of Boston history, this was the site of the home of Anne Hutchinson, the religious dissident who was expelled from the Massachusetts Bay colony and co-founded the Rhode Island colony. The current brick building dates to 1718, when it served as a pharmacy and residence. Today the storefront houses a fast

food restaurant, which seems somewhat less lofty than its earlier incarnations.

OLD SOUTH MEETING HOUSE
HISTORIC BUILDING

Map p236 (www.osmh.org; 310 Washington St; adult/child $6/1; ⊙9:30am-5pm Apr-Oct, 10am-4pm Nov-Mar; TDowntown Crossing or State) 'No tax on tea!' That was the decision on December 16, 1773, when 5000 angry colonists gathered here to protest British taxes, leading to the Boston Tea Party. Visit the graceful meeting house to check out an exhibit about the history of the building and listen to an audio reenactment of the historic pre–Tea Party meeting.

This brick meeting house, with its soaring steeple, was also used as a church house back in the day. In fact, Ben Franklin was baptized here. Which is why he found it so abhorrent when – after the Tea Party – British soldiers used the building for a stable and riding practice. The Old South congregation moved to a new building in Back Bay in 1875, when Ralph Waldo Emerson and Julia Ward Howe gathered support to convert the church into a museum.

⊙ Waterfront

NEW ENGLAND AQUARIUM
AQUARIUM

See p81.

CUSTOM HOUSE
MUSEUM

Map p236 (www.marriott.com; 3 McKinley Sq; observation deck $5; ⊙observation deck 2pm Sat-Thu; TAquarium) Begun in 1837, the lower portion of the Custom House resembles a Greek temple. But the federal government wanted something grander, so in 1913 it exempted itself from local height restrictions and financed a 500ft tower. Nowadays there are many taller buildings, but the 22ft illuminated clock makes this gem the most recognizable part of the city skyline.

One of Boston's first skyscrapers, the Custom House now houses a Marriott hotel. But that doesn't mean you have to dole out big bucks to appreciate the building's history and aesthetics. The public is welcome to the 1st-floor rotunda, a work of art in itself, which houses a small exhibit of maritime art and artifacts from Salem's Peabody Essex Museum (p170). Even better, the public is welcome to enjoy the spectacular views from the 26th-floor **observation deck** when weather permits.

EATING

✖ Faneuil Hall, Quincy Market & Around

Faneuil Hall and its environs are packed with touristy places touting baked beans, live lobsters and other Boston specialties. It's hard to get off the beaten track, but that doesn't mean you won't find some fun, funky and delicious places to eat.

QUINCY MARKET   FOOD COURT $
Map p236 (www.faneuilhallmarketplace.com; Congress St; ⊙10am-9pm Mon-Sat, noon-6pm Sun; 🛜🚲♿; ⊤Haymarket) Behind Faneuil Hall, this food court offers a variety of places under one roof: the place is packed with about 20 restaurants and 40 food stalls. Choose from chowder, bagels, Indian, Greek, baked goods and ice cream, and take a seat at one of the tables in the central rotunda.

KOY   KOREAN $$
Map p236 (☑857-991-1483; www.koyboston.com; 16 North St; mains $15-28; ⊙11am-midnight Sun-Thu, to 1am Fri & Sat; 🛜; ⊤Haymarket) It's unusual that something so classy, so contemporary and so cosmopolitan should find a home in historic Blackstone Block. But here it is: Korean fusion. There are traditional dishes, including excellent bibimbap, but

the 'twists' are what make mouths water, not to mention the original cocktails. Soju Sangria is potent.

DURGIN PARK   AMERICAN $$
Map p236 (www.durgin-park.com; North Market, Faneuil Hall; mains lunch $9-15, dinner $15-30; ⊙11:30am-9pm; ♿; ⊤Haymarket) Known for no-nonsense service, Durgin Park hasn't changed much since the restaurant opened in 1827. Nor has the menu, which features New England standards such as prime rib, fish chowder, chicken pot pie and Boston baked beans, with Indian pudding for dessert. Be prepared to make friends with the other parties seated at your table.

UNION OYSTER HOUSE   SEAFOOD $$$
Map p236 (www.unionoysterhouse.com; 41 Union St; mains lunch $15-20, dinner $22-32; ⊙11am-9:30pm; ⊤Haymarket) The oldest restaurant in Boston, ye olde Union Oyster House has been serving seafood in this historic red-brick building since 1826. Countless history-makers have propped themselves up at this bar, including Daniel Webster and John F Kennedy. (Apparently JFK used to order the lobster bisque.) Overpriced but atmospheric.

✖ Downtown Crossing & Financial District

CASA RAZDORA   ITALIAN $
Map p236 (www.casarazdora.com; 115 Water St; mains $7-10; ⊙11am-4pm Mon-Wed, to 5pm Thu & Fri; 🖋; ⊤State) The line is usually out the door, but it's worth the wait for amazing Italian food, just like your nonna made. Pick a pasta (all made fresh on the premises) and top it with the delicious sauce of your choosing. Or select one of the chef's mouthwatering daily specials. Seats are limited, so snag one if you can!

PEDRO'S TACOS   MEXICAN $
Map p236 (www.pedrostacos.com; 55 Bromfield St; tacos $3-5; ⊙7am-6pm Mon-Fri; 🖋♿; ⊤Park St) Imagine a sweet, surfside taco shop in Southern California, transplanted to downtown Boston. That's Pedro's, complete with boards on the wall, chilled-out ambience and to-die-for fish tacos. But there's one thing this joint has that SoCal taquerias don't: lobster tacos. Why didn't somebody think of *that* before?

CHACARERO
SANDWICHES **$**

Map p236 (www.chacarero.com; 101 Arch St; mains breakfast $4-6, lunch $7-10; ☺8am-6pm Mon-Fri; ⊤Downtown Crossing) A *chacarero* is a traditional Chilean sandwich made with grilled chicken or beef, Muenster cheese, fresh tomatoes, guacamole and the surprise ingredient – steamed green beans. Stuffed into homemade bread, the sandwiches are a favorite for lunch around Downtown.

SAM LA GRASSA'S
DELI **$**

Map p236 (www.samlagrassas.com; 44 Province St; sandwiches $12-13; ☺11am-3:30pm Mon-Fri; 🍴📶; ⊤Downtown Crossing) Step up to the counter and place your order for one of Sam La Grassa's signature sandwiches, then find a spot at the crowded communal table. You won't be disappointed by the famous Romanian pastrami or the 'fresh from the pot' corned beef. All of the sandwiches are so well stuffed that they can be tricky to eat, which is part of the fun.

FALAFEL KING
MIDDLE EASTERN **$**

Map p236 (48 Winter St; mains $5-7; ☺11am-8pm Mon-Fri, to 4pm Sat; 🍴; ⊤Downtown Crossing) Two words: free falafels. That's right, everyone gets a little free sample before ordering. There is no disputing that this carry-out spot is indeed the falafel king of Boston. The sandwiches are fast, delicious and cheap, and you're only a half a block from a picnic on the Common. If you prefer to sit inside, there's another location nearby on **Summer St** (Map p236; 62 Summer St; mains $5-7; ☺11am-7:30pm Mon-Fri; 🍴; ⊤Downtown Crossing).

JM CURLEY
PUB FOOD **$$**

Map p236 (www.jmcurleyboston.com; 21 Temple Pl; mains lunch $8-10, dinner $13-20; ☺11:30am-1am; ⊤Downtown Crossing) This dim, inviting bar is a perfect place to settle in for a Dark & Stormy on a dark and stormy night. The fare is bar food like you've never had before: curley's cracka jack (caramel corn with bacon); mac 'n' cheese (served in a cast-iron skillet); and fried pickles (yes, you read that right). That's why they call it a gastropub.

The place is named for Boston's beloved four-term (including one term – his last – that he served from prison) mayor.

MARLIAVE
AMERICAN, FRENCH **$$$**

Map p236 (www.marliave.com; 10 Bosworth St; sandwiches $14-16, mains $22-38; ☺11am-10pm; 🍴; ⊤Park St) Dating to 1885, the Marliave has all of its vintage architectural quirks still intact, from the mosaic floor to the tin ceilings. The wide-ranging menu includes quirky cocktails, a raw bar, delicious egg dishes, house-made pastas, and old-fashioned Sunday dinners (eg, Wellington). Best bargain: half-price oysters from 4pm to 6pm and from 9pm to 10pm daily.

LOCAL KNOWLEDGE

TO MARKET, TO MARKET

Local foodies are buzzing about the long-awaited opening of the Boston Public Market, the city's first permanent local farmers market. The location is just a few steps from Haymarket, and a few more steps from Faneuil Hall and Quincy Market, which is the city's historic marketplace. As such, the new public market anchors a vibrant 'market district' in downtown Boston.

Boston Public Market (BPM; Map p236; www.bostonpublicmarket.org; 136 Blackstone St; ☺May-Nov; ⊤Haymarket) A locavore's longtime dream-come-true, the Boston Public Market is a daily farmers market, housed in a brick-and-mortar building, that gives shoppers access to fresh foodstuffs, grown and harvested right here in New England. Any day – spring, summer or fall – come for seasonal produce, fresh seafood, meats and poultry from local farms, artisan cheeses and dairy products, maple syrup and other sweets.

The BPM is due to open in the summer of 2015.

Haymarket (Map p236; Blackstone & Hanover Sts; ☺7am-5pm Fri & Sat; ⊤Haymarket) Touch the produce at Haymarket and you risk the wrath of the vendors, but nowhere in the city matches these prices on ripe-and-ready fruits and vegetables. And nowhere matches Haymarket for local charm. Operated by the Haymarket Vendors Association, this outdoor market is an outlet for discount produce that was purchased from wholesalers.

LOCAL KNOWLEDGE

BOSTON CREAM PIE

Wondering where to go to sample Boston's namesake dessert? At the Omni Parker House, they could write a book about Boston Cream Pie, as the hotel's pastry chefs invented this creamy, cakey delight. Literally. For a special occasion dessert, hunker down at the **Last Hurrah** (p89) for an individual-sized Boston Cream Pie, artfully presented and masterfully paired with a glass of Cava. Delightful!

DRINKING & NIGHTLIFE

After the department store at Downtown Crossing locks up for the night, the street life quiets considerably. There is a cluster of bars around Faneuil Hall and Blackstone Block, but most of them actively cater to the tourist crowd and have an underwhelming, generic vibe. Embedded nearby are some perennial favorites, some of them quite crowded on weekends.

THINKING CUP   CAFE

Map p236 (www.thinkingcup.com; 165 Tremont St; ⊙7am-10pm Mon-Wed, to 11pm Thu-Sun; TBoylston) 🍴 There are a few things that make the Thinking Cup special. One is the French hot chocolate – *ooh la la*. Another is the Stumptown Coffee, the Portland brew that has earned accolades from coffee-drinkers around the country. But the best thing? It's across from the Boston Common, making it a perfect stop for a post–Frog Pond warm-up.

HIGHBALL LOUNGE   COCKTAIL BAR, LOUNGE

Map p236 (www.highballboston.com; 90 Tremont St; ⊙5pm-2am; TPark St) Go out to play! Well stocked with board games, the Highball Lounge has yours, whether you're on a date (Connect Four) or in a group (Jenga). The Viewmaster is for looking at the menu, which features local beers, creative cocktails and intriguing snack foods (tater tot nachos, crispy brussel sprouts). This place will make you feel like a kid again. Except you can drink.

SIP CAFÉ   CAFE

Map p236 (www.sipboston.com; Post Office Sq; ⊙6:30am-6pm Mon-Fri Apr-Nov, to 5pm Dec-Mar; 🍴; TDowntown Crossing) Enclosed by glass and surrounded by the greenery of Post Office Sq, Sip Café is a delightful place to stop for lunch or a caffeinated beverage. There's outdoor seating in warm weather, but even in winter, the high ceilings and streaming sunlight will warm your heart. As will the George Howell coffee, daily-changing soups and yummy sandwiches.

SILVERTONE   PUB

Map p236 (www.silvertonedowntown.com; 69 Bromfield St; ⊙11:30am-2am Mon-Fri, 6pm-2am Sat; TPark St) Black-and-white photos and retro advertising posters create a nostalgic atmosphere at this still-trendy pub and grill. The old-fashioned comfort food is always satisfying (the steak tips come highly recommended), as is Miller High Life in a bottle (and local beers on tap). Popular after-work spot.

CAFFE NERO   CAFE

Map p236 (http://us.caffenero.com; 560 Washington St; ⊙7am-9:30pm; 🍴; TChinatown or Downtown Crossing) Italian coffee. Antique Alsatian bar. Comfy couches and cozy fireplace. Cosmopolitan clientele. This place is oozing Old World ambience, and we mean that in the most modern, sophisticated way. Espresso drinks are top-notch, and there's sidewalk seating in warm weather.

FROST ICE BAR   BAR

Map p236 (www.frosticebar.com; Faneuil Hall Marketplace; adult/child $12/6; ⊙2-9pm Mon-Thu, noon-10pm Fri & Sat, to 8pm Sun; THaymarket) Don your puffy, insulated parka and enter the coolest bar in Boston. How cool is it? Twenty-one degrees. This entire place is carved out of ice, including the bar, the furniture and the Boston-themed sculptures. The bar serves overpriced cocktails ($11) in ice glasses. Kind of hokey, but kind of fun. Young people (under 21) are not admitted after 5pm.

MR DOOLEY'S BOSTON TAVERN   IRISH PUB

Map p236 (www.somerspubs.com; 77 Broad St; ⊙11:30am-2am Mon-Fri, 9am-2am Sat & Sun; TState) With Irish bands playing traditional tunes from Friday to Sunday and a decent list of appropriate beers, this warm and inviting bar is one of the most welcoming joints in the area. Sit in a wooden booth and linger over a copy of the *Irish Immigrant* or *Boston Irish Reporter* to learn about current events on the other side of the Atlantic.

GOOD LIFE   CLUB
Map p236 (www.goodlifebar.com; 28 Kingston St; cover $5-10; ☺11:30am-2am Mon-Fri, 5pm-2am Sat; ⓉDowntown Crossing) The Good Life means a lot of things to a lot of people – solid lunch option, after-work hangout, trivia night etc. But the top reason to come to the Good Life is to get your groove on. Three bars and two dance floors, with great DJs spinning tunes Thursday to Saturday.

LAST HURRAH   HOTEL BAR
Map p236 (www.omnihotels.com; 60 School St; ☺11:30am-1am Mon-Fri, 6am-1am Sat; ⓉPark St) It's now named for the 1956 novel about former Boston mayor James Michael Curley, but the elegant lobby bar of the Omni Parker House hotel was a hallowed haunt for Boston's 19th-century intelligentsia and politicians. Enjoy a dish of hot nuts and drink a bourbon at this throwback to Old Boston.

BIDDY EARLY'S PUB   DIVE BAR
Map p236 (141 Pearl St; ☺10am-2am; ⓉSouth Station) If dive bars are your thing, you'll be happy here. In fact, Biddy's is sometimes called the 'best' dive bar in Boston (a town that has no shortage of them). We're not sure what that means (Dirtiest bathrooms? Cheapest beer?), but needless to say, you'll find a dart board, a juke box, buckets of beers and very friendly faces on both sides of the bar.

ALLEY BAR   GAY
Map p236 (www.thealleybar.com; 14 Pi Alley; ⓉDowntown Crossing) If you can find this secret spot, you will be welcomed in. No matter if you are petite, effeminate (or female) or even straight. This place is known as a 'bear bar,' but most of these big gruff guys are friendly – very friendly. Enjoy the cheap beer and laid-back atmosphere.

Pi Alley is a tiny pedestrian lane that runs between Washington St and Court Sq.

UMBRIA PRIME   CLUB
Map p236 (www.umbriaristorante.com; 295 Franklin St; cover $20; ☺10pm-2am Fri & Sat; ⓉState) On weekends, the upper floors of this Italian restaurant are transformed into a swank nightclub, featuring plush couches,

crowded dance floors, an LED wall and a great line-up of DJs. An international designer crowd queues up, starting around midnight. Go online to get yourself on the guestlist and look sharp. Free admission if you eat at the restaurant.

☆ ENTERTAINMENT

OPERA HOUSE   LIVE PERFORMANCE
Map p236 (www.bostonoperahouse.com; 539 Washington St; ⓉDowntown Crossing) This lavish theater has been restored to its 1928 glory, complete with mural-painted ceiling, gilded molding and plush velvet curtains. The glitzy venue regularly hosts productions from the Broadway Across America series, and is also the main performance space for the Boston Ballet.

PARAMOUNT CENTER   DANCE, THEATER
Map p236 (www.paramountboston.org; 559 Washington St; ⓉChinatown or Downtown Crossing) This art-deco masterpiece, restored by Emerson College, re-opened in 2010. Originally a 1700-seat, single-screen cinema, it was owned by Paramount Pictures (thus, the name). The new facility includes a cinema and a black-box stage, as well as the more traditional but still grand main stage.

DICK'S BEANTOWN COMEDY   COMEDY
Map p236 (www.dickdoherty.com; 184 High St; admission $15-20; ☺7:30pm Thu & Sat, 8pm Fri & Sun; ⓉAquarium) In the basement of a nightclub, local comedian Dick Doherty and a collection of regular helpers work the room into painful howls with surgical precision. Sunday nights are open mic, and the pain you feel on such occasions might feel very different than on other days.

SIMONS IMAX THEATRE   CINEMA
Map p236 (www.neaq.org; Central Wharf; adult/child $10/8; ☺10am-10pm; ♿; ⓉAquarium) At the New England Aquarium, this IMAX bad boy plays lots of educational films on a six-story screen, in 3D. That way, when you have a gander at *Sharks,* you'll actually feel like you're about to be eaten. It occasionally plays IMAX versions of popular fare.

MODERN THEATRE   CINEMA, THEATER
Map p236 (www.suffolk.edu; 525 Washington St; ⓉDowntown Crossing) The Modern Theatre dates to 1876 and showed Boston's first 'talkie' in 1928. Nearly a century later,

DOWNTOWN & WATERFRONT ENTERTAINMENT

the building has opened its doors again as a venue for Suffolk University, holding an intimate 185-seat theater. Only the facade remains from the original building, but it looks stellar – another step in the revival of a mini theater district on lower Washington St.

 # SHOPPING

Downtown Crossing is an outdoor pedestrian mall. Many of the stores are outlets of national chains, although a few local yokels are still keeping it real. The Faneuil Hall and Quincy Market area is possibly Boston's most popular tourist shopping spot: upward of 15 million people visit annually. The five buildings are filled with 100-plus tourist-oriented shops, pushcart vendors and national chain stores.

BRATTLE BOOK SHOP BOOKS
Map p236 (www.brattlebookshop.com; 9 West St; ☺9am-5:30pm Mon-Sat; Ⓣ Park St) Since 1825, the Brattle Book Shop has catered to Boston's literati: it's a treasure trove crammed with out-of-print, rare and first-edition books. Ken Gloss – whose family has owned this gem since 1949 – is an expert on antiquarian books, moonlighting as a consultant and appraiser (see him on *Antiques Roadshow*). Don't miss the bargains on the outside lot.

GREENWAY OPEN MARKET ART MARKET
Map p236 (www.newenglandopenmarkets.com; Rose Kennedy Greenway; ☺11am-5pm Sat May-Oct; ☎; Ⓣ Aquarium) This Saturday-only artist market brings dozens of vendors to display their wares in the open air. Look for unique, handmade gifts, jewelry, bags, paintings, ceramics and other arts and crafts – most of which are locally and ethically made. Food trucks are always on hand to cater to the hungry.

LUCY'S LEAGUE CLOTHING
Map p236 (www.rosterstores.com/lucysleague; North Market, Faneuil Hall; ☺10am-9pm Mon-Sat, to 6pm Sun; Ⓣ Government Center) We're not advocating those pink Red Sox caps, but sometimes a girl wants to look good while she's supporting the team. At Lucy's League, fashionable sports fans will find shirts, jackets and other gear sporting the local teams' logos in super-cute styles designed to flatter the female figure.

MAKE WAY FOR DUCKLINGS CHILDREN, BOOKS
Map p236 (www.makewayforducklings.com; North Market, Faneuil Hall; ☺10am-9pm Mon-Sat, 11am-7pm Sun; 🏃; Ⓣ Haymarket) The legacy of Robert McClosky's ducklings lives on at this children's bookstore in Faneuil Hall Marketplace. The friendly shop has a super selection of books and toys for little people, including many written by local authors. Story times and sing-alongs are regular events.

SOCK IT TO ME ACCESSORIES
Map p236 (www.sockittomeboston.com; South Market, Faneuil Hall; ☺11am-9pm Mon-Sat, noon-6pm Sun; Ⓣ State) You know you want a pair of Boston Terrier socks to remember your visit. Not your dog? Don't worry, some 25 breeds are available. There are also cat socks, lobster socks, shoe socks and – of course – Red Sox. Whether you choose fancy, funky or funny, they are all functional and fun. It's the perfect souvenir, really.

DESIGN MUSEUM BOSTON STORE ARTS
Map p236 (www.designmuseumboston.org; 70 East India Row; ☺11am-6pm Tue-Sat; Ⓣ Aquarium) The Design Museum is a pop-up museum ('Design is everywhere. So are we.'), but the museum shop is always here, overlooking the Greenway, selling quirky T-shirts, cool tote bags and attractive coffee-table books. The gallery also showcases some rad pieces by partner designers. Drop in to find out about design exhibits and events all around town.

LOCAL CHARM JEWELRY
Map p236 (www.localcharm.net; South Market, Faneuil Hall; ☺10am-9pm Mon-Sat, 11am-7pm Sun; Ⓣ State) Here's something to make you cynical: Local Charm is a chain store, with outlets in five states. Once you clear up that misunderstanding, you can appreciate the exquisite things on offer in this tiny jewelry boutique. The jewelry is tasteful, artful and interesting. And some of it is even crafted by local artisans.

GEOCLASSICS JEWELRY
Map p236 (www.geoclassics.com; North Market, Faneuil Hall; ☺10am-9pm Mon-Sat, noon-6pm Sun; Ⓣ State) Geoclassics showcases minerals, fossils and gemstones in jewelry and other decorative settings. The natural beau-

ty of the stones is enhanced by their artistic presentation. The collection of fossils – from dinosaur eggs to dragonflies – is incredible.

REVOLUTIONARY
BOSTON MUSEUM STORE SOUVENIRS

Map p236 (www.revolutionaryboston.org; Quincy Market; ⊙10am-9pm Mon-Sat, 11am-6pm Sun; ⊤State) Souvenirs with an Americana theme: woven throws featuring flags, eagles and other all-American goodness; reproductions of Paul Revere's depiction of the Boston Massacre; patriotic coffee mugs etc. The cleverest souvenirs are in the food aisle: Boston Harbor Tea, Stars & Stripes pasta and other treats to enliven your next July 4 cookout.

JEWELERS EXCHANGE BUILDING JEWELRY

Map p236 (www.jewelersbuildingboston.com; 333 Washington St; ⊙8am-6pm Mon-Sat; ⊤Downtown Crossing) With over 100 jewelers, this historic building is the first stop for many would-be grooms. Some jewelers have retail space on the 1st floor, other less conspicuous artisans work upstairs. If you're overwhelmed by too many options, go to Boston Ring and Gem (BRAG) on the 2nd floor. The Zargarian family has been designing and crafting the sparkly stuff for seven generations.

BOSTON PEWTER COMPANY SOUVENIRS

Map p236 (www.bostonpewtercompany.com; 5 South Market, Faneuil Hall; ⊙10am-9pm Mon-Sat, noon-6pm Sun; ⊤State) This specialty shop is pretty much what the name says. Think tableware, picture frames and light fixtures, all crafted from the elegant metal. The collection is supplemented with other New England collectibles like scrimshaw, copper weather vanes and hand-blown glass.

🏃 SPORTS & ACTIVITIES

⭐**NEW ENGLAND AQUARIUM**
WHALE WATCH WHALE WATCHING

Map p236 (www.neaq.org; Central Wharf; adult/child/infant $49/33/16; ⊙times vary Apr-Oct; ⛟; ⊤Aquarium) 🚢 Board the *Voyager III* for the journey out to Stellwagen Bank, a rich feeding ground for whales, dolphins and marine birds. Onboard naturalists can answer all your questions, plus they have keen eyes. Whale sightings are guaranteed, otherwise you'll receive a coupon for a free trip at a later date.

NPS FREEDOM TRAIL TOUR WALKING TOUR

Map p236 (www.nps.gov/bost; Faneuil Hall; ⊙10am & 2pm Apr-Oct; ⊤State) **FREE** Show up at least 30 minutes early to snag a spot on one of the free, ranger-led Freedom Trail tours provided by the National Park Service. Tours depart from the visitor center in Faneuil Hall, and follow a portion of the Freedom Trail (not including Charlestown), for a total of 90 minutes. Each tour is limited to 30 people.

LIBERTY FLEET CRUISE

Map p236 (✆617-742-0333; www.libertyfleet.com; Central Wharf; adult $30-35, child $19-24; ⊙times vary Jun-Sep; ⊤Aquarium) Th 125ft *Liberty Clipper* and the smaller *Liberty Star* take passengers out for a two-hour, 12-mile cruise around the harbor. The schooners sail several times a day, sometimes offering history reenactments, brunch or sunsets. Purchase tickets online or from the office on Long Wharf.

CODZILLA BOATING

Map p236 (www.bostonharborcruises.com; 1 Long Wharf; adult/child $29/25; ⊙times vary May-Sep; ⛟; ⊤Aquarium) 'Boating' may not be the proper word to describe this activity, which takes place on a 2800HP speedboat that cruises through the waves at speeds of up to 40mph. Painted like a multicolored shark with a big toothy grin, the boat has a unique hull design that enables it to do the ocean version of doughnuts. Warning: you will get wet.

Boston by Water

With the expansive Boston Harbor at its front door and the winding River Charles at its back, Boston offers endless opportunities for beach bumming, boat rides, seaside strolls and riverside relaxation. Whatever aquatic activity you choose, don't miss a chance to feel the breeze and soak up the stunning views.

1

5

STEVE DUNWELL/GETTY IMAGES ©

1. Zakim Bunker Hill Bridge (p53)
Zakim Bunker Hill Bridge over the Charles River.

2. Seaport District (p133)
Dining at waterfront Liberty Wharf.

3. Harborside Boston (p85)
View of Boston Harbor and skyline.

4. Charles River (p110)
Sailing on the Charles River.

5. Boston on the Water (p85)
Boston's magnificent waterfront skyline.

4

JEAN-PIERRE LESCOURRET/GETTY IMAGES ©

3

DWIGHT NADIG/GETTY IMAGES ©

South End & Chinatown

SOUTH END | CHINATOWN | THEATER DISTRICT | LEATHER DISTRICT

Neighborhood Top Five

1 Hitting Chinatown (p99) for pork buns, dumplings and other dim sum delights.

2 Browsing at the **SoWa Open Market** (p103) and **SoWa Vintage Market** (p104) followed by Sunday brunch in the South End.

3 Packing into **Wally's Café** (p102) for old-time jazz and blues.

4 Sampling the stylish vintage threads at **Bobby from Boston** (p103).

5 Dressing to the nines and going out for a night in the Theater District, whether for comedy at the **Wilbur Theatre** (p103), opera at the **Shubert Theatre** (p103) or dance at the **Wang Theatre** (p103).

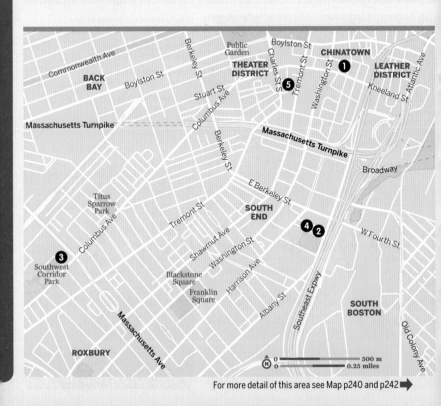

For more detail of this area see Map p240 and p242 ➡

Explore South End & Chinatown

Four side-by-side neighborhoods are home to Boston's lively theater scene, hip-hop-happening nightclubs and its best international and contemporary dining.

Once downtrodden, the South End was claimed and cleaned up by the gay community, and now everyone wants to live there. And why not? The neighborhood boasts the country's largest concentration of Victorian row houses, the city's most innovative and exciting options for dining out, and a vibrant art scene.

Although tiny by New York standards, Boston's Theater District has long served as a pre-Broadway staging area. Many landmark theaters have received facelifts in recent years, and their colorful marquees and posh patrons make for a festive night out on the town. The Theater District is also Boston's club hub.

Nearby, Chinatown is overflowing with ethnic restaurants, live-poultry and fresh-produce markets, teahouses and textile shops. As well as the Chinese, this tight-knit community also includes Cambodians, Vietnamese and Laotians. Chinatown is a popular stop for lunch, a pre-theater dinner or a post-clubbing munch.

East of Chinatown, the Leather District is a pocket of uniform brick buildings that also shelters some fine restaurants. In all four neighborhoods, there is a dearth of traditional 'sights' to see, but there is a superabundance of eating and entertainment options.

Local Life

➡ **First Fridays** On the first Friday of the month, get thee to the open studios at SoWa Artists Guild (p96) to chat with the resident creatives.
➡ **Hang-outs** Southenders hang out at Delux Café (p101) and Franklin Café (p97).
➡ **Chinese Chess** Local residents congregate in the shadow of the Chinatown Gate (p96) for fierce chess competitions and friendly Cantonese chatter.

Getting There & Away

➡ **Metro** For the South End, take the orange line to Back Bay station or New England Medical Center station. Chinatown is served by its eponymous station, also on the orange line. The green-line Boylston station is handy for the Theater District, while the Leather District is easiest to access from the red-line South Station.
➡ **Bus** Good for the South End, the silver-line bus runs down Washington St from South Station (SL4) or Downtown Crossing (SL5).

Lonely Planet's Top Tip

Budget travelers will find Boston's best restaurant bargains in Chinatown at lunchtime. Go straight to Kneeland St to take advantage of amazing lunch specials. Chow down on soup and a main course for less than $10 – bargain!

 ### Best Places to Eat

➡ O Ya (p101)
➡ Toro (p97)
➡ Gourmet Dumpling House (p99)
➡ Q Restaurant (p100)
➡ B&G Oysters (p97)

For reviews, see p96

Best Places to Drink

➡ Gallows (p101)
➡ Beehive (p101)
➡ Delux Café (p101)

For reviews, see p101

Best Places to Dance

➡ Whisky Saigon (p102)
➡ Tunnel (p102)
➡ Candibar (p102)
➡ Emerald Lounge (p102)

For reviews, see p102

SOUTH END & CHINATOWN

SIGHTS

South End

SOWA ARTISTS GUILD · GALLERY
Map p240 (www.sowaartistsguild.com; 450 Harrison Ave; ⊙5-9pm 1st Fri of month; 🚆SL4 or SL5, 🇹New England Medical Center) The brick-and-beam buildings along Harrison Ave were originally used to manufacture goods ranging from canned food to pianos. Now, these factories turn out paintings and sculptures instead. The SoWa Artists Guild houses about 70 artist studios and more than a dozen galleries.This is the epicenter of the South End art district. There is a SoWa Open Studios event on the first Friday of every month, while many artists also welcome visitors during the **SoWa Sundays** (www.sowasundays.com; Harrison Ave; ⊙10am-4pm Sun May-Oct).

CATHEDRAL OF THE HOLY CROSS · CHURCH
Map p240 (www.holycrossboston.com; 1400 Washington St; ⊙service 9am Mon-Sat, 8am & 11:30am Sun; 🚆SL4 or SL5, 🇹Back Bay) When this neo-Gothic cathedral was built in 1875, it was America's largest Catholic cathedral, and as big as London's Westminster Abbey. It serves as the main cathedral for the archdiocese of Boston and the seat of the archbishop. The exquisite rose window features King David playing his harp, while the rest of the cross-shaped building is peppered with stained-glass windows.

Chinatown

CHINATOWN GATE · LANDMARK
Map p242 (cnr Beach St & Surface Rd; 🇹Chinatown) The official entrance to Chinatown is the decorative gate, or *paifong,* a gift from the city of Taipei. It is symbolic – not only as an entryway for guests visiting Chinatown, but also as an entryway for immigrants who are still settling here, as they come to establish relationships and put down roots in their newly claimed home. Surrounding the gate and anchoring the southern end of the Rose Kennedy Greenway is the new **Chinatown Park**. A bamboo-lined walkway runs through the modern gardens. The plaza is often populated by local residents engaged in *Xiangqi* (Chinese chess).

SOWA ART WALK

SoWa Art Walk (www.sowaartwalk.com; ⊙11am-6pm, 1st Sun in May; 🇹New England Medical Center) There's more to SoWa than Open Markets and Open Studios. The biggest event of the year is the annual SoWa Art Walk, which draws thousands of visitors (and visiting artists) to the neighborhood. Many artists (in the Artists Guild and elsewhere) open their studios, while others set up booths at the outdoor art market. Local galleries also get in on the festive event.

EATING

South End

BLUNCH · SANDWICHES $
Map p240 (www.eatblunch.com; 59 E Springfield St; sandwiches $5-10; ⊙8am-3pm Mon-Fri, 9am-3pm Sat; 🥗; 🇹Massachusetts Ave) This is a tiny place with counter service, blackboard menu and a-MAZ-ing chocolate chip cookies. The sandwiches are also delish, especially the eggs-ellent fluffy breakfast sandwiches, which are available all day long.

PICCO · PIZZA $
Map p240 (www.piccorestaurant.com; 513 Tremont St; mains $10-15; ⊙11am-10pm Sun-Wed, to 11pm Thu-Sat; 🍴🥗👶; 🇹Back Bay) The crust of a Picco pizza undergoes a two-day process of cold fermentation before it goes into the oven and then into your mouth. The result is a thin crust with substantial texture and rich flavor. You can add toppings to create your own pie.

MIKE'S CITY DINER · DINER $
Map p240 (www.mikescitydiner.com; 1714 Washington St; mains $6-12; ⊙6am-3pm; 👶; 🚆SL4 or SL5, 🇹Massachusetts Ave) Start the day with a big breakfast of eggs, bacon, toast and other old-fashioned goodness, topped with a bottomless cup of coffee. If you need to refuel at lunchtime, go for classics such as meatloaf and mashed potatoes or fried chicken and biscuits. Service is friendly and fast.

FRANKLIN CAFÉ
AMERICAN $$

Map p240 (www.franklincafe.com; 278 Shawmut Ave; mains $15-20; ⏱5pm-2am; 🅿; 🚇SL4 or SL5, Ⓣ Back Bay) The Franklin is probably the South End's longest-standing favorite neighborhood joint – and that's saying something in this restaurant-rich neighborhood. It's at once friendly and hip. The menu is New American comfort food prepared by a gourmet chef: surely turkey meatloaf with fig gravy and chive mashed potatoes does a body good.

TORO
TAPAS $$

Map p240 (☎617-536-4300; www.toro-restaurant.com; 1704 Washington St; tapas $10-15; ⏱noon-10pm Mon-Thu, to midnight Fri, 5pm-midnight Sat, 10:30am-10pm Sun; 🅿; 🚇SL4 or SL5, Ⓣ Massachusetts Ave) 🍴 True to its Spanish spirit, this place is bursting with energy, from the open kitchen to the lively bar to the communal butcher-block tables. The menu features simple but sublime tapas – grilled chilies with sea salt, corn on the cob dripping with lemon and butter, and delectable, garlicky shrimp. For accompaniment, try rioja, sangria or any number of spiced-up mojitos and margaritas.

COPPA
ITALIAN $$

Map p240 (☎617-391-0902; www.coppaboston.com; 253 Shawmut Ave; small plates $10-16, pasta $16-27; ⏱noon-10pm Mon-Thu, to 11pm Fri, 5-11pm Sat, 3-10pm Sun; 🚇SL4 or SL5, Ⓣ Back Bay) This South End *enoteca* (wine bar) recreates an Italian dining experience with authenticity and innovation, serving up *salumi* (cured meats), antipasti, pasta and other delicious small plates. Wash it all down with an Aperol spritz and you might be tricked into thinking you're in Venice.

MYERS & CHANG
ASIAN $$

Map p240 (☎617-542-5200; www.myersandchang.com; 1145 Washington St; small plates $10-18; ⏱11:30am-10pm Sun-Thu, to 11pm Fri & Sat; 🅿; 🚇SL4 or SL5, Ⓣ New England Medical Center) This super-hip Asian spot blends Thai, Chinese and Vietnamese cuisines, which means delicious dumplings, spicy stir-fries and oodles of noodles. The kitchen staff does amazing things with a wok, and the menu of small plates allows you to sample a wide selection of dishes.

GASLIGHT, BRASSERIE DU COIN
FRENCH $$

Map p240 (☎617-422-0224; www.gaslight560.com; 560 Harrison Ave; mains $17-27; ⏱9am-

3pm Sat & Sun, 5-11pm daily; 🅿🍴; 🚇SL4 or SL5, Ⓣ New England Medical Center) Gaslight is the friendly and affordable 'brasserie on the corner' that we all wish we had in our own neighborhood. Mosaic tiles, wood-beam ceilings and cozy booths set up the comfortable, convivial atmosphere, which is enhanced by classic French fare and an excellent selection of wines by the glass.

SOUTH END BUTTERY
BAKERY, CAFE $$

Map p240 (www.southendbuttery.com; 314 Shawmut Ave; mains café $4-8, brunch $10-19, dinner $15-22; ⏱6:30am-10pm; 🅿🖐; 🚇SL4 or SL5, Ⓣ Back Bay) 🍴 This is a three-in-one affair, with side-by-side café, restaurant and market. The café has counter service, outdoor seating and amazing cupcakes. The restaurant has exposed brick walls, sophisticated food presentations and alcohol. And the market has baked goods and prepared foods that you can take back to your hotel and eat at midnight. Take your pick!

B&G OYSTERS
SEAFOOD $$$

Map p240 (☎617-423-0550; www.bandgoysters.com; 550 Tremont St; single oysters $3, mains $25-35; ⏱11:30am-11pm Mon-Sat, noon-10pm Sun; 🍴; Ⓣ Back Bay) Patrons flock to this casually cool oyster bar to get in on the raw delicacies offered by chef Barbara Lynch. Sit inside at the marble bar or outside on the peaceful terrace, and indulge in the freshest oysters from local waters. An extensive list of wines and a modest menu of mains and appetizers (mostly seafood) are ample accompaniment for the oysters.

LOCAL KNOWLEDGE

SOUTH END RESTAURANT DEALS

Dining in the South End can be pricey, but even hipsters appreciate a bargain.

➨ **Gaslight, Brasserie du Coin** (p97) offers a 3-course prix-fixe dinner ($30) from 5pm to 6pm.

➨ Gaslight also has a prix-fixe brunch ($10) all day Saturday and from 9am to 11am on Sunday.

➨ On Monday and Tuesday evenings from 5pm to 10pm, head to **Myers & Chang** (p97) for Cheap Date Night ($45 for two people).

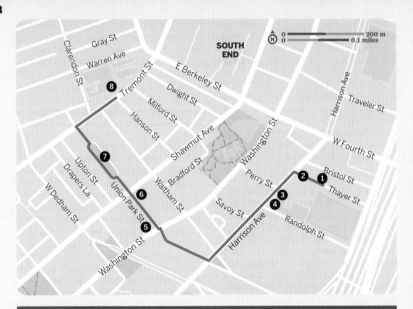

Local Life
South End Art Stroll

Boston's main art district is the South End. The artistic community has moved into the once-barren area south of Washington St (now known as SoWa), converting old warehouses into studios and galleries. For best results, do this walk on a Sunday in summer or in the evening on the first Friday of the month (year-round).

❶ SoWa Artists Guild

This is the epicenter of the South End art scene, where artists have carved out studios and gallery space from the former warehouses and factories on Harrison Ave. The SoWa Artists Guild (p96) hosts an Open Studios event on the first Friday of every month and SoWa Sundays (p96) in summer months.

❷ Thayer Street

Bromfield Art Gallery (Map p240; www.bromfieldgallery.com; 450 Harrison Ave; ⊗noon-5pm Wed-Sat; ⊤New England Medical Center) is a long-running artist-run gallery that features New England artists. But there are dozens of art venues in the former warehouses at 450 and 460 Harrison Ave.

❸ Boston Sculptors Gallery

Peek into this unusual cooperative gallery, which has been going strong for 20-plus years. Three dozen local artists run the innovative **Boston Sculptors Gallery** (Map p240; www.bostonsculptors.com; 486 Harrison Ave; ⊗noon-6pm Wed-Sun; ⊤New England

Medical Center), dedicated to three-dimensional art in all media.

❹ Ars Libri

Ring the doorbell: **Ars Libri** (Map p240; www.arslibri.com; 500 Harrison Ave; ⊗9am-6pm Mon-Fri, 11am-5pm Sat; ⊒SL4 or SL5, ⊤New England Medical Center) is an art bookstore extraordinaire, specializing in rare and out-of-print books. The former warehouse is filled from floor to ceiling with books on all aspects and eras of art, architecture and design. If you love books, and especially books about art, you'll love Ars Libri.

❺ The Gallows

Head over to Washington St and mosey into the Gallows (p101). It's hard to say whether it's a restaurant with amazing cocktails and a cozy, crowded, convivial atmosphere; or a pub with irresistible and innovative food. Either way, it's a fave among trendy, friendly South Enders.

SoWa Artists Guild

6 South End Buttery

If it's too early for drinks and appetizers, head up the street to the South End Buttery (p97) for coffee and cupcakes. A portion of revenue goes to a local animal shelter, coffee drinks feature shade-grown organic beans, and packaging materials are made from recycled paper. Now that your conscience is eased, indulge!

7 Union Park

Continue up Union Park St to get a glimpse of the neighborhood's charming Victorian rowhouses, clustered around a tree-lined, fountain-filled park. This is South End architecture at its best.

8 Boston Center for the Arts

Finish your walk at the Boston Center for the Arts, home of the **Mills Gallery** (Map p240; www.bcaonline.org; 539 Tremont St; ⊙noon-5pm Wed & Sun, to 9pm Thu-Sat; T Back Bay) This venue for visual arts hosts cutting-edge art exhibits, as well as artist and curator talks. Exhibits feature established and emerging artists from Boston and around the country.

KITCHEN AMERICAN $$$

Map p240 (www.kitchenbostonmass.com; 560 Tremont St; mains brunch $12-18, dinner $24-38; ⊙11am-3pm Thu-Sun & 5-10pm daily; T Back Bay) Kitchen may be the only place in Boston that serves 'supper.' Cooking under the tagline *Old is New,* this sweet spot offers classic American fare with panache. This is where you'll find old-fashioned New England dishes (pork and beans, lobster thermidor) that you'll actually be tempted to order – and be glad that you did.

Don't miss the chance to eat doughnuts for dessert. Quintessential Boston.

BUTCHER SHOP FRENCH, ITALIAN $$$

Map p240 (☎617-423-4800; www.thebutchershopboston.com; 552 Tremont St; petite charcuterie $17, mains lunch $15-25, dinner $21-59; ⊙noon-10am Sun & Mon, to 11pm Tue-Thu, to midnight Fri & Sat; T Back Bay) Only in the South End does the neighborhood butcher shop double as an elegant eatery and wine bar. The cases filled with tantalizing cuts of meat, fresh foie gras and homemade sausages give a glimpse of the ingredients and provide the decoration at this bistro (not a good place for vegetarians). There is a nice selection of artisanal wines.

✖ Chinatown

Chinatown is overflowing with authentic restaurants (many open late-night), bakeries and markets. It's not just Chinese, but also Vietnamese, Japanese, Korean, Thai, Malaysian and more. This is some of Boston's best budget eating.

GOURMET DUMPLING HOUSE CHINESE, TAIWANESE $

Map p242 (52 Beach St; dumplings $2-8, mains $10-15; ⊙11am-1am; ✐; T Chinatown) *Xiao long bao.* That's all the Chinese you need to know to take advantage of the specialty at the Gourmet Dumpling House (or GDH, as it is fondly called). They are Shanghai soup dumplings, of course, and they are fresh, doughy and delicious. The menu offers plenty of other options, including scrumptious crispy scallion pancakes. Come early or be prepared to wait.

TAIWAN CAFE TAIWANESE $

Map p242 (34 Oxford St; mains lunch $8, dinner $10-15; ⊙11am-1am; ✐; T Chinatown) Taiwan Cafe is a few steps off the main drag, so

STEVE DUNWELL/GETTY IMAGES ©

you might not have to wait quite as long for the excellent *xiao long bao* and other Taiwanese specialties. Regulars rave about the roast beef scallion pancakes.

XINH XINH
VIETNAMESE **$**

Map p242 (7 Beach St; mains $8-12; ⊙10am-10pm; ☑; Ⓣ Chinatown) Wins the award for Boston's favorite *pho* (pronounced 'fuh'), the sometimes exotic, always fragrant and flavorful Vietnamese noodle soup. These hot, hearty meals come in big bowls and warm you from the inside out.

AVANA SUSHI
SUSHI **$**

Map p242 (www.avanasushi.com; 42 Beach St; sushi & sashimi $4-7; ⊙11am-10pm; Ⓣ Chinatown) This place is essentially unmarked from the street, tucked into a tiny, cramped food court. There's only a handful of seats, and the tableware is all plastic and paper. But the sushi is fresh, delicious and affordable.

MY THAI VEGAN CAFÉ
THAI **$**

Map p242 (3 Beach St; mains $8-15; ⊙11am-10pm; ☑; Ⓣ Chinatown) This welcoming café is up a sketchy staircase, tucked into a sun-lit second-story space. It's an animal-free zone – but good enough that meat-eaters will enjoy eating here, too. The menu has a Thai twist, offering noodle soups, dumplings, excellent spring rolls and pad thai.

WINSOR DIM SUM CAFE
DIM SUM **$**

Map p242 (10 Tyler St; items $2-8; ⊙9am-10pm; ☑; Ⓣ Chinatown) The downside is that there are no pushcarts to choose your food from – the place is so small the pushcarts would have nowhere to go. Instead you have to pre-order from a menu with photographs. The upside is that the food is freshly made to order and it is delicious. Shrimp dumplings and steamed pork buns are recommended.

CAFÉ DE LULU
CHINESE **$**

Map p242 (www.cafe-de-lulu.com; 42 Beach St; mains $6-10; ⊙8am-9pm Sun-Thu, to 10pm Fri & Sat; ☎; Ⓣ Chinatown) Tucked into a tiny basement. Food served on plastic dishes. Hong Kong soap operas on the tube. With over 200 menu items, you're bound to find something to sate you.

PEACH FARM
CHINESE, SEAFOOD **$**

Map p242 (4 Tyler St; mains $7-18; ⊙11am-3am; ☑; Ⓣ Chinatown) Popular wisdom says that if you don't know where to eat in Chinatown, you should ask some locals where *they* like

to eat. Chances are they will direct you to the Peach Farm, an old-school Chinatown haunt that has been around for ages.

★ Q RESTAURANT
ASIAN **$$**

Map p242 (www.thequsa.com; 660 Washington St; hot pot $12-25; ⊙11:30am-11pm Sun-Thu, to 1am Fri & Sat; ☎☑☷; Ⓣ Chinatown) Hip and hungry patrons flock to this trendy hot-pot spot in Chinatown. Q is unusual for its spacious interior and upscale atmosphere, but it's also a unique, interactive eating experience. Choose your broth, choose your morsels of meat and veggies, cook them in the pot and eat them as you go.

SHŌJŌ
ASIAN FUSION **$$**

Map p242 (www.shojoboston.com; 9a Tyler St; mains $18-26; ⊙5:30-11pm Mon-Wed, 11am-11pm Thu, 11am-2am Fri & Sat; Ⓣ Chinatown) Clean, contemporary and super cool, Shojo is unique in Chinatown for its trendy vibe. The menu picks and chooses from all over Asia (and beyond), effortlessly blending disparate elements into original, enticing fare.

KAZE SHABU SHABU
ASIAN **$$**

Map p236 (www.kazeshabushabu.com; 1 Harrison Ave; mains $15-22; ⊙11:30am-1am Sun-Thu, to 2am Fri & Sat; ☑☷) Offering a hands-on approach to dinner, 'Shabu-shabu' is also known as hot-pot cuisine, where you cook your meal at your table in a big family-style pot. Choose from a variety of seafood, poultry and meats, fresh vegetables and an array of homemade broths, then cook it up the way you like it.

✕ Theater District

MIKE & PATTY'S
SANDWICHES **$**

Map p242 (www.mikeandpattys.com; 12 Church St; sandwiches $7-9; ⊙7:30am-2pm Wed-Sun; ☑; Ⓣ New England Medical Center or Arlington) Tucked away in Bay Village, this tiny gem of a corner sandwich shop does amazing things between two slices of bread. There's only eight options and they're all pretty perfect, but the hands-down favorite is the Fancy (fried egg, cheddar cheese, bacon and avocado on multigrain).

FINALE DESSERTERIE
CAFE **$**

Map p244 (www.finaledesserts.com; 1 Columbus Ave; desserts $9-14; ⊙11am-midnight; ☑; Ⓣ Arlington) Choose from a long list of tempting treats, from crème brûlée to chocolate soufflé, and enjoy them with coffee, wine or port. Mirrors over the pastry chefs' workstation allow patrons to watch their magic.

BISTRO DU MIDI
FRENCH $$

Map p244 (☏617-426-7878; www.bistrodumidi.com; 272 Boylston St; mains cafe $12-24, dining room $24-37; ⊙cafe 11am-10pm Sun-Wed, to 11pm Thu-Sat, dining room 5-10pm; ⊤Arlington) The upstairs dining room is exquisite, but the downstairs café exudes warmth and camaraderie, inviting casual callers to linger over wine and snacks. The Provençal fare is artfully presented and simply delicious.

TROQUET
FRENCH $$$

Map p234 (☏617-695-9463; www.troquetboston.com; 140 Boylston St; mains $28-40; ⊤Boylston) Overlooking the Boston Common, this sophisticated French restaurant has an unbeatable location and a highly lauded wine program, including an amazing menu of wines by the glass for better sampling.

✖ Leather District

SOUTH STREET DINER
DINER $

Map p242 (www.southstreetdiner.com; 178 Kneeland St; mains $6-12; ⊙24hr; ☏; ⊤South Station) A divey diner that does what a diner is supposed to do – that is, serve bacon and eggs and burgers and fries, at any time of the day or night. Plonk yourself into a vinyl-upholstered booth and let the sass-talking waitstaff satisfy your midnight munchies.

★O YA
SUSHI $$$

Map p242 (☏617-654-9900; www.oyarestaurant-boston.com; 9 East St; nigiri & sashimi pieces $12-28; ⊙5-10pm Tue-Sat; ☏; ⊤South Station) Who knew that raw fish could be so exciting? Each piece of nigiri or sashimi is dripped with something unexpected but exquisite, ranging from honey truffle sauce to banana pepper mousse. Shrimp tempura is topped with a bacon truffle emulsion. Foie gras is drizzled in balsamic chocolate kabayaki.

🍷 DRINKING & NIGHTLIFE

🍷 South End

This neighborhood contains some of Boston's hippest bars. The South End serves as home base for much of Boston's gay community, but the number of spots catering specifically to the fellas has dwindled in recent years. In any case, both gays and lesbians are usually well represented at any place in the ' hood.

★GALLOWS
PUB

Map p240 (www.thegallowsboston.com; 1395 Washington St; ⊙5pm-midnight Mon-Wed, 11:30am-midnight Thu-Sat, 11am-11pm Sun; ☒SL4 or SL5, ⊤New England Medical Center) It's only four years old, but already a South End favorite. The dark woody interior is inviting and the bartenders are truly talented. The gastropub grub includes such interesting fare as the 'carpet burger' topped with fried oysters and pickles, the enticing Scotch egg, and scrumptious vegetarian poutine. Solid beer selection, delectable cocktails.

★BEEHIVE
COCKTAIL BAR

Map p240 (☏617-423-0069; www.beehiveboston.com; 541 Tremont St; ⊙5pm-1am Mon-Wed, to 2am Thu & Fri, 10am-2am Sat & Sun; ⊤Back Bay) The Beehive has transformed the basement of the Boston Center for the Arts into a 1920s Paris jazz club. This place is more about the scene than the music, which is often provided by students from Berklee College of Music.

DELUX CAFÉ
DIVE BAR

Map p240 (☏617-338-5258; 100 Chandler St; ⊙5pm-1am Mon-Sat; ⊤Back Bay) The South End's best – and perhaps only – hipster dive bar. Now under new ownership, this long-standing favorite has been cleaned up (a little), but the decor is still mainly Christmas lights and the atmosphere is still totally laid-back. The kitchen still turns out an incredible grilled cheese sandwich, and they still don't accept credit cards.

🍷 Chinatown

JACOB WIRTH
BEER HALL

Map p242 (☏617-338-8586; www.jacobwirth.com; 31-37 Stuart St; ⊙11:30am-9:30pm Sun-Wed, to 10:30pm Thu, to 12:30am Fri & Sat; ☒; ⊤Boylston) Boston's second-oldest eatery is this atmospheric Bavarian beer hall. The menu features Wiener schnitzel, *sauerbraten,* potato pancakes and pork chops (mains $16 to $24), but the highlight is the beer – almost 30 different drafts, including Jake's House Lager and Jake's Special Dark. From Thursday to Sunday (from 8pm), Jake hosts a sing-along that rouses the *haus.*

INTERMISSION TAVERN PUB

Map p242 (www.intermissiontavern.com; 228 Tremont St; ⊗11am-2am; ⊤Boylston) Enter beneath the masks of Comedy and Tragedy into the dimly lit interior, where show posters adorn the brick walls. This tiny, theatrically themed tavern is a cozy, casual spot for a drink or a bite to eat before or after a show.

⚑ Theater District

STAGE NIGHTCLUB CLUB

Map p242 (www.stagenightclub.com; 19 Boylston Pl; ⊗9pm-2am Fri & Sat; ⊤Boylston) Here's something new and different. Stage is a Vaudeville-themed club that hosts a nonstop show of burlesque dancers, jugglers, aerialists, acrobats and more, unfolding on four stages and all around you. Remember to dress up to go on Stage.

WHISKY SAIGON CLUB

Map p234 (www.whiskysaigon.com; 116 Boylston St; cover free-$15; ⊗10pm-2am Fri & Sat; ⊤Boylston) Whisky Saigon is undoubtedly the hottest dance spot in Boston at the time of writing, and with good reason. Who can resist bubbles and fog on the dance floor? It's classy, with upscale decor, good looking patrons and top-notch sound system.

TUNNEL CLUB

Map p242 (www.tunnelboston.com; 100 Stuart St; cover $10-20; ⊗9:30pm-2am Tue & Thu-Sat; ⊤Boylston) This is a slick lounge – albeit a tiny one – in the basement of the W hotel. The 'tunnel' is the effect of the LED lights on the ceiling, which lead the way through the chic lounge and back to the dance floor. Tunnel is the rare nightclub where bouncers and bartenders are actually friendly.

EMERALD LOUNGE LOUNGE, CLUB

Map p242 (www.emeraldnightlife.com; 200 Stuart St; cover free-$20; ⊗10pm-2am Wed-Sun;

ℹ NIGHTCLUB GUEST LISTS

If you plan to hit any nightclubs in the Theater District (or anywhere), definitely go online and get yourself on the guest list. This normally will ensure entry, instead of leaving it to the whims of the bouncer. Sometimes it will get you a reduced cover charge.

⊤Boylston) You have to navigate a maze to get into this place, but once you do, you'll find an excellent club that's at once upscale and unpretentious. People of all ages and sizes hang out in the shiny, green lounge in the Revere Hotel. For a change, there's plenty of seating.

CANDIBAR CLUB

Map p242 (www.candibarboston.com; 271 Tremont St; cover $10-20; ⊗10pm-2am Fri-Sun; ⊤New England Medical Center) Welcome to the future, where the walls and ceiling are covered with multicolored lights that throb in time with the music. A state-of-the-art sound system gets you moving on the dance floor. And when you need a break, you can find a seat on the shapely plastic furniture. In a word, surreal.

⚑ Leather District

LES ZYGOMATES WINE BAR

Map p242 (www.winebar.com; 129 South St; ⊗11:30am-10pm Mon-Thu, to 11pm Fri, 5:30-11pm Sat; ⊤South Station) This late-night Parisian bistro serves up live jazz alongside classic but contemporary French cuisine. The clientele is sophisticated but not stuffy. Dinner is pricey, but the tempting selection of starters and cocktails make it a perfect pre- or post-theater spot.

☆ ENTERTAINMENT

★WALLY'S CAFÉ BLUES, JAZZ

Map p240 (www.wallyscafe.com; 427 Massachusetts Ave; ⊗noon-2am; ⊤Massachusetts Ave) When Wally's opened in 1947, Barbadian immigrant Joseph Walcott became the first African American to own a nightclub in New England. Old-school, gritty and small, it still attracts a racially diverse crowd to hear jammin' jazz music 365 days a year. Wally's is the kind of place where someone on stage will recognize a high-caliber out-of-town musician in the crowd and convince them to play.

BOSTON CENTER FOR THE ARTS THEATER

Map p240 (www.bcaonline.org; 539 Tremont St; ⊤Back Bay) There's rarely a dull moment at the BCA, which serves as a nexus for excellent small theater productions. Each year over 20 companies present more than 45 separate productions, from comedies and drama to modern dance and musicals. The BCA occupies a complex comprising several buildings, including a cyclorama from 1884 built to display panoramic paintings, a former organ factory and the Mills Gallery.

CHARLES PLAYHOUSE
THEATER

Map p242 (74 Warrenton St; TBoylston) Built in 1839, the Charles Playhouse was originally a speakeasy, later a jazz club and finally a theater. With its backstreet location and underground ambience, it has always been home to offbeat and unusual performances. Nowadays, that means the ever-popular, indefinable **Blue Man Group** (www.blueman.com; 74 Warrenton St; tickets $60-120; TBoylston) and the long-running improv comedy show **Shear Madness** (Map p242; ☑617-426-5225; www.shearmadness.com; 74 Warrenton St; admission $50; TBoylston).

CUTLER MAJESTIC THEATRE
THEATER, DANCE

Map p242 (☑617-824-8000; www.cutlermajestic.org; 219 Tremont St; TBoylston) This beautiful beaux-arts-style opera house dates to 1903. One century after its construction, the theater was sumptuously renovated and reopened by Emerson College. Today, the performances that take place here are diverse, including seasonal celebrations.

WILBUR THEATRE
COMEDY

Map p242 (www.thewilburtheatre.com; 246 Tremont St; tickets $20-50; TBoylston) The colonial Wilbur Theatre dates to 1914, and over the years has hosted many prominent theatrical productions. These days it is Boston's premier comedy club.

CITI PERFORMING ARTS CENTER
MUSIC, DANCE

Map p242 (☑617-482-9393; www.citicenter.org; 270 Tremont St; TBoylston) Boston's biggest music and dance venue, the Citi Performing Arts Center is comprised of two theaters that face off across Tremont St. The main stage is the enormous, opulent **Wang Theatre**, built in 1925. The Wang hosts extravagant music and modern dance productions, as well as occasional giant-screen movies (the center was built as a movie palace).

SHUBERT THEATRE
OPERA

Map p242 (www.citicenter.org; 265 Tremont St; TBoylston) With 1600 seats, the Shubert is smaller and more intimate than some of the other Theater District venues, thus earning the moniker 'Little Princess.' The Shubert

COMPANY ONE

Company One (Map p240; www.companyone.org; 539 Tremont St; TBack Bay) is a radical theater company striving to be at the 'intersection of art and social change' by offering provocative performances and fostering socially engaged artists. Critics are crazy for C1, which has racked up a slew of awards and nominations for its innovative productions. Most shows are performed in the Boston Center for the Arts theaters.

is the place to see the **Boston Lyric Opera** (Map p242; www.blo.org).

JACQUES CABARET
GAY, CABARET

Map p242 (www.jacques-cabaret.com; 79 Broadway; admission $7-10; ⊙11am-midnight, show times vary; TArlington) Head to this dive on a dark side street to experience the gay culture of the South End before gentrification took over. A shaded-lamp and pool-table kind of place, Jacques hosts outstanding low-budget drag shows every night. We think Mizery is the cat's pyjamas.

🛍 SHOPPING

The South End is the only neighborhood in Boston that has more boutiques for men than women. If you are a straight guy in need of a queer eye, take a walk to the South End. SoWa is also home to Boston's edgiest, up-and-coming art scene.

SOWA OPEN MARKET
HANDICRAFTS, MARKET

Map p240 (www.newenglandopenmarkets.com; Thayer St; ⊙10am-4pm Sun May-Oct; ⊒SL4 or SL5, TNew England Medical Center) Part flea market and part artists' market, this weekly outdoor event is a fabulous opportunity for strolling, shopping and people-watching. More than 100 vendors set up shop under white tents. It's never the same two weeks in a row, but there's always plenty of arts and crafts, as well as edgier art, vintage clothing, jewelry, local farm produce and homemade sweets.

★BOBBY FROM BOSTON
CLOTHING, VINTAGE

Map p240 (19 Thayer St; ⊙noon-6pm Mon-Sat; ⊒SL4 or SL5, TNew England Medical Center) Bobby is one of Boston's coolest cats. Men from all over the greater Boston area come to the South End to peruse Bobby's amazing selection of classic clothing from another era. Smoking jackets, bow ties, bomber jackets and more.

OLIVES & GRACE
GIFTS

Map p240 (www.olivesandgrace.com; 623 Tremont St; ⊙10am-7pm; TBack Bay) This little shoebox of a store offers an eclectic array of gift items made with love and thoughtfulness by artisans. The most enticing items are the foodstuffs, including chocolate bars, hot sauces, raw honey, salt water taffy and beef jerky.

SAULT NEW ENGLAND
CLOTHING, GIFTS

Map p240 (www.saultne.com; 577 Tremont St; ⊙11am-7pm Tue-Sun; TBack Bay) Blending prepster and hipster, rustic and chic, this little basement boutique packs in a lot of intriguing stuff. The eclectic mix runs the gamut from new and vintage clothing to coffee-table books and terrariums.

SOWA VINTAGE MARKET
MARKET, VINTAGE

Map p240 (www.sowavintagemarket.com; 460 Harrison Ave; ⊙10am-4pm Sun, also 5-9pm first Fri of month; SL4 or SL5, TNew England Medical Center) Where the Open Market is for cool hand-made stuff, the Vintage Market is for cool old stuff. It's like an indoor flea market, with dozens of vendors selling clothes, furniture, posters, housewares and loads of other trash and treasure.

GRACIE FINN
GIFTS

Map p240 (www.graciefinn.com; 18 Union Park St; ⊙10am-6pm; TBack Bay) This is essentially a stationery store, with contemporary, cool, hand-pressed cards. There's the never-ending array of Aunt Sadie's scented candles (all-time bestseller: Tree in a Can), a great selection of tote bags, funny magnets, and other things you didn't know you needed.

CALAMUS BOOKSTORE
BOOKS

Map p242 (www.calamusbooks.com; 92 South St; ⊙9am-7pm Mon-Sat, noon-6pm Sun; TSouth Station) The Greek deity Calamus was transformed with grief into a reed when his lover drowned. The character inspired Walt Whitman's 'Calamus' poems, which celebrate gay love. And now, he has inspired Boston's biggest and best GLBT bookstore.

UNIFORM
CLOTHING

Map p240 (www.uniformboston.com; 511 Tremont St; ⊙11am-8pm Tue-Sat, noon-5pm Sun; TBack Bay) With its cool collection of men's casual wear, Uniform caters to all the metrosexuals in this hipster 'hood. Guys leave this place decked out in designers like Ben Sherman, with Freitag bag slung over shoulder.

LEKKER HOME
HOMEWARES

Map p240 (www.lekkerhome.com; 1313 Washington St; ⊙10am-6pm Mon-Wed & Sat, to 7pm Thu & Fri, noon-5pm Sun; SL5, TTufts Medical Center) If you are into Scandinavian design, get into Lekker. Look for crisp, clean lines, attractive yet practical gadgets, stainless steel and monochrome color patterns and plenty of modern chic.

🏃 SPORTS & ACTIVITIES

CHINATOWN MARKET TOUR
WALKING TOUR

(☑617-523-6032; www.bostonfoodtours.com; tour $65; ⊙9:30am-1pm Thu & Sat) Is it a walking tour or a cooking class? Let local chef Jim Becker guide you through the crowded, chaotic streets of Chinatown, with stops at a produce market, a Chinese bakery, a herbal pharmacy and a traditional teahouse, with plenty of shopping and cooking tips.

EXHALE SPA
SPA, YOGA

Map p244 (☑617-532-7000; www.exhalespa.com; 28 Arlington St; ⊙6am-9pm Mon-Fri, 8am-8pm Sat & Sun; TArlington) If you are waiting to exhale, now you can do it at this spa for mind and body. Offering up to 10 classes a day, Exhale focuses on core fusion, barre and yoga basics. Exhale also offers acupuncture, nutrition consulting and other healing services.

GRUB STREET
COURSE

Map p234 (www.grubstreet.org; 160 Boylston St; ⊙9am-5pm Mon-Fri; TBoylston) Designed to offer a supportive environment for would-be writers, Grub Street sponsors long-term writing workshops, seminars and countless readings and other events.

BOSTON CENTER FOR ADULT EDUCATION
COURSE

Map p242 (www.bcae.org; 122 Arlington St; ⊙9am-5pm Mon-Fri; TArlington) The Boston Center for Adult Education offers everything from historical tours to writing classes to massage courses for couples.

Back Bay

Neighborhood Top Five

❶ Admiring Boston's most evocative and archetypal architecture in Copley Sq, with **Trinity Church** (p107) reflecting in the facade of the **John Hancock Tower** (p110) at one end, and the **Boston Public Library** (p107) anchoring the other end.

❷ Strolling, cycling or running along the **Charles River Esplanade** (p110).

❸ Window shopping and gallery hopping on **Newbury St** (p114).

❹ Feeling yourself at the center of the world in the unusual **Mapparium** (p111).

❺ Indulging in afternoon tea at **Courtyard** (p112) in the BPL.

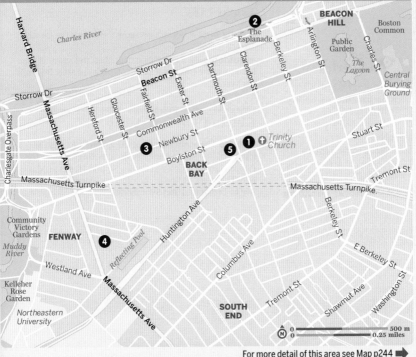

For more detail of this area see Map p244 ➡

Lonely Planet's Top Tip

Visit **BosTix** (www.bostix.org; ⊙10am-6pm Tue-Sat, 11am-4pm Sun) on Copley Sq for same-day, half-price tickets to local theater, comedy and music events.

🍴 Best Places to Eat

➡ Courtyard (p112)
➡ Lolita Cocina (p112)
➡ Piattini (p112)
➡ L'Espalier (p113)
➡ Douzo (p113)

For reviews, see p111 ➡

🍷 Best Places to Drink

➡ Sofá Café (p113)
➡ Corner Tavern (p113)
➡ Bukowski Tavern (p113)
➡ Brahmin (p113)

For reviews, see p113 ➡

👁 Best Galleries

➡ Gallery Naga (p110)
➡ Barbara Krakow Gallery (p110)
➡ Copley Society of Art (p110)
➡ Alpha Gallery (p110)
➡ Society of Arts & Crafts (p115)

For reviews, see p110 ➡

Explore Back Bay

Back Bay is not as old as some other Boston neighborhoods, nor is it as historically significant. But thanks to magnificent Victorian brownstones and high-minded civic plazas, it is certainly among the loveliest – and a required destination for all Boston visitors.

Copley Sq represents the best of Back Bay architecture, as it gracefully blends disparate elements such as the Renaissance Revival Boston Public Library, the Richardsonian Romanesque Trinity Church and the modernist John Hancock Tower. Copley Sq should be your first stop in Back Bay, good for whiling away an hour or even a day.

After admiring the architecture and browsing the books, you are perfectly placed for an afternoon of window shopping or gallery hopping. Swanky Newbury St is famous among fashion mavens, art aficionados and music lovers, for it is lined with boutiques and galleries (and one legendary music store).

Not surprisingly, this bustling retail and residential center is also a drinking and dining wonderland, with sidewalk cafes, trendy bars and chic restaurants on nearly every block. It's not quite the same slick scene as the trendsetting South End, but there are still places to see and be seen in Back Bay.

Local Life

➡ **Hang-outs** It doesn't get more local than the Corner Tavern (p113).
➡ **Outdoors** Perfect for picnic lunches and summertime lounging, the Charles River Esplanade (p110) is Boston's backyard.

Getting There & Away

➡ **Metro** The main branch of the green line runs the length of Boylston St, with stops at Arlington near the Public Garden, Copley at Copley Sq and Hynes at Mass Ave. The green E-line branch follows along Huntington Ave to Prudential and Symphony.

TOP SIGHT
TRINITY CHURCH

A masterpiece of American architecture, Trinity Church is the country's ultimate example of Richardsonian Romanesque. The granite exterior, with a massive portico and side cloister, uses sandstone in colorful patterns. The interior is an awe-striking array of vibrant murals and stained glass, most by artist John LaFarge, who cooperated closely with architect Henry Hobson Richardson to create an integrated composition of shapes, colors and textures. Free architectural tours are offered following Sunday service at 11:15am.

The footprint of Trinity Church is a Greek cross, with chancel, nave and transepts surrounding the central square. The wide-open interior was a radical departure from traditional Episcopal architecture, but it embodies the democratic spirit of the congregation in the 1870s.

The walls of the great central tower are covered by two tiers of **murals**, soaring more than 100ft. Prior to this commission, LaFarge did not have experience with mural painting on this scale. The result – thousands of square feet of exquisite, jewel-toned encaustic paintings – established his authority as the father of the American mural movement.

The 33 **stained-glass windows** in the church represent diverse styles: most of them were executed by different glass workshops. The jewels of the church are the work of LaFarge, who was not commissioned until 1883. His windows are distinctive for their use of layered opalescent glass, resulting in an unprecedented richness of shades and dimensions. LaFarge's first commission was *Christ in Majesty,* the spectacular three-panel clerestory window at the west end that is now considered one of America's finest examples of stained-glass art.

DON'T MISS

→ Sunlight streaming through John La-Farge's stained-glass windows

→ Free pipe organ concerts on Fridays at 12:15pm, from September to June

→ Reflection of Trinity Church in the facade of the John Hancock Tower

PRACTICALITIES

→ www.trinitychurch boston.org

→ 206 Clarendon St

→ adult/child $7/free

→ ⊘9am-4:30pm Mon, Fri & Sat, to 5:30pm Tue-Thu, 1-5pm Sun

→ Ⓣ Copley

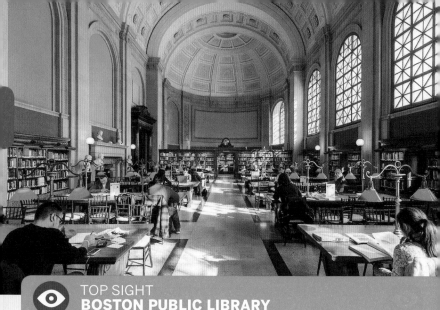

JULIEN HAUTCOEUR/SHUTTERSTOCK ©

TOP SIGHT
BOSTON PUBLIC LIBRARY

Dating from 1852, the esteemed Boston Public Library (BPL) was built as a 'shrine of letters,' lending credence to Boston's reputation as the Athens of America. The old McKim building is notable for its magnificent facade (inspired by Italian Renaissance *palazzi*) and exquisite interior art. Pick up a free brochure and take a self-guided tour; alternatively, free guided tours depart from the entrance hall (times vary).

Puvis de Chavannes Gallery

From the main entrance, a marble staircase leads past Pierre Puvis de Chavannes' inspirational murals. The artist titled his composition *The Muses of Inspiration Hail the Spirit, the Harbinger of Light*. The mural depicts poetry, philosophy, history and science, which he considered 'the four great expressions of the human mind.'

Don't miss the mighty lions posed on their pedestals, carved by Saint-Gaudens to honor the Massachusetts Civil War infantries.

Upstairs, at the entrance to Bates Hall, there is another Puvis de Chavannes mural, also *The Muses*. Here, the nine muses from Greek mythology are honoring a male figure, the Genius of the Enlightenment.

Bates Hall

The staircase terminates at the splendid Bates Hall Reading Room, where even mundane musings are elevated by the barrel-vaulted, 50ft coffered ceilings.

Bates Hall is named for Joshua Bates, the BPL's original benefactor in 1852. After spending his childhood browsing in bookstores, Bates appreciated the potential for, and importance of, self-education through reading. He donated $50,000 to the city of Boston,

DON'T MISS...

➡ Mora and Saint-Gaudens' carving of Minerva, goddess of wisdom, on the central keystone on the facade
➡ *Frieze of the Prophets* by John Singer Sargent
➡ Peaceful Italianate courtyard

PRACTICALITIES

➡ www.bpl.org
➡ 700 Boylston St
➡ ⊙9am-9pm Mon-Thu, to 5pm Fri & Sat year-round, also 1-5pm Sun Oct-May
➡ Ⓣ Copley

with the stipulations that 'the building shall be...an ornament to the city, that there shall be a room for 100 to 150 persons to sit at reading tables, and that it be perfectly free to all.'

Abbey Room

The Abbey Room is among the library's most sumptuous, with its oak wainscoting, marble flooring and elaborate fireplace. The room is named for the author of the 1895 murals, which recowunt Sir Galahad's *Quest and Achievement of the Holy Grail.*

Elliott Room

The two 2nd-floor lobbies borrow their artistic elements from Pompeii and Venice, respectively. Off the Venetian lobby, the relatively plain study room is named for painter John Elliott, who did the ceiling mural. *The Triumph of Time* depicts 12 angelic figures, representing the 12 hours on the clock, while the male figure in the cart is Father Time. He is flanked on either side by the Hours of Life and Death. The 20 horses are the centuries since the birth of Christ.

Sargent Gallery

The pièce de résistance of the BPL artwork is on the 3rd floor, which features John Singer Sargent's unfinished Judaic and Christian murals entitled *The Triumph of Religion.*

The theme is surprising for an institution of secular learning. The mural traces the history of Western religion from the primitive worship of pagan gods to the foundation of the Law of Israel to the commencement of the Messianic Age with the birth of Christ. Some scholars argue that the sequence depicts a progression toward religious subjectivity and individualist spiritual pursuits. Others have interpreted that the artist portrayed Christianity as being more evolved than Judaism. Most controversial was Sargent's use of a strong and steadfast figure for *Church,* in contrast with the weak and blindfolded figure for *Synagogue.*

A final painting of the Sermon on the Mount was intended for the vacant space above the stairwell; the mural was never completed, due in part to the strong reaction from the Jewish community. When the installation was unveiled in 1919, critics called it anti-Semitic. Sargent (by all accounts, dismayed) was unable to appease his critics.

The murals were largely (and perhaps intentionally) forgotten for the remainder of the century. They were finally restored and unveiled in 1999.

BPL EVENTS

See the Boston Public Library website for a schedule of free events, which range from author talks to musical performances.

The Boston Public Library was the first free municipal library in the world, as well as being the first library to allow its patrons to borrow books and materials. The BPL was also the first library to establish a branch system, when it opened a branch in East Boston in 1870 (and 20 more in subsequent years). And in 1895, BPL became the first library with a designated children's area.

TOTS & TEENS & IN-BETWEENS

The BPL offers loads of entertaining and educational resources for kids and teenagers, including homework help, book lists, movie nights and even video games. Of course there is a dedicated children's area, but older kids will want to hang out in the fun and funky Teen Lounge.

⊙ SIGHTS

TRINITY CHURCH CHURCH
See p107.

BOSTON PUBLIC LIBRARY LIBRARY
See p108

COMMONWEALTH AVENUE STREET
(TArlington, Copley or Hynes) The grandest of Back Bay's grand boulevards is Commonwealth Ave (more commonly Comm Ave). Boston's Champs Élysées, the dual-carriageway connects the Public Garden with the Back Bay Fens, a green link in Olmsted's Emerald Necklace. The grassy mall is dotted with grand elms and lined with stately brownstones. The eclectic array of public art honors – among others – a Civil War hero, a First Lady, an abolitionist, a suffragist, a maritime historian, an Argentine statesman and a Viking explorer.

★CHARLES RIVER ESPLANADE PARK
(www.esplanadeassociation.org; ♿; TCharles/ MGH or Kenmore) The southern bank of the Charles River Basin is an enticing urban escape, with grassy knolls and cooling waterways, all designed by Frederick Law Olmsted. It stretches almost 3 miles along the Boston shore of the Charles River, from the Museum of Science to BU Bridge. The park is dotted with public art, including an oversized bust of Arthur Fiedler, long-time conductor of the Boston Pops. Paths along the river are ideal for bicycling, jogging or walking.

GIBSON HOUSE MUSEUM HISTORIC BUILDING
(www.thegibsonhouse.org; 137 Beacon St; tours adult/child $9/3; ⊘tours 1pm, 2pm & 3pm Wed-Sun; TArlington) Catherine Hammond Gibson was considered quite the pioneer when she moved to this Italian Renaissance row house in 1860 (that she was a female homeowner in this 'New Land' was even more unusual). The Gibson House attempts to preserve a piece of Victorian-era Boston, showcasing the antique furniture and art collected by the Gibson family.

ARLINGTON STREET CHURCH CHURCH
(www.ascboston.org; 351 Boylston St; ⊘service 11am Sun; TArlington) The first public building erected in Back Bay in 1861, this graceful church features extraordinary Tiffany windows and 16 bells in its steeple. The church's Unitarian Universalist ministry is purely progressive, as it has been since Rev William Ellery Channing preached here in the early 19th century. (A statue in his honor is across the street in the Public Garden.)

BARBARA KRAKOW GALLERY GALLERY
(www.barbarakrakowgallery.com; 10 Newbury St; ⊘10am-5:30pm Tue-Sat; TArlington) FREE Established in 1964, this is one of Boston's most prominent galleries, with a catalogue of artists that reads like something from a major museum. The gallery represents the estates of Sol LeWitt and Fred Sandbeck, and also shows many others.

COPLEY SOCIETY OF ART GALLERY
(CoSo; www.copleysociety.org; 158 Newbury St; ⊘11am-6pm Mon-Sat, noon-5pm Sun; TCopley) FREE Dating to 1879, CoSo is the country's oldest non-profit art association. With more than 500 members, the showings in the three exhibit spaces are rich and varied. There are usually 15 to 20 exhibits each year, including shows featuring new members, small works and Boston-themed pieces.

ALPHA GALLERY GALLERY
(www.alphagallery.com; 37 Newbury St; ⊘10am-5:30pm Tue-Sat, 11am-5:30pm Sun; TArlington) FREE Presenting the work of some headline-grabbing artists (sometimes local, sometimes international), this starkly minimalist gallery mostly shows oils (some figurative, some abstract), though occasionally you'll see sculpture, mixed media and prints. In addition to Milton Avery, whose estate is represented here, Alpha has special shows of masters such as Max Beckmann and Pablo Picasso.

GALLERY NAGA GALLERY
(www.gallerynaga.com; 67 Newbury St; ⊘10am-5pm Tue-Sat; TArlington) FREE Inside the Gothic digs of the Church of the Covenant, Gallery Naga exhibits contemporary painters, featuring many highly regarded local and regional artists. You can also see varied prints, photographs and sculpture, as well as some impressive examples of holography. One special and noteworthy niche is unique and limited-edition furniture.

JOHN HANCOCK TOWER NOTABLE BUILDING
(200 Clarendon St; TCopley) Constructed with more than 10,000 panels of mirrored glass, the 62-story John Hancock Tower was designed in 1976 by Henry Cobb. It is the tallest and most beloved skyscraper on the Boston skyline – despite the precarious

falling panes of glass when it was first built. The Hancock offers an amazing perspective on Trinity Church, reflected in its facade.

NEW OLD SOUTH CHURCH   CHURCH
(www.oldsouth.org; 645 Boylston St; ⊘8am-7pm Mon-Fri, 10am-4pm Sat, 8:30am-7pm Sun; ⊤Copley) This magnificent puddingstone Venetian Gothic church on Copley Sq is called the 'new' Old South because up until 1875, the congregation worshipped in the Old South Church on Milk St (now the Old South Meeting House). The Congregational church has an impressive collection of stained-glass windows, all shipped from London, and an organ that was rescued from a Minneapolis church just before demolition.

PRUDENTIAL CENTER SKYWALK
OBSERVATORY   LOOKOUT
(www.skywalkboston.com; 800 Boylston St; adult/child $16/11; ⊘10am-10pm Mar-Oct, to 8pm Nov-Feb; P♿; ⊤Prudential) Technically called the Shops at Prudential Center, this landmark Boston building is not much more than a fancy shopping mall. But it does provide a bird's-eye view of Boston from its 50th-floor skywalk. Completely enclosed by glass, the skywalk offers spectacular 360-degree views of Boston and Cambridge, accompanied by an entertaining audio tour (with a special version catering to kids). Alternatively, enjoy the same view from Top of the Hub (p114).

MARY BAKER EDDY LIBRARY &
MAPPARIUM   LIBRARY
(www.marybakereddylibrary.org; 200 Massachusetts Ave; adult/child $6/free; ⊘10am-4pm Tue-Sun; ♿; ⊤Symphony) The Mary Baker Eddy Library houses one of Boston's hidden treasures. The intriguing Mapparium is a room-size, stained-glass globe that visitors walk through on a glass bridge. It was created in 1935, which is reflected in the globe's geopolitical boundaries. The acoustics allow everyone in the room to hear even the tiniest whisper.

Besides the Mapparium, the library has an odd amalgam of exhibits related to its full name, the MBE Library for the Betterment of Humanity. Second-floor galleries deal with the 'search for the meaning of life,' both on a personal and global level. The heart of the library's collections, Eddy's papers and transcripts, are on the top floors and accessible by permission.

WEATHER OR NOT

Steady blue, clear view/Flashing blue, clouds are due/Steady red, rain ahead/ Flashing red, snow instead.

Since 1950, Bostonians have used this simple rhyme and the weather beacon atop the old Hancock tower (next to the new John Hancock Tower) to determine if they need to take their umbrella when they leave the house. And yes, the beacon has been known to flash red in midsummer, but that is not a warning of some extremely inclement New England weather, but rather an indication that the Red Sox game has been canceled for the night.

CHRISTIAN SCIENCE CHURCH   CHURCH
(www.christianscience.com; 175 Huntington Ave; ⊘noon-4pm Tue, 1-4pm Wed, noon-5pm Thu-Sat, 11am-3pm Sun, service 10am Sun; ⊤Symphony) Known to adherents as the 'Mother Church,' this is the international home base for the Church of Christ, Scientist (Christian Science), founded by Mary Baker Eddy in 1866. Tour the grand classical revival basilica, which can seat 3000 worshippers, listen to the 14,000-pipe organ, and linger on the expansive plaza with its 670ft-long reflecting pool.

✗ EATING

FLOUR   BAKERY $
(www.flourbakery.com; 131 Clarendon St; mains $5-10; ⊘7am-8pm Mon-Fri, 8am-6pm Sat, 9am-5pm Sun; 🔊📶♿; ⊤Back Bay/South End) Joann Chang's beloved bakery is taking over Boston. This newest outlet – on the edge of Back Bay – has the same flaky pastries and rich coffee that we have come to expect, not to mention sandwiches, soups, salads and pizzas.

SWEETGREEN   VEGETARIAN $
(www.sweetgreen.com; 659 Boylston St; mains $6-10; ⊘10:30am-10:30pm; 📶♿; ⊤Copley) Vegetarians, gluten-free eaters, health nuts and all human beings will rejoice in the goodness that is served at Sweetgreens. Choose a salad or a wrap, then custom-design your own, or choose one of the unexpected, delicious, fresh combos that have already been invented, including seasonal specialties.

PARISH CAFÉ
SANDWICHES $

(www.parishcafe.com; 361 Boylston St; sandwiches $12-15; ☉noon-2am; ☑; ⓣArlington) Sample the creations of Boston's most famous chefs without exhausting your expense account. The menu at Parish features a rotating roster of salads and sandwiches, each designed by a local celebrity chef, including Lydia Shire, Ken Oringer and Barbara Lynch. The place feels more 'pub' than 'café' with a long bar backed by big TVs and mirrors.

TRIDENT
BOOKSELLERS & CAFÉ
INTERNATIONAL $

(www.tridentbookscafe.com; 338 Newbury St; mains $8-12; ☉8am-midnight; ☏☑; ⓣHynes) Is Trident a bookstore with an amazingly eclectic menu or a café with a super selection of reading material? The collection of books is wide, but leans toward political and New Age themes. The food menu is equally varied, ranging from the comforting (muffins, soups, smoothies) to the daring (spinach *arancini*, Tibetan dumplings). Vegetarians rejoice over the vegan cashew chili.

★COURTYARD
MODERN AMERICAN $$

(www.thecateredaffair.com; 700 Boylston St; mains $17-22; ☉11:30am-4pm Mon-Fri; ☑; ⓣCopley) The perfect destination for an elegant luncheon with artfully prepared food is – believe it or not – the Boston Public Library. Overlooking the beautiful Italianate courtyard, this grown-up restaurant serves seasonal, innovative and exotic dishes (along with a few standards). After 2pm, the Courtyard serves afternoon tea ($32), with a selection of sandwiches, scones and sweets.

★LOLITA COCINA
MEXICAN $$

(www.lolitatequilabars.com; 271 Dartmouth St; tacos $11-15, mains $17-26; ☉5pm-1am, bar to 2am; ☑; ⓣCopley) This spicy little Mexican number is full of surprises (which we won't ruin for you). We will reveal that the menu is packed with unusual and enticing Mexican fare that does not disappoint: lobster enchiladas, charred sweet corn and spicy *mojo* tuna. Oh, and there's all-you-can-eat tacos for $7 on Monday nights.

SALTY PIG
ITALIAN $$

(www.thesaltypig.com; 130 Dartmouth St; charcuterie $6-8, mains $13-21; ⓣBack Bay) With prosciutto, paté, *rillettes, testa* (head cheese), *sanguinaccio* (blood sausage), *porchetta* (pork shoulder) and more, you'll feel like you're in one of those cultures that eats every part of the animal. The 'Salty Pig Parts' get paired with stinky cheeses and other accompaniments for amazing charcuterie plates. There's pizza and pasta for the less adventurous, and cocktails and craft beers for the thirsty.

PIATTINI
ITALIAN $$

(www.piattini.com; 226 Newbury St; small plates $9-15, mains $18-25; ☉11:30am-10pm Sun-Thu, to 11pm Fri & Sat; ☑; ⓣCopley) If you have trouble deciding what to order, Piattini can help. The name means 'small plates,' so you don't have to choose just one. The list of wines by the glass is extensive, each accompanied by tasting notes and fun facts. This intimate *enoteca* (wine bar) is a delightful setting to sample the flavors of Italy, and you might just learn something while you're here.

CODA
PUB FOOD $$

(www.codaboston.com; 329 Columbus Ave; mains lunch $9-15, dinner $13-24; ☉11:30am-11pm Sun-Thu, to 1am Fri & Sat; ☏; ⓣBack Bay) Coda does the essentials, and does them right. The menu changes seasonally, but you'll often find grilled salmon, *steak frites* and bone-in chicken breast, all prepared to perfection. The Coda burger (offered with add-ons to please epicureans) does not disappoint. Understated interior. Hip clientele. Potent cocktails. Good times.

CASA ROMERO
MEXICAN $$

(☑617-536-4341; www.casaromero.com; 30 Gloucester St; mains $18-25; ☉5-10pm Mon-Thu, to 11pm Fri & Sat, 11am-9pm Sun; ☑; ⓣHynes) The entrance to this hidden treasure is in the public alley off Gloucester St. Step inside and find yourself in a cozy *casa* – filled with folk art and Talavera tiles – which is wonderful and warm during winter months. In pleasant weather, dine under the stars on the delightful patio.

This is not your average *taquería* – be prepared to pay for the experience (unless you arrive before 6pm, in which case you can take advantage of the early bird special, a three-course meal for $22).

BARLOLA
TAPAS $$

(www.barlola.com; 160 Commonwealth Ave; tapas $6-12; ☉4pm-1am; ⓣCopley) This authentic Spanish eatery is tucked into a subterranean space on residential Commonwealth Ave. The menu is exclusively tapas, prepared by a team of chefs trained in España. Mural-painted walls and flamenco music create an inviting old-world ambience; the lively, Spanish-speaking crowd and pitchers of sangria add to it. Live flamenco dancing Sundays at 8pm.

L'ESPALIER
FRENCH $$$

(⌂617-262-3023; www.lespalier.com; 774 Boylston St; lunch mains $28, 3-course prix-fixe dinner $95, degustation $115; ⊙11:30am-10:30pm; ⊤Prudential) This tried-and-true favorite remains the crème de la crème of Boston's culinary scene, thanks to impeccable service and a variety of prix-fixe and tasting menus. The menus change daily, but usually include a degustation of caviar, a degustation of seasonal vegetables, and recommended wine pairings.

DOUZO
SUSHI $$$

(⌂617-859-8886; www.douzosushi.com; 131 Dartmouth St; sushi & sashimi $4-10, mains lunch $10-15, dinner $20-30; ⊙11:30am-11:30pm; ⊤Back Bay) Easy on the eyes, easy on the palate. Douzo fills its loungey interior with attractive urbanites sipping fancy cocktails and feasting on fresh raw fish. The place buzzes with an atmosphere of see-and-be-seen, but attentive eaters are also paying close attention to the mini masterpieces coming from the sushi bar.

DEUXAVE
FRENCH $$$

(⌂617-517-5915; www.deuxave.com; 371 Commonwealth Ave; mains $28-41; ⊙5-10pm Sun-Wed, to 11pm Thu-Sat; ✎; ⊤Hynes) At the corner of Mass Ave and Comm Ave (get it?) this is a highly lauded addition to Boston's dining scene. It's all very elegant, with chandeliers, dark wood furniture and big picture windows overlooking the two avenues. The menu is nouvelle cuisine, offering modern interpretations of French flavors. The place gets raves for lobster gnocchi and nine-hour French onion soup.

ATLANTIC FISH CO
SEAFOOD $$$

(www.atlanticfishco.com; 761 Boylston St; mains lunch $12-22, dinner $22-38; ⊙11:30am-11pm Sun-Thu, to midnight Fri & Sat; ⊤Copley) New England clam chowder in a bread bowl: for a perfect lunch at Atlantic Fish Co, that's all you need to know. For non-believers, we will also seafood *fra diavolo,* lobster ravioli and local Jonah crabcakes. There's more, of course, and the menu is printed daily to showcase the freshest ingredients. Enjoy it in the seafaring dining room or on the flower-filled sidewalk patio.

🍷 DRINKING & NIGHTLIFE

WIRED PUPPY
CAFE

(www.wiredpuppy.com; 250 Newbury St; ⊙6:30am-7:30pm; ☂; ⊤Hynes) Delicious organic coffee, welcoming atmosphere and free wi-fi or computer use. Surely, that's all you need. But there's also the cozy, exposed-brick interior and awesome outdoor patio.

BRAHMIN
LOUNGE

(www.thebrahmin.com; 33 Stanhope St; ⊙4:30pm-2am Mon-Sat; ⊤Back Bay) You may have never heard of *Nightclub & Bar Magazine,* but apparently they named this Back Bay original as the best lounge in the whole country! We understand why. The elegant atmosphere is enhanced by chandeliers and leather couches, the menu of small plates is thoughtful, and we love the seamless transition to dance club (Friday and Saturday).

BUKOWSKI TAVERN
DIVE BAR

(www.bukowskitavern.net; 50 Dalton St; ⊙11am-2am; ⊤Hynes) This sweet bar lies inside a parking garage next to the canyon of the Mass Pike. Expect sticky wooden tables, loud rock, lots of black hoodies, plenty of cussing, a dozen different burgers and dogs and more than 100 kinds of beer.

SOFÁ CAFÉ
CAFE

(www.sofacafeusa.com; 217 Newbury St; ⊙7am-8pm; ☂✎; ⊤Copley) A transplant from São Paolo, this Newbury St newcomer is attracting dedicated coffee-drinkers to sample its aromatic Brazilian espresso drinks. The specialty flavors are truly enticing. The Ventura is iced coffee with sugar and lime that will cool you off on a hot day.

CITY BAR
COCKTAIL BAR

(www.citybarboston.com; 710 Boylston St; ⊙4:30pm-2am; ⊤Copley) For an intimate atmosphere and sweet selection of cocktails, you can't go wrong at this swish bar in the Lenox Hotel. It's not exactly a destination in and of itself, but it's ideal for after-work or early-evening drinks.

CORNER TAVERN
PUB

(www.thecornerboston.com; 421 Marlborough St; ⊙11:30am-2am; ⊤Hynes) A true neighborhood bar, the Corner Tavern has a decent beer selection, satisfying food and a welcoming laid-back atmosphere. It's convivial, but not overly crowded. The Sox are on the TVs, but the volume is down.

MINIBAR
COCKTAIL BAR

(www.minibarboston.com; 51 Huntington Ave; ⏰5pm-2am; 🚇Copley) Located in the posh Copley Square Hotel, Minibar is much more enticing than your typical hotel bar. It's a swank space with cushy couches, sexy people and good vibes. Most importantly, the bartenders mix deadly delicious cocktails. Come for happy hour (5pm to 7pm Monday to Thursday) and feast on juicy $2 sliders.

TOP OF THE HUB
BAR

(☎617-536-1775; www.topofthehub.net; 800 Boylston St; ⏰11:30am-1am; 📷; 🚇Prudential) Yes, it's touristy. And overpriced. And a little bit snooty. But the head-spinning city view makes it worthwhile to ride the elevator up to the 52nd floor of the Prudential Center. Come for spectacular sunset drinks and stay for free live jazz. Beware the $24 per person minimum after 8pm.

POUR HOUSE
DIVE BAR

(www.pourhouseboston.com; 907 Boylston St; ⏰8am-2am; 🚇Hynes) For years, young college students have introduced themselves to urban nightlife by enjoying cheap drinks and cheaper burgers in this pleasantly ratty bar.

STORYVILLE
CLUB

(www.storyvilleboston.com; 90 Exeter St; ⏰9:30pm-2am Wed, Fri & Sat; 🚇Copley) The legendary Storyville jazz club occupied this same spot in the 1950s, when it hosted the likes of Dave Brubeck and Billie Holiday (who even recorded an album here). The contemporary nightclub recalls that era with its loungey atmosphere and sexy New Orleans bordello–inspired vibe.

CLUB CAFÉ
GAY

(www.clubcafe.com; 209 Columbus Ave; ⏰11am-2am; 🚇Back Bay) It's a club! It's a café! It's cabaret! Anything goes at this glossy, gay nightlife extravaganza. There is live cabaret in the Napoleon Room five nights a week, while the main dance and lounge area has tea parties, salsa dancing, trivia competitions, karaoke and good old-fashioned dance parties, depending on the night.

☆ ENTERTAINMENT

★RED ROOM @ CAFÉ 939
LIVE MUSIC

(www.cafe939.com; 939 Boylston St; ⏰8-11pm Wed-Sun; 🚇Hynes) Run by Berklee students, the Red Room @ 939 has emerged as one of Boston's least predictable and most enjoyable music venues. The place has an excellent sound system and a baby grand piano; most importantly, it books interesting, eclectic up-and-coming musicians. Check out wicked local Wednesdays to sample the local sound. Buy tickets in advance at the Berklee Performance Center.

BERKLEE PERFORMANCE CENTER
BLUES, JAZZ

(www.berklee.edu/bpc; 136 Massachusetts Ave; tickets $8-45; 🚇Hynes) For high-energy jazz recitals, smoky-throated vocalists and oddball sets by keyboard-playing guys who look like they dabble at being dungeon masters, the performance hall at this notable music college hosts a wide variety of performers. Depending on the night, you'll hear student recitals, invited musicians, instructors or the Ultra Sonic Rock Orchestra.

HATCH MEMORIAL SHELL
CONCERT VENUE

(www.hatchshell.com; Charles River Esplanade; 🚇Charles/MGH or Arlington) Free summer concerts take place at this outdoor bandstand on the banks of the Charles River. Most famously, there's Boston's biggest annual music event, the Boston Pops' July 4 concert. But throughout the summer, there are also Friday-night movies, Wednesday-night orchestral ensembles and the occasional oldies concert.

SHOPPING

★SIKARA & CO
JEWELRY

(www.sikara.com; 250 Newbury St; ⏰10am-7pm Mon-Sat, 11am-6pm Sun; 🚇Hynes) Mousumi travels the world to seek inspiration for the amazing 'modern fusion jewelry' you'll find in Sikara & Co. From her native India to countries the world around, she works with designers to incorporate semi-precious stones, precious metals and exotic design elements into these miniature pieces of art!

CONVERSE
SHOES, CLOTHING

(www.converse.com; 348 Newbury St; ⏰10am-7pm Mon-Fri, to 8pm Sat, 11am-6pm Sun; 🚇Hynes) Converse started making shoes right up the road in Malden, Massachusetts way back in 1908. Chuck Taylor joined the 'team' in the 1920s and the rest is history. This retail store (one of three in the country) carries sneakers, denim and other gear. The iconic shoes come in all colors and

LOCAL KNOWLEDGE

BOSTON FASHION

Lunarik Fashions (279 Newbury St; ⊙11am-7pm Mon-Fri, 10am-8pm Sat, noon-6pm Sun; ⓉHynes) Like a modern woman's handbag, Lunarik is packed with useful stuff, much of it by local designers. Look for whimsical collage-covered pieces by Jenn Sherr, beautiful hand-crafted jewelry by Dasken Designs, and the best-selling richly colored leather handbags by Saya Cullinan. Who wouldn't want to pack their stuff into that!

Daniela Corte (www.danielacorte.com; 211 Newbury St; ⊙11am-7pm Mon-Sat; ⓉCopley) Daniela Corte attended the Boston School of Fashion Design before launching her own line and opening this understated boutique on Newbury St. Browse her collection of silky tops, fun-loving dresses and skin-hugging leggings.

patterns; make them uniquely your own at the in-store customization area.

IBEX   CLOTHING
(www.ibex.com; 303 Newbury St; ⊙10am-7pm Mon-Sat, 11am-6pm Sun; ⓉHynes) Based in snowy, cold Vermont, Ibex makes outdoor clothing from soft, warm, breathable merino wool. It's not the itchy stuff you remember – this wool is plush and pleasurable, thanks to the fineness of the fiber. Categorized as base layer, midlayer or outerlayer, the clothing is guaranteed to keep you cozy, even through the coldest, snowiest Vermont winter. Bonus: it looks good, too.

BALL & BUCK   MEN'S CLOTHING
(www.ballandbuck.com; 144 Newbury St; ⊙11am-8pm; ⓉCopley) The hunter logo is indicative of Ball & Buck's target audience – manly men who are not afraid to wear camouflage and look good in it, too. These attractive, durable duds are meant to be worn, for work or play, trekking through the woods or strolling city streets. Every item in the shop is made in the US of A.

FAIRY SHOP   GIFTS
(www.thefairyshop.com; 272 Newbury St; ⊙vary; ⓉHynes) Don't bother coming here unless you believe in fairies. But if you do believe, stop in for pixie dust, pet unicorns, magical trinkets and Wonderland souvenirs. You'll find fairies and gnomes in every shape and size. So if you'd rather be 'chillin' with your gnomies,' here's where.

MARATHON SPORTS   SPORTS
(www.marathonsports.com; 671 Boylston St; ⊙10:30am-7:30pm Mon-Fri, 10am-6pm Sat, noon-6pm Sun; ⓉCopley) Specializing in running gear, this place could not have a bet-

ter location: it overlooks the finish line of the Boston Marathon. It's known for attentive customer service, as staff work hard to make sure you get a shoe that fits. They also work hard to support the running community, with a weekly running club and a calendar of other events.

TRIDENT BOOKSELLERS & CAFÉ   BOOKS
(www.tridentbookscafe.com; 338 Newbury St; ⊙9am-midnight; ☎; ⓉHynes) Pick out a pile of books and retreat to a quiet corner of the café to decide which ones you really want to buy. You'll come away enriched, as Trident's stock tends toward New Age titles. But there's a little bit of everything here, as the 'hippie turned back-to-the-lander, turned Buddhist, turned entrepreneur' owners know how to keep their customers happy.

NEWBURY COMICS   MUSIC
(www.newburycomics.com; 332 Newbury St; ⊙10am-10pm Mon-Fri, to 11pm Sat, 11am-8pm Sun; ⓉHynes) How does a music store remain relevant in this age of MP3? One word: vinyl. In addition to the many cheap CDs and DVDs, there's a solid selection of new release vinyl. Incidentally, they do sell comic books, as well as action figures and other silly gags. No wonder everyone is having such a wicked good time.

SOCIETY OF ARTS & CRAFTS   HANDICRAFTS
(www.societyofcrafts.org; 175 Newbury St; ⊙10am-6pm Tue-Sat; ⓉCopley) This prestigious nonprofit gallery was founded in 1897. With retail space downstairs and exhibit space upstairs, the society promotes emerging and established artists, and encourages innovative handicrafts. The collection changes constantly, but you'll find lovely weaving, leather, ceramics, glassware, furniture and other hand-crafted items.

CLOSET, INC
CLOTHING

(www.theclosetboston.com; 175 Newbury St; 10am-6pm Tue-Sat; ⊤Copley) For shoppers with an eye for fashion, but without a pocketbook to match. Closet, Inc (and it does feel like some fashion maven's overstuffed closet) is a secondhand clothing store that carries high-quality suits, sweaters, jackets, jeans, gowns and other garb by acclaimed designers. The longer the item sits in the store, the bigger the discount.

CONDOM WORLD
ACCESSORIES

(www.condomworldboston.com; 332 Newbury St; 11am-8pm Mon-Thu, to 10pm Fri & Sat, noon-7pm Sun; ⊤Hynes) There's a good selection of condoms in all sizes, colors and textures. Cinnamon-flavored condoms are not the only way to spice up your sex life, however. Friendly staff can also help you pick out lubricants, adult toys and other basic sex paraphernalia. And for the easily amused: provocatively shaped ice-cube trays, pasta and straws; X-rated fortune cookies etc.

COPLEY PLACE
MALL

(www.simon.com; 100 Huntington Ave; 10am-8pm Mon-Sat, noon-6pm Sun; ⊤Back Bay) Half the fun of Back Bay shopping is the unique boutiques and local shops that line Newbury St. The other half is the super-swank designer stores that populate Copley Place. This urban mall includes 75 shops, most of them with big names such as Neiman Marcus, Barneys New York, Tiffany & Co, Jimmy Choo, Christian Dior etc.

HEMPEST
CLOTHING, HOMEWARES

(www.hempest.com; 207 Newbury St; 11am-8pm Mon-Sat, noon-6pm Sun; ⊤Copley) 🌿 The Hempest is not a well-stocked smoke shop, as it's more about stylish clothing, organic soaps and lotions, and fun home-furnishing items. Most of the products are made from cannabis hemp, the botanical cousin of marijuana. Hemp is a versatile, renewable resource that is economically and environmentally beneficial, and now some enlightened politicians are poised to make it legal to grow in the US. Stay tuned.

PRUDENTIAL CENTER
MALL

(www.prudentialcenter.com; 800 Boylston St; 10am-9pm Mon-Sat, 11am-8pm Sun; 🛜; ⊤Prudential) One of Boston's most distinctive landmarks, the Prudential Center has something for everyone: shops, restaurants, a ho-

tel, a chapel and an amazing city view from the top-floor Skywalk (p111).

🏃 SPORTS & ACTIVITIES

BACK BAY YOGA STUDIO
YOGA

(☑617-375-9642; www.backbayyoga.com; 364 Boylston St; yoga class $15; 6am-9pm Mon-Fri, 9:30am-8pm Sat, 8am-8pm Sun; ⊤Arlington) Services from massage to meditation, as well as all forms of yoga. Seven to ten classes are offered daily, with a particularly full schedule on Monday. One-hour vinyasa classes are $10, and there are daily community classes for only $5. With three studios painted in jewel tones, it's a warm and attractive space for your sun salutations.

G2O SPA & SALON
SPA

(☑617-262-2220; www.g2ospasalon.com; 278 Newbury St; 8am-9pm Mon-Fri, to 6pm Sat, 10am-6pm Sun; ⊤Hynes) Spend some time at this 'Day Spa Resort' and your body will thank you. The offerings include facials, massage, acupuncture and so much more. There are (relatively) simple pleasures, such as the Skylight Hot Tub and the Rooftop Terrace.

SOUTHWEST CORRIDOR
CYCLING

(www.swcpc.org; ⊤Back Bay) Extending for almost 5 miles, the Southwest Corridor is a paved walkway, running between and parallel to Columbus and Huntington Aves. It's an ideal urban cycling route, leading from Back Bay, through the South End and Roxbury, to Forest Hills in Jamaica Plain. Borrow a bike from the Hubway (p209) or rent one at **Community Bicycle Supply** (www.communitybicycle.com; 496 Tremont St; per day $25-35; 10am-7pm Mon-Sat year-round, also noon-5pm Sun Apr-Sep; ⊤Back Bay).

KINGS
BOWLING

(www.kingsbackbay.com; 50 Dalton St; bowling per person per game $5.50-7, shoe rental $4; 3pm-1am Mon-Wed, noon-1am Thu-Sat, noon-11pm Sun; ♿; ⊤Hynes) For an over-the-top tenpin experience, roll a few at Kings, where high-tech lanes are lined with neon lights and surrounded by trippy graphics. Behind deck is an enormous cocktail lounge done up in a style reminiscent of *The Jetsons*. If bowling is not your game, there is also billiards, shuffleboard and skeeball.

Kenmore Square & Fenway

Neighborhood Top Five

1 Spending a day at the **Museum of Fine Arts** (p120), immersing yourself in the Art of the Americas and lunching at the New American Cafe, then dedicating the afternoon to exploring other treasures, especially the Impressionist and post-Impressionist paintings.

2 Watching the Red Sox whip their opponents at **Fenway Park** (p119).

3 Venerating the artistic, aesthetic and cultural legacy of Isabella Stewart Gardner at her namesake **museum** (p122).

4 Hearing the world-renowned **Boston Symphony Orchestra** (p127) play in the acoustically perfect Symphony Hall.

5 Hitting **Lansdowne St** (p126) for a night of drinking, music and merry-making.

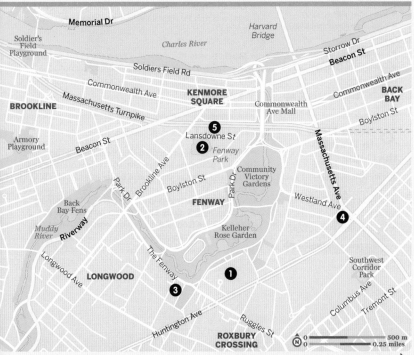

For more detail of this area see Map p247 ➡

Lonely Planet's Top Tip

If you can't score tickets to the baseball game, you can still watch the action and soak up the atmosphere at one of the bars on Lansdowne St (they all definitely have TVs). You can even hear the gasps and the cheers from the fans inside the ballpark.

✖ Best Places to Eat

➡ Island Creek Oyster Bar (p125)

➡ El Pelon (p125)

➡ Gyro City (p125)

➡ Audubon Boston (p125)

For reviews, see p125 ➡

🍷 Best Places to Drink

➡ Bleacher Bar (p126)

➡ Lower Depths Tap Room (p126)

➡ Hawthorne (p126)

➡ Pavement Coffeehouse (p127)

For reviews, see p126 ➡

⊙ Best Places to Watch the Game

➡ Bleacher Bar (p126)

➡ Tasty Burger (p126)

➡ Boston Beer Works (p126)

➡ Lansdowne Pub (p127)

For reviews, see p126 ➡

Explore Kenmore Square & Fenway

Kenmore Sq is the epicenter of student life in Boston. In addition to the Boston University behemoth, there are more than a half-dozen colleges in the area. As such, Kenmore Sq has a disproportionate share of nightlife, inexpensive eateries and dormitories disguised as brownstones.

Come to Kenmore Sq to cavort at cool clubs and devour cheap food. If you get the timing right, you can do so before or after the Red Sox game. Watch the boys battle it out from your perch at one of the local sports bars or, if you're lucky, at Fenway Park.

While Kenmore Sq is best for baseball and beer, the southern part of this neighborhood is dedicated to more high-minded pursuits. Dubbed 'Avenue of the Arts,' Huntington Ave represents a concentrated area of major and minor artistic and cultural venues, including Symphony Hall, two universities and two museums. Artlovers should devote a day to exploring one of Boston's celebrated art venues (although deciding which one will be a challenge).

Local Life

➡ **Cheap Grub** Locals know that Peterborough St (p125) is a hub for affordable eating. Ethnic eateries and take-out joints line the little residential street, making it a sort of urban food court.

➡ **Music Scene** Buy tickets in advance to see national acts at the House of Blues (p128), but hang out at Church (p128) any night of the week for a glimpse of the local music scene.

Getting There & Away

➡ **Metro** West of the center, the green line of the T forks into four branches, so you have to pay attention not only to the color of your train, but also its letter (B, C, D or E). To reach Kenmore Sq or Fenway Park, take any of the green-line trains except the E-line to Kenmore T station. Sights along Huntington Ave in Fenway are accessible from the E-line Museum station or the orange-line Ruggles station.

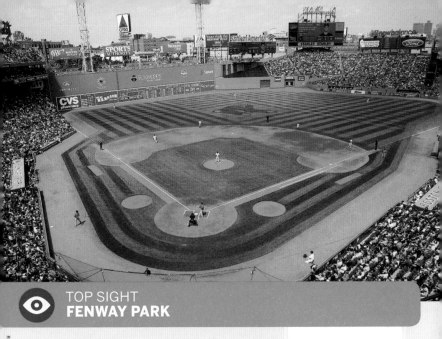

RICH GAGNON/GETTY IMAGES ©

TOP SIGHT
FENWAY PARK

What is it that makes Fenway Park 'America's Most Beloved Ballpark'? It's not just that it's the home of the Boston Red Sox. Open since 1912, it is the oldest operating baseball park in the country. As such, the park has many quirks that make for a unique experience.

The **Green Monster**, the 37ft-high wall in left field, is the most famous feature at Fenway Park. It's only 310ft away from home plate (compared to the standard 325ft). It's a popular target for right-handed hitters, who can score an easy home run with a high hit to left field. On the other hand, a powerful line drive – which might normally be a home run – bounces off the Monster. As all Red Sox fans know, 'the wall giveth and the wall taketh away.'

The Green Monster was painted green only in 1947. But since then, it has become a patented part of the Fenway experience. Literally. The color is officially known as Fence Green and the supplier will not share the recipe.

The **Pesky Pole**, Fenway's right-field foul pole, is named for former shortstop Johnny Pesky. Until his death in 2012, 'Mr Red Sox' Johnny Pesky was associated with the team for 12 years as a player and 46 years as a manager or coach.

The Triangle, in the deepest darkest corner of centre field where the walls form a triangle, is – at 425ft – the furthest distance from home plate.

The bleachers at Fenway Park are green, except for the **lone red seat**: seat 21 at section 42, row 37. This is supposedly the location of the longest home run ever hit at Fenway Park – officially 502ft, hit by Ted Williams in 1946.

The best way to experience Fenway Park is to catch a game (p128). Otherwise, see these highlights on a **Ballpark Tour**. Avoid afternoon tours on game days; crowds are huge and tours shortened.

DON'T MISS

→ Sitting atop the Green Monster

→ Original seats that are more than a century old

→ Fenway's beloved manual scoreboard

PRACTICALITIES

→ Map p247

→ www.redsox.com

→ 4 Yawkey Way

→ tours adult/child $18/12

→ ⏰10am-5pm

→ 🚻

→ Ⓣ Kenmore

TOP SIGHT
MUSEUM OF FINE ARTS

Since 1876, the Museum of Fine Arts (MFA) has been Boston's premier venue for showcasing art by local, national and international artists. Nowadays, the museum's holdings encompass all eras, from the ancient world to contemporary times, and all areas of the globe, making it truly encyclopedic in scope. Most recently, the museum has added gorgeous new wings dedicated to the Art of the Americas and to contemporary art, contributing to Boston's emergence as an art center in the 21st century.

Art of the Americas

The centerpiece of the MFA is the four-story Americas wing, which includes 53 galleries exhibiting art from the pre-Columbian era up through the 20th century.

Some of the newest, most intriguing acquisitions are on the lower level, which houses the pre-Columbian and Native American artwork. There are also a few rooms dedicated to colonial America and the maritime trade, with a wonderful collection of model ships.

Level one showcases 18th- and 19th-century art, with several rooms dedicated to neoclassicism and revolutionary Boston. Thomas Sully's depiction of Washington's *Passage of the Delaware* is a highlight. The MFA also has the world's largest holding of Copley paintings; don't miss the alarming *Watson and the Shark*.

The second level is, perhaps, the richest part of the wing. An entire gallery is dedicated to John Singer Sargent, including his iconic painting *The Daughters of Edward Darley Boit*. Highlights in the American Impressionism

DON'T MISS

➡ *The Daughters of Edward Darley Boit* by John Singer Sargent
➡ *Boston Common at Twilight* by Childe Hassam
➡ *Where Do We Come From?* by Paul Gauguin
➡ Buddhist Temple room
➡ *Black River* by El Anatsui

PRACTICALITIES

➡ MFA
➡ Map p247
➡ www.mfa.org
➡ 465 Huntington Ave
➡ adult/child $25/10
➡ ⏲10am-5pm Sat-Tue, to 10pm Wed-Fri
➡ ♿
➡ ⓣMuseum or Ruggles

galleries include pieces by Mary Cassat and the perennial local favorite, *Boston Common at Twilight* by Childe Hassam.

The top floor is devoted to modernism, with wonderful pieces by Alexander Calder, Frank Stella and Georgia O'Keefe. There are also impressive additions by Latin American artists.

Art of Europe

Located in the museum's northern wing, the MFA's collection of European art spans the centuries from the Middle Ages to the 20th century. The Italian Renaissance is well represented, with gilded icons and paintings by Botticelli, Titian and Tintoretto. Also in the house is the Golden Age of Dutch painting, with five paintings by Rembrandt. The highlight of the European exhibit is no doubt the Impressionists and post-Impressionists, with masterpieces by Degas, Gauguin, Renoir and Van Gogh, as well as the largest collection of Monets outside Paris.

Art of Asia, Oceania & Africa

One of the MFA's strongest areas, the collection of Asian art is located in the southwestern wing, along with art from the South Pacific and Africa. The centerpiece of the exhibit is the serene Buddhist Temple room on the 2nd floor, just one exhibit in a vast array of Japanese art, including prints and metal works. There is also an extensive display of Chinese paintings, calligraphy and ceramics.

Art of the Ancient World

In the southeastern part of the museum, the MFA's ancient-art collection dates from 6000 BC to 600 AD and covers a huge geographic spectrum. The highlight is certainly the Egyptian galleries, especially the two rooms of mummies. The Etruscan painted tombs are also impressive. Greek, Roman and Nubian pieces occupy the second level, with plenty of perfectly sculpted Greek gods and Roman emperors.

Linde Wing for Contemporary Art

Opened in 2011, this is the newest part of the 'new' MFA. The renovation of the west wing – originally designed by IM Pei – nearly tripled the exhibition space for contemporary art. There are galleries dedicated to video, multimedia art and decorative arts in addition to the more traditional media.

The darling of museum patrons is *Black River,* a fantastic woven tapestry of discarded bottle caps, by Ghanaian artist El Anatsui. But the most compelling piece is perhaps the blue neon sign by Maurizio Nannucci, which spells out 'All Art Has Been Contemporary.'

FOR KIDS

Children under the age of 17 are admitted free after 3pm on weekdays and all day on weekends – a fantastic family bargain.

The murals in the rotunda and above the main staircase were painted by John Singer Sargent in the 1920s. The main rotunda painting depicts the Greek goddess of wisdom, Athena, turning back Time.

GET A GUIDE

For a guided tour in one of seven languages, rent the museum's multimedia guide (adult/child $6/4), which uses video, audio and animation to provide extra insight into the highlights of the MFA collection.

The Linde wing features upscale dining at the restaurant Bravo, as well as a café and cafeteria. In the Shapiro Courtyard, sample Ken Oringer's menu of modern American cuisine at the New American Café.

TOP SIGHT
ISABELLA STEWART GARDNER MUSEUM

The magnificent Venetian-style palazzo that houses this museum was home to 'Mrs Jack' Gardner herself until her death in 1924. A monument to one woman's taste for acquiring exquisite art, the Gardner is filled with some 2500 priceless objects, primarily European, including outstanding tapestries and Italian Renaissance and 17th-century Dutch paintings. The four-story greenhouse courtyard is a masterpiece and a tranquil oasis that alone is worth the price of admission.

Courtyard

The centerpiece of the Gardner Museum is the gorgeous courtyard, filled with lush greenery, vibrant blooms and evocative sculpture. Almost every room gives a different perspective on this masterpiece of landscape design. The plantings change seasonally. Come in early spring to see the courtyard draped in stunning nasturtium blooms (reportedly Isabella's favorite).

Cloisters

The most striking room on the 1st floor is the Spanish Cloister, with its Islamic tile. At one end, a Moorish arch frames John Singer Sargent's picture of a Gypsy dance. At the other end, a wrought-iron gate leads into the Spanish Chapel, hung with Spanish religious art. Other cloisters encircle the courtyard, sprinkled with sculptures and stone work.

Several smaller rooms are stuffed with paintings, including work by James McNeill Whistler, Henri Matisse, Edgar Degas and Anders Zorn. Mrs Gardner was a patron of John Singer Sargent, and many of his paintings hang in these rooms.

DON'T MISS

➡ Ancient art and seasonal landscaping in the courtyard
➡ *Portrait of Isabella Stewart Gardner* by John Singer Sargent
➡ *Rape of Europa* by Titian
➡ Newly restored Tapestry Room

PRACTICALITIES

➡ Map p247
➡ www.gardnermuseum.org
➡ 280 The Fenway
➡ adult/child $15/free
➡ ⊙11am-5pm Mon, Wed & Fri-Sun, to 9pm Thu
➡ ♿
➡ Ⓣ Museum

Second Floor

On the 2nd floor, the Dutch room contains Mrs Gardner's small collection of Dutch and Flemish art, including a self-portrait by Rembrandt and another portrait by Rubens. Note the empty frames, where the stolen paintings once hung.

The majestic Tapestry Room evokes a castle hall, hung with 10 allegorical tapestries. One series depicts scenes from the Life of Cyrus the Great, while the other recounts the Life of Abraham.

The Raphael Room shows off two paintings by the namesake Renaissance painter, as well as two gorgeous *cassoni* (Italian wedding chests).

Third Floor

The 3rd floor contains the highlights of this rich collection. The sumptuous Veronese Room is so named for the stunning ceiling painting, but this room is filled with treasures, including pastels by James McNeill Whistler.

The museum's most celebrated gallery is the Titian Room, where Mrs Gardner displayed her passion for all things Venetian. The gallery is centered on Titian's famous rendition of *Europa,* which was much loved by the collector.

Your final stop is the Gothic Room, featuring Sargent's remarkable (and rather controversial) portrait of Mrs Gardner herself. This room was never open to the public when Mrs Gardner was alive, but she did allow Sargent to use it as a studio.

Piano Building

In 2012, the Gardner Museum opened the doors of a greatly anticipated, hotly contested new building, designed by architect Renzo Piano. Mrs Jack's will stipulated that her art-filled palazzo never be altered, so the project required much negotiation (including a special permission from the Massachusetts Supreme Court). The end result allows the palazzo to better serve its originally intended purpose, which is to share Isabella's love for art and culture with the community. The new space includes a lovely concert hall, as well as additional exhibit space which supports a vibrant art-in-residency program.

ART HEIST

On March 18, 1990, two thieves disguised as police officers broke into the Isabella Stewart Gardner Museum. They left with nearly $200 million worth of artworks. The most famous painting stolen was Vermeer's *The Concert,* but the loot also included three works by Rembrandt, and others by Manet and Degas, not to mention French and Chinese artifacts. The crime was never solved. Since Mrs Gardner's will stipulated that the exhibit should never be altered, the empty frames still hang on the walls.

Take a free one-hour tour of museum highlights on weekdays at noon and 2pm. Introductory talks take place in Calderwood Hall on weekdays at 12:30pm and 2:30pm. Alternatively, printed room guides provide descriptions of the art work in each room.

MUSEUM CONCERTS

Elegant Calderwood Hall is the setting for concerts – from classical to contemporary – on the third Thursday of the month (5:30pm to 9pm) and Sunday afternoons (1:30pm).

SIGN OF THE TIMES

London has Big Ben, Paris has the Eiffel Tower, and Boston has the **Citgo Sign** (Map p247). It's an unlikely landmark in this high-minded city, but Bostonians love the bright-blinking 'trimark' that has towered over Kenmore Sq since 1965. Every time the Red Sox hit a home run over the leftfield wall at Fenway Park, Citgo's colorful logo is seen by thousands of fans. It also symbolizes the end of the Boston Marathon, as it falls at mile 25 in the race.

For whatever reason, Bostonians have claimed these neon lights as their own. The sign was turned off in 1979 to conserve energy, and after four years, Citgo decided to dismantle the deteriorating sign. But local residents rallied, arguing it was a prime example of urban neon art. They fought to bestow landmark status on the sign to preserve it. And the Citgo sign stayed.

The sign was renovated in 2005, replacing the neon lights with LEDs (which are more durable, more energy-efficient and easier to maintain). Indeed, the previous version of the sign required more than 5 miles of neon tubing to light its 60ft-by-60ft face. Featured in film, photographs and song, the Citgo sign continues to shine.

⊙ SIGHTS

⊙ Kenmore Square

FENWAY PARK STADIUM
See p119.

MUGAR MEMORIAL LIBRARY LIBRARY
Map p247 (Howard Gotlieb Archival Research Center; www.bu.edu/archives; 771 Commonwealth Ave; ⊙9am-5pm Mon-Fri; T BU Central) FREE The special collections of BU's Mugar Memorial Library are housed in the Howard Gotlieb Archival Research Center, an outstanding 20th-century archive that balances pop culture and scholarly appeal. Rotating exhibits showcase the holdings, including papers from Arthur Fiedler's collection, the personal correspondance of Julius and Ethel Rosenberg, or the correspondence of BU alumnus Dr Martin Luther King, Jr.

⊙ Fenway

MUSEUM OF FINE ARTS MUSEUM
See p120.

ISABELLA STEWART GARDNER MUSEUM MUSEUM
See p122.

BACK BAY FENS PARK
Map p247 (Park Dr; ⊙dawn-dusk; T Museum) The Back Bay Fens, or the Fenway, follows the Muddy River, an aptly named creek that is choked with tall reeds. The Fens features well-cared-for community gardens, the elegant Kelleher Rose Garden, and plenty of space to toss a Frisbee, play pick-up basketball or lie in the sun.

MASSART GALLERY
Map p247 (Massachusetts College of Art; www.massart.edu; 621 Huntington Ave, South Bldg; ⊙noon-6pm Mon, Tue & Thu-Sat, to 8pm Wed; T Longwood Ave) FREE This is the country's first and only four-year independent public art college. There's always some thought-provoking or sense-stimulating exhibits to see at one of seven galleries on campus. In the South Building, the Bakalar and Paine galleries host nationally and internationally known artists – as well as emerging talents – as a complement to the school's curricula. Other campus galleries usually showcase student and faculty work.

MassArt is one of the country's oldest art schools and – as such – was the first to grant an art degree. Originally the Massachusetts Normal Art School, the institution was part of a plan by civic leaders to promote fine arts and technology, in an attempt to ensure the state's continued economic growth. Other parts of this plan included establishing the Museum of Fine Arts (founded in 1870) and Massachusetts Institute of Technology (1860).

SYMPHONY HALL HISTORIC BUILDING
Map p247 (www.bso.org; 301 Massachusetts Ave; ⊙tours 4pm Wed & 2pm Sat, reservation required) This majestic building has been the home of the Boston Symphony Orchestra

since 1900, when it was built by McKim, Mead & White (of BPL fame). See the hall's public spaces and go behind the scenes on a free, one-hour tour.

Symphony Hall is often lauded for its perfect acoustics, and the architects did in fact engage a Harvard physics professor to achieve this. The sloped stage walls, shallow side balconies and coffered ceiling all help distribute the sound around the hall. To truly appreciate the physics, you'll have to come for a concert.

EATING

Kenmore Square

Most places in Kenmore Sq target the large local student population, meaning cheap ethnic eats and divey sandwich shops, but a few upscale restaurants have found their way here, too.

INDIA QUALITY   INDIAN $

Map p247 (www.indiaquality.com; 484 Commonwealth Ave; mains lunch $8, dinner $12-15; ⊙11:30am-11pm; ⚡♿; TKenmore) India Quality has been serving chicken curry and lamb *saag* to hungry students, daytime professionals and baseball fans since 1983 – and it repeatedly tops the lists of Boston's best Indian food. The place is rather nondescript, but the food is anything but, especially considering the reasonable prices (look for lunch specials under $10). Service is reliably fast and friendly.

UBURGER   BURGERS $

Map p247 (www.uburgerboston.com; 636 Beacon St; burgers $5-7; ⊙11am-11pm; TKenmore) The way burgers were meant to be. The beef is ground fresh daily on the premises and burgers are made to order, with fancy (grilled mushrooms and Swiss cheese) or basic (American cheese and pickles) toppings. The french fries and onion rings are hand-cut and crispy-crunchy good. Also available: chicken sandwiches, hot dogs and salads, but why would you do that?

AUDUBON BOSTON   PUB FOOD $$

Map p247 (www.audubonboston.us; 838 Beacon St; sandwiches $9-12, mains $15-17; ⊙11:30am-midnight, bar to 1am; ⚡; TSt Mary's) Audubon is a long-standing Fenway favorite, now with a new menu, a new name and new

management. The place has retained its minimalist decor and casual-cool vibe, but it has added a cocktail program and interesting menu items like corn husk flounder and Cajun cauliflower heart. Highly recommended for a bite before the Sox game.

PETIT ROBERT BISTRO   FRENCH $$

Map p247 (www.petitrobertbistro.com; 468 Commonwealth Ave; mains lunch $12-18, dinner $17-27; ⊙11am-11pm; TKenmore) Once upon a time the legendary Maison Robert represented the finest dining in Boston. The ultrachic institution has now closed, but chef Jacky Robert has reapplied his talents to this welcoming, working-class bistro. The French fare is straightforward and hearty, with daily specials posted on the blackboard. The surroundings are casual-chic but crowded, including a tiny patio.

★ISLAND CREEK OYSTER BAR   SEAFOOD $$$

Map p247 (⚡617-532-5300; www.islandcreekoysterbar.com; 500 Commonwealth Ave; oysters $2.50-4, mains lunch $18-21, dinner $25-35; ⊙4pm-1am; TKenmore) Island Creek has united 'farmer, chef and diner in one space' – and what a space it is. ICOB serves up the region's finest oysters, along with other local seafood, in an ethereal new-age setting. The specialty – lobster roe noodles topped with braised short ribs and grilled lobster – lives up to the hype.

Fenway

The quiet streets between the Back Bay Fens and Fenway Park are home to a few neighborhood favorites.

★EL PELON   MEXICAN $

Map p247 (www.elpelon.com; 92 Peterborough St; mains $6-8; ⊙11am-11pm; ⚡♿; TMuseum) If your budget is tight, don't miss this chance to fill up on Boston's best burritos, tacos and tortas, made with the freshest ingredients. The *tacos de la casa* are highly recommended, especially the *pescado,* made with Icelandic cod and topped with chili mayo. Plates are paper and cutlery is plastic.

GYRO CITY   GREEK $

Map p247 (www.gyrocityboston.com; 88 Peterborough St; mains $7-10; ⊙11am-11pm; ⚡♿; TMuseum) This authentic *gyrotico* is a newcomer to Peterborough St (aka Fenway's restaurant row), but it fits right in with cheap, scrumptious, filling food. There are a variety of gyros, each with a delightful twist (eg, French fries on the traditional pork gyro) – as well as baklava made by a real live Greek mama. Counter seating inside, patio seating outside.

TASTY BURGER
BURGERS $

Map p247 (www.tastyburger.com; 1301 Boylston St; burgers $4-6; ⊙11am-2am; ☻; ⊤Fenway) Once a Mobile station, it's now a retro burger joint, with picnic tables outside and a pool table inside. The name of the place is a nod to *Pulp Fiction,* as is the poster of Samuel L Jackson on the wall. You won't find a half-pound of Kobe beef on your bun, but you will have to agree, 'That's a tasty burger.' Aside from the burgers, this is a fun place to drink cheap beer and watch sports on TV.

TRATTORIA TOSCANA
ITALIAN $$

Map p247 (www.trattoriatoscanafenway.com; 130 Jersey St; mains $15-25; ⊙5-10pm Mon-Sat; ⊤Museum) This tiny trattoria welcomes all comers as if they are old friends, serving up Tuscan wines, rich soups and delicious pastas, with the gnocchi a particular highlight. The tantalizing aromas and intimate atmosphere delight the neighborhood crowd at this hidden gem. It's a small place that does not take reservations, but your patience will be rewarded.

CITIZEN PUBLIC HOUSE
MODERN AMERICAN $$

Map p247 (✆617-450-9000; www.citizenpub. com; 1310 Boylston St; mains $15-23; ⊙5pm-2am Mon-Sat, 11am-2am Sun; ⊤Fenway) This is a modern, urban gastropub with food and drinks for a sophisticated palate. There is an eye-catching and daily-changing raw bar, while the selective list of main dishes focuses on roasts and grills. The food is top-notch, and it's all complemented by an extensive bar menu, featuring 75 varieties of whisky.

🍷 DRINKING & NIGHTLIFE

Most bars in the vicinity of mecca (otherwise known as Fenway Park) cater to sports fans. While many are forgettable, a few complement and enhance the hysteria.

🍷 Kenmore Square

★BLEACHER BAR
SPORTS BAR

Map p247 (www.bleacherbarboston.com; 82a Lansdowne St; ⊙11am-1am Sun-Wed, to 2am Thu-Sat; ⊤Kenmore) Tucked under the bleachers at Fenway Park, this classy bar offers a view onto center field. It's not the best place to watch the game, as the place gets packed, but it's a fun way to experience America's oldest ballpark, even when the Sox are not playing. Gentlemen: enjoy the view from the loo! If you want a seat in front of the window, get your name on the waiting list an hour or two before game time; once seated, diners have 45 minutes in the hot seat.

LOWER DEPTHS TAP ROOM
BAR

Map p247 (www.thelowerdepths.com; 476 Commonwealth Ave; ⊙11:30am-1am; ⊤Kenmore) This subterranean space is a beer-lovers' paradise. It has all the atmosphere (and beer knowledge) of its sister establishment, Bukowski Tavern, but the Lower Depths classes it up just a little. Besides the impressive beer selection, the kitchen turns out excellent comfort food, including one-dollar Fenway Franks with exotic one-dollar toppings. Cash only.

HAWTHORNE
COCKTAIL BAR

Map p247 (www.thehawthornebar.com; 500a Commonwealth Ave; ⊙5pm-2am; ⊤Kenmore) Located in the basement of the Hotel Commonwealth, this is a living room–style cocktail lounge that attracts the city's sophisticates. Sink into the plush furniture and sip a custom cocktail.

EASTERN STANDARD
COCKTAIL BAR

Map p247 (www.easternstandardboston.com; 528 Commonwealth Ave; ⊙7am-2am; ⊤Kenmore) Whether you choose to sit in the sophisticated, brassy interior or on the heated patio (open year-round), you're sure to enjoy the upscale atmosphere at this Kenmore Sq favorite. French bistro fare, with a hint of New American panache (mains $20 to $30), caters to a pregame crowd that prefers wine and cheese to peanuts and crackerjacks. Great people-watching on game nights.

BOSTON BEER WORKS
BREWERY

Map p247 (www.beerworks.net; 61 Brookline Ave; ⊙11:30am-1am; ⊤Kenmore) Decked out with scads of TVs, which form a ring around the bar, this place is in a prime location –

directly across the street from all the action at Fenway Park. Most importantly, there is a rotating menu of 15-plus delicious beer flavors. The slick, modern room uses blonde-wood tones and simple trim stools to create an appealing design effect.

CORNWALL'S PUB
Map p247 (www.cornwalls.com; 654 Beacon St; ⊙noon-2am Mon-Sat; TKenmore) It's not a sports bar, or a dive bar, or a cocktail bar. It's a pub. An English pub. You can tell it's English by the extensive list of English beers, both draft and bottled. It's a friendly, family-run place, with board games, darts and pool tables to keep the drinkers entertained.

LANSDOWNE PUB IRISH PUB
Map p247 (www.lansdownepubboston.com; 9 Lansdowne St; cover $5; ⊙4pm-2am Mon-Fri, 10am-2am Sat & Sun; TKenmore) Disclaimer: this place gets packed with college kids on weekends and on game nights. If you can stand the happy, sweaty people, it's a great vibe, especially if the Sox are winning. If you're not into baseball, maybe you'll like the live-band karaoke (Thursday) or cover band dance parties (Friday and Saturday).

BILL'S BAR CLUB
Map p247 (www.billsbarboston.com; 5½ Lansdowne St; ⊙5pm-2am; TKenmore) The self-dubbed Dirty Rock Club is an obligatory stop if you're clubbing on Lansdowne St. Not your first stop, though, as the scene only starts to pick up around 11pm. This scrubby joint is reminiscent of the Lansdowne St of bygone days.

🍸 Fenway

PAVEMENT COFFEEHOUSE CAFE
Map p247 (www.pavementcoffeehouseboston. com; 1096 Boylston St; ⊙7am-7pm Mon-Fri, 8am-7pm Sat & Sun; 🛜; THynes) Exposed brick walls hung with art create a bohemian atmosphere at this coffee-lovers' dream. Berklee students and other hipsters congregate for fair-trade coffee, free wi-fi and bagel sandwiches.

MACHINE GAY
Map p247 (Ramrod; www.machine-boston. com; 1256 Boylston St; ⊙10pm-2am Wed-Mon; THynes) This long-standing gay favorite practically guarantees a fun night out, partially because it's two clubs in one, upstairs

and downstairs. So there are two different entertainment options nearly every night of the week, including Tantric Tuesdays, Wishful Wednesdays and Throwdown Thursdays. (Alliteration is alright!) Other events include karaoke, Latin night, drag night and a hot dyke night.

⭐ ENTERTAINMENT

★BOSTON SYMPHONY ORCHESTRA CLASSICAL MUSIC
Map p247 (BSO; ☎617-266-1200; www.bso.org; 301 Massachusetts Ave; tickets $30-115; TSymphony) Flawless acoustics match the ambitious programs of the world-renowned Boston Symphony Orchestra. From September to April, the BSO performs in the beauteous Symphony Hall (p124), featuring an ornamental high-relief ceiling and attracting a fancy-dress crowd. In summer, the BSO retreats to Tanglewood in Western Massachusetts.

BOSTON POPS CLASSICAL MUSIC
Map p247 (☎617-266-1200; www.bostonpops. org; 301 Massachusetts Ave; tickets $30-111; TSymphony) Playing out of the auditorily and visually delightful Symphony Hall, the Boston Pops arranges crowd-pleasers for the orchestra to tackle. Usually this means Christmas carols, movie scores and thematic mischief. The business is conducted by the dashing Keith Lockhart, making Boston hearts swoon since 1995.

HUNTINGTON THEATRE
COMPANY
THEATER

Map p247 (Boston University Theatre; www.huntingtontheatre.org; 264 Huntington Ave; ⊤Symphony) Boston's leading award-winning theater company, the Huntington specializes in developing new plays, staging many shows before they're transferred to Broadway (several of which have won Tonys). Seven major works by August Wilson were performed by the Huntington before going on to fame in New York. The company's credentials also include more than 50 world premieres of works by playwrights such as Tom Stoppard and Christopher Durang.

CHURCH
LIVE MUSIC

Map p247 (www.churchofboston.com; 69 Kilmarnock St; cover $10-12; ⊙5pm-2am; ⊤Museum or Kenmore) Say a prayer of thanks for this neighborhood music venue. It books cool bands five nights a week, which is the most important thing. But it's also stylish, with pool tables, a pretty slick restaurant (open till midnight) and attractive people. And plasma TVs, of course. Music starts most nights at 8pm.

HOUSE OF BLUES
LIVE MUSIC

Map p247 (www.hob.com/boston; 15 Lansdowne St; ⊤Kenmore) The HOB is bigger and better than ever. Well, it's bigger. Never mind the ridiculously tight security measures, this is where national acts play if they can't fill the Garden (eg the Bosstones, Dropkick Murphys etc). The balcony seating offers an excellent view of the stage, while fighting the crowds on the mezzanine can be brutal.

MUSEUM OF FINE ARTS
CINEMA

Map p247 (www.mfa.org; 465 Huntington Ave; adult/student $11/9; ⊤Museum or Ruggles) If you packed your thinking cap, the MFA screens highbrow film events. The museum also hosts film festivals dedicated to every ethnicity on the planet (Jewish, Iranian, African, French etc) as well as a gay and lesbian film festival and the Human Rights Watch film festival.

NEW ENGLAND
CONSERVATORY
CLASSICAL MUSIC

Map p247 (Jordan Hall; www.necmusic.edu; Jordan Hall, 30 Gainsborough St; ⊤Northeastern or Symphony) FREE Founded in 1867, the NEC is the country's oldest music school. The conservatory hosts professional and student chamber and orchestral concerts in

SHOPPING FOR VINYL

Nuggets (Map p247; www.nuggets records.com; 486 Commonwealth Ave; ⊙11:30am-7pm Tue-Sat, noon-5pm Sun; ⊤Kenmore) A little slice of 'old' Kenmore Sq. With a constantly shifting collection of vinyl, CDs and DVDs, Nuggets is a great place to browse. Many a Red Sox fan has popped in on the way to Fenway and ended up carting a sack of albums to the baseball game.

the acoustically superlative Jordan Hall, which dates from 1904. Admission is usually free.

SPORTS & ACTIVITIES

★FENWAY PARK
BASEBALL

Map p247 (www.redsox.com; 4 Yawkey Way; bleachers $12-40, grandstand $29-78, box $50-75; ⊤Kenmore) From April to September you can watch the Red Sox play at Fenway Park (p119), the nation's oldest and most storied ballpark. Unfortunately, it is also the most expensive – not that this stops the Fenway faithful from scooping up the tickets. There are sometimes game-day tickets on sale starting 90 minutes before the opening pitch.

Head to Gate E on Lansdowne St; arrive early (but no earlier than five hours before game time) and be prepared to enter the ballpark as soon as you purchase your tickets. Otherwise, you can always get tickets in advance from online vendors or on game-day from scalpers around Kenmore Sq. If the Sox are doing well, expect to pay two times the face value (less if you wait until after the game starts).

JILLIAN'S & LUCKY STRIKE
BOWLING

Map p247 (www.jilliansboston.com; 145 Ipswich St; ⊙11am-2am Mon-Sat, noon-2am Sun; ⊕; ⊤Kenmore) Bowling, billiards, and gettin' jiggy with it. That's what you can do at this enormous (but usually packed), three-story entertainment complex, which also has seven bars and a full-service menu. On the 2nd floor, the 24 pool tables are in pristine condition. Upstairs, the high-tech bowling alley has only 16 flashy lanes, so it's often a long wait.

Seaport District & South Boston

SEAPORT DISTRICT | SOUTH BOSTON

Neighborhood Top Five

1 Spending an afternoon at the striking waterfront site of the **Institute of Contemporary Art** (p131), contemplating the artistic curiosities on display within and admiring the stunning harbor and city views without.

2 Boarding the **Boston Tea Party Ships** (p132) and tossing crates of tea overboard.

3 Admiring the view and feasting on the creatures of the sea at **Legal Harborside** (p133).

4 Wriggling, crawling and climbing on the three-story climbing structure at the **Boston Children's Museum** (p132).

5 Sidling up to the bar at **Drink** (p135) for some serious cocktail swilling.

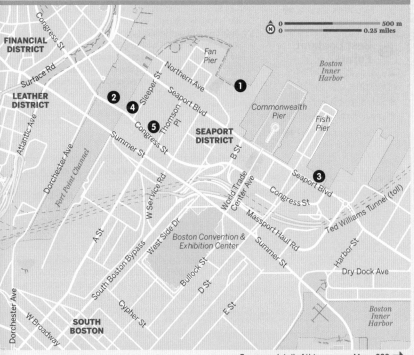

For more detail of this area see Map p239 ➡

Lonely Planet's Top Tip

Thursday nights are free at the ICA, while Friday nights at the Boston Children's Museum are only $1. The reduced admission is from 5pm to 9pm, in both cases.

✕ Best Places to Eat

➡ Row 34 (p133)

➡ Yankee Lobster Co (p133)

➡ Sam's (p133)

➡ Sportello (p133)

For reviews, see p133 ➡

🍷 Best Places to Drink

➡ Drink (p135)

➡ Lucky's Lounge (p135)

➡ Croke Park Whitey's (p135)

For reviews, see p135 ➡

◉ Best Lookout Points

➡ Founder's Gallery in the ICA (p131)

➡ Sam's (p133)

➡ Legal Harborside (p133)

For reviews, see p132 ➡

Explore Seaport District & South Boston

Separated from Boston proper by the jellyfish-laden Fort Point Channel, the Seaport District has always afforded a spectacular vista of the Boston Harbor and downtown Boston. Now this hot district offers all kinds of opportunities to see and savor it.

On the east side of the Fort Point Channel, follow the HarborWalk around the Moakley Federal Courthouse to enjoy the landscaped parks and fantastic views from Fan Pier, eventually ending up at the Institute of Contemporary Art (ICA). Spend an afternoon admiring art and feasting on fish and you've got a pretty good sense of what the Seaport District is all about.

Further east, the wharves are dominated by fish-processing facilities and a marine industrial center. But change is afoot, as restaurants, bars and retail outlets open in the new buildings. For visitors, it's worth strolling past the Fish Pier to catch a whiff of what this area used to be, and what it is becoming.

Meanwhile, the rest of South Boston remains well off the beaten path. Former stomping ground of Whitey Bulger and preferred setting for Boston-based mafia movies, 'Southie' lives large in local and national lore. Despite its reputation, South Boston has its own charm. The waterside community offers great harbor views, as well as Boston's best city beaches. On a hot summer day, Castle Island is a windy, welcoming waterside playscape for families and outdoorsy types.

The 'hood is packed with Irish pubs, but there are also a few notable 'New American' restaurants, should you care to drink something other than Guinness or PBR. This area is getting a glimpse of the gentrification that has transformed other parts of the city, but Southie is still unapologetically old-school.

Local Life

➡ **Drinking joint 1** You know it's a local hangout when they don't bother to put a proper sign outside, as is the case at Lucky's Lounge (p135).

➡ **Drinking joint 2** For a picture of local South Boston, chat up the regulars at Croke Park Whitey's (p135).

Getting There & Away

➡ **Metro** It's a 10-minute walk from South Station (red line) to the Seaport District; Broadway Station (also red line) sits at the top of South Boston's main street.

➡ **Bus** Connected to the metro system, the silver-line bus (SL1 or SL2) travels from South Station through the Seaport District, with stops at Courthouse, the World Trade Center and Silver Line Way.

TOP SIGHT
INSTITUTE OF CONTEMPORARY ART

Boston is fast becoming a focal point for contemporary art in the 21st century, with the Institute of Contemporary Art leading the way. The building is a work of art in itself – a striking glass structure cantilevered over a waterside plaza. The spacious light-filled interior allows for multimedia presentations, educational programs and studio space. More importantly, it provides the venue for the development of the ICA's permanent collection of 21st-century art.

Arguably, the ICA building is as much of an attraction as the art itself. Opened in 2006, the structure skillfully incorporates its surroundings into the architecture. In the **Founders Gallery**, which spans the entire width of the building, a glass wall virtually eliminates any barrier between viewer and seascape.

The **Mediatheque** is the museum's digital media center, where visitors can use the computer stations to learn more about featured art and artists. The terraced room also has a wall of windows at the front, but the room's unique perspective shows only the dancing and rippling of water, with no horizon in sight.

In 2000 the ICA began to develop a permanent collection. More than a decade later, the ICA now has the space to display its collection, which continues to grow. It showcases both national and international artists, including the likes of graffiti-artist Shepard Fairey; video artist Christian Jankowski; photographer Boris Mikhailov; local boy Josiah McElhany; and sculptors Tara Donovan, Mona Hatoum and Cornelia Parker. Look for all manner of art, from paintings to video to multidimensional mixed-media mash-ups.

DON'T MISS

➡ Fineberg Art Wall in the lobby
➡ *Peace Goddess* and other powerful pieces by Shepard Fairey
➡ *Hanging Fire* by Cornelia Parker
➡ View from the Foundation Gallery

PRACTICALITIES

➡ ICA
➡ Map p239
➡ www.icaboston.org
➡ 100 Northern Ave
➡ adult/child $15/free
➡ ⊙10am-5pm Tue, Wed, Sat & Sun, to 9pm Thu & Fri
➡ 🚻
➡ 🚌SL1 or SL2, Ⓣ South Station

◉ SIGHTS

◉ Seaport District

INSTITUTE OF
CONTEMPORARY ART   MUSEUM
See p131.

BOSTON CHILDREN'S MUSEUM   MUSEUM
Map p239 (www.bostonchildrensmuseum.org;
300 Congress St; admission $14, Fri 5-9pm $1;
⊘10am-5pm Sat-Thu, to 9pm Fri; ⊛; ⓉSouth
Station) ⏩ The interactive, educational exhibits at the delightful Children's Museum
keep kids entertained for hours. Highlights
include a bubble exhibit, rock-climbing
walls, a hands-on construction site and
intercultural immersion experiences. The
light-filled atrium features an amazing
three-story climbing maze.

The museum building utilizes loads of
green technology, including salvaged and
recycled construction materials and a fuel-
efficient heating system that incorporates a
green roof. Rain water run-off is collected
and used for irrigation and plumbing.

★BOSTON TEA PARTY
SHIPS & MUSEUM   MUSEUM
Map p236 (www.bostonteapartyship.com; Congress St Bridge; adult/child $25/15; ⊘10am-5pm,
last tour 4pm; ⊛; ⓉSouth Station) 'Boston Harbor a teapot tonight!' To protest unfair tax-
es, a gang of rebellious colonists dumped
342 chests of tea into the water. The 1773
protest set into motion the events leading
to the Revolutionary War. Nowadays, replica Tea Party Ships are moored at the re-
constructed Griffin's Wharf, alongside an
excellent experiential museum dedicated to
the revolution's most catalytic event.

Visitors can board the fully rigged *Elea-
nor* and the whaler *Beaver* to experience life
aboard an 18th-century vessel. Would-be rebels can throw crates of tea into the harbor,
in solidarity with their fiery forebears.

Using re-enactments, multimedia and
other fun exhibits, the museum addresses
all aspects of the Boston Tea Party, as well
as the events that followed. To hear both
sides of the story, visitors can witness a vir-
tual debate between Sam Adams and King
George III (though in reality they never
met). The museum's one actual artifact – a
tea crate known as the Robinson Half Chest
– is highlighted with an audio presentation.

Save a couple of dollars by purchasing
tickets online.

FORT POINT ARTS COMMUNITY   GALLERY
Map p239 (FPAC; www.fortpointarts.org; 300
Summer St; ⊘10am-6pm Wed-Fri; ⓉSouth Station) FREE This refurbished big-windowed
warehouse is the hub of the Fort Point Arts
Community, which contains a gallery featuring work from the talented collective.
See huge psychedelic oils, prints inspired
by 14th-century Venetian laces, lampshades
made from birch, and mixed-media films.
Several times a year, FPAC hosts popular
open-studio events that allow you to see the
artists' working spaces and creations.

◉ South Boston

CASTLE ISLAND & FORT
INDEPENDENCE   PARK, FORT
(Marine Park; ⊘dawn-dusk May-Sep; ⊛; ◻11,
ⓉBroadway) FREE The 19th-century Fort
Independence sits on 22 acres of parkland
called Castle Island (a misnomer, as it's
connected to the mainland). A paved path-
way follows the perimeter of the peninsula
– good for strolling or cycling – and there
is a small swimming beach. From the Seaport District, walk south on Summer St for
about a half-mile, then turn left on E 1st St
and continue to the waterfront.

DORCHESTER HEIGHTS   MONUMENT
(btwn G & Old Harbor Sts; ⊘dawn-dusk; ◻11,
ⓉBroadway) High above the Boston Harbor,
this strategic spot played a crucial role in
overcoming the British occupation. The
Georgian revival tower that stands today

GOT MILK?
Up there with the Citgo sign and the
Steaming Kettle, the giant **Hood Milk
Bottle** is emblematic of Boston. Tow-
ering 40ft over Fort Point Channel, it
would hold 50,000 gallons of milk if
it could hold a drop (that's 800,000
glasses of milk, if anybody's counting).
This unlikely wooden milk bottle was
built in 1934 to house an ice-cream
stand, which it did for 30-odd years
before it was abandoned. The milk bottle was finally purchased by Hood Milk,
New England's largest and oldest dairy,
and moved to its current location in
1977. It's now back in business (in summer) selling sandwiches and ice cream.

was built in 1898. To reach the monument, walk southeast along West Broadway from the T station, turn right onto Dorchester St and head up any of the little streets.

In the winter of 1776, rebel troops dragged 59 heavy cannons to Boston from Fort Ticonderoga in upstate New York. On the night of March 4, they perched them high atop Dorchester Heights, from where the British warships in the Harbor were at their mercy. The move caught the British completely by surprise, and ultimately convinced them to abandon Boston.

EATING

Seaport District

There was a time when hanging around the Seaport District meant you were eating seafood, because there was no other reason to be here. With the opening of the Boston Convention & Exhibition Center and the Institute of Contemporary Art, however, this district is quickly developing as a hotspot for new restaurants.

YANKEE LOBSTER CO   SEAFOOD $
Map p239 (www.yankeelobstercompany.com; 300 Northern Ave; mains $11-20; ⊙10am-9pm Mon-Sat, 11am-6pm Sun; ⌷SL1 or SL2, ⊤South Station) The Zanti family has been fishing for three generations, so they definitely know their stuff. A relatively recent addition is this retail fish market, scattered with a few tables in case you want to dine in. And you do. Order something simple like clam chowder or a lobster roll, along with a cold beer, and you will not be disappointed.

FLOUR   BAKERY, CAFE $
Map p239 (www.flourbakery.com; 12 Farnsworth St; pastries $2-4, salads & sandwiches $8-10; ⊙7am-8pm Mon-Fri, 8am-6pm Sat, 9am-5pm Sun; ⌷⌷; ⊤South Station) 🌿 Flour implores patrons to 'make life sweeter...eat dessert first!' It's hard to resist at this pastry-lover's paradise. If you can't decide – and it can be a challenge – go for the melt-in-your-mouth sticky buns; delicious sandwiches, soups, salads and pizzas are also available.

★ROW 34   SEAFOOD $$
Map p239 (☑617-553-5900; www.row34.com; 383 Congress St; oysters $2-3, lunch mains $13-18, dinner $21-28; ⊙11:30am-10pm Mon-Fri, 5-10pm Sat & Sun; ⊤South Station) In the heart of the new Seaport District, this is a 'work-ingman's oyster bar' (by working man, they mean yuppie). Set in a sharp, post-industrial space, the place offers a dozen types of raw oysters and clams, alongside an amazing selection of craft beers. There's also a full menu of cooked seafood, ranging from the traditional to the trendy.

SPORTELLO   ITALIAN $$
Map p239 (☑617-737-1234; www.sportelloboston.com; 348 Congress St; mains $21-26; ⊙11:30am-11pm; ⊤South Station) Modern and minimalist, this brainchild of Barbara Lynch fits right into this up-and-coming urban 'hood. At the *sportello* (lunch counter) suited yuppies indulge in sophisticated soups and salads and decadent polenta and pasta dishes. It's a popular spot, which means it's usually a tight squeeze, but the attentive waitstaff ensure that everybody is comfortable and content.

LEGAL HARBORSIDE   SEAFOOD $$
Map p239 (www.legalseafoods.com; 270 Northern Ave; mains $13-24; ⊙11am-10pm Sun-Thu, to 11pm Fri & Sat; ⌷; ⌷SL1 or SL2, ⊤South Station) This vast glass-fronted waterfront complex offers three different restaurant concepts on three floors. Our favorite is the 1st floor – a casual restaurant and fish market that is a throwback to Legal's original outlet from 1904. The updated menu includes a raw bar, small plates, seafood grills and plenty of international influences (including sushi). There is outdoor seating in the summer months.

BARKING CRAB   SEAFOOD $$
Map p239 (www.barkingcrab.com; 88 Sleeper St; sandwiches $9-17, mains $19-29; ⊙11:30am-10pm; ⌷SL1 or SL2, ⊤South Station or Aquarium) Big buckets of crabs (bairdi, king, snow, Dungeness etc), steamers dripping in lemon and butter, paper plates piled high with all things fried... The food is plentiful and cheap, and you eat it at communal picnic tables overlooking the water. Beer flows freely. Service is slack, but the atmosphere is jovial. Be prepared to wait for a table if the weather is warm.

SAM'S   MODERN AMERICAN $$$
Map p239 (☑617-295-0191; www.samsatlouis.com; 22 Liberty Dr; sandwiches $13-18, mains $22-30; ⊙11:30am-10pm Mon-Thu, to 11pm Fri & Sat, to 9pm Sun; ⌷⌷⌷; ⌷SL1 or SL2, ⊤South Station) Unarguably, the highlight of Sam's is the three walls of windows, yielding a

WORTH A DETOUR

COLUMBIA POINT

Columbia Point juts into the harbor south of the city center in Dorchester, one of Boston's rougher neighborhoods. The location is unexpected, but it does offer dramatic views of the sea. It's a four-mile stroll or ride along the HarborWalk between Castle Island and Columbia Point. Otherwise, take the red line to JFK/UMass and catch a free shuttle bus (departures every 20 minutes) to Columbia Point.

John F Kennedy Library & Museum (www.jfklibrary.org; Columbia Point; adult/child $14/10; ⊙9am-5pm; ⊤JFK/UMass) The legacy of JFK is ubiquitous in Boston, but the official memorial to the 35th president is the presidential library and museum – a striking, modern, marble building designed by IM Pei. The architectural centerpiece is the glass pavilion, with soaring 115ft ceilings and floor-to-ceiling windows overlooking Boston Harbor. The museum is a fitting tribute to JFK's life and legacy. The effective use of video recreates history for visitors who may or may not remember the early 1960s. A highlight is the museum's treatment of the Cuban Missile Crisis: a short film explores the dilemmas and decisions that the president faced.

Edward Kennedy Institute for the US Senate (EMK Institute; www.emkinstitute.org; Columbia Point; adult/child $16/8; ⊙9am-5pm Tue-Sat, 10am-5pm Sun; ⊤JKF/UMass) Ted Kennedy served in the US Senate for nearly half a century. It is fitting, therefore, that his legacy should include an institute and museum designed to teach the public about the inner workings of democracy. Brand new in 2015, this state-of-the-art facility uses advanced technology, multimedia exhibits and interactive designs to engage visitors and demonstrate the functioning (and sometimes non-functioning) of the legislative process. The museum centerpiece is a full-scale replica of the Senate chamber. Exhibits cover how a bill becomes a law ('I'm just a bill... and I'm sitting here on Capitol Hill...'), the great debates and accomplishments of the Senate in history, contemporary hot topics, and ways for concerned citizens to get involved.

Commonwealth Museum (☏617-727-9268; www.commonwealthmuseum.org; 220 Morrissey Blvd, Columbia Point; ⊙9am-5pm Mon-Fri, 9am-3pm Sat & Sun May-Oct; ⊤JFK/UMass) The Commonwealth Museum exhibits documents dating to the early days of colonization. The permanent exhibit, *Our Common Wealth*, uses interactive multimedia technologies to trace the history of the colony and state using the rich materials from the on-site Massachusetts Archives. *Tracing our Roots*, explores the state's heritage following four families: Native American, English, African American and Irish.

180-degree view of city and sea. A chrome and leather, post-industrial decor complements the spectacular view. In summer, there's patio seating. It's a delightfully casual-chic place, with an interesting, innovative menu to match. Live music on Friday nights. Lots of small plates on offer.

MENTON   FRENCH, ITALIAN $$$
Map p239 (☏617-737-0099; www.mentonboston.com; 354 Congress St; 4-course prix-fixe dinner $95; ⊙5:30-10pm Mon-Sat, to 9pm Sun; ⊤South Station) Boston's favorite celebrity chef Barbara Lynch has outdone herself at this high-class conglomeration of classic European cuisine and modern American innovation. She has set her latest venture in a revamped warehouse in the edgy, eclectic Seaport District.

✖ South Boston

SULLIVAN'S   FAST FOOD $
(www.sullivanscastleisland.com; 1080 Day Blvd; mains $3-10; ⊙8:30am-10pm Mar-Nov; 🚻; 🚍11, ⊤Broadway) A Southie tradition since 1951, Sullivan's is beloved for hotdogs in the casing, known as 'Sully's snappers.' In 60-plus years of business, the price of those dogs has increased by more than 10 times – making them a whopping $1.90.

LOCAL 149   MODERN AMERICAN $$
(www.local149.com; 149 P St; mains $16-22; ⊙4-10pm Mon-Thu, 11am-11pm Fri-Sun, bar to 1am; 🚍11, ⊤Broadway) Southie's first gastropub puts a curious, local-with-a-Southern-twist on things, which might catch you off guard.

But why wouldn't you want a lobster Mac-Muffin for brunch or fried chicken and waffles for dinner? Besides the interesting menu, there is a great beer list, including nearly 20 selections on draft.

🍺 DRINKING & NIGHTLIFE

🍷 Seaport District

★ DRINK
COCKTAIL BAR
Map p239 (www.drinkfortpoint.com; 348 Congress St; ⊘4pm-1am; 🚇SL1 or SL2, 🇹South Station) There is no cocktail menu at Drink. Instead you have a little chat with the bartender, and he or she will whip something up according to your specifications.

LUCKY'S LOUNGE
COCKTAIL BAR
Map p239 (www.luckyslounge.com; 355 Congress St; ⊘11am-2am Sun-Fri, 6pm-2am Sat; 🚇SL1 or SL2, 🇹South Station) One of Boston's top-notch bars, Lucky's earns street cred by having no sign to speak of. Step into a delightfully gritty lounge that looks like it's straight out of 1959. Enjoy well-priced drinks, excellent martinis and cover bands playing tunes (Thursday to Sunday).

HARPOON BREWERY & BEER HALL
BREWERY
Map p239 (www.harpoonbrewery.com; 306 Northern Ave; tours $5; ⊘beer hall 11am-7pm Sun-Wed, to 11pm Thu-Sat, tours noon-5pm Sun-Wed, to 6pm Thu-Sat; 🚇SL1 or SL2, 🇹South Station) This brewery is the largest beer facility in the state. Take a tour (hourly) to see how the beer is made and to sample some of the goods. Or just take a seat at the bar in the beer hall and watch the action from above.

🍷 South Boston

Head deeper into South Boston for an authentic Boston Irish experience. Pubs galore line E and W Broadway.

CROKE PARK WHITEY'S
DIVE BAR
(268 W Broadway; 🇹Broadway) Whitey's is everything a dive bar is supposed to be, with cheap beer, free pool, free popcorn and a cast of colorful local characters propping up the bar. This is old-school Southie, and it's not nearly as scary as it's made out to be in the movies.

☆ ENTERTAINMENT

LAUGH BOSTON
COMEDY
Map p239 (www.laughboston.com; 425 Summer St; admission $8-25; ⊘times vary Wed-Sun; 🚇SL1 or SL2, 🇹South Station) The funny guys over at Improv Asylum decided that Boston needed a few more laughs, so they opened this premier, stand-up comedy club in the Westin Hotel. The place has a swanky, happy atmosphere, and there are shows scheduled five nights a week.

INSTITUTE OF CONTEMPORARY ART
CINEMA, PERFORMING ARTS
Map p239 (ICA; www.icaboston.org; 100 Northern Ave; 🚇SL1 or SL2, 🇹South Station) The Barbara Lee Family Foundation Theater is one of the ICA's coolest features. With wooden floor and ceiling and glass walls, the two-story venue is an extension of the boardwalk outside. It's a remarkable backdrop for edgy theater, dance, music and other performance art.

BLUE HILLS BANK PAVILION
LIVE MUSIC
Map p239 (www.bluehillsbank.com; 290 Northern Ave; 🚇SL1 or SL2, 🇹South Station) A white sail-like tent with sweeping harbor views, this is a great venue for summer concerts. It seats about 5000 people, so you can actually see the smiling faces of the performers.

🛍 SHOPPING

MADE IN FORT POINT
HANDICRAFTS
Map p239 (www.fortpointarts.org; 315 A St; ⊘11am-6pm Mon-Fri, noon-4pm Sat; 🚇SL1 or SL2, 🇹South Station) This little boutique is the retail outlet for the Fort Point Arts Community (p132). Not exactly a gallery, it is more like a gift shop, featuring jewelry, prints, photographs, T-shirts, pottery, housewares and other cool, creative stuff.

🏃 SPORTS & ACTIVITIES

CARSON BEACH
BEACH
(Day Blvd; ⊘dawn-dusk; 🚸; 🚌11, 🇹Broadway) Heading west from Castle Island, 3 miles of beaches offer opportunities for swimming in an urban setting. L and M St beaches are adjacent to each other along Day Blvd, while Carson Beach is further west.

Seafood Capital

Nowadays, one can eat seafood anywhere in the world, even when the sea is hundreds of miles away. So what's so special about seafood in Boston? As one local restaurant used to boast, 'the fish is so fresh it jumps out of the water and onto your plate.' This means the texture is preserved and the flavor is enhanced. And a view of the harbor or a breeze off the water makes it all the more delectable.

BEST PLACES FOR CLAM CHOWDER

→ Legal Harborside (p133)
→ Island Creek Oyster Bar (p128)
→ Neptune Oyster (p62)
→ Union Oyster House (p86)
→ Barking Crab (p133)

Chowder

Ask 10 locals for Boston's best chowder and you'll get 10 different answers. This thick, cream-based soup is chock-full of clams or fish, although clam chowder, using the meaty insides of giant surf clams, is more prevalent.

Clams & Oysters

Many seafood restaurants showcase their shellfish at a raw bar, where a dedicated bartender works to shuck oysters and clams to be served on the half-shell. Any self-respecting raw bar will have a selection of hard-shelled clams, or 'quahogs,' including littlenecks and cherrystones. The most famous type of oysters are Wellfleet oysters from Cape Cod; they're eaten raw, with a dollop of cocktail sauce and a few drops of lemon

1. New England clam chowder – a Boston specialty
2. Buying oysters at Union Oyster House (p86)
3. Lobster – Boston's favorite crustacean

juice. For a raw-bar experience, head to Row 34 (p133) or Neptune Oyster (p62).

You can also get clams deep-fried (great hangover food) or steamed (aka 'steamers'). They also get tossed into spicy seafood stew, like that served at Giacomo's Ristorante (p62).

Lobster

Back in the day, the seemingly endless supply of lobster was the food of poor people and prisoners. Times have changed; seafood lovers now pay big bucks for the crustaceans. Traditionally, lobsters are steamed or boiled, then it's up to the patron to crack the shell to get the succulent meat out. A less labor-intensive choice is a lobster roll, where the lobster meat is dressed with a little mayonnaise and stuffed into a grilled, buttered

hot-dog roll. Either way, you can't go wrong at Yankee Lobster Co (p133).

Lobster also makes a decadently delicious bisque, and it's downright sinful when tossed into pasta, such as lobster mac 'n' cheese (again, try the Yankee Lobster Co) or lobster *fra diavolo* (try Daily Catch; p62).

Fish

Atlantic codfish has played such an important role in the region's culture and economy that it is known as the 'sacred cod,' and a carved wooden effigy hangs in the Massachusetts State House. Cod, haddock, hake and other white-fleshed fish are sometimes called 'scrod.' Other fresh local fishes appearing on Boston menus in summer include bluefin tuna, bluefish and striped bass.

Cambridge

HARVARD SQUARE | CENTRAL & KENDALL SQUARES

Neighborhood Top Five

1 Browsing the bookstores, rifling through the records and trying on vintage clothing in Harvard Sq (p151), then camping out in a local cafe (preferably with sidewalk seating) to watch the world go by.

2 Cycling the **Minuteman Bikeway** (p153) from urban Cambridge to idyllic Bedford.

3 Checking out the varied collection and superb architecture at the **Harvard Art Museums** (p142).

4 Exploring the **MIT campus** (p141) and discovering its fantastic, eclectic collection of public art.

5 Strolling around the **Mt Auburn Cemetery** (p143) in search of famous gravestones, impressive artwork and elusive birds.

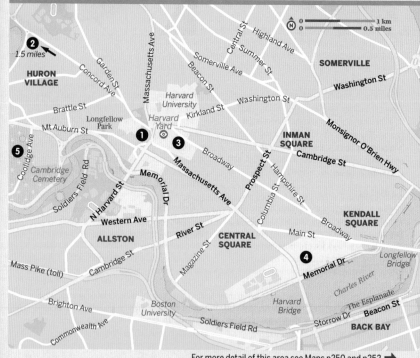

For more detail of this area see Maps p250 and p252 ➡

Explore Cambridge

Here, we count Cambridge as one among many 'neighborhoods' in Boston. But truth be told, this independent town has the historical and cultural offerings to rival many major cities. Certainly, it matches Boston for quality (if not quantity) and diversity of drinking, dining and entertainment options. Exploring museums, historic sites and university landmarks, you could just as easily spend a day as spend a year.

Much of life in Cambridge is centered on the universities – Harvard and MIT – each of which occupies its respective corner of town, with restaurants, shops and clubs clustered around each campus. If you have limited time in Cambridge, you'll probably want to choose one or the other, as there is plenty of activity around either campus to fill a day. (Harvard or MIT...? Harvard or MIT...? Now you know what it's like for the brainiacs who have to decide where they want to go to school.)

Both universities offer excellent (free) campus tours – Harvard is packed with history, while MIT boasts a wealth of public art and innovative architecture. Both universities have interesting and unusual museums showcasing cutting-edge art and science. Both universities have excellent dining and entertainment options in their vicinities. So take your pick.

All that said, only Harvard has Harvard Sq. Overflowing with coffee houses and pubs, bookstores and record stores, street musicians and sidewalk artists, panhandlers and professors, Harvard Sq exudes energy, creativity and nonconformity – and it's all packed into a handful of streets between the university and the river. Even if you have your heart set on exploring MIT and its environs, it's worth setting aside a few hours to hang out up the road in Harvard Sq.

Local Life

→ **Student bars** Local life is student life. To see it in action go to Shay's Pub (p147) in Harvard Sq.

→ **Campus corners** JFK Park is a favorite local spot for picnics, dogs and Frisbee, while the area outside the MIT Stratton Center attracts students and pigeons.

→ **Sidewalk seating** The sidewalk cafe at the Smith Campus Center (p144) gives a front-row seat to watch the buskers, beggers, chess-players, good-deed-doers and other Harvard Sq hullabaloo.

Getting There & Away

→ **Metro** Take the red line to Harvard station for Harvard Sq, Central station for Central Sq and Kendall/MIT for Kendall Sq.

Lonely Planet's Top Tip

The **Harvard Bookstore** (p152) hosts lectures, author talks and book readings almost every night, Monday to Friday, presenting a cool opportunity to hobnob with local writers and scholars.

 Best Places to Eat

→ Alden & Harlow (p146)
→ Clover Food Lab (p143)
→ Life Alive (p146)
→ Hungry Mother (p147)

For reviews, see p143 ➡

 Best Places to Drink

→ Café Pamplona (p147)
→ Beat Hotel (p147)
→ Green Street Grill (p148)
→ State Park (p148)
→ LA Burdick (p147)

For reviews, see p147 ➡

Best University Museums

→ Harvard Art Museums (p142)
→ MIT Museum (p141)
→ Harvard Museum of Natural History (p142)
→ Peabody Museum of Archaeology & Ethnology (p142)

For reviews, see p14

CAMBRIDGE

JANNIS TOBIAS WERNER/SHUTTERSTOCK ©

TOP SIGHT
HARVARD YARD

Founded in 1636 to educate men for the ministry, Harvard is America's oldest college. The original Ivy League school has eight graduates who went on to be US presidents, not to mention dozens of Nobel Laureates and Pulitzer Prize winners. It educates 6500 undergraduates and about 12,000 graduates yearly in 10 professional schools. The geographic heart of Harvard University is Harvard Yard.

Massachusetts Hall & Harvard Hall

Flanking Johnston Gate are the two oldest buildings on campus. South of the gate, Massachusetts Hall houses the offices of the President of the University. Dating to 1720, it is the oldest building at Harvard and the oldest academic building in the country. North is Harvard Hall, which dates to 1766 and originally housed the library.

John Harvard Statue

The focal point of the yard is the John Harvard statue, where every Harvard hopeful has a photo taken (and touches the statue's shiny shoe for good luck). Daniel Chester French's sculpture, inscribed 'John Harvard, Founder of Harvard College, 1638,' is known as the statue of three lies: it does not actually depict Harvard (since no image of him exists), but a random student; John Harvard was not the founder of the college, but its first benefactor in 1638; and the college was actually founded two years earlier in 1636. The Harvard symbol hardly lives up to the university's motto, *Veritas* ('Truth').

DON'T MISS

➜ Free campus tours from the **Harvard Information Center** (Map p250; ☎617-495-1573; www.harvard.edu/visitors; 1350 Massachusetts Ave; ◷9am-5pm Mon-Sat), inside the Smith Campus Center.

➜ Cambridge Open Market – an art market on the plaza in front of the Science Center – on Friday afternoons in July and August.

PRACTICALITIES

➜ Map p250
➜ www.harvard.edu
➜ Massachusetts Ave
➜ tours free
➜ ◷tours hourly 10am-3pm Mon-Sat
➜ ⓣHarvard

SONGQUAN DENG/GETTY IMAGES ©

TOP SIGHT
MASSACHUSETTS INSTITUTE OF TECHNOLOGY

The Massachusetts Institute of Technology (MIT) offers a completely novel perspective on Cambridge academia: proudly nerdy, but not quite as tweedy as Harvard. A recent frenzy of building has resulted in some of the most architecturally intriguing structures you'll find on either side of the river.

Leave it to the mischievous brainiacs at MIT to come up with the city's quirkiest museum – the **MIT Museum** (Map p252; www.web.mit.edu/museum; 265 Massachusetts Ave; adult/child $10/5; ⊙10am-6pm Jul & Aug, to 5pm Sep-Jun; P 🚻; Ⓣ Central). You can meet humanoid robots such as observant Cog and personable Kismet and decide for yourself if they are smarter than humans. Another highlight: the fantastic Jeweled Net, drawing on the world's largest exhibit of holograms.

The stated goal of the **List Visual Arts Center** (Map p252; http://listart.mit.edu; 20 Ames St, Weisner Bldg; donation $5; ⊙noon-6pm Tue, Wed & Fri-Sun, to 8pm Thu; Ⓣ Kendall/MIT) is to explore the boundaries of artistic inquiry – to use art to ask questions about culture, society and science. Rotating exhibits push the contemporary-art envelope in painting, sculpture, photography and video. This is also where you can pick up a map of MIT's public art, proof enough that this university supports artistic as well as technological innovation. If you want a professional opinion, book a free tour. Of all the funky buildings on the MIT campus, none has received more attention than the **Stata Center** (CSAIL; Map p252; www.csail.mit.edu; 32 Vassar St; Ⓣ Kendall/MIT) 🌿, an avant-garde edifice that was designed by architectural legend Frank Gehry.

DON'T MISS

➜ Campus tours, departing from MIT Information Center at 11am and 3pm, Monday to Friday.

➜ MIT's signature sculpture, *La Grande Voile* by Alexander Calder

➜ Henry Moore's bronze reclining figures

➜ Stata Center

PRACTICALITIES

➜ MIT

➜ Map p252

➜ www.mit.edu

➜ 77 Massachusetts Ave

➜ Ⓣ Kendall/MIT

⊙ SIGHTS

⊙ Harvard Square

HARVARD YARD   UNIVERSITY
See p140.

CHRIST CHURCH   CHURCH
Map p250 (www.cccambridge.org; 0 Garden St; ⊙services 7:45am & 10:15am Sun; Ⓣ Harvard) Cambridge's oldest church was designed in 1761 by America's first formally trained architect, Peter Harrison (who also designed King's Chapel in Boston). Washington's troops used it as a barracks after its Tory congregation fled. Adjacent to the church, the Old Burying Ground is a tranquil revolutionary-era cemetery, where Harvard's first eight presidents are buried.

CAMBRIDGE COMMON   PARK
Map p250 (cnr Massachusetts Ave & Garden St; Ⓣ Harvard) Opposite the main entrance to Harvard Yard, Cambridge Common is the village green where General Washington took command of the Continental Army on July 3, 1775. The traffic island at the south end, known as Dawes Island, pays tribute to the 'other rider,' William Dawes, who rode through here on April 18, 1775, to warn that the British were coming (look for the bronze hoofprints embedded in the sidewalk).

The excellent **playground** at the northern end features a Viking ship, a climbing web and plenty of water play.

★ HARVARD ART MUSEUMS   MUSEUM
Map p250 (www.harvardartmuseums.org; 32 Quincy St; adult/child $15/free; ⊙10am-5pm; Ⓣ Harvard) Architect extraordinaire Renzo Piano has overseen a renovation and expansion of Harvard's art museums, allowing the university's massive 250,000-piece collection to come together under one very stylish roof. Harvard's art spans the globe, with separate collections devoted to Asian and Islamic cultures (formerly the Arthur M Sackler Museum), Northern European and Germanic cultures (formerly the Busch-Reisinger Museum) and other Western art, especially European modernism (formerly the Fogg).

HARVARD MUSEUM OF
NATURAL HISTORY   MUSEUM
Map p250 (www.hmnh.harvard.edu; 26 Oxford St; adult/child $12/8; ⊙9am-5pm; ♦; 🚌86, Ⓣ Harvard) This esteemed institution is famed for its botanical galleries, featuring more than 3000 lifelike pieces of handblown glass flowers and plants. At the intersection of art and science, the collection of intricately crafted flora is truly amazing. Nearby, the zoological galleries house an unbelievable number of stuffed animals and reassembled skeletons, as well as an impressive fossil collection. Other cool exhibits feature climate change, sparkling gemstones and arthropods (yes, cockroaches).

The price of admission includes entry into the Peabody Museum of Archaeology & Ethnology, which is in the same building.

PEABODY MUSEUM OF
ARCHAEOLOGY & ETHNOLOGY   MUSEUM
Map p250 (www.peabody.harvard.edu; 11 Divinity Ave; adult/child $12/8; ⊙9am-5pm; ♦; 🚌86, Ⓣ Harvard) The centerpiece of the Peabody is the impressive Hall of the North American Indian, which traces how native peoples

---

CAR TALK

Tom and Ray Magliozzi were never your typical auto-repair guys, nor were they your typical public radio fare. 'Click and Clack, the Tappett Brothers' were East Cambridge natives and MIT graduates. For 35 years, they led listeners under the hood and unraveled the mysteries of internal gas combustion, while engaging in nonstop playful banter and sibling rivalry.

At their peak, Car Talk was heard by more than four million listeners on over 700 radio stations each week. The show inspired an animated TV series and a musical. And it's credited with changing the character of public radio.

In Cambridge, it was unanimously declared the end of an era when the Car Talk guys retired in 2012. And when Tom Magliozzi died in 2014, the city mourned. But the Best of Car Talk continues to be broadcast on public radio; and crack-ups Click and Clack will not soon be forgotten. Nor will their sage advice: 'Don't drive like my brother. Don't drive like my brother.'

responded to the arrival of Europeans from the 15th to the 18th centuries. Other exhibits examine indigenous cultures throughout the Americas, including a fantastic comparison of cave paintings and murals of the Awatovi (New Mexico), the Maya (Guatemala) and the Moche (Peru).

The price of admission includes entry to the neighboring Harvard Museum of Natural History.

COLLECTION OF HISTORICAL SCIENTIFIC INSTRUMENTS
MUSEUM

Map p250 (www.chsi.harvard.edu; 1 Oxford St; ⊙9am-5pm Mon-Fri; T Harvard) FREE Science lovers and history buffs can geek out at this small but fascinating museum. Located inside the Harvard Science Center, it showcases a selection of the 20,000 items in the university collection, some of which date to the 15th century. Look for the geometric sector designed by Galileo, and the clocks illustrating the development of modern timekeeping. The collection was actually compiled by one Benjamin Franklin, so add that to his resume.

The exhibition is housed on three floors. The 1st-floor Putnam Gallery actually opens later than the others, so start upstairs if you arrive before 11am.

LONGFELLOW HOUSE
HISTORIC BUILDING

Map p250 (www.nps.gov/long; 105 Brattle St; ⊙tours 9:30am-4:30pm Wed-Sun Jun-Oct, grounds dawn-dusk year-round; 🚌71 or 73, T Harvard) FREE Brattle St's most famous resident was Henry Wadsworth Longfellow, whose stately manor is now a National Historic Site. The poet lived here for 45 years, from 1837 to 1882, writing many of his most famous poems including *Evangeline* and *The Song of Hiawatha*. Accessible by guided tour, the Georgian mansion contains many of Longfellow's belongings as well as lush period gardens.

Incidentally, one reason Longfellow was so taken with this house was its historical significance. During the Revolutionary War, General Washington appropriated this beauty from its absent Loyalist owner and used it as his headquarters.

TORY ROW
STREET

Map p250 (Brattle St; T Harvard) Heading west out of Harvard Sq, Brattle St is the epitome of colonial posh. Lined with mansions that were once home to royal sympathizers, the street earned the nickname Tory Row.

★ MT AUBURN CEMETERY
CEMETERY

(www.mountauburn.org; 580 Mt Auburn St; ⊙8am-7pm May-Sep, to 5pm Oct-Apr; 🅿; 🚌71 or 73, T Harvard) FREE This delightful spot at the end of Brattle St is worth the 30-minute walk west from Harvard Sq. Developed in 1831, it was the first 'garden cemetery' in the US. Maps pinpoint the rare botanical specimens and notable burial plots. Famous long-term residents include Mary Baker Eddy (founder of the Christian Science Church), Isabella Stewart Gardner (socialite and art collector), Winslow Homer (19th-century American painter), Oliver Wendell Holmes (US Supreme Court Justice) and Henry W Longfellow (19th-century writer).

⊙ Central & Kendall Squares

MASSACHUSETTS INSTITUTE OF TECHNOLOGY
UNIVERSITY
See p141.

✕ EATING

✕ Harvard Square

Harvard Sq has coffeehouses, sandwich shops, ethnic eateries and upscale restaurants to suit every budget and taste. There is also a decent food court in the mini-mall known as the Garage (p145).

★ CLOVER FOOD LAB
VEGETARIAN $

Map p250 (www.cloverfoodlab.com; 7 Holyoke St; mains $6-7; ⊙7am-midnight Mon-Sat, to 7pm Sun; 🚇🖋🅿; T Harvard) 🌱 Clover is on the cutting edge. It's all high-tech with its 'live' menu updates and electronic ordering system. But it's really about the food – local, seasonal, vegetarian food – that is cheap, delicious and fast. How fast? Check the menu. Interesting tidbit: Clover started as a food truck (and still has a few trucks making the rounds).

DARWIN'S LTD
SANDWICHES $

Map p250 (www.darwinsltd.com; 148 Mt Auburn St; mains $8-12; ⊙6:30am-9pm; 🚇🖋🅿; T Harvard) Punky staff serve fat sandwiches, fresh soup and salads, and delicious coffee and pastries, all with a generous helping of attitude. The limited seating is often

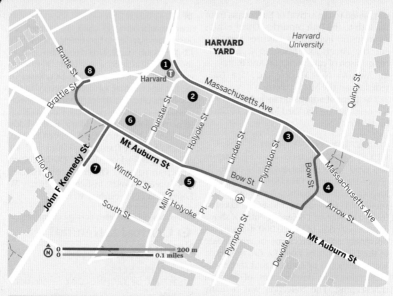

Local Life
Offbeat Harvard Square

Harvard Sq is overflowing with cafes, bookstores, record shops and street musicians. Although many Cantabrigians rightly complain that the area has lost its edge, Harvard Sq still has a thriving counterculture, if you know where to look.

❶ The Pit

Start your tour in the center of Harvard Sq, where Out of Town News (p153) has been selling newspapers and magazines from around the world since 1955. The sunken area nearby, aka 'the Pit,' is a popular spot for street artists, skateboarders and counterculture youth to congregate.

❷ Smith Campus Center

The sidewalk cafe in front of the **Smith Campus Center** (Map p250; www.harvard. edu/visitors; 1350 Massachusetts Ave; ⊘9am-5pm Mon-Sat; T̄Harvard) has hosted an ongoing chess tournament for 30 years and counting – look for the 'Play the Chessmaster' sign. It also offers a front-row seat to watch the buskers, beggars and other Harvard Sq hullabaloo.

❸ Harvard Bookstore

The Harvard Bookstore (p152) is not just a bookstore, but a reading community. Come in to browse the stacks and check out dis-

counted 'seconds' in the basement. Next door, **Grolier Poetry Bookshop** (Map p250; www.grolierpoetrybookshop.org; 6 Plympton St; ⊘11am-7pm Tue & Wed, to 6pm Thu-Sat; T̄Harvard) is the oldest – and perhaps most famous – poetry bookstore in the US. Through the years, TS Eliot, ee cummings, Marianne Moore and Allen Ginsberg have all passed through these doors.

❹ Café Pamplona

For sustenance, make your way to this hidden gem. This no-frills European cafe (p147) in a cozy cellar has been serving coffee and tea to Cantabrigian bohemians since 1959.

❺ In Your Ear

IYE (Map p250; www.iye.com; 72 Mt Auburn St; ⊘11am-7pm Mon-Sat, noon-6pm Sun; T̄Harvard) is located in the basement of a Harvard social club. It's totally disorganized, dusty and crammed with LPs and 45s, as well as CDs, DVDs and even eight-tracks.

Bookstore near Harvard Square

❻ The Garage

This gritty **mini-mall** (Map p250; 36 John F Kennedy St; ⊙10am-9pm Mon-Sat, to 10pm Sun; ⊤Harvard) – formerly a parking garage – houses an eclectic collection of offbeat shops. Try on sweet streetwear at Kulturez, listen to tunes at Newbury Comics, or get some ink at Chameleon Tattoo & Body Piercing.

❼ Raven Used Books

Tucked into a tiny basement, **Raven** (Map p250; www.ravencambridge.com; 52 John F Kennedy St; ⊙10am-9pm Mon-Sat, 11am-8pm Sun; ⊤Harvard) knows its audience: its 14,000 books focus on scholarly titles, especially in the liberal arts.

❽ Brattle Square

A few steps from the historic **Brattle Theatre** (p149), this intersection is a main stage for street performers. Tracy Chapman played here in the 1980s and Amanda Palmer was a living statue here in the 1990s. Puppeteer Igor Fokin also put on shows here until his unexpected death in 1996. Look for the bronze memorial marionette, erected 'in celebration of all street performers.'

occupied by students who are in for the long haul (thanks to wi-fi access). So unless you intend to surf, take your lunch out to enjoy JFK Park or Radcliffe Yard to enjoy.

MR BARTLEY'S
BURGER COTTAGE   BURGERS $

Map p250 (www.mrbartley.com; 1246 Massachusetts Ave; burgers $10-15; ⊙11am-9pm Mon-Sat; ⊡; ⊤Harvard) Packed with small tables and hungry college students, this burger joint has been a Harvard Sq institution for more than 50 years. Bartley's offers at least 40 different burgers; sweet-potato fries, onion rings, thick frappés and raspberry-lime rickeys complete the classic American meal. Be aware that this place is old-school: credit cards not accepted; no bathroom on site.

CAMBRIDGE, 1   PIZZA $$

Map p250 (www.cambridge1.us; 27 Church St; pizzas $10-23; ⊙11:30am-midnight; ⊘; ⊤Harvard) Set in the old fire station, this pizzeria's name comes from the sign chiseled into the stonework out front. The interior is sleek, sparse and industrial, with big windows overlooking the Old Burying Ground in the back. The menu is equally simple: pizza, soup, salad, dessert. These oddly shaped pizzas are delectable, with crispy crusts and creative topping combos.

RUSSELL HOUSE
TAVERN   MODERN AMERICAN $$

Map p250 (www.russellhousecambridge.com; 14 John F Kennedy St; mains lunch $12-16, dinner $19-26; ⊙11am-1am Mon-Fri, 10am-1am Sat & Sun; ⊤Harvard) Smack dab in the middle of Harvard Sq, this attractive gastropub has a classy, classic atmosphere, enhanced by good-looking, effervescent patrons. The menu includes a raw bar and a list of intriguing but irresistible small plates, not to mention a well-selected all-American wine list and killer cocktails.

NIGHT MARKET   ASIAN $$

Map p250 (www.nightmkt.com; 75 Winthrop St; dishes $6-12; ⊙11:30am-2pm Thu & Fri, 5-10pm Sun-Thu, to 11pm Fri & Sat; ⊘) All of Boston is talking about this super-hip subterranean spot, serving up skewers, noodles and other smallish servings that you might find at an Asian market. There's an interesting selection of beers, as well as irresistible sake slushies. The food gets mixed reviews for consistency and authenticity, but everyone loves the clever concept, the graffiti-covered walls and the spot-on service.

CAMBRIDGE EATING

★ALDEN & HARLOW   MODERN AMERICAN $$$

Map p250 (☑617-864-2100; www.aldenharlow.com; 40 Brattle St; small plates $9-17; ⊗5pm-1am Sun-Wed, to 2am Thu-Sat; ☑; Ⓣ Harvard) This spanking-new place in a cozy subterranean space is offering a brand-new take on American cooking. The small plates are made for sharing, so everyone in your party gets to sample. And you will want to sample, because these local ingredients are prepared in ways you've never seen before. By the way, it's no secret that the 'Secret Burger' is amazing.

✕ Central & Kendall Squares

★LIFE ALIVE   VEGETARIAN $

Map p252 (www.lifealive.com; 765 Massachusetts Ave; mains $8-10; ⊗8am-10pm Mon-Sat, 11am-7pm Sun; ☑ ⛎; Ⓣ Central) ✐ Life Alive offers a joyful, healthful, purposeful approach to fast food. The unusual combinations of ingredients yield delicious results, most of which come in a bowl (like a salad) or in a wrap. There are also soups, sides and smoothies, all served in a funky, colorful, light-filled space.

In addition to all the feel-good, there's also a cozy, kiddie play space downstairs. So your children will feel good, too.

BON ME   VIETNAMESE $

Map p252 (www.bonmetruck.com; 1 Kendall Sq; mains $6-7; ⊗11am-8pm Mon-Thu, to 9pm Fri & Sat; Ⓣ Kendall/MIT) Bon Me started as a food truck that catered to the Kendall Sq crowd, and you'll still see the trucks tooling around town. This little storefront sells the same, simple, fresh, insanely good Vietnamese fare. Choose your dish (sandwich, rice or noodles). Choose your filling (chicken, pork or tofu). Choose your extras (edamame, papaya, greens or deviled eggs). Eat up and enjoy!

TOSCANINI'S   ICE CREAM $

Map p252 (www.tosci.com; 899 Main St; ice cream from $4; ⊗8am-11pm Mon-Fri, 9am-11pm Sat & Sun; ☎⛎; Ⓣ Central) People come from miles around for Tosci's burnt-caramel ice cream, which apparently was invented as the result of an accident (you can imagine). Besides the dozens of delicious ice-cream flavors, there is also excellent coffee.

VEGGIE GALAXY   DINER $

Map p252 (www.veggiegalaxy.com; 450 Massachusetts Ave; mains $8-15; ⊗7am-10pm Mon-Fri, 9am-10pm Sat & Sun; ☑⛎; Ⓣ Central) What does the word 'diner' mean to you? All-day breakfast? Check. Burgers and milkshakes? Check. Counter seating and comfy booths? Got those, too. A circular glass display case showing off desserts? Yes, complete with tangy, delicious lemon meringue pie. In short, Veggie Galaxy does everything that a diner is supposed to do, but they do it without meat. There's also an amazing vegan bakery – now that's going above and beyond diner duty!

FRIENDLY TOAST   DINER $

Map p252 (www.thefriendlytoast.com; 1 Kendall Sq; mains $8-12; ⊗8am-10pm Sun-Thu, to midnight Fri & Sat; ☑⛎; Ⓣ Kendall/MIT) Some people think that this retro funky diner is one of the best places to eat breakfast in the entire country. (Yes, the toast really is that friendly.) Decadent delights such as pumpkin pancakes and loads of vegetarian and vegan options have hungry folks lining up out the door for weekend brunch.

But here's the bonus: breakfast isn't just for breakfast anymore. At the Friendly Toast, it's served all day long, along with burgers, burritos and more.

MIRACLE OF SCIENCE
BAR & GRILL   AMERICAN $

Map p252 (www.miracleofscience.us; 321 Massachusetts Ave; mains $10-14; ⊗11am-midnight; Ⓣ Central) With all the decor of your high-school science lab, this bar and grill was a pioneer of chic-geek. The menu takes the form of the periodic table posted on the wall, so you get the idea. Join the MIT wannabes for burgers, kabobs and other grilled fare, as well as a choice selection of beers on tap.

EMMA'S PIZZA   PIZZA $$

Map p252 (www.emmaspizza.com; 40 Hampshire St; sandwiches $6-9, pizzas $12-20; ⊗11:30am-10pm Mon-Fri, 4-10pm Sat, 3-9pm Sun; ☑; Ⓣ Kendall/MIT) Before or after a flick at the nearby Kendall Sq Cinema, make a point of stopping at this friendly neighborhood pizzeria, which instills a maniacal devotion in its customers. Crispy thin crusts and creative topping combinations mean Emma's is consistently rated among the city's best pizza. Slices and salads are also sold from the front window.

AREA FOUR
CAFE, PIZZA $$

Map p252 (www.areafour.com; 500 Technology Sq; pizza $18-28; ⊘11:30am-10pm Mon-Fri, 10:30am-10pm Sat & Sun; 🛜🖉; T Kendall/MIT) 🏴 The post-industrial vibe at Area Four is perfect for the high-tech block where it is located (and for which it is named). Doubling as a cool cafe and modern pizzeria, Area Four offers strong coffee and fresh pastries by day, and local brews, sustainable wines and wood-fired pizzas by night. Eat and drink your way around the clock.

CAFÉ ARTSCIENCE
MODERN FRENCH $$

Map p252 (www.cafeartscience.com; 650 E Kendall St; mains $19-24; ⊘11am-10pm Mon-Fri, 5-10pm Sat; 🛜🖉; T Kendall) Before David Edwards was a restaurateur, he was an MIT professor and an inventor, dreaming up novelties such as Wikipearl (edible food wrapper) and oPhone (an aroma gadget). Now he's channeling his energies into the 'artscience' of food. It's not as gimmicky as it sounds, though there is some futurism here (cocktails involving vaporized alcohol and variously flavored ice cubes, for instance). Mostly, though, it's just innovative food that looks like it was plated with surgical instruments.

★ HUNGRY MOTHER
SOUTHERN $$$

Map p252 (☑617-499-0090; www.hungrymother-cambridge.com; 233 Cardinal Medeiros Ave; mains $19, 4-course prix-fixe dinner $52; ⊘5-10:30pm Tue-Sun; T Kendall/MIT) Who knew that Bostonians would take so well to grits? No wonder, Hungry Mother does Southern fare right, using fresh local ingredients and classic French cooking techniques. It's a cozy crowded space that feels like somebody's country house, with lots of little rooms, and eclectic art and photos on the walls.

🍷 DRINKING & NIGHTLIFE

🍸 Harvard Square

★ CAFÉ PAMPLONA
CAFE

Map p250 (12 Bow St; ⊘11am-midnight; T Harvard) Located in a cozy cellar on a backstreet, this no-frills European cafe is the choice among old-time Cantabrigians. In addition to tea and coffee drinks, Pamplona has light snacks such as gazpacho, sandwiches and biscotti.

COOKING COURSES

Patron food-saint Julia Child, long-time Cambridge resident and star of many cooking shows, spent four decades teaching people to cook before she died in 2004. If you want to embody Julia's *bon vivant, bon appétit* spirit, take a cooking class.

The recreation division of this professional **Cambridge School of Culinary Arts** (www.cambridgeculinary.com; 2020 Massachusetts Ave; T Porter) offers one-time courses focusing on seasonal meals such as 'An American Gathering' or on crucial cooking skills such as 'All You Knead' (basic breads). Several times a week there are special 'Cooking Couples' classes, teaching tapas, sushi, dinner parties and more.

BEAT HOTEL
BAR

Map p250 (www.beathotel.com; 13 Brattle St; ⊘4pm-midnight Mon-Wed, to 2am Thu & Fri, 10am-2am Sat, to midnight Sun; T Harvard) A great addition to Harvard Sq, this vast, underground bistro packs in good-looking patrons for international food, classy cocktails and live jazz and blues. It's inspired by the Beat Generation writers – and named for a rundown Parisian motel where they hung out.

LA BURDICK
CAFE

Map p250 (www.burdickchocolate.com; 52d Brattle St; ⊘8am-9pm Sun-Thu, to 10pm Fri & Sat; T Harvard) This boutique chocolatier doubles as a cafe, usually packed full of happy patrons drinking hot cocoa. Whether you choose dark or milk, it's sure to be some of the best chocolate you'll drink in your lifetime.

SHAYS PUB & WINE BAR
PUB

Map p250 (www.shayspubandwinebar.com; 58 John F Kennedy St; ⊘11am-1am Mon-Sat, noon-1am Sun; T Harvard) A charming basement-level bar, Shays is a long-standing favorite among Harvard graduate students that has fancied itself up and expanded its wine list. Inside, it's a small wooden pub where you'll sit on a stool and pretend to look thoughtful. Out front is a small brick patio full of sunners and smokers jockeying for a table and watching the sidewalk goings-on.

CHARLIE'S KITCHEN
DIVE BAR

Map p250 (www.charlieskitchen.com; 10 Eliot St; ⊙11am-1am Sun-Wed, to 2am Thu-Sat; Ⓣ Harvard) Charlie's is a three-in-one. Downstairs is a lovable greasy spoon serving burgers and bargain-price lobster rolls late into the night; upstairs is a long-standing and much beloved dive bar blasting the Cars from the jukebox. For 40-some years, that's all there was. Recently, though, this family-run institution rocked Harvard Sq by opening a beer garden with 18 taps. Drink beer outside, y'all!

ALGIERS COFFEE HOUSE
CAFE

Map p250 (40 Brattle St; ⊙8am-midnight; ⓢ; Ⓣ Harvard) Although the pace of service can be glacial, the palatial Middle Eastern decor makes this an inviting rest spot. The one good thing about the relaxed service is that you won't be rushed to finish your pot of Arabic coffee or mint tea.

⚑ Central & Kendall Squares

GREEN STREET GRILL
COCKTAIL BAR

Map p252 (www.greenstreetgrill.com; 280 Green St; ⊙5:30pm-1am; Ⓣ Central) Gritty on the outside, cozy on the inside, the Green Street Grill is a longstanding neighborhood joint that still manages to be thoroughly up to date – thanks in part to bartenders in flannel and killer cocktails. The urban bar and grill hints at upscale, but keeps it real with affordable prices (all cocktails under $10), tried-and-true American fare and no snoot.

STATE PARK
BAR

Map p252 (www.statepark.is; 1 Kendall Sq; ⊙11:30am-1am Tue & Wed, to 2am Thu & Fri, 5pm-1am Sat-Mon; Ⓣ Kendall) This is a popular, rowdy, almost divey bar, where wood paneling and carpeting cover the walls and Miller High Life is an ingredient in the 'official' cocktail. It's not a dive, though. The quirky, kitschy decor is carefully calculated and playfully ironic. And the heightened Southern comfort food is superb – as you would expect from the folks behind the Hungry Mother.

VOLTAGE COFFEE & ART
CAFE

Map p252 (www.voltagecoffee.com; 295 Third St; ⊙7am-7pm Mon-Fri, 9am-3pm Sat & Sun; ⓢ; Ⓣ Kendall/MIT) The place promises 'Coffee & Art,' but we are left to wonder – what's the difference? The lattes are beautiful to look at and they inspire deep thoughts. The

artwork is deliciously dark and it stimulates the brain. Art aficionados and coffee drinkers, come to Voltage for a little of both.

BRICK & MORTAR
COCKTAIL BAR

Map p252 (www.brickmortarltd.com; 569 Massachusetts Ave; ⊙5pm-1am Sun-Wed, to 2am Thu-Sat; Ⓣ Central) Enter through the unmarked door (next to Central Kitchen) and climb the dark stairs to cool cocktail heaven. No pretenses here – just a pared down setting and a choice list of craft cocktails and beers. The staff is knowledgeable and friendly, so if you don't see something you like, ask for advice.

RIVER GODS
BAR

Map p252 (www.rivergodsonline.com; 125 River St; ⊙3pm-1am; Ⓣ Central) The decor of this small, cramped room (max 45 people) leans toward kitsch, with a cluttered assortment of seasonal holiday decorations, sparkly leather stools and gothic red-velvet chairs. Art-house movies and documentary footage project silently on the wall, while DJs spin from a second-story alcove. The DJs work their magic every night, with a few sessions each week dedicated to new music.

HAVANA CLUB
CLUB

Map p252 (www.havanaclubsalsa.com; 288 Green St; weeknight/weekend $5/12; ⊙8pm-midnight Mon & Thu, 9pm-2am Fri & Sat; Ⓣ Central) On Friday and Saturday nights, this old social club on a back street in Central Sq transforms into the Boston area's most happening salsa dance party. It's an international crowd – not just Latino – and the first hour is devoted to lessons. DJs change things up for Bachata Monday.

PLOUGH & STARS
IRISH PUB

Map p252 (www.ploughandstars.com; 912 Massachusetts Ave; ⊙11:30am-1am Sun-Wed, to 2am Thu-Sat; ⓢ; Ⓣ Central) The Plough & Stars is real-deal Irish, serving up bangers, eggs and gastropub fare in a cozy wooden room with stout on tap and in bottles. Weekend soccer matches are on the telly and stringed bands play Irish tunes. Actually, there's music every night of the week – not only Irish, but also jazz, blues, rockabilly, funk and other indefinable genres.

MIDDLESEX
CLUB

Map p252 (www.middlesexlounge.us; 315 Massachusetts Ave; cover $10; ⊙7pm-2am Thu-Sat; Ⓣ Central) Sleek and sophisticated, Middlesex brings the dance crowd to the Cambridge side of town. Black modular furniture sits on heavy casters, allowing the cubes to be rolled aside when the place transforms from lounge to club, making space for the movers and groovers to become entranced with DJs experimenting with hip-hop and electronica. Less about the scene, all about the dancing.

CAMBRIDGE BREWING CO   BREWERY

Map p252 (www.cambridgebrewingcompany.com; 1 Kendall Sq; ⊙11:30am-midnight; ⊤Kendall/MIT) ✐ This jovial microbrewery is often crowded, as students and other beer-lovers like to imbibe fresh local beer. Flavors include Regatta Golden, Cambridge Amber and Charles River Porter (love that dirty water). Note that CBC was a microbrewery before microbreweries were cool – since 1989 to be exact.

☆ ENTERTAINMENT

☆ Harvard Square

★CLUB PASSIM   LIVE MUSIC

Map p250 (☎617-492-7679; www.clubpassim.org; 47 Palmer St; tickets $15-30; ⊤Harvard) Folk music in Boston seems to be endangered outside of Irish bars, but the legendary Club Passim does such a great job booking top-notch acts that it practically fills in the vacuum by itself. The colorful, intimate room is hidden off a side street in Harvard Sq, just as it has been since 1969.

★LIZARD LOUNGE   LIVE MUSIC

(www.lizardloungeclub.com; 1667 Massachusetts Ave; cover $5-10; ⊙8pm-1am Sun-Wed, to 2am Thu-Sat; ⊤Harvard) The underground Lizard Lounge doubles as a jazz and rock venue. The big drawcard is the Sunday night poetry slam, featuring music by the jazzy Jeff Robinson Trio. Also popular are the Monday open-mic challenge and regular appearances by local favorite Club d'Elf. The bar stocks an excellent list of New England beers, which are complemented by the sweet-potato fries.

Located a quarter-mile north of Cambridge Common (the park), below Cambridge Common (the restaurant).

★COMEDY STUDIO   COMEDY

Map p250 (www.thecomedystudio.com; 1238 Massachusetts Ave; tickets $10-12; ⊙show 8pm Tue-Sun; ⊤Harvard) The 3rd floor of the Hong Kong noodle house contains a low-budget comedy house with a reputation for hosting cutting-edge acts. This is where talented future stars (such as Brian Kiley, who became a writer for Conan O'Brien) refine their racy material. Each night has a different theme; on Tuesday, for instance, you can usually see a weird magic show.

SINCLAIR   LIVE MUSIC

Map p250 (www.sinclaircambridge.com; 52 Church St; tickets $15-18; ⊙5pm-1am Mon, 11am-1am Tue-Sun; ⊤Harvard) Great small venue to hear live music. The acoustics are excellent and the mezzanine level allows you to escape the crowds on the floor. The club attracts a good range of local and regional bands and DJs.

BRATTLE THEATRE   CINEMA

Map p250 (www.brattlefilm.org; 40 Brattle St; ⊤Harvard) The Brattle is a film lover's *cinema paradiso*. Film noir, independent films and series that celebrate directors or periods are shown regularly in this renovated 1890 repertory theater. Some famous (or infamous) special events include the annual Valentine's Day screening of *Casablanca* and occasional cartoon marathons.

AMERICAN REPERTORY THEATER   PERFORMING ARTS

Map p250 (ART; ☎617-547-8300; www.americanrepertorytheater.org; 64 Brattle St; tickets $40-75; ⊤Harvard) There isn't a bad seat in the house at the Loeb Drama Theater, where the prestigious ART stages new plays and experimental interpretations of classics. Artistic Director Diane Paulus encourages a broad interpretation of 'theater,' staging interactive murder mysteries, readings of novels in their entirety and robot operas. The ART's musical productions, in particular, have been racking up the Tonies.

TOAD   LIVE MUSIC

(www.toadcambridge.com; 1912 Massachusetts Ave; ⊙5pm-1am Mon-Wed, to 2am Thu-Sat, 3pm-1am Sun; ⊤Porter) This tiny, laid-back place is beloved for its excellent line-up of music (seven nights a week) and its no-cover-charge policy. (Ever. At all.) There are a dozen beers on tap and 'all sorts of booze available.' No food, but it's okay to bring something to nosh from next door.

About a mile north of Harvard Sq, across from the Porter Sq shopping plaza.

HARVARD FILM ARCHIVE

CINEMATHEQUE
CINEMA

Map p250 (www.hcl.harvard.edu/hfa; 24 Quincy St; tickets $9-12; ⊙screenings Mon, Wed & Fri-Sun; ⊤Harvard) Five nights a week, the Cinematheque presents retrospectives of distinguished actors, screenings of rare films, thematic groupings and special events featuring the filmmakers themselves. The screenings – which often sell out – take place in the 200-seat theater in the esteemed Carpenter Center for the Arts (designed by Le Corbusier). Tickets go on sale 45 minutes ahead of show times.

CLUB OBERON
PERFORMING ARTS

Map p250 (www.cluboberon.com; 2 Arrow St; ⊤Harvard) The second stage of the American Repertory Theater, this black box is ideally suited to flashy song and dance performances and interactive, acrobatic theater. The long-running favorite is the Shakespearean disco, *The Donkey Show,* but you might also see *Rocky Horror Live* or *Abbey Road: An Erotic, Thrilling Interpretation.* Indeed, 'erotic' and 'thrilling' seem to be consistent themes across performances.

REGATTABAR
JAZZ

Map p250 (☎617-395-7757; www.regattabarjazz.com; 1 Bennett St; tickets $15-35; ⊤Harvard) Why does Boston have such clean jazz clubs? Regattabar looks just like a conference room in a hotel – in this case the Charles Hotel. They get big enough names (Virginia Rodrigues, Keb Mo) to transcend the mediocre space, though.

WORTH A DETOUR

SOMERVILLE THEATRE

Somerville Theatre (☎617-625-5700; www.somervilletheatreonline.com; 55 Davis Sq; ⊤Davis) is a classic neighborhood movie house. It dates from 1914 and features plenty of well-preserved gilding and pastel murals of muses. On offer are first- and second-run Hollywood hits, live performances by chamber orchestras and world musicians, and the Independent Film Festival of Boston screenings. The main theater is the biggest, best and oldest, and has the added treat of a balcony.

This gem is in Davis Sq, just a hop and a skip north from Cambridge.

CAMBRIDGE FORUM
LECTURES

Map p250 (www.cambridgeforum.org; 3 Church St; ⊙talks 7pm Wed; ⊤Harvard) This excellent (free) series brings speakers on a weekly basis to talk in the meeting house at First Parish in Cambridge. Recent speakers have included luminaries like Nobel Prize–winning economist Paul Krugman, poet laureate Robert Pinsky, beloved biologist of the people, EO Wilson and former Secretary of Labor Robert Reich.

LONGY SCHOOL OF MUSIC
CLASSICAL MUSIC

Map p250 (www.longy.edu; 27-33 Garden St; ⊤Harvard) George Longy was an oboist with the Boston Symphony Orchestra before he decided to found the Longy School of Music in 1915. Now more than a century old, Longy is a well-respected training ground for classical musicians. Students and faculty show off the goods on an almost daily basis, often free of charge. Longy is just northwest of Cambridge Common.

SANDERS THEATRE AT MEMORIAL HALL
CONCERT VENUE

Map p250 (www.harvard.edu/arts; 45 Quincy St; ⊤Harvard) Set inside the magnificent Memorial Hall, this beautiful, 1166-seat, wood-paneled theater is known for its acoustics. It is frequently used for classical musical performances by local chorales and ensembles, as well as occasional concerts by jazz and world musicians. Buy tickets at the booth inside the Smith Campus Center.

☆ Central & Kendall Squares

★LILY PAD
PERFORMING ARTS

Map p252 (www.lilypadinman.com; 1353 Cambridge St; ☐91, ⊤Central) Lily Pad is a tiny space that fills up with music and performance art, whether it's tango dancing or narrated jazz storytelling. You might also hear indie, avant-garde, folk and even chamber music. The space is stripped down – basically folding chairs in a room – which adds to the underground ambience. There's also beer and wine!

RYLES JAZZ CLUB
JAZZ, CLUB

Map p252 (☎617-876-9330; www.rylesjazz.com; 212 Hampshire St; cover $10-15; ⊙5pm-1am Mon & Tue, to 2am Wed-Sat, 10am-1am Sun; ⊤Central) Bonus: Ryles is not in a hotel. It is a dark lounge with low lighting and big windows, offering an intimate atmosphere to hear great music. This includes the house band – Ryles Jazz Orchestra – which plays monthly, as well as other local talent and the occasional big name. The Sunday jazz brunch is super popular: reserve if possible.

No matter what's going down on the 1st floor, there is dancing upstairs. And it usually has a Latin beat. Salsa Sunday, Noche Latina Tuesday, Viernes de Vacilon...

**LANDMARK KENDALL
SQUARE CINEMA**   CINEMA
Map p252 (www.landmarktheatres.com; 1 Kendall Sq; adult/child $9.75/7.50; Ⓣ Kendall/MIT) This cinema screens popular foreign films and the usual collection of hits from the Sundance Festival. Seats are steeply sloped and the concession stand serves cappuccino. New releases sell out on Friday nights, so buy your tickets before dinner.

IMPROV BOSTON   COMEDY
Map p252 (www.improvboston.com; 40 Prospect St; ☺ Wed-Sat; 🚹; Ⓣ Central) This group has been making things up and making people laugh for more than a quarter of a century. The troupe's funny shows feature not just improv, but also comedy competitions, slapstick storytelling and nude stand-up.

MIDDLE EAST   LIVE MUSIC
Map p252 (www.mideastoffers.com; 472 Massachusetts Ave; cover $10-30; Ⓣ Central) The Middle East is as good as the bands it books, which means it varies wildly. This is the preferred venue for local garage bands (hit or miss, by definition), as well as 1980s rockers and fun Euro-pop artists.

In addition to the two stages, creatively known as 'Upstairs' and 'Downstairs', there are two bar-restaurant areas serving decent Middle Eastern food (go figure). All four areas are venues for DJs and dance parties, depending on the night.

CANTAB LOUNGE   LIVE MUSIC
Map p252 (www.cantab-lounge.com; 738 Massachusetts Ave; cover free-$10; Ⓣ Central) The

Cantab is one of the neighborhood's divier dives (and that's saying something in Central Sq). But the eclectic music line-up attracts an awesome mixed crowd that likes to get its groove on. Tuesday night is the area's best bluegrass night, Wednesday is the poetry slam, and Thursday is the famous, funky Chickenslacks. Friday is a get-down, old-timer sweaty dance party. Cash only.

🛍 SHOPPING

🛍 Harvard Square

Harvard Sq is home to upward of 150 shops, all within a few blocks of the university campus. The area used to boast an avant-garde sensibility and dozens of independent stores, and vestiges of this free spirit remain. Certainly, there are still more bookstores in Harvard Sq than anywhere else in the Boston area. However, many of the funkier shops have been replaced by chains, leading critics to complain that the square has become an outdoor shopping mall.

★ WARD MAPS   MAPS, SOUVENIRS
(www.wardmaps.com; 1735 Massachusetts Ave; ☺ 10am-6pm Mon-Sat, noon-5pm Sun; Ⓣ Porter) If you're into maps, you'll be into Ward Maps. They have an incredible collection of original antique and reproduction maps, with a special focus on Boston, Cambridge and Somerville. What's more, they print the maps on coffee mugs, mouse pads, journals and greeting cards, creating unique and personal gifts. There's also an awesome selection of T station signs and other vintage MBTA paraphernalia.

★ TAYRONA   ACCESSORIES
Map p250 (www.tayrona1156.com; 1156 Massachusetts Ave; ☺ 10am-7pm Mon-Sat, noon-7pm Sun; Ⓣ Harvard) Tayrona is named for an ancient indigenous culture that inhabited the mountains of Colombia. But the items that Tayrona carries are by no means limited to South American–influenced styles. The jewelry runs the gamut from clunky costume jewels to delicate gold and silver. Beaded handbags, batik scarves and handcrafted gift items reflect an exotic, international, but thoroughly sophisticated, style.

CAMBRIDGE ARTISTS' COOPERATIVE
HANDICRAFTS

Map p250 (www.cambridgeartistscoop.com; 59a Church St; 10am-6pm Mon-Wed, Fri & Sat, to 8pm Thu, noon-8pm Sun; T Harvard) Owned and operated by Cambridge artists, this three-floor gallery displays an ever-changing exhibit of their work. The pieces are crafty – handmade jewelry, woven scarves, leather products and pottery. The craftspeople double as sales staff, so you may get to meet the creative force behind your souvenir.

CURIOUS GEORGE STORE
BOOKS, TOYS

Map p250 (www.thecuriousgeorgestore.com; 1 John F Kennedy St; 10am-6pm Sun-Wed, to 8pm Thu-Sat; T Harvard) Find your favorite story about that mischievous monkey, but there are also thousands of other books and toys.

HARVARD BOOKSTORE
BOOKS

Map p250 (www.harvard.com; 1256 Massachusetts Ave; 9am-11pm Mon-Sat, 10am-10pm Sun; T Harvard) Family-owned and operated since 1932, the Harvard Bookstore is not officially affiliated with the university, but it is the university community's favorite place for browsing. While the shop maintains an academic focus, there is plenty of fiction for the less lofty, as well as used books and bargain books in the basement.

Harvard Bookstore hosts author talks and other interesting lectures, often in conjunction with Cambridge Forum.

BERK'S
SHOES

Map p250 (www.berkshoes.com; 50 John F Kennedy St; 10am-9pm Mon-Sat, 11am-7pm Sun; T Harvard) Berk's is a little store with a great selection of shoes – half for your sensible feet and half for your fancy feet. Prices can

---

WORTH A DETOUR

CAMBRIDGE ANTIQUE MARKET

Cambridge Antique Market (Map p252; www.marketantique.com; 201 Monsignor O'Brien Hwy; 11am-6pm Tue-Sun; T Lechmere), in an old brick warehouse in East Cambridge, looks foreboding from the outside, but inside is an antiquer's paradise. With more than 150 dealers on five floors, the market is a trove of trash and treasure. The constant turnover of dealers lends a flea-market feel, guaranteeing that you never know what you will find.

---

be prohibitively high, unless you manage to strike the awesome end-of-season sales. You know they're going on when you see tables on the sidewalks piled high with shoes.

FORTY WINKS
CLOTHING

Map p250 (www.shopfortywinks.com; 56 John F Kennedy St; 10am-7pm Mon-Sat, noon-6pm Sun; T Harvard) Forty Winks is a little slice of luxurious lingerie heaven. The items are pricey, but they are also soft, silky and oh-so-sexy. And the staff is graciously determined to help you find the perfect fit for body and soul. So if you're looking to treat yourself – or your favorite lady friend – this is an excellent place to start.

SCHOENHOF'S FOREIGN BOOKS
BOOKS

Map p250 (www.schoenhofs.com; 76a Mt Auburn St; 10am-6pm Mon-Wed, Fri & Sat, to 8pm Thu; T Harvard) Since 1856, Schoenhof's has been providing Boston's foreign-language-speaking literati with reading material. Special booklists keep regulars abreast of new arrivals in their language of choice, whether it's scholarly or literary works, language instruction materials or children's books. If you are wondering which languages and dialects are available, the official count is over 700, so Schoenhof's has you covered.

OONA'S EXPERIENCED CLOTHING
CLOTHING

Map p250 (www.oonasboston.com; 1210 Massachusetts Ave; 11am-8pm; T Harvard) At Oona's you'll find stylish clothes from all eras – not necessarily big-name designers, but distinctive, vintage wear that's elegant and affordable. Operating since 1972, Oona's is the oldest resale clothing shop in the Boston area.

DICKSON BROS
HOMEWARES

Map p250 (www.dicksonbros.com; 26 Brattle St; 8:30am-6pm Mon-Sat, 10am-4pm Sun; T Harvard) Locals know that you can find just about anything you need for your home at this old-timer hardware store. From house paint to cleaning supplies, from kitchen accessories to storage bins, it's all crammed into this three-story space in the heart of Harvard Sq.

CARDULLO'S GOURMET SHOP
FOOD & DRINK

Map p250 (www.cardullos.com; 6 Brattle St; 9am-9pm Mon-Sat, 10am-7pm Sun; T Harvard) We've never seen so many goodies packed into such a small space. You'll find every sort of imported edible your heart desires, from caviar to chocolate. The excellent selection of New England products is a good source of souvenirs. Take home some Taza chocolate from Somerville, Effie's oatcakes from Boston, and even clam chowder from Maine.

OUT OF TOWN NEWS   NEWSSTAND

Map p250 (Harvard Sq; ☺6am-10pm Sun-Thu, to 11pm Fri & Sat; ⓉHarvard) Dating to 1955, Out of Town News is a national historic landmark. This quintessential newsstand sells newspapers from every major US city, as well as dozens of cities around the world. Even if you're not looking for reading material, you need to know this place; it's the top spot to hook up with friends coming off the T.

🏠 Central & Kendall Squares

★WEIRDO RECORDS   MUSIC

Map p252 (www.weirdorecords.com; 844 Massachusetts Ave; ☺11am-9pm; ⓉCentral) Not to be confused with Cheapo Records up the street, this place is not particularly cheap, but it sure is weird. And we mean that in the best possible way. The shop is packed with thousands of records, most of which are out of print, from another country, or on obscure or defunct labels.

It just got weirder...the tiny record store hosts a monthly show, usually on a Tuesday, featuring local comedians and other weirdos, plus free prizes and free alcohol. Shazam.

CHEAPO RECORDS   MUSIC

Map p252 (www.cheaporecords.com; 538 Massachusetts Ave; ☺11am-7pm Mon-Wed & Sat, to 9pm Thu & Fri, to 5pm Sun; ⓉCentral) With tunes blasting out onto the sidewalk, Cheapo Records lures in music-lovers to browse through its huge selection of vinyl and decent selection of CDs. The staff know their stuff, and the collection spans all genres, with a fun box of new arrivals for the regulars. And yes, they really are cheap-o.

GARMENT DISTRICT   CLOTHING

Map p252 (www.garmentdistrict.com; 200 Broadway; ☺11am-8pm Sun-Fri, 9am-8pm Sat; ⓉKendall/MIT) If your memories of the fashion-conscious '60s and '70s have faded like an old pair of jeans, this store will bring it all back. The upstairs is organized by decade and filled with highly wearable vintage

duds. Downstairs, Dollar-a-Pound offers piles of clothes that are priced by the pound.

Also in the same location, **Boston Costume** (Map p252; www.bostoncostume.com; 200 Broadway; ☺11am-8pm Sun-Fri, 9am-8pm Sat; ⓉKendall/MIT) can dress you up like your favorite superhero, sports mascot, literary character or historical figure.

🏃 SPORTS & ACTIVITIES

★MINUTEMAN BIKEWAY   CYCLING

(www.minutemanbikeway.org; 🚴; ⓉAlewife or Davis) The best of Boston's bicycle trails starts near Alewife station and leads 5 miles to historic Lexington Center, then traverses an additional 4 miles of idyllic scenery and terminates in the rural suburb of Bedford. The wide, straight, paved path gets crowded on weekends. Rent a bike at the Bicycle Exchange (p210).The Minuteman Bikeway is also accessible from Davis Sq in Somerville (Davis T station) via the 2-mile Community Path to Alewife.

CHARLES RIVER CANOE & KAYAK CENTER   CANOEING, KAYAKING

Map p252 (www.ski-paddle.com; 500 Broad Canal Way; per hr canoe $20, kayak $15-20; ☺noon-8pm Mon-Fri, 9am-8pm Sat & Sun May-Oct; 🚴; ⓉKendall/MIT) Besides canoe and kayak rental, Charles River Canoe & Kayak offers classes and organized outings. Experienced kayakers can venture out to the harbor, but the river and basin are lovely for skyline views and fall foliage. There is another outlet in

Allston (near Harvard Sq), which allows for an excellent one-way five-mile trip between the two rental centers.

CHARLES RIVER BIKE PATH   CYCLING

(Storrow Dr & Memorial Dr; 🚴; Ⓣ Harvard, Kendall/MIT, Charles/MGH or Science Park) A popular cycling circuit runs along both sides of the Charles River between the Museum of Science and the Mt Auburn St Bridge in Watertown center (5 miles west of Cambridge). The round trip is 17 miles, but 10 bridges in between offer ample opportunities to turn around and shorten the trip. Rent a bike at Cambridge Bicycle (p210) or Back Bay Bicycles (p210). This trail is not particularly well maintained and is often crowded with pedestrians.

HAHVAHD TOUR   WALKING TOUR

(Trademark Tours; www.harvardtour.com; tour $10; Ⓣ Harvard) This company was founded by a couple of Harvard students who shared the inside scoop on history and student life at the University. Now the company offers a whole menu of Boston tours, but the funny, offbeat Hahvahd Tour is the trademark.

Tours depart from the Cambridge Visitor Information Kiosk in Harvard Sq; see the website for schedule details.

KARMA YOGA STUDIO   YOGA

Map p250 (www.karmayogastudios.com; 1120 Massachusetts Ave; yoga cass $10-20; ⊘6am-10pm Mon-Fri, 8am-8pm Sat & Sun; Ⓣ Harvard) This studio offers about 10 yoga classes a day, mostly variations on hatha and vinyasa yoga. There is also a fully equipped gym upstairs. The set-up is gorgeous, with hard-

> **WORTH A DETOUR**
>
> ### CANDLEPIN BOWLING
>
> Founded in 1939, **Flatbread Co & Sacco's Bowl Haven** (www.flatbread-company.com; 45 Day St, Somerville; per lane per hr $25; ⊘9am-midnight Mon-Sat, to 10:30pm Sun; 🚴; Ⓣ Davis) is a Somerville institution – old-time candlepin bowling lanes that managed to survive into the 21st century. The place was overtaken and updated by Flatbread Co, who brightened the space and added clay ovens, but preserved most of the lanes and the good-time atmosphere. Now you can enjoy delicious organic pizzas and cold craft beers with your candlepins.

wood floors and imported Indian art and furniture. The quaint cafe serves organic tea and vegan treats. All classes before noon or after 8pm are only $10.

COMMUNITY ICE SKATING
@ KENDALL SQUARE   SKATING

Map p252 (www.skatekendall.com; 300 Athenaeum St; adult/child $5/1, rental $8; ⊘noon-8pm Mon-Thu, 11am-9pm Fri & Sat, to 6pm Sun Dec-Mar; 🚴; Ⓣ Kendall/MIT) Perhaps Kendall Sq does not have the same charm as the Boston Common, but this smallish rink has many other benefits. Mainly, there are usually fewer people, which means more room for your pirouettes (or whatever you do on the ice). The rental skates are in excellent condition and the staff are helpful.

CAMBRIDGE CENTER
FOR ADULT EDUCATION   COURSE

Map p250 (www.ccae.org; 42 Brattle St; Ⓣ Harvard) The Cambridge Center for Adult Education offers everything from historical tours to writing classes to massage courses for couples.

RINK AT THE CHARLES   SKATING

Map p250 (www.charleshotel.com; 1 Bennett St; adult/child $5/3, rental $5/3; ⊘4-7pm Mon-Fri, 10am-6pm Sat & Sun Dec-Mar; 🚴; Ⓣ Harvard) The plaza in front of the Charles is an unexpected location for skating, with H-Square passers-by enjoying the music and admiring the talent on the ice. It's a small rink, but not nearly as crowded as the Frog Pond..

FLAT TOP JOHNNY'S   POOL HALL

Map p252 (www.flattopjohnnys.com; 1 Kendall Sq; pool per hr $12; ⊘3pm-1am Sat-Wed, noon-1am Thu & Fri; Ⓣ Kendall/MIT) Twelve red-felt tournament tables are set in a tall-ceilinged space surrounded by brick walls and comic-book murals. There are 16 beers on tap, plus darts and pinball for while you're waiting on a table. Pool is half-price before 6pm.

FRESH POND GOLF COURSE   GOLF

(☎617-349-6282; www.freshpondgolf.com; 691 Huron Ave; 9 holes $23-26; ⊘6am-8pm; 🚗71, 73 or 78) About 2 miles west of Harvard Sq, the Fresh Pond is a nine-hole public course that wraps around the city's reservoir. It's easily accessible, but the setting is suburban. Drive west on Mt Auburn St and turn right on the Fresh Pond Parkway and left on Huron Ave.

Streetcar Suburbs

BROOKLINE | JAMAICA PLAIN

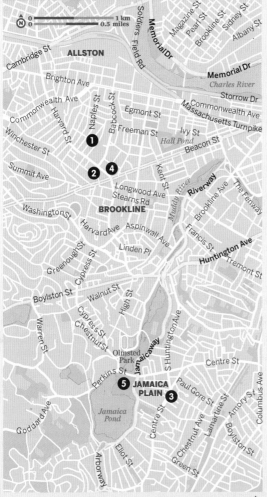

Neighborhood Top Five

1 Taking a pilgrimage to the **birthplace of John F Kennedy** (p157), touring the home and listening to Rose Kennedy's reminiscence of her family's time, and then following the NPS walking tour to see the schools, churches and other places from Kennedy lore.

2 Sitting in the balcony at the **Coolidge Corner Theatre** (p161) and catching an art-house flick.

3 Enjoying an evening of delightful food, music and camaraderie at **Tres Gatos** (p159).

4 Browsing the stacks, listening to a lecture or finding a bargain at the **Brookline Booksmith** (p161).

5 Cycling along the **Emerald Necklace** (p158), from downtown Boston to Franklin Park.

For more detail of this area see Maps p254 and p255 ➡

Lonely Planet's Top Tip

The Coolidge Corner Theatre (p161) is not just a cinema. It offers a wide variety of programming for all segments of the population, including @fter Midnite (horror and comedy for the late-night set), Opera at the Cinema (high-def screenings straight from the world's best opera houses), Off the Couch (film accompanied by psychoanalytic discussion), Sounds of Silents (silent-film classics accompanied by live music).

 Best Places to Eat

➡ Ten Tables (p160)

➡ Tres Gatos (p159)

➡ Michael's Deli (p158)

➡ Zaftigs Delicatessen (p159)

For reviews, see p158 ➡

 Best Places to Drink

➡ Brendan Behan Pub (p160)

➡ Publick House (p160)

➡ Haven (p161)

➡ Samuel Adams Brewery (p161)

For reviews, see p160 ➡

Best Urban Oases

➡ Arnold Arboretum (p157)

➡ Forest Hills Cemetery (p157)

➡ Frederick Law Olmsted National Historic Site (p157)

➡ Jamaica Pond (p162)

➡ Franklin Park Zoo (p158)

For reviews, see p157 ➡

STREETCAR SUBURBS

Explore Streetcar Suburbs

Brookline and Jamaica Plain (among others) are streetcar suburbs, residential areas that developed around Boston in the late 19th century. They are geographically isolated from other parts of Boston, though transitionally connected, yes, by streetcar (or metro now). Both JP and Brookline maintain distinct identities and unique 'neighborhood' atmospheres that make them attractive, off-the-beaten-path destinations for travelers.

Brookline was built as a modest, middle-income neighborhood, suitable for young families, which explains the draw to Joseph and Rose Kennedy, who moved here in 1914. Today, JFK admirers and history buffs make the pilgrimage to Beals St near Coolidge Corner to see the birthplace of the 35th president of the United States. The tour only takes an hour, but it's easy to while away the rest of the afternoon lunching at local Jewish delis and browsing the boutiques and bookstores.

By day, Coolidge Corner is a hub of shopping and eating. After dark, things quiet down, although the local cinema – a retro movie house – draws crowds for its arty international films and balcony seating. For a more raucous good time, check out the music clubs up the street in Allston and Brighton.

Further south, Jamaica Plain was actually a summertime retreat for wealthy Bostonians who built stately homes overlooking the quaint glacial pond. JP's open spaces are still part of this outer neighborhood's appeal, along with the cooling breezes off Jamaica Pond, the diverse flora at Arnold Arboretum, the solemn landscaping of Forest Hills Cemetery and the extensive recreational facilities at Franklin Park. If you want to enjoy the great outdoors, but you can't leave the city, head to Jamaica Plain instead.

Downtown JP is Centre St – that's where you'll find an eclectic assortment of eateries and delightful neighborhood shopping, as well as some drinking options.

Local Life

➡ **Brookline Local** Eat breakfast at Kupel's Bakery (p159) or lunch at Michael's Deli (p158).

➡ **JP Local** Go jogging around Jamaica Pond (p162) or take the dog for a drink at Brendan Behan Pub (p160).

Getting There & Away

➡ **Metro** Two branches of the green line traverse Brookline. Take the C-line to Coolidge Corner or the D-line to Brookline Village. Traveling to Jamaica Plain, orange-line stations such as Green St and Stony Brook provide the easiest access to Centre St and Jamaica Pond. Use Forest Hills station to reach JP's major sights, which are further out.

⊙ SIGHTS

⊙ Brookline

PHOTOGRAPHIC
RESOURCE CENTER   GALLERY
Map p254 (PRC; www.bu.edu/prc; 832 Commonwealth Ave; donation $5; ⊙10am-5pm Tue-Fri, noon-4pm Sat; TBU West) The independent Photographic Resource Center is one of the few centers in the US devoted exclusively to this art form. The PRC's rotating exhibits lean toward the modern and experimental, often featuring work by amateur members. Other resources include educational programs, online exhibits, a well-stocked library and unique events.

JOHN F KENNEDY NATIONAL
HISTORIC SITE   HISTORIC SITE
Map p254 (www.nps.gov/jofi; 83 Beals St; ⊙9:30am-5pm Wed-Sun May-Oct; TCoolidge Corner) FREE Four of the nine Kennedy children were born and raised in this modest house, including Jack, who was born in the master bedroom in 1917. Matriarch Rose Kennedy oversaw the restoration of the house in the late 1960s; today her narrative sheds light on the Kennedys' family life. Guided tours allow visitors to see furnishings, photographs and mementos that have been preserved here.

A self-guided walking tour of the surrounding neighborhood sets the scene for the Kennedy family's day-to-day life, including church, school and shopping.

LARZ ANDERSON AUTO
MUSEUM & PARK   MUSEUM
(www.larzanderson.org; 15 Newton St; adult/child $10/5; ⊙10am-4pm Tue-Sun; ☐51, TForest Hill or Reservoir) Larz and Isabel Anderson, a high-society couple, bought their first automobile in 1899: a Winton Runabout. It was the first of 32 autos that they would purchase over the next 50 years. 'America's oldest motorcar collection' is now on display in the carriage house on the grounds of the estate (now Larz Anderson Park). Take bus 51 from Forest Hill (orange) or Reservoir (green D-line).

FREDERICK LAW OLMSTED NATIONAL
HISTORIC SITE   HISTORIC SITE
(☑617-566-1689; www.nps.gov/frla; 99 Warren St; ⊙grounds dawn-dusk year-round, exhibits noon-4pm Wed-Fri Jan-Mar, noon-4pm Wed & Thu, 10am-4pm Fri & Sat Apr-Jun & Oct-Dec, 10am-4pm Wed-Sun Jul-Sep; ☐60 from Kenmore, TBrookline Hills) FREE Widely considered the father of landscape design, Frederick Law Olmsted ran his operation from his home 'Fairsted,' which is now a National Historic Site. The gorgeous grounds are open to casual callers. Take a tour to visit Olmsted's home and office, which remain as they were a century ago. You can peruse his designs for the country's most beloved green spaces, which include the Emerald Necklace in Boston, Central Park in New York City, many national parks, and more.

From Brookline Hills, walk two blocks south on Cypress St and three blocks west on Walnut St, then turn south on Warren.

⊙ Jamaica Plain

ARNOLD ARBORETUM   PARK
(www.arboretum.harvard.edu; 125 Arborway; ⊙dawn-dusk; ♿; TForest Hills) FREE Under a public-private partnership with Harvard University, the 265-acre Arnold Arboretum is planted with over 15,000 exotic trees and flowering shrubs. This gem is pleasant year-round, but it's particularly beautiful in the bloom of spring. Dog walking, Frisbee throwing, bicycling, sledding and general contemplation are encouraged (but picnicking is not allowed). The southern Forest Hills gate is located on the Arborway just west of the metro station.

A **visitor center** (⊙10am-5pm Thu-Tue Apr-Oct, noon-4pm Nov-Mar) is located at the main gate, just south of the rotary at Rte 1 and Rte 203. Free one-hour walking tours are offered several times a week from April to November.

FOREST HILLS CEMETERY   CEMETERY
(www.foresthillstrust.org; 95 Forest Hills Ave; ⊙8:30am-dusk; ℗; TForest Hills) Dating to 1848, Forest Hills is a gorgeous, green cemetery that is filled with art and whimsy. It is still an active burial ground, but it also plays the role of open-air museum. The walking paths are lined with sculptures paying tribute to individuals and causes from times past, while a contemporary sculpture path winds its way around the historic gravestones, connecting then and now. Gravestones include such famous figures as revolutionary heroes William

EMERALD NECKLACE

The **Emerald Necklace** (www.emeraldnecklace.org; ⓣForest Hills) is an evocative name for a series of parks and green spaces that weave some 7 miles through Boston, from the Boston Common to Franklin Park. Designed by Frederick Law Olmsted in the late 19th century, the Emerald Necklace treats city residents to a bit of fresh air, green grass and flowing water, right within the city limits. It's well suited to cycling, so hop on a bike and go for the green.

Olmsted Park (Map p255) features a paved path that hugs the banks of Leverett Pond and Ward's Pond in Jamaica Plain. The idyllic spring-fed **Jamaica Pond** (p162), on the west side of the Jamaicaway, is more than 50ft deep and great for boating, fishing, jogging and picnicking. Beautifully landscaped and wonderfully serene, the **Arnold Arboretum** (p157) will appeal not only to green thumbs and plant lovers, but also to anyone who can take time to smell the roses. Check the website to see what's blooming when you're visiting.

Franklin Park, at 500-plus acres, is an underutilized resource – partly because it borders a sketchy neighborhood, and partly because it is so huge. Still, on weekend afternoons the park is full of families from the nearby neighborhoods of Jamaica Plain, Dorchester and Roxbury. Take the orange line to Stony Brook, Green St or Forest Hills and walk about a half-mile east to the park's edge. The **Franklin Park Zoo** is also contained within the park.

North of Jamaica Plain, other green links in the Emerald Necklace include the **Back Bay Fens** (p124), the **Commonwealth Ave mall** (p110) and the **Public Garden** (p69), with the terminus at the **Boston Common** (p70).

Dawes and Joseph Warren, abolitionist William Lloyd Garrison and suffragette Lucy Stone, poets ee cummings and Anne Sexton, sculptors Daniel Chester French and Martin Milmore, and playwright Eugene O'Neill. The on-site Forsyth Chapel is a spot for peaceful contemplation surrounded by vaulted wood ceilings and stained-glass windows, in the midst of the greenery. Concerts, poetry readings and other events are often held in this exquisite space. Walk east along the Arborway a half-mile from Forest Hills station.

FRANKLIN PARK ZOO   ZOO
(www.zoonewengland.com; 1 Franklin Park Rd; adult/child $18/12; ◷10am-5pm Apr-Sep, to 4pm Oct-Mar; ⓟⓗ; ⓠ22 or 28, ⓣRuggles) Tucked into Franklin Park, the zoo features a half-dozen different habitats, as well as special exhibits devoted to birds and butterflies. The zoo's highlight is the well-designed Tropical Forest pavilion, complete with lush vegetation, waterfalls, lowland gorillas and over 30 species of free flight birds. The Australian Outback Trail allows visitors to walk among red kangaroos and wallabies.

Several exhibits are devoted to life on the savannah, showcasing an African lion, as well as giraffes, zebras and wildebeests.

Franklin Farms lets kids get up close and personal with sheep and goats. Take bus 22 or 28 from Ruggles station.

EATING

Brookline

Brookline is worth the trip for an eclectic assortment of dining options, including kosher delis, Russian restaurants and many other ethnic eats. Coolidge Corner, which is around the intersection of Harvard and Beacon Sts, is the hub for the Brookline dining scene.

MICHAEL'S DELI   DELI $
Map p254 (www.michaelsdelibrookline.com; 256 Harvard St; sandwiches $8-12; ◷9am-5:30pm Mon-Sat, to 3pm Sun; ⓣCoolidge Corner) There are two things you need to know: corned-beef Reuben; sour pickle. That said, there are dozens of sandwiches on the menu and you really can't go wrong (but don't forget the pickle). The sammies are generously stuffed and the service is superfriendly. On the downside, there's limited seating and they don't accept credit cards.

KUPEL'S BAKERY
BAKERY $

Map p254 (www.kupelsbakery.com; 421 Harvard St; mains $3-8; ⊘6am-8pm Sun-Thu, to 1hr before sundown Fri; ✔; ⊤Coolidge Corner) Kupel's has 16 kinds of chewy bagels and 16 kinds of decadent cream cheese. We're not good at math, but that's a lot of breakfast goodness. Lines are out the door on Sunday mornings, but it's worth the wait for a sesame, toasted, with chive cream cheese and lox. Not only is this place kosher, it's also vegan friendly.

ZAFTIGS DELICATESSEN
DELI, DINER $

Map p254 (www.zaftigs.com; 335 Harvard St; mains $10-15; ⊘8am-9pm Sun-Wed, to 10pm Thu-Sat; ✔; ⊤Coolidge Corner) 'Let us be your Jewish mother,' Zaftigs implores. And on Saturday and Sunday mornings, patrons craving potato pancakes with smoked salmon, challah French toast and cheese blintzes line up out the door to oblige. Fortunately, breakfast is served all day, so no one has to miss it. Otherwise, the deli turns out a huge selection of sandwiches, including classics like Reubens, egg salad and pastrami.

FUGAKYU
SUSHI $$$

Map p254 (✆617-734-1268; www.fugakyu.net; 1280 Beacon St; lunch $12-18, sushi boat $65; ⊘11:30am-1:30am; ✔; ⊤Coolidge Corner) The name aptly translates as 'house of elegance.' Upscale and over-the-top, Fugakyu offers a gorgeous array of sushi and sashimi, served by staff dressed in kimonos. The food is beautiful to look at and delicious to eat, especially the expertly plated sushi boats. Don't fall in the koi pond.

✖ Jamaica Plain

Funky, progressive Jamaica Plain hosts an ever-growing restaurant scene. The neighborhood's diverse population enjoys a variety of spunky cafes and international eateries, with many veg-friendly options.

JP LICKS
ICE CREAM $

Map p255 (www.jplicks.com; 659 Centre St; ice cream from $4; ⊘6am-midnight; 🕾; ⊤Green St) 'JP' stands for Jamaica Plain: this is the flagship location of the ice-creamery that's now all over Boston. You can't miss the happy Holstein head looking down over Centre St. And you shouldn't miss the white-coffee ice cream, either. Expensive, but worth it.

EL ORIENTAL DE CUBA
CUBAN $

Map p255 (www.elorientaldecuba.net; 416 Centre St; sandwiches $6-10, plates $12-16; ⊘8am-9pm Mon-Thu, to 10pm Fri & Sat, to 8pm Sun; ⊤Stony Brook) Lunchtime lines often run out the door as hungry patrons wait patiently for the specialty Cuban sandwich. Roast pork, Swiss cheese and ham are stuffed into a roll, and served with a side of *maduros* (fried plantains). Wash it down with a tropical shake or a sugar-cane juice, and you can be forgiven for thinking you're in Havana.

★ TRES GATOS
TAPAS $$

Map p255 (✆617-477-4851; www.tresgatosjp. com; 470 Centre St; brunch $8-13, tapas $8-16; ⊘5:30-10pm Mon-Wed, to 11pm Thu & Fri,10am-11pm Sat & Sun; ✔; ▢39, ⊤Stony Brook) This small space is not only a tapas bar, but also a bookstore and music store. It all feels like you are eating, browsing books and listening to music in somebody's living room, but that somebody is a gracious, fun host, and somehow it works. The menu features charcuterie, cheeses and a selection of authentic Spanish tapas and wine.

VEE VEE
INTERNATIONAL $$

Map p255 (✆617-522-0145; www.veeveejp.com; 763 Centre St; mains $18-24; ⊘5:30-10pm Tue-Sat, 10:30am-10pm Sun; ✔; ⊤Green St) Vee Vee stands for Valachovic, the last name of the two creative genii behind this sweet spot on Centre St. The decor is minimalist and modern, but not too trendy for granola-loving Jamaica Plain. The menu is limited to seafood and vegetarian items. Veggies should come on Wednesday for a $26 three-course prix-fixe bargain.

BELLA LUNA MILKY WAY
PIZZA $$

Map p255 (www.milkywayjp.com; 284 Amory St; mains $12-20; ⊘5-11pm Sun-Wed, to 1am Thu & Fri, noon-1am Sat; ✔; ⊤Stony Brook) Now housed in an old brewery building, Bella Luna Milky Way is a neighborhood haunt that has long enticed JP residents with its colorfully painted walls and sci-fi decor. Regulars keep coming back, year after year, for crispy thin-crust pizza pies with interesting combinations of toppings, such as the all-time favorite Gypsy King, with spinach, ricotta and caramelized onions.

While waiting for pizza, regulars keep themselves entertained with pool, Connect Four and vintage video games. After 9pm, there's trivia (Monday), two-stepping (Tuesday), comedy (Wednesday) and live music (Thursday to Saturday).

STREETCAR SUBURBS EATING

ETHNIC EATING 101: ALLSTON

Ethnic food lovers take note: one segment of one Boston neighborhood packs in 40 ethnic restaurants spanning more than 20 different cuisines. To reach this corner in Allston, take bus 66 from Harvard Sq, or walk from the B-line Harvard Ave T-stop.

The crossroads of Harvard Ave and Brighton Ave in Allston is the city's epicenter of ethnic eating. There's a choice of Afghan, Brazilian, Burmese, Cantonese, Colombian, Egyptian, Guatemalan, Indian, Israeli, Italian, Japanese, Korean, Lebanese, Mexican, Pakistani, Salvadoran, Shanghainese, Taiwanese, Thai, Turkish or Vietnamese.

This colorful neighborhood is home to a mélange of immigrants and students, a demographic formula that has resulted in an eating paradise:

Bibim (Map p254; 166 Harvard Ave; mains $10-18; ⊙11am-10:30pm; 🍴; 🚌66, 🚇Harvard Ave, B-line) Bibim transformed a little restaurant with yellow walls into a spacious, light-filled oasis of authentic Korean delights. The namesake bibimbap is filled with colorful veggies and fresh nutritious goodness. The tofu soups are recommended.

Jo Jo TaiPei (Map p254; www.jojotaipeiboston.com; 103 Brighton Ave; mains $7-14; ⊙11:30am-11pm Mon-Sat, to 10pm Sun; 🍴; 🚇Harvard Ave, B-line) Jo Jo TaiPei is the keystone of Boston's 'Little Taiwan' – a Taiwanese bakery and a bubble-tea cafe are across the street. Try the three cups tofu – a perfect combination of flavors.

Shanghai Gate (Map p254; www.shanghaigateboston.com; 204 Harvard Ave; mains $8-12; ⊙11:30am-10pm Wed-Mon; 🍴; 🚌66, 🚇Harvard Ave, B-line) The menu here offers regional dishes that will redefine your concept of what constitutes Chinese food. Cold appetizers such as the five-spice tofu or the scallion jellyfish preface the meal like a perfect aperitif, and the 'lion's head' casserole elevates the modest meatball to new heights.

Yoma Burmese Restaurant (www.yomaboston.com; 5 North Beacon St; mains $10-12; ⊙4-9pm; 🍴; 🚌66, 🚇Harvard Ave, B-line) Boston is one of the few US cities that boasts a Burmese restaurant. Yoma's *la phet thot* (green-tea leaf salad) is rich in the hearty taste called umami. And the freshly ground, complexly flavored Burmese curry powder makes the chicken curry the best in town across all cuisines.

STREETCAR SUBURBS DRINKING & NIGHTLIFE

TEN TABLES INTERNATIONAL $$$
Map p255 (📞617-524-8810; www.tentables.net; 597 Centre St; mains $22-32; ⊙5:30-10pm Mon-Sat, 5-9pm Sun; 🍴; 🚇Green St) 🌱 True to its name, this gem has only 10 tables. The emphasis here is on simplicity – appropriate for a restaurant that specializes in traditional cooking techniques. The menu is short, but changes frequently to highlight local, organic produce, handmade pasta, fresh seafood and homemade sausages.

🍺 DRINKING & NIGHTLIFE

🍸 Brookline

PUBLICK HOUSE BEER BAR
(www.thepublickhousebeerbar.com; 1648 Beacon St; ⊙5pm-2am Mon-Fri, noon-2am Sat & Sun; 🛜; 🚇Washington Square) This loud, friendly pub is buzzing with good vibes, thanks to the superb selection of brews (30-plus drafts rotating). The specialty is the good stuff from Belgium, most of which seems to have a high alcohol content. The place gets crowded on weekends, so be prepared to wait if you want to sample the mussels or mac 'n' cheese.

🍸 Jamaica Plain

BRENDAN BEHAN PUB IRISH PUB
Map p255 (www.brendanbehanpub.com; 378 Centre St; ⊙noon-1am; 🚇Stony Brook) Candlelit tables, stained glass and old liquor cabinets make this dark den an attractive destination for regulars of all ages and origins (including dogs). The beer list is not massive, but it's thoughtful and diverse. There are a few things that make this place unique: no food (but you can bring it in), no TVs, no credit cards.

HAVEN PUB

Map p255 (www.thehavenjp.com; 2 Perkins St; ⊙noon-1am Mon-Fri, 10:30am-1am Sat & Sun; 🛜; 🚋Stony Brook) If you can't stand to drink in another Irish pub, this is your Haven: a Scottish pub. There are more than a dozen Scottish craft beers, haggis, and men in kilts. Trivia, movies and live music keep the troops entertained, and the food gets rave reviews, especially the burgers and the Scotch egg.

SAMUEL ADAMS BREWERY BREWERY

Map p255 (www.samueladams.com; 30 Germania St; donation $2; ⊙10am-3pm Mon-Thu & Sat, to 5:30pm Fri; 🚋Stony Brook) Learn about Sam Adams (the patriot and the beer). See how they make the ales and lagers, and sample a few, too. Tours last about one hour and end at the gift shop and tour center (aka bar). Arrive early in the day, as tours do fill up.

 ENTERTAINMENT

COOLIDGE CORNER THEATRE CINEMA

Map p254 (www.coolidge.org; 290 Harvard St; tickets $9-11; 🚋Coolidge Corner) An art-deco neighborhood palace, this old theater blazes with exterior neon. Inside, view select Hollywood hits, cult flicks, popular independent fare and special events. Fifty cents of every ticket sale goes to the upkeep of the building.

MIDWAY CAFÉ LIVE MUSIC

(www.midwaycafe.com; 3496 Washington St; cover $5; ⊙4pm-2am; 🚋Green St) In addition to hosting a kick-ass dyke night (Thursday), this queer-friendly rock and punk bar books some of Boston's finest independent music, ranging from rockabilly to dub. Inside, find Pabst beer signs of antique vintage, some longhorn skulls, pinball and a genuinely friendly atmosphere. Cash only.

 SHOPPING

Centre St (JP) is edgy and urban, while Coolidge Corner (Brookline) is sophisticated and suburban.

★**BROOKLINE BOOKSMITH** BOOKS

Map p254 (www.brooklinebooksmith.com; 279 Harvard St; ⊙8:30am-10pm Mon-Thu, to 11pm Fri & Sat, 9am-9pm Sun; 🚋Coolidge Corner) Year after year, this independent bookstore wins

'Best Bookstore in Boston.' Customers love the line-up of author talks and poetry readings, the emphasis on local writers and the Used Book Cellar in the basement. Extralong hours are also a perk.

★**SALMAGUNDI** ACCESSORIES

Map p255 (www.salmagundiboston.com; 765 Centre St; ⊙noon-8pm Tue-Fri, 11am-8pm Sat, to 6pm Sun & Mon; 🚋Green St) In our humble opinion, every man should own at least one fedora. And if not a fedora, some other fun and functional head-topper. If you are intrigued by this idea, head to Salmagundi, where style-mavens Jessen and Andria can help you find a hat just made for your head, no matter what your gender identification.

EUREKA PUZZLES GAMES

Map p254 (www.eurekapuzzles.com; 1349 Beacon St; ⊙10am-7pm Mon-Sat, 11am-6pm Sun; ♿; 🚋Coolidge Corner) Puzzles, of course. But even better, this place has board games. And card games. And many other kinds of games. The folks at Eureka know and love games so much that they will scour their shop to find a game that you will love, too. A cool souvenir idea: City Squares – a block puzzle featuring six artistic images of historic Boston.

BOING! TOYS

Map p255 (www.boingtoys.com; 667 Centre St; ⊙10am-6pm Mon-Sat, to 5pm Sun; ♿; 🚋Green St) Boing! is fun. It's fun that they have an exclamation point at the end of their name and crazy colorful creatures adorning their facade. And it's really fun inside, where kids and parents can find educational, age-appropriate toys, games and activities with the help of knowledgeable, caring staff. Favorite aunts love this place.

ON CENTRE GIFTS, JEWELRY

Map p255 (www.oncentrejp.com; 676 Centre St; ⊙11am-7pm Mon-Fri, 10am-6pm Sat, noon-5pm Sun; 🚋Green St) The friendly folks at this little boutique can help you find the perfect gift. The jewelry is inexpensive and highly original; much of it is designed by local artists. But if your special person is not into origami earrings, never fear: there are funky reusable shopping bags and designer T-shirts, as well as cool, colorful glassware, rugs and other stuff for the home.

WORTH A DETOUR

MUSIC THEORY 101: ALLSTON/BRIGHTON

If you care to sample the Boston music scene, venture west to Allston/Brighton, the gritty 'student ghetto.' Some of Boston's best music clubs are located in these innocuous alleys and subterranean spaces.

Great Scott (Map p254; www.greatscottboston.com; 1222 Commonwealth Ave; cover $5-12; 66, Harvard Ave) A music palace for rock and indie. Get up close and personal with the bands, hang out with them after the set and buy them some beers. The sound system is not perfect and the bathrooms are nasty, but this is where you can hear the future of music. On Friday nights, the place turns into a comedy club known as the Gas (7pm).

Brighton Music Hall (Map p254; www.crossroadspresents.com; 158 Brighton Ave; tickets $10-20; Harvard Ave) This reincarnation of Harpers Ferry is now owned and operated by Crossroads (the force behind the Paradise Rock Club and House of Blues), which bodes well. The cavernous space attracts great local bands, cool world-music acts and touring national bands.The interior hasn't changed much from the HF days and thankfully the pool tables remain.

Paradise Rock Club (Map p254; www.crossroadspresents.com; 967 Commonwealth Ave; tickets $20-40; Pleasant St) Top bands rock at this landmark club – like U2, whose first gig in the USA was on this stage. Nowadays, you're more likely to hear the likes of the Del Fuegos, Los Compesiños, Trombone Shorty, and plenty of Boston bands that made good, but still come home to play the Dise.

Scullers Jazz Club (617-642-4111; www.scullersjazz.com; 400 Soldiers Field Rd; tickets $20-45; 47 or 70, Central) A more mature music experience, this club books big names (Dave Brubeck, Dr John, Michael Franks) in a small room. Though it enjoys impressive views over the Charles, the room itself lacks the grit you might hanker for in a jazz club. It feels like it's inside a Doubletree Hotel (which it is). Book in advance.

GOOD VIBRATIONS
SEX SHOP

Map p254 (www.goodvibes.com; 308a Harvard St; 10am-9pm Sun-Thu, to 10pm Fri & Sat; Coolidge Corner) Down a narrow alley and marked by a discrete sign, this woman-focused sex shop is worth seeking out. The tasteful and tantalizing boutique offers sex-positive products, not to mention newsletters, workshops and pleasure parties. No question is too probing for the women at Good Vibes. And it would seem that no product is either.

HATCHED
CHILDREN

Map p255 (www.hatchedboston.com; 668 Centre St; 10am-6pm Mon-Sat, to 3pm Sun; Green St) A baby is surely one of nature's most incredible creations, so why muff it up with synthetic fabrics and toxic toys? If you prefer to dress your little bundle of natural goodness in unbleached cloth diapers and adorable organic clothing, you'll find an excellent selection at 'Boston's first ecobaby store' (but you can't buy an ecobaby here).

SPORTS & ACTIVITIES

JAMAICA POND
SAILING, FISHING

Map p255 (www.jamaicapond.com; 507 Jamaica Way; boat rental per hr $15; boathouse noon-sunset Mon-Thu, 10am-sunset Fri-Sun Apr-Oct; Green St) Once a summer destination for city residents, Jamaica Pond is now a tranquil urban oasis, perfect for paddling or rather tame sailing. A 1.4-mile paved path circles the glacial kettlehole. Rowboats and sailboats are available for rental at the 1913 Tudor boathouse.

BROOKLINE GOLF CLUB
AT PUTTERHAM
GOLF

(www.brooklinegolf.com; 1281 West Roxbury Pkwy; 18 holes weekday/weekend $32/43) You probably can't get on the famous Brookline Country Club green, but you can play golf next door at Putterham, a less famed but perfectly pleasant public course. Wide fairways and a lack of water hazards make it a suitable course for all levels.

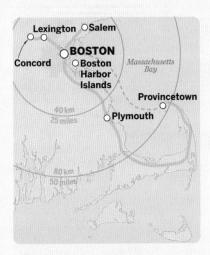

Day Trips from Boston

Boston Harbor Islands p164
These offshore islands are inviting for walking trails, rocky beaches, wild berries and one highly explorable abandoned fort.

Lexington & Concord p166
Now serene suburbs, these twin towns were the site of the dramatic kickoff to the War for Independence on April 19, 1775.

Salem p169
In addition to the many witchy sites in 'Witch City,' Salem showcases a proud maritime history and unique artistic legacy.

Plymouth p171
Settled by the Pilgrims in 1620, Plymouth is now home to *Mayflower II*, a replica of their ship, and Plimoth Plantation, a replica of their settlement.

Provincetown p172
Provincetown is a perfect summertime destination, with vast stretches of sandy beaches, miles of seaside bicycle trails, and an eclectic strip of art galleries and seafood restaurants.

Boston Harbor Islands

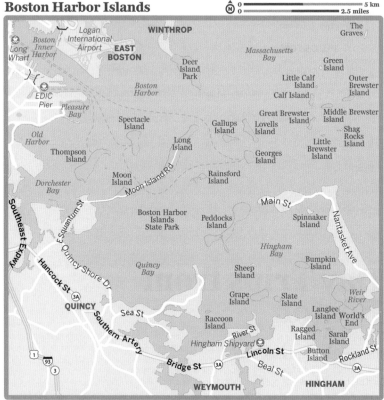

Boston Harbor Islands

Explore

Boston Harbor is sprinkled with 34 islands, many of which are open for trail walking, bird-watching, fishing and swimming. You can't visit them all in one day, so consider the activities on offer and plan accordingly.

Hop on the first ferry to Georges Island, where you can spend the morning exploring Fort Warren. After lunch, take the shuttle to one of the other islands. Hit Spectacle Island for good walking trails and marvelous city views. Head to Lovells to catch some rays and cool off in the refreshing Atlantic waters. Or venture to Grape Island to hunt for wild berries.

Catch a shuttle (if necessary) and ferry back to the mainland from Spectacle or Georges. Don't try to visit more than two or three islands in one day: you'll end up spending all your time riding on or waiting for boats.

The Best...
➡ **Sight** Fort Warren (p165)
➡ **Place to Hike** Spectacle Island (p165)
➡ **Place to Swim** Lovells (p165) or Spectacle (p165) beaches

Top Tip

Georges and Spectacle Islands have snack shacks (10am to 5pm), but there is no food or water on the other islands. Pack a picnic!

Getting There & Away
➡ **Boat** To reach most of the islands, Boston Harbor Cruises (p211) offers

seasonal ferry service from Long Wharf. Purchase a round-trip ticket to Georges Island or Spectacle Island (adult/child $15/9), where you catch another boat to the smaller islands. Make sure you check the schedule in advance and plan your day accordingly.

....

Need to Know

➜ **Area Code** 617

➜ **Location** Scattered around the Boston Harbor, 20 to 40 minutes from Downtown Boston

➜ **Tourist Office** Boston Harbor Islands Pavilion (p216)

SIGHTS

GEORGES ISLAND
ISLAND, FORT

(early May–mid-Sep; ; from Long Wharf or Hull) Georges Island is one of the transportation hubs for the islands. It is also the site of **Fort Warren**, a 19th-century fort and Civil War prison. While National Park Service (NPS) rangers give guided tours of the fort and there is a small museum, it is largely abandoned, with many dark tunnels, creepy corners and magnificent lookouts to discover. This is one of the only islands with facilities like a snack bar and rest rooms.

The extensive picnic area attracts large groups of kids, as do the family programs like children's theater and family fun days. In summer, there are Friday-night barbecues and other special events.

SPECTACLE ISLAND
ISLAND

(dawn-dusk early May–mid-Sep; ; from Long Wharf) A Harbor Island hub, Spectacle Island has a large marina, a solar-powered visitor center, a healthy snack bar, and sandy, supervised beaches. Five miles of walking trails provide access to a 157ft peak overlooking the harbor. Special events include Sunday-afternoon jazz concerts and Thursday-evening clambakes. There are also ranger-led kayak tours on Monday and Wednesday. Spectacle Island is relatively close to the city and a ferry runs here directly from Long Wharf (hourly in July and August, less frequently in June and September).

LOVELLS ISLAND
ISLAND

(mid-Jun–early Sep; from Georges) Two deadly shipwrecks may bode badly for seafarers, but that doesn't seem to stop recreational boaters, swimmers and sunbathers from lounging on Lovells' long rocky beach. Some of the former uses of Lovells are evident: European settlers used the island as a rabbit run, and descendent bunnies are still running this place; Fort Standish dates from WWI, but has yet to be excavated. With facilities for camping and picnicking, Lovells is one of the most popular Harbor Island destinations.

BUMPKIN ISLAND
ISLAND

(early May–mid-Sep; from Georges or Hull) This small island has served many purposes over the years, first farming then fish drying and smelting. In 1900 it was the site of a children's hospital, but it was taken over for navy training during WWI. You can still explore the remains of a stone farmhouse and the hospital. The beaches are not the best for swimming, as they are slate and seashell. A network of trails leads through fields overgrown with wildflowers. It's one of three islands with camping facilities.

GRAPE ISLAND
ISLAND

(mid-Jun–early Sep; from Georges or Hingham) Grape Island is rich with fruity goodness – not grapes, but raspberries, bayberries and elderberries, all growing wild amid the scrubby wooded trails. The wild fruit attracts abundant bird life. Unlike many of the Harbor Islands, Grape Island has no remains of forts or military prisons, although during the Revolutionary War, it was the site of a skirmish over hay, known as the Battle of Grape Island.

PEDDOCKS ISLAND
ISLAND

(mid-Jun–early Sep; from Georges or Long Wharf) One of the largest Harbor Islands, Peddocks consists of four headlands connected by sandbars. Hiking trails wander through marsh, pond and coastal environs. But the dominant feature of Peddocks Island is the remains of **Fort Andrews**, a large facility with more than 20 buildings. Peddocks' proximity to the mainland ensured its use as a military stronghold, from the Revolutionary War right through WWII.

LITTLE BREWSTER ISLAND
ISLAND, LIGHTHOUSE

(617-223-8666; Fri-Sun Jun-Sep; from Fan Pier) Little Brewster is the country's oldest light station and site of the iconic **Boston Light**, dating from 1783. To visit Little Brewster, you must take an organized tour (reservations required). Learn about Boston's maritime history during a one-hour sail around the harbor, then spend two hours exploring the island. Adventurous travelers can climb the 76 steps to the top of the lighthouse for a close-up view of the rotating light and a far-off view of the city skyline.

Tours depart from Moakley Courthouse Dock in the Seaport District.

DEER ISLAND   PARK

(☑617-660-7607; www.mwra.com; ☉dawn-dusk) Funny thing about Deer Island: it's not actually an island. A hurricane in 1938 created the causeway that now connects the 'island' to the mainland. The other funny thing about Deer Island is that it is dominated by a gigantic sewage treatment plant, which is one of the keys to the clean-up of Boston Harbor. The facility is surrounded by 60 acres of parkland, with 5 miles of trails. Tours of the waste-water treatment facility are available with advance arrangements. Deer Island is accessible only by car.

THOMPSON ISLAND   ISLAND

(☑617-328-3900; www.thompsonisland.org; ☉noon-5pm Sat & Sun Jun-Aug; ⛴from EDIC Pier) Thompson Island was settled as early as 1626 by a Scotsman, David Thompson, who set up a trading post to do business with the Neponset Indians. Today this island is privately owned by Thompson Island Outward Bound, a nonprofit organization that develops fun and challenging physical adventures, especially for training and developing leadership skills. As such, the public can explore its 200-plus acres only on weekends, when it's wonderful for walking, fishing and birding.

A dedicated ferry leaves from EDIC Pier in the Seaport District; see the website for details.

WORLD'S END   PARK

(www.thetrustees.org; 250 Martin's Lane, Hingham; adult/child $6/free; ☉8am-dusk) Not exactly an island, this 251-acre peninsula was originally designed by Frederick Law Olmsted for residential development in 1889. Carriage paths were laid out and trees were planted, but the houses were never built. Instead, wide grassy meadows attract butterflies and grass-nesting birds. Today management by the Trustees of Reservations guarantees continued serenity and beauty.

The 4-plus miles of tree-lined carriage paths are perfect for walking, mountain biking or cross-country skiing – download a map from the Trustees website.

World's End is accessible by car from Hingham.

Lexington & Concord

....

Explore

Students of history and lovers of liberty can trace the events of the fateful day that started a revolution – April 19, 1775. Follow in the footsteps of British troops and colonial Minutemen, who tromped out to Lexington to face off on the town green, then continued on to Concord for the battle at the Old North Bridge. Concord is the bigger town, with many more sights to see, so don't dally in Lexington.

This day trip is an excellent bicycle outing: the paved Minuteman Bikeway covers the route from Cambridge to Lexington, while the more rugged Battle Rd (within the Minute National Historic Park) continues from Lexington to Concord. If you don't feel like pedaling back, you can take your bicycle on the commuter rail. Otherwise, you will probably need a car (or the Liberty Ride) to see both towns in one day.

....

The Best...
➡ **Sight** Walden Pond (p168)
➡ **Place to Eat** Country Kitchen (p169)
➡ **Place to Drink** 80 Thoreau (p169)

....

Top Tip
If you don't have your own wheels, consider catching the **Liberty Ride** (www.libertyride.us; adult/child $28/12; ☉10am-4pm daily Jun-Oct, Sat & Sun Apr & May), a hop-on hop-off trolley, which includes all of the major sites in both towns. Buy tickets at the Lexington Visitors Center.

....

Getting There & Away
➡ **Bicycle** The Minuteman Bikeway runs for 6 miles from Alewife, in Cambridge, to Lexington. From Lexington you can follow the Battle Rd Trail to Concord.

➡ **Bus** MBTA buses 62 and 76 run from the red-line T terminus at Alewife through to Lexington center hourly on weekdays, less frequently on Saturday (no Sunday service).

➡ **Car** On Rte 2, drive about 20 minutes west from Cambridge to Waltham St (exit 54) for Lexington and Walden St (Rte 126) for Concord.

➡ **Train** MBTA commuter-rail trains ($8.50, 40 minutes, 10 daily) run between Boston's North Station and the Concord Depot on the Fitchburg/South Acton line.

Need to Know

➡ **Area Code** ☑781

➡ **Location** 12 miles west of Boston (Lexington), 18 miles west of Boston (Concord)

➡ **Tourist Offices Lexington Visitors Center** (Lexington Chamber of Commerce; www.lexingtonchamber.org; 1875 Massachusetts Ave; ⊙9am-5pm); **Concord Chamber of Commerce & Visitors Center** (www.concordchamberofcommerce.org; 58 Main St; ⊙10am-4pm Mar-Oct)

◉ SIGHTS

◉ Lexington

BATTLE GREEN HISTORIC SITE
(Massachusetts Ave) The historic Battle Green is where the skirmish between patriots and British troops jumpstarted the War for Independence. The **Lexington Minuteman Statue** (crafted by Henry Hudson Kitson in 1900) stands guard at the southeast end of Battle Green, honoring the bravery of the 77 Minutemen who met the British here in 1775, and the eight who died.

The **Parker Boulder**, named for their commander, marks the spot where the Minutemen faced a force almost 10 times their strength. It is inscribed with Parker's instructions to his troops: 'Stand your ground. Don't fire unless fired upon. But if they mean to have a war, let it begin here.' Across the street, history buffs have preserved the **Old Belfry** that sounded the alarm signaling the start of the revolution.

BUCKMAN TAVERN MUSEUM
(www.lexingtonhistory.org; 1 Bedford Rd; adult/child $8/5; ⊙10am-4pm mid-Mar–Nov) Facing the Battle Green, the 1709 Buckman Tavern was the headquarters of the Minutemen. Here, they spent the tense hours between the midnight call to arms and the dawn arrival of the Redcoats. Today, the tavern has been restored to its 18th-century appearance, complete with bar, fireplace and bullet holes resulting from British musket fire.

★**MINUTE MAN NATIONAL HISTORIC PARK** PARK
(www.nps.gov/mima; 250 North Great Rd, Lincoln; ⊙9am-5pm Apr-Oct; ♿) **FREE** Two miles west of Lexington center, the route that British troops followed to Concord has been designated the Minute Man National Historic Park. Within the park, Battle Rd is a five-mile wooded trail that connects the historic sites related to the battles – from Meriam's Corner, where gunfire erupted while British soldiers were retreating, to the Paul Revere capture site. It's well marked and quite fascinating, besides being a lovely walk.

The visitor center at the eastern end of the park shows an informative multimedia presentation depicting Paul Revere's ride and the ensuing battles.

◉ Concord

OLD NORTH BRIDGE HISTORIC SITE
(www.nps.gov/mima; Monument St; ⊙dawn-dusk) A half-mile north of Memorial Sq in Concord center, the wooden span of Old North Bridge is the site of the 'shot heard around the world' (as Emerson wrote in his poem *Concord Hymn*). Daniel Chester French's first statue, *Minute Man,* presides over the park from the opposite side of the bridge. On the far side of the bridge, the Buttrick mansion contains the **visitor center** (www.nps.gov/mima; Liberty St; ⊙9am-5pm Apr-Oct, to 3pm Mar & Nov), where you can see a video about the battle and admire the Revolutionary War brass cannon known as the Hancock.

On your way up to Old North Bridge, look for the yellow **Bullet Hole House** (262 Monument St), at which British troops purportedly fired as they retreated from North Bridge.

OLD MANSE HISTORIC SITE
(www.thetrustees.org; 269 Monument St; adult/child $8/5; ⊙noon-5pm Tue-Sun May-Oct, Sat & Sun only Mar, Apr, Nov & Dec) Right next to Old North Bridge, the Old Manse was built in 1769 by Ralph Waldo's grandfather, the

WORTH A DETOUR

DECORDOVA MUSEUM & SCULPTURE PARK

Located near Walden Pond, the magical **Decordova Museum & Sculpture Park** (www.decordova.org; 51 Sandy Pond Rd; adult/child $14/free; ⊙10am-5pm) encompasses 35 acres of green hills, providing a spectacular natural environment for a constantly changing exhibit of outdoor artwork. As many as 75 pieces are on display at any given time. Inside the complex, a museum hosts rotating exhibits of sculpture, painting, photography and mixed media.

There's free admission on the first Wednesday of the month.

Reverend William Emerson. Today it's filled with mementos, including those of Nathaniel and Sophia Hawthorne, who lived here for a few years. A highlight of Old Manse is the gorgeously maintained grounds – the fabulous organic garden was planted by Henry Thoreau as a wedding gift to the Hawthornes.

★CONCORD MUSEUM   MUSEUM
(www.concordmuseum.org; 200 Lexington Rd; adult/child $10/5; ⊙9am-5pm Mon-Sat, noon-5pm Sun Apr-Dec, 11am-4pm Mon-Sat, 1-4pm Sun Jan-Mar; ♿) Southeast of Monument Sq, the Concord Museum brings the town's diverse history under one roof. The museum's prized possession is one of the 'two if by sea' lanterns that hung in the steeple of the Old North Church in Boston as a signal to Paul Revere. It also has the world's largest collection of Henry David Thoreau artifacts, including his writing desk from Walden Pond.

RALPH WALDO EMERSON
MEMORIAL HOUSE   HISTORIC SITE
(28 Cambridge Turnpike; adult/child $7/free; ⊙10am-4:30pm Thu-Sat, 1-4:30pm Sun mid-Apr-Oct) The Ralph Waldo Emerson Memorial House is where the philosopher lived for almost 50 years (1835–82). Emerson was the paterfamilias of literary Concord, one of the great literary figures of his age and the founding thinker of the Transcendentalist movement. The house often hosted his renowned circle of friends and still contains many original furnishings.

ORCHARD HOUSE   HISTORIC SITE
(www.louisamayalcott.org; 399 Lexington Rd; adult/child $10/5; ⊙10am-4:30pm Mon-Sat, 1-4:30pm Sun Apr-Oct, 11am-3pm Mon-Fri, 10am-4:30pm Sat, 1-4:30pm Sun Nov-Mar) Louisa May Alcott (1832–88) was a junior member of Concord's august literary crowd, but her work proved to be durable: *Little Women* is among the most popular young-adult books ever written. The mostly autobiographical novel is set in Concord. Orchard House, her fully furnished childhood home, is across from the Emerson Memorial House and is open for guided tours.

SLEEPY HOLLOW CEMETERY   CEMETERY
(www.friendsofsleepyhollow.org; Bedford St; ⊙dawn-dusk) This is the final resting place for the most famous Concordians. Though the entrance is only a block east of Monument Sq, the most interesting part, Authors' Ridge, is a 15-minute walk along Bedford St. You'll find Thoreau and his family buried here, as well as the Alcotts and the Hawthornes.

Emerson's tombstone is the large uncarved rock of New England marble, an appropriate Transcendentalist symbol.

★WALDEN POND   STATE PARK
(www.mass.gov/dcr/parks/walden; 915 Walden St; parking $5; ⊙dawn-dusk) FREE Thoreau took the naturalist beliefs of Transcendentalism out of the realm of theory and into practice when he left the comforts of town and built a rustic cabin at Walden Pond. Now a state park, the glacial pond is surrounded by acres of forest preserved by the nonprofit Walden Woods project. The site of Thoreau's cabin is on the northeast side, marked by a cairn and signs.

✕ EATING & DRINKING

✕ Lexington

VIA LAGO CAFÉ   CAFE $
(www.vialagocatering.com; 1845 Massachusetts Ave; mains $5-8; ⊙7am-9pm Mon-Sat; ♿) This cafe has high ceilings, intimate tables, a scent of fresh-roasted coffee and a great deli case. You'll often see cyclists in here kicking back with the daily paper, a cup of exotic java or tea, and a sandwich of roasted turkey, Swiss and sprouts.

✖ Concord

Myriad cafes and restaurants are located on the streets immediately surrounding Memorial Sq, but the really special places to eat are located slightly out of the center, near the train depot.

BEDFORD FARMS   ICE CREAM **$**
(www.bedfordfarmsicecream.com; 68 Thoreau St; ice cream from $4; ⊘11am-9:30pm Mar-Nov, noon-6pm Dec-Feb; 🖢) Dating to the 19th century, this local dairy specializes in delectable ice cream, and frozen yogurt that tastes like delectable ice cream. If prices seem a tad high, it's because the scoops are gigantic. Besides their trademark Moosetracks (vanilla ice cream, chocolate swirl, peanut-butter cups), most of the flavors are pretty standard. Conveniently next to the train depot.

COUNTRY KITCHEN   SANDWICHES **$**
(181 Sudbury Ave; sandwiches $8-10; ⊘6am-4pm Mon-Fri; 🖢) At lunchtime, this little yellow house often has a line out the door, which is testament to its tiny size, as well as its amazing sandwiches. The Thanksgiving sandwich is the hands-down favorite, with roasted turkey carved straight off the bird. They don't accept credit cards and there's no seating, save the picnic table out front.

80 THOREAU   MODERN AMERICAN **$$$**
(☏978-318-0008; www.80thoreau.com; 80 Thoreau St; mains $21-29; ⊘5:30-10:30pm Mon-Thu, to 11:30pm Fri & Sat) Understated and elegant, this modern restaurant is an anomaly in historic Concord – but that's a good thing. The menu – short but sweet – features deliciously unexpected combinations of flavors, mostly using seasonal, local ingredients. There's also a busy bar area, which offers a short selection of classic cocktails and a long list of wines by the glass.

Salem

Explore

A lot of history is packed into this gritty city. There is much more than a day's worth of sights and activities, so be selective when planning your time here.

Your starting point should be the Salem Maritime National Historic Site, which includes a smattering of historic buildings and the impressive ship *Friendship*. This overview of the city's maritime exploits is the perfect introduction to the Peabody Essex Museum, which is Salem's unrivaled highlight.

Dubbed 'Witch City,' Salem is also infamous as the site of the witch trials in 1692, when 19 people were hanged as a result of witch-hunt hysteria. There are dozens of witch-themed sights, as well as an excellent trial re-enactment. Most of these destinations are more about fun than authenticity, so choose wisely.

....

The Best...

➤ **Sight** Peabody Essex Museum (p170)
➤ **Place to Eat** New England Soup Factory (p170)
➤ **Place to Drink** Gulu-Gulu Café (p170)

....

Top Tip

During the month of October, the **Haunted Happenings Halloween festival** (www.hauntedhappenings.org) includes special exhibits, parades, concerts, pumpkin carvings, costume parties and trick-or-treating.

....

Getting There & Away

➤ **Boat** Boston Harbor Cruises (Salem Ferry; www.bostonharborcruises.com; 10 Blaney St; round-trip adult/child $27/22; ⊘May-Oct) operates the ferry from Long Wharf to Salem (one hour, five daily).
➤ **Bus** MBTA buses 450 and 455 from Boston's Haymarket Sq are slower than the train.
➤ **Car** Take MA 128 north from Boston, then take MA 114 east into Salem center (one hour).
➤ **Train** Both the Newburyport and Rockport lines of the MBTA commuter rail ($7, 30 minutes, hourly) run from Boston's North Station to Salem Depot.

....

Need to Know

➤ **Area Code** ☏978
➤ **Location** 20 miles northeast of Boston
➤ **Tourist Office NPS Regional Visitors Center** (www.nps.gov/sama; 2 New Liberty St; ⊘9am-5pm)

◉ SIGHTS

★ SALEM MARITIME NATIONAL HISTORIC SITE
HISTORIC SITE

(www.nps.gov/sama; 193 Derby St; ⊙9am-5pm) **FREE** Salem's glory days occurred in the late 18th century, when it was a center for clipper-ship trade with China, started by Elias Hasket Derby. The Salem Maritime National Historic Site comprises the customhouse, the ship *Friendship* and the wharves, as well as other buildings along Derby St that are remnants of the shipping industry once thriving along this stretch of Salem.

In all, the site comprises 10 different historic locations within a two-block area. Check in at the visitor center for a schedule of ranger-led tours.

★ PEABODY ESSEX MUSEUM
ART MUSEUM

(www.pem.org; 161 Essex St; adult/child $18/free; ⊙10am-5pm Tue-Sun; 👶) The world-class Peabody Essex Museum grew out of Salem's thriving maritime trade. Predictably, the collection of Asian art is particularly strong, and includes Yin Yu Tang, a house that was shipped from southeastern China. The museum also has extensive collections focusing on New England decorative arts and maritime history, and there is a fascinating exhibit dedicated to Native American art.

After Elias Derby's ship *Grand Turk* rounded the Cape of Good Hope, many Salem vessels followed course. Soon the merchants founded the East India Marine Society to provide warehousing services. The new company's charter required the establishment of a museum 'to house the natural and artificial curiosities' brought back by member ships. Thus the museum was born.

HOUSE OF THE SEVEN GABLES
HISTORIC SITE

(www.7gables.org; 54 Turner St; adult/child $12.50/7.50; ⊙10am-7pm Jul-Oct, to 5pm Nov-Jun) The House of the Seven Gables was made famous in Nathaniel Hawthorne's 1851 novel of the same name. The novel brings to life the gloomy Puritan atmosphere of early New England and its effect on the psyches of the residents; the house does the same. Look for wonderful seaside gardens, many original furnishings and a mysterious secret staircase.

WITCH HOUSE
HISTORIC SITE

(Jonathan Corwin House; www.witchhouse.info; 310 Essex St; adult/child $8.25/4.25, tour extra $2; ⊙10am-5pm Mar-Nov) The most authentic of more than a score of witchy sites is Witch House – once the home of Jonathan Corwin, a local magistrate who was called on to investigate witchcraft claims. He examined several accused witches, possibly in the 1st-floor rooms of this house. Hours are extended in October.

✕ EATING & DRINKING

NEW ENGLAND SOUP FACTORY
SOUP $

(www.nesoupfactorysalem.com; 140 Washington St; soup $5-10, sandwiches $4-8; ⊙11am-8pm Mon-Fri, to 7pm Sat, noon-7pm Sun; 🍴 👶) When there's a chill in the air, nothing warms body and soul like a bowl of hot soup. That's when you head straight to the New England Soup Factory. It's not much to look at, and tableware is paper and plastic, but there are 10 divine soup options every day (rotating).

Favorites include chicken pot pie soup (topped with a puff pastry) and pumpkin lobster bisque, but you're welcome to sample before deciding. In summer, they serve cold soups, of course.

RED'S SANDWICH SHOP
DINER $

(www.redssandwichshop.com; 15 Central St; mains $5-8; ⊙5am-3pm Mon-Sat, 6am-1pm Sun) This Salem institution has been serving eggs and sandwiches to faithful customers for over 50 years. The food is hearty and basic, but the real attraction is Red's old-school decor, complete with counter service and friendly faces. It's housed in the old London Coffee House building (around since 1698).

★ GULU-GULU CAFÉ
CAFE

(www.gulugulucafe.com; 247 Essex St; ⊙8am-1am; 📶) Gulu-gulu means 'gulp, gulp' in French and it's named after a now-defunct cafe in Prague. That is an indication of how eclectic this place is, featuring (in no particular order) delicious coffee, art-adorned walls, a fantastic beer selection, live music, sinful crêpes and board games. Come for a snack or stay all day.

Plymouth

Explore

Neatly contained and historically significant, Plymouth is the perfect day trip. Start the day at *Mayflower II* to experience life aboard the 17th-century sailing vessel. Make the obligatory stop at Plymouth Rock to see where the Pilgrims (might have) first stepped ashore. Then climb the hill into town, which is lined up along Main St. This is an opportunity to stop for lunch, before moving on to spend the afternoon at Plimoth Plantation to experience what life was like for the Pilgrims once they were settled here.

Not surprisingly, Plymouth has a handful of historic houses and other micromuseums that are also open for visitors. The best is Pilgrim Hall (America's oldest museum!), which contains some cool artifacts and excellent educational exhibits.

The Best...

➡ **Sight** Plimoth Plantation (p171)

➡ **Place to Eat Burgers** Nosh Tavern (p172)

➡ **Place to Eat Seafood** Blue-Eyed Crab (p172)

Top Tip

If you plan to visit both *Mayflower II* and Plimoth Plantation, consider purchasing a combination ticket, which is good for admission to Plimoth Plantation on two consecutive days and to *Mayflower II* for any one day within a year.

Getting There & Away

➡ **Boat** The 90-minute **Plymouth-to-Provincetown Express Ferry** (www.p-townferry.com; State Pier, 77 Water St) departs Plymouth at 10am and leaves Provincetown at 4:30pm (late June to mid-September).

➡ **Bus Plymouth & Brockton** (P&B; www.p-b.com) buses travel to South Station in Boston (adult/child $15/8, hourly). Heading south, these buses continue as far as Provincetown. **GATRA buses** (www.gatra.org; one-way/day-pass $1/3) connect the P&B terminal and the train station at Cordage Park to the town center, while another

link runs from the center to Plimoth Plantation.

➡ **Car** Take I-93 South to MA 3. It's a one-hour drive.

➡ **Train** MBTA (www.mbta.com) commuter trains ($10.50, one hour, four daily) to Plymouth leave from South Station.

Need to Know

➡ **Area Code** ☑508

➡ **Location** 40 miles south of Boston

➡ **Tourist Office Destination Plymouth** (www.seeplymouth.com; 130 Water St; ☺9am-8pm Jun-Aug, to 5pm Apr, May & Sep-Nov)

 SIGHTS

PLYMOUTH ROCK   MONUMENT

(Water St) Historic Plymouth, 'America's Home Town,' is synonymous with Plymouth Rock. Thousands of visitors come here each year to look at this weathered granite ball and to consider what it was like for the Pilgrims, who stepped ashore on this strange land in the autumn of 1620.

We don't really know that the Pilgrims landed on Plymouth Rock, as it's not mentioned in any early written records, but it stands today as an enduring symbol of the quest for religious freedom.

MAYFLOWER II   HISTORIC SITE

(www.plimoth.org; State Pier, Water St; adult/child $12/8; ☺9am-5pm Apr-Nov; 🚼) If Plymouth Rock tells us little about the Pilgrims, *Mayflower II* speaks volumes. Climb aboard this replica of the small ship in which they made the fateful voyage, where 102 people lived together for 66 days as the ship passed through stormy North Atlantic waters. Actors in period costume are often on board, recounting harrowing tales from the journey.

★**PLIMOTH PLANTATION**   MUSEUM

(www.plimoth.org; 137 Warren Ave; adult/child $26/15; ☺9am-5pm Apr-Nov; 🚼) The Plimoth Plantation, a mile or so south of Plymouth Rock, authentically recreates the Pilgrims' 1627 settlement. Everything in the village – costumes, implements, vocabulary, artistry, recipes and crops – has been painstakingly researched and remade. Hobbamock's (Wampanoag) Homesite replicates the life of a Native American community in the area at the same time.

PILGRIM HALL MUSEUM   MUSEUM

(www.pilgrimhall.org; 75 Court St; adult/child $8/5; ⏱9:30am-4:30pm Feb-Dec; ♿) Claiming to be the oldest continually operating public museum in the country, Pilgrim Hall Museum was founded in 1824. Its exhibits are not reproductions, but real objects that the Pilgrims and their Wampanoag neighbors used in their daily lives – from Governor Bradford's chair to Constance Hopkins' beaver hat. The exhibits are dedicated to correcting the misrepresentations about the Pilgrims that have been passed down through history.

 EATING

NOSH TAVERN   MODERN AMERICAN $$
(www.noshfoodgroup.com; 15 Main St Ext; lunch & brunch mains $7-12, dinner $12-22; ⏱11:30am-12:30am Mon-Fri, 9am-12:30am Sat & Sun; 🛜) 'America's Hometown' has emerged from the 17th century with a thoroughly modern gastropub. It's all-American fare with flair. The obligatory turkey dinner is here, but it's cinnamon-brined turkey, served with butternut risotto and candied pecans. The burgers are here – four different versions – and one comes with truffles. The beer is here, too – a slew of craft brews served in dedicated glasses.

BLUE-EYED CRAB   SEAFOOD $$$
(www.blue-eyedcrab.com; 170 Water St; sandwiches $10-13, dinner mains $20-30; ⏱11:30am-9pm Sun-Thu, to 10pm Fri, noon-10pm Sat) There are a few tried-and-true seafood restaurants clustered around Town Wharf. But if you like a little innovation with your fish (and perhaps a cocktail or a glass of wine), head a bit further west to this fun and funky joint, with sea-blue walls and fish floating from the ceiling.

You can still get clam chowder and lobster rolls, but you can also try squid chilli, seafood stew with chorizo, or a crispy crab burger.

Provincetown

Explore

Provincetown is far out. We're not just talking geographically (though it does occupy the outermost point on Cape Cod), we're also talking about the flamboyant street scenes, brilliant art galleries and unbridled nightlife. Once an outpost for fringe writers and artists, Provincetown has morphed into the hottest gay and lesbian destination in the Northeast.

Even if you're only in town for a day, you'll want to spend part of it admiring the art and watching the street life on Commercial St. If you are lucky enough to be here at night, you can also partake in some diverse dining, and singing and dancing until dawn.

But that's only half the show. As part of the Cape Cod National Seashore, Provincetown's untamed coastline and vast beaches beg exploring. A network of bicycle trails wind through picturesque sand dunes and a beach backed by sea and sky (and a lighthouse or two).

The Best...

➡ **Sight** Cape Cod National Seashore (p173)
➡ **Place to Eat** Mews Restaurant & Cafe (p174)
➡ **Place to Drink** Harbor Lounge (p174)

Top Tip

The best way to get around Provincetown is by bicycle (free parking everywhere you go). Bring a bicycle on the ferry from Boston for only $6, or rent one from Ptown Bikes.

Getting There & Away

➡ **Air** Cape Air flies several times a day to Provincetown's Municipal Airport (one way $120, 25 minutes).

➡ **Boat** Both **Bay State Cruise Co** (Map p239; www.boston-ptown.com; Commonwealth Pier, Seaport Blvd; round-trip adult/child $88/65; 🚇SL1 or SL2, Ⓣ South Station) and **Boston Harbor Cruises** (Map p236; www.bostonharborcruises.com; 1 Long Wharf; round-trip adult/child $88/65; Ⓣ Aquarium) operate ferries between Boston and Provincetown. Both companies run the 90-minute trip two or three times a day during the peak summer season.

➡ **Bus** The **Plymouth & Brockton** (P&B; www.p-b.com) bus (adult/child $31/16, 3½ hours), which terminates at the Chamber of Commerce, operates several times a day from Boston, stopping at other Cape towns along the way. From late May to mid-October, the shuttle buses (one-trip/day pass $1/3) travel up and down Bradford St, and to MacMillan Wharf, Herring Cove Beach and North Truro.

➡ **Car** Allow 2½ hours to make the drive from Boston; weekend traffic can be brutal and will surely slow you down.

Need to Know
➡ **Area Code** 508
➡ **Location** 115 miles southeast of Boston
➡ **Tourist Office Provincetown Chamber of Commerce** (www.ptownchamber.com; 307 Commercial St; ⊙9am-6pm)

⊙ SIGHTS

PROVINCE LANDS
VISITOR CENTER   BEACH
(www.nps.gov/caco; Race Point Rd; car/bike/pedestrian $15/3/3; ⊙9am-5pm; P) Even with all the art and history, the main attraction at Provincetown is the **Cape Cod National Seashore**, which includes eight miles of exhilarating mountain-bike trails leading through sand dunes and coastal forest. Two spurs lead to the pounding surf at Race Point Beach and the calmer waters of Herring Cove. Rent bikes at **Ptown Bikes** (www.ptownbikes.com; 42 Bradford St; bicycles per day $23; ⊙9am-6pm).

When the weather is fine, swimmers and sun-worshippers set up camp near the entrances to these two beaches. But the seashore stretches for miles and miles in either direction, so take a hike to find your own private patch of sea and sand.

COMMERCIAL STREET   STREET
The main artery of the town, walking down Commercial St is a top attraction in Provincetown. On any given day you may see cross-dressers, leather-clad motorcyclists, barely clad in-line skaters, same-sex couples strolling hand-in-hand and heterosexual tourists wondering what they've stumbled into on their way to a whale-watch.

★PROVINCETOWN ART
ASSOCIATION & MUSEUM   MUSEUM
(PAAM; www.paam.org; 460 Commercial St; adult/child $10/free; ⊙11am-8pm Mon-Thu, to 10pm Fri, to 5pm Sat & Sun) Founded in 1914 to celebrate the town's thriving art community, this museum showcases the works of hundreds of artists who have found their inspiration on the Lower Cape. Chief among them are Charles Hawthorne, who led the early Provincetown art movement, and Edward Hopper, who had a home and gallery in the Truro dunes.

✕ EATING & DRINKING

CANTEEN   SEAFOOD, AMERICAN $
(www.thecanteenptown.com; 225 Commercial St; mains $8-15; ⊙11am-9pm Thu-Sun May-Dec;) Cool and casual, but unmistakeably gourmet, here is your optimal P-town lunch stop. Choose from classics like lobster rolls and BBQ pulled-pork sandwiches, or innovations like cod *bahn-mi* and shrimp sliders. Accompany with crispy Brussels

GLBTQ PROVINCETOWN

While other cities have their gay districts, in Provincetown the entire town is the gay district.

Boatslip Resort (www.boatslipresort.com; 161 Commercial St; ⊙4-7pm) Hosts wildly popular afternoon tea dances (May to October), often packed with gorgeous guys.

A-House (Atlantic House; www.ahouse.com; 4 Masonic Pl; ⊙pub noon-1am, club 10pm-1am) P-town's gay scene got its start here and it's still a go-to place, especially for dancing. Includes an intimate 1st-floor pub with fireplace, as well as a dance club and leather bar upstairs.

Pied Bar (www.piedbar.com; 193 Commercial St; ⊙noon-1am May-Oct) This woman-owned waterfront lounge is a popular dance spot for all genders. The main event is the 'After Tea T-Dance,' so folks head here after the Boatslip. Also hosts 'Women's Week' in October.

Crown & Anchor (www.onlyatthecrown.com; 247 Commercial St; ⊙hours vary) The queen of the scene, this multiwing complex has a nightclub, a video bar, a leather bar and a steamy cabaret that takes it to the limit.

Provincetown

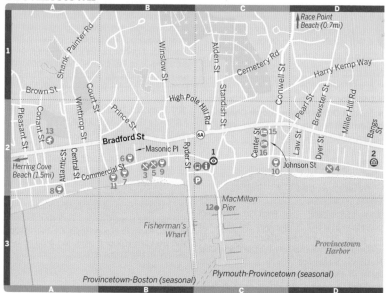

sprouts and cold beer. Take a seat at the communal picnic table on the sand. Devour.

ROSS' GRILL
AMERICAN, FRENCH $$
(☎508-487-8878; www.rossgrillptown.com; 237 Commercial St; sandwiches $10-15, mains $16-32; ☺11:30am-10:30pm daily May-Oct, 3-9pm Fri-Sun Nov-Apr; ☎) A much beloved hideaway tucked above Whalers Wharf, this casual bar and grill has spectacular views of the harbor, an impressive wine list and impeccable, traditional steaks and seafood. Regulars rave about the French onion soup, which could be a meal in and of itself. Large portions make dessert a challenge, but try to save room for banana-bread pudding.

★MEWS RESTAURANT & CAFE
MODERN AMERICAN $$$
(☎508-487-1500; www.mews.com; 429 Commercial St; bistro mains $13-22, restaurant $27-31; ☺5:30-10pm) A fantastic water view, the hottest martini bar in town and scrumptious food add up to Provincetown's finest dining scene. There are two sections: opt to dine gourmet on lobster risotto or roasted duck downstairs, where you're right on the sand; or go casual with a juicy Angus burger from the bistro menu upstairs.

HARBOR LOUNGE
COCKTAIL BAR
(www.theharborlounge.com; 359 Commercial St; ☺noon-10pm) The Harbor Lounge takes full advantage of its seaside setting, with floor-to-ceiling windows and a boardwalk stretching out into the bay. Candlelit tables and black leather sofas constitute the decor – nothing else is needed. The cocktails are surprisingly affordable, with many martini concoctions to sample.

AQUA BAR
BAR
(207 Commercial St; ☺10am-1am) Imagine a food court where the options include a raw bar, sushi, gelato and other international delights. Add a fully stocked bar with generous tenders pouring the drinks. Now put the whole place in a gorgeous seaside setting, overlooking a little beach and beautiful harbor. Now, imagine this whole scene at sunset. That's no fantasy, that's Aqua Bar.

🏃 ACTIVITIES

★DOLPHIN FLEET WHALE WATCH
WHALE-WATCHING
(☎800-826-9300; www.whalewatch.com; MacMillan Wharf; adult/child $46/31; ☺Apr-Oct; ⓘ) ⚲ Provincetown is the closest port to Stell-

DAY TRIPS FROM BOSTON PROVINCETOWN

PROVINCETOWN

◎ Sights

1 Commercial Street C2

2 Provincetown Art Association &
     Museum D2

◎ Eating

3 Canteen B2

4 Mews Restaurant & Cafe D2

5 Ross' Grill B2

◎ Drinking & Nightlife

6 A-House B2

7 Aqua Bar B2

8 Boatslip Resort A2

9 Crown & Anchor B2

10 Harbor Lounge C2

11 Pied Bar B2

◎ Sports & Activities

12 Dolphin Fleet Whale Watch C3

13 Ptown Bikes A2

◎ Sleeping

14 Cape Codder F3

15 Carpe Diem C2

16 Christopher's by the Bay C2

wagen Bank, the offshore feeding grounds of whales, dolphins and other sea creatures. This recommended outfit offers up to nine tours daily in peak season, each lasting three to four hours.

🛏 SLEEPING

Provincetown has a hundred or so delightful small inns and guesthouses lining Commercial St and the side roads. Most require reservations in summer, but inquire at the Chamber of Commerce if you arrive without a booking.

CAPE CODDER   MOTEL **$**

(☏508-487-0131; www.capecodderguests.com; 570 Commercial St; r $65-90; ⊘Apr-Nov; 🛜🐾🐕) Definitely think budget – this is a very simple place that makes no pretense at being anything more. There are four bathrooms shared between 14 rooms, no TVs or phones, and the occasional wall crack and threadbare bedspread. But for these prices in this town it's a steal. You can't beat the private beach and sundeck.

CHRISTOPHER'S BY THE BAY   B&B **$$**

(☏508-487-9263; www.christophersbythebay. com; 8 Johnson St; r with shared/private bathroom from $105/155; 🛜🐕) Tucked away on a quiet side street, this welcoming inn is a top-value option. Local art on the walls and personal recommendations from the owners add a homey Provincetown flavor. Rooms on the 2nd floor are the largest and snazziest, but the 3rd-floor rooms, which share a bathroom, get the ocean view.

★ CARPE DIEM   BOUTIQUE HOTEL **$$$**

(☏508-487-4242; www.carpediemguesthouse. com; 12 Johnson St; r incl breakfast $279-469; 🌼@🛜) Sophisticated yet relaxed, this boutique inn blends a soothing mix of smiling Buddhas, orchid sprays and artistic decor. Each guest room is inspired by a different gay literary genius; the room themed on poet Raj Rao, for example, has sumptuous embroidered fabrics and hand-carved Indian furniture. The on-site spa includes a Finnish sauna, hot tub and massage therapy.

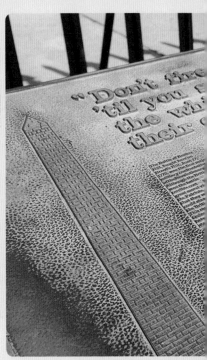

CHRISTIAN DELBERT/SHUTTERSTOCK ©

1. Old North Bridge, Concord (p167) **2.** Bunker Hill Monument (p53), Freedom Trail **3.** Boston Tea Party Ships & Museum (p132) **4.** George Washington Monument, Public Garden (p69)

JORGE SALCEDO/SHUTTERSTOCK ©

Revolutionary Boston

There's a good reason why Boston is called the birthplace of the American Revolution. Here, the Sons of Liberty railed against British policies of taxation without representation, the conflict's first blood was shed, and the 'shot heard around the world' launched a war that would spawn a nation.

Freedom Trail

Follow this 2.5-mile walking trail (p26) from the Boston Common to Bunker Hill to see where history unfolded – where protests were staged, battles were fought and heroes were lain to rest.

Boston Tea Party Ships

Protesting an unfair tax on tea, an angry mob of colonists dumped 342 crates of tea into the Boston Harbor in 1773. The **Boston Tea Party Ships & Museum** (p132) recalls the catalytic event, inviting visitors to participate in the protest and witness its aftermath.

Patriots' Day

On April 19, 1775, rebellious Minutemen stood up to British Regulars and sparked the first battles of the Revolution. Celebrated on the third Monday in April, Patriots' Day commemorates the event with historic re-enactments and parades (not to mention the Boston Marathon).

Lexington & Concord

The Minutemen first faced the Regulars at Lexington Common (now called Battle Green), and then later at the Old North Bridge in Concord. These sites and the surrounding countryside constitute the Minute Man National Historic Park – still peppered with contemporary buildings and packed with historical significance.

Sleeping

Boston offers a wide range of accommodations, from inviting guesthouses in historic quarters to swanky hotels with all the amenities. Considering that Boston is a city filled with students, there are surprisingly few accommodation options targeting budget travelers and backpackers.

Rates

Most hotels have no set rates. Instead, rates fluctuate seasonally, if not daily. High season is roughly defined as April through October, although prices are more accurately driven by occupancy and high-profile events. Holidays, university graduations, baseball games and pride parades all affect hotel prices. Often the most expensive period is from mid-September to mid-October.

Boutique Hotels

In recent years, Boston has become a hotspot for boutique hotels – small, stylish hotels, usually with personalized service and contemporary flair. The classiest boutique hotels are not cheap, but most offer competitive rates to attract tourists and businesspeople.

Budget Lodgings

Inexpensive accommodations are rare, but the savvy traveler should have no problem locating an acceptable option. Boston has only a few hostels catering to traditional backpacking travelers, but some guesthouses also offer simple accommodation and personal service at budget prices. There are also myriad options for staying in private homes, booked through services like airbnb and couchsurfing.

Apartments & B&Bs

Many B&Bs and inns are housed in historic or architecturally significant buildings. Contact B&Bs direct, or better yet, contact an agency that will try to match your neighborhood desires with the thickness of your wallet.

Accommodation Websites

Even the highest-end hotels post promotions and off-season sales on their websites. Several agencies manage B&Bs and apartments for short-term rental.

➡ **Lonely Planet** (lonelyplanet.com/usa/boston/hotels) Includes reviews and booking service.

➡ **B&B Agency of Boston** (www.boston-bnbagency.com) Fully furnished vacation rentals for daily, weekly or monthly let.

➡ **Bed & Breakfast Associates Bay Colony** (www.bnbboston.com) A huge database of unhosted, furnished rooms and apartments.

➡ **Inn Boston Reservations** (www.innbostonreservations.com) Studios and apartments for rent in Boston's best neighborhoods.

Longer-Term Rentals

With hordes of students and other transients moving around town, Boston, Brookline and Cambridge are full of summer sublets and longer-term apartments available to rent. Signs are often posted at coffee shops, bookstores and other student hang outs. University housing offices are also good sources of information.

➡ **Boston Apartments** (www.bostonapartments.com) Includes listings for long- and short-term, furnished and unfurnished, and a search by neighborhood.

➡ **Rental Beast** (www.rentalbeast.com) Rental properties all over town. Search by neighborhood or requirements.

Lonely Planet's Top Choices

Liberty Hotel (p181) You'll want to throw away the key.

Verb Hotel (p186) It needs to be said. This place rocks.

HI-Boston (p183) Sets the standard for urban hostels.

Gryphon House (p186) Indulge your senses at this gorgeous riverside brownstone.

Oasis Guest House (p185) Offers the best value for your midrange dollars.

Best by Budget

$

Friend Street Hostel (p181) Make some friends.

HI-Boston (p183) New in the heart of Chinatown.

40 Berkeley (p183) Lay your head in Boston's hip 'hood.

$$

Chandler Inn (p183) Fresh rooms offering excellent value.

Copley House (p184) Friendly, family-run guesthouse.

Oasis Guest House (p185) Homey urban oasis.

John Jeffries House (p182) Affordable suites.

$$$

Revere Hotel (p183) New and artistic in the Theater District.

XV Beacon (p182) Pinnacle of stylish luxury.

Inn @ St Botolph (p185) Affordable luxury, artful design.

Best Green Hotels

Seaport Boston Hotel (p186) Good Earthkeeping award winner.

Lenox Hotel (p185) Green trailblazer.

Hotel Marlowe (p188) Green Key certified.

HI-Boston (p183) LEED certified.

Irving House (p187) EPA Energy Star award winner.

Best for Families

Constitution Inn (p181) Attached to a giant play area.

Colonnade (p185) Rubber duckies and a rooftop pool.

Charles Hotel (p187) Smarty Pants package includes the Museum of Natural History.

Omni Parker House (p183) Kids receive fun-filled backpacks and cookies and milk.

Hotel Commonwealth (p186) Family package includes a tour of Fenway Park.

Best for Baseball Fans

Verb Hotel (p186) Tucked in behind Fenway Park.

Hotel Commonwealth (p186) Baseball packages.

Hotel Buckminster (p186) Views into the ballpark from some rooms.

Gryphon House (p186) Discounts for Sox ticket holders.

Best B&Bs

Gryphon House (p186) Beautiful riverside brownstone.

Clarendon Square Inn (p184) Victorian beauty.

Taylor House (p188) Sitting pretty Pondside.

La Cappella Suites (p181) North End original.

Encore (p183) Contemporary with a theatrical theme.

Truly Original

Green Turtle (p181) Drift off on a boat.

Liberty Hotel (p181) Spend the night in jail.

Verb Hotel (p186) Rock out.

NEED TO KNOW

Price Ranges
Prices quoted are for a double room in high season. Unless otherwise noted, rates include private bathroom, but exclude breakfast and tax.

$ less than $100
$$ $100 to $250
$$$ over $250

Taxes
Massachusetts levies a 5.7% hotel tax, while Boston levies a 6% hotel tax and a 2.75% convention-center fee, bringing your total tax to 14.45%. Note that there's no room tax on B&Bs with fewer than three rooms.

Tipping
It's customary to tip housekeeping $2 to $5 per day, depending on the standard of the accommodation. It's best to tip on a daily basis, as there might be different staff on duty.

SLEEPING

Where to Stay

Neighborhood	For	Against
Charlestown	Relatively affordable; neighborhood charm; great skyline views	Removed from city center; limited transportation options
West End & North End	Relatively affordable; close to major sights; convenient transportation to other neighborhoods; dining and shopping in North End	Few sleeping options in North End; desolate atmosphere in West End
Beacon Hill & Boston Common	Neighborhood charm; close proximity to major sights; great dining and shopping	Expensive
Downtown & Waterfront	Close to major sights and waterfront; convenient transportation to other neighborhoods; hustle-and-bustle atmosphere	Expensive; hustle-and-bustle city atmosphere (noisy, no neighborhood charm)
South End & Chinatown	Neighborhood charm; close proximity to major sights; convenient transportation to other neighborhoods; great dining, shopping and nightlife; hustle-and-bustle city atmosphere	Some areas can be dangerous for solo travelers and late-night revelers who are not cautious; hustle-and-bustle city atmosphere (noisy)
Back Bay	Neighborhood charm; close to major sights; convenient transportation to other neighborhoods; great dining, shopping and nightlife	None
Kenmore Square & Fenway	Close \to major sights; convenient transportation to other neighborhoods; great dining and nightlife	None
Seaport District & South Boston	Close proximity to airport and waterfront; great harbor and skyline views	Removed from city center; can feel desolate at night; limited transportation options
Cambridge	Neighborhood charm; close proximity to some sights; convenient transportation to other neighborhoods; great dining, shopping and nightlife	Removed from city center
Streetcar Suburbs	Relatively affordable; neighborhood charm; close to some sights; convenient transportation to other neighborhoods; great dining, shopping and nightlife	Removed from city center

🛏 Charlestown

CONSTITUTION INN   HOTEL $$

Map p229 (☑617-241-8400; www.constitution
inn.org; 150 Third Ave; d $209-219; 🅿⚹🚻🚗;
🚈93 from Haymarket, 🚢F4 from Long Wharf)
Housed in a granite building in the historic
Charlestown Navy Yard, this excellent, affordable hotel accommodates active and
retired military personnel, but you don't
have to have a crew cut to stay here. The
rooms are clean, crisp, modern and freshly
painted, and decorated with plain cherry
furniture; some have kitchenettes. Guests
gain free access to the fitness center.

GREEN TURTLE   B&B $$$

Map p229 (☑617-337-0202; www.greenturtlebb.
com; Pier 8, 13th St; r $260; 🅿⚹🛜; 🚢F4 from
Long Wharf) It's not just a B&B, but a floating
B&B. If you want to be lulled to sleep by the
sound of waves lapping and wake up to the
cry of seagulls, maybe you should be sleeping on a houseboat. The two contemporary
guest rooms are surprisingly spacious, complete with kitchenettes. Hot coffee and fresh
pastries are served in your room.

🛏 West End & North End

The North End's close-knit Italian community is not known for welcoming visitors –
for dinner, yes, but not to spend the night.
Save for one or two small places, all of the
accommodations are in the West End.

FRIEND STREET HOSTEL   HOSTEL $

Map p230 (☑617-248-8971; www.friend-
streethostel.com; 234 Friend St; dm $45-50;
@🛜; 🚈North Station) We believe them when
they say it's the friendliest hostel in Boston.
But there are other reasons to love this af-
fable hostelry, such as the spick-and-span
kitchen and the comfy common area with
the huge flatscreen TV. Sleeping six to 10
people each, dorm rooms have painted
brick walls, wide-plank wood floors and
bunk beds with thin mattresses.

LA CAPPELLA SUITES   B&B $$

Map p232 (☑617-523-9020; www.lacappellas-
uites.com; 290 North St; ste $170-225; ⚹🛜;
🚈Haymarket) 'La Cappella' refers to the
small chapel of La Societá di San Calogero
di Sciacca that previously occupied this
red-brick building. Now it is a private home

with three spacious guest suites on the upper floors, topped off by a shared roof deck.
Italian marble flooring, skyline views and
access to a kitchen and common areas.

★LIBERTY HOTEL   HOTEL $$$

Map p230 (☑617-224-4000; www.libertyhotel.
com; 215 Charles St; r from $375; 🅿⚹🚻🛜;
🚈Charles/MGH) It is with intended irony
that the notorious Charles Street Jail has
been converted into the luxurious Liberty
Hotel. Today, the spectacular lobby soars
under a 90ft ceiling. Guest rooms boast
floor-to-ceiling windows with amazing
views of the Charles River and Beacon Hill,
not to mention luxurious linens and high-
tech amenities such as LCD televisions and
iPod docking stations.

Off the lobby, there's a small exhibit on
the building's history. Over the years, the
jail housed many famous residents, including the anarchists Sacco and Vanzetti,
black liberationist Malcolm X and Boston's
own James Michael Curley.

BRICCO SUITES   APARTMENT $$$

Map p232 (☑617-248-6800; www.bricco.com;
241 Hanover St; d/ste from $259/299; 🚻🛜;
🚈Haymarket) Immerse yourself in the Italian American Boston experience with a
stay in a lovely, light-filled apartment in the
heart of the North End. The DePasquales
rent 15 studios and apartments – all of them
decked out with polished hardwood floors,
marble bathrooms, Italian linens and gas
fireplaces. There's no elevator, but it's worth
the climb.

ONYX HOTEL   BOUTIQUE HOTEL $$$

Map p230 (☑617-557-9955; www.onyxhotel.com;
155 Portland St; d $269-299; 🅿🚻🛜🚗; 🚈North
Station) 🐾 Done up in jewel tones and
contemporary furniture, the Onyx exudes
warmth and style – two elements that do not
always go hand in hand. Attractive features
of the hotel (a member of the Kimpton Hotel
Group) include morning car service and an
evening wine reception. 'Pet-friendly' goes
to a new level with gourmet doggy biscuits
and a dog-sitting service.

BOXER HOTEL   BOUTIQUE HOTEL $$$

Map p230 (☑617-624-0202; www.theboxer-
boston.com; 107 Merrimac St; r from $279;
🅿⚹@🛜🚗; 🚈North Station) Exemplifying
the up-and-coming character of this once-
downtrodden district, this new boutique
hotel occupies a fully restored 19th-century

flatiron building on the western edge of the Bulfinch Triangle. Design elements like open-frame wardrobes and plaid bedding exhibit a subtly masculine sophistication. Technology perks include Keurig coffee makers, iHomes and flatscreen TVs. Unfortunately, the staff are stretched pretty thin, which may result in some frustration.

🛏 Beacon Hill & Boston Common

JOHN JEFFRIES HOUSE
HOTEL $$

Map p234 (☏617-367-1866; www.johnjeffrieshouse.com; 14 David Mugar Way; s/d $135/164, ste $189-199; P✷❄; T Charles/MGH) Reproduction furnishings, original molding, hardwood floors and mahogany accents recall the era when Dr John Jeffries founded what is now the world-renowned Massachusetts Eye & Ear Infirmary. Many patients reside here when they come to town for treatment, as do travelers. Complimentary breakfast is served in the parlor, but you can also whip up your own meal in your in-room kitchenette.

XV BEACON
BOUTIQUE HOTEL $$$

Map p234 (☏617-670-1500; www.xvbeacon.com; 15 Beacon St; r from $355; P✷❄🍴; T Park St) Housed in a turn-of-the-20th-century beaux-arts building, XV Beacon sets the standard for Boston's boutique hotels. Guest-room decor is soothing, taking advantage of color schemes rich with taupe, espresso and cream. You'll find custommade gas fireplaces and built-in mahogany entertainment units, alongside heated towel racks and rainforest shower heads in the bathrooms, and romantic canopy beds dressed in Frette linens.

BEACON HILL HOTEL & BISTRO
BOUTIQUE HOTEL $$$

Map p234 (☏617-723-7575; www.beaconhillhotel.com; 25 Charles St; r $295-365, ste $425; P✷❄; T Charles/MGH) This upscale European-style inn blends into its namesake neighborhood without flash or fanfare. Carved out of former residential buildings typical of Beacon Hill, the hotel has 12 very small but stylish rooms, individually decorated with black-and-white photographs, louvered shutters and a designer's soothing palette of paint choices. Added perks include the exclusive roof deck, and complimentary breakfast at the urbane, on-site bistro.

🛏 Downtown & Waterfront

NINE ZERO
BOUTIQUE HOTEL $$$

Map p236 (☏617-772-5810; www.ninezero.com; 90 Tremont St; r from $309; P✷❄❄; T Park St) ⏺ This chic boutique hotel appeals to a broad audience, courting business travelers with a complimentary shoe-shine service and ergonomic workspace; active travelers with complimentary bikes and in-room yoga mats; and animal lovers with Kimpton's signature pet service. All of the above enjoy excellent customer service and marvelous views of the State House and the Granary from the upper floors.

INTERCONTINENTAL HOTEL
HOTEL $$$

Map p236 (☏617-747-1000; www.intercontinentalboston.com; 510 Atlantic Ave; r from $325; P✷❄❄; T South Station) ⏺ The Inter-Continental has it going on. Service is on point. The rooms are sumptuous and sophisticated. And the location – perched on the edge of the Seaport District – is ideal. You'll pay more for a water view, but what a water view! The marble bathrooms alone are worth the price of staying in this first-class hotel.

AMES HOTEL
BOUTIQUE HOTEL $$$

Map p236 (☏617-979-8100; www.ameshotel.com; 1 Court St; r from $309; P✷❄; T State) It's easy to miss this understated hotel, tucked behind the granite facade of the historic Ames Building (Boston's first skyscraper). Starting in the lobby and extending to the guest rooms, the style is elegant but eclectic, artfully blending modern minimalism and old-fashioned ornamental details. The upper floors yield wonderful views over the city.

HARBORSIDE INN
BOUTIQUE HOTEL $$$

Map p236 (☏617-723-7500; www.harborsideinn-boston.com; 185 State St; r from $269; P✷@❄; T Aquarium) Steps from Faneuil Hall and the waterfront, this boutique hotel inhabits a respectfully renovated 19th-century mercantile warehouse. The 116 rooms are on the small side, but comfortable and appropriately nautically themed. Note that Atrium Rooms face the atrium (ahem) and Cabin Rooms have no windows at all. Add $20 for a city view (worth it).

MILLENNIUM
BOSTONIAN HOTEL   HOTEL $$$
Map p236 (☑617-523-3600; www.millennium-hotels.com; 26 North St; d from $250; P☀☏; ⊤Haymarket) The Bostonian proudly touts its roots as part of the Blackstone Block, the city's oldest block. From the moment you enter the cool, contemporary lobby, to the time you step out onto your balcony overlooking the bustle of Haymarket, you'll appreciate this hotel's singular position. All-new rooms feature high-def TVs, Frette linens and other luxuries.

OMNI PARKER HOUSE   HISTORIC HOTEL $$$
Map p236 (☑617-227-8600; www.omnihotels.com; 60 School St; r from $359; P☀@☏; ⊤Park St) History and Parker House go hand in hand like JFK and Jackie O (who got engaged here). Malcolm X was a busboy here; Ho Chi Minh was a pastry chef here; and Boston cream pie, the official state dessert, was created here. The lovely guest rooms are decorated in rich red and gold tones and equipped with all the high-tech gadgetry.

🛏 South End & Chinatown

All of the accommodation options are located in the South End and the Theater District (although isn't it nice to have Chinatown nearby when you get the munchies at 2am?).

HI-BOSTON   HOSTEL $
Map p242 (☑617-536-9455; www.bostonhostel.org; 19 Stuart St; dm $55-65, d $199; ☀@☏; ⊤Chinatown or Boylston) 🍃 HI-Boston sets the standard for urban hostels, with its new, ecofriendly facility in the historic Dill Building. Purpose-built rooms are comfortable and clean, as are the shared bathrooms. Community spaces are numerous, from fully equipped kitchen to trendy ground-floor cafe, and there's a whole calendar of activities on offer. The place is large, but it books out, so reserve in advance.

40 BERKELEY   HOSTEL $
Map p240 (☑617-375-2524; www.40berkeley.com; 40 Berkeley St; s/d/tr/q from $95/103/121/130; ☏; ⊤Back Bay) Straddling the South End and Back Bay, this safe, friendly hostelry was the first YWCA in the country. It's no longer a Y, but it still rents some 200 basic rooms (some overlooking the lovely garden) to guests on a nightly and long-term basis. Bathrooms are shared, as are other useful facilities including the telephone, library, TV room and laundry.

★ENCORE   B&B $$
Map p240 (☑617-247-3425; www.encorebandb.com; 116 W Newton St; r $230-270; P☀☏; ⊤Back Bay) If you love the theater, or if you love innovative contemporary design, or if you just love creature comforts and warm hospitality, you will love Encore. Co-owned by an architect and a set designer, this 19th-century South End town house sets a stage for both of their passions.

Exposed brick walls are adorned with exotic masks, interesting art and theatrical posters; bold colors and contemporary furniture pieces furnish the spacious guest rooms. All three rooms have a sitting area or private deck that offers a sweet skyline view. Continental breakfast included.

CHANDLER INN   HOTEL $$
Map p240 (☑617-482-3450; www.chandlerinn.com; 26 Chandler St; r from $179; ☀☏; ⊤Back Bay) Small but sleek rooms show off a designer's touch, giving them a sophisticated, urban glow. Travelers appreciate the plasma TVs and iPod docks, all of which come at relatively affordable prices. As a bonus, congenial staff provide super service. Across the street, the inn rents out 11 newly renovated, modern apartments of various sizes, under the moniker **Chandler Studios** (Map p240; www.chandlerstudiosboston.com; 54 Berkeley St; ste from $269; ☀☏; ⊤Back Bay).

MILNER HOTEL   HOTEL $$
Map p242 (☑617-453-1731, 617-426-6220; www.milner-hotels.com; 78 Charles St S; s/d from $159/179; P☏☒; ⊤Boylston) Mr Milner said it himself back in 1918: 'A bed and a bath for a buck and a half.' Prices have gone up since then, but the Milner Hotel still offers excellent value for this central location. Itinerant actors and international travelers frequent this affordable Theater District hostelry, which offers threadbare rooms with passable decor. The price includes a continental breakfast.

REVERE HOTEL   DESIGN HOTEL $$$
Map p242 (☑617-482-1800; www.revereho-tel.com; 200 Stuart St; d from $379; P☀☏; ⊤Boylston) It's hard to enter the circular lobby without contemplating the centerpiece Serra-inspired sculpture. But that's just the beginning of the artistic flare at the

Revere Hotel, as the rooms are replete with furniture, light fixtures and other contemporary design elements that marry form and function. City views are wonderful, especially from the rooftop lounge.

CLARENDON SQUARE INN B&B $$$

Map p240 (☑617-536-2229; www.clarendonsquare.com; 198 W Brookline St; d $298; P❋☎; T Prudential) Located on a quiet residential street in the South End, this completely renovated brownstone is a designer's dream. Guest room details might include Italian marble wainscoting, French limestone floors, a silver-leaf barrel-vaulted ceiling or a hand-forged iron-and-porcelain washbasin. Common areas are decadent (for example, the roof-deck hot tub); continental breakfast is served in the paneled dining room and butler's pantry.

🛏 Back Bay

★NEWBURY GUEST HOUSE GUESTHOUSE $$

Map p244 (☑617-437-7666, 617-437-7668; www.newburyguesthouse.com; 261 Newbury St; d from $209; P❋☎; T Hynes or Copley) Dating to 1882, these three interconnected brick and brownstone buildings offer a prime location in the heart of Newbury St. A recent renovation has preserved the charming features like ceiling medallions and in-room fireplaces, but now the rooms feature clean lines, luxurious linens and modern amenities. Each morning, a complimentary continental breakfast is laid out next to the marble fireplace in the salon.

CHARLESMARK HOTEL BOUTIQUE HOTEL $$

Map p244 (☑617-247-1212; www.thecharlesmark.com; 655 Boylston St; r $219-269; P❋☎; T Copley) The Charlesmark's small but sleek rooms are at the crossroads of European style and functionality. The design is classic modernism, and the effect is upscale, urbane and relatively affordable. This hip hotel is backed by a small group of warmly efficient staff that see to every detail. The downstairs lounge spills out onto the sidewalk where the people-watching is tops. Complimentary continental breakfast.

COPLEY HOUSE APARTMENT $$

Map p244 (☑617-236-8300; www.copleyhouse.com; 239 W Newton St; s/d from $135/165; ❋☎; T Prudential) Copley House occupies four different buildings, straddling Back Bay

and the South End. A judicious use of antique wood and big windows beaming with light make this Queen Anne–style inn a place of respite, while the location makes it a handy base of operations for exploring Boston. The simple kitchenette rooms are not large, but they offer exceptional value.

COMMONWEALTH COURT
GUEST HOUSE GUESTHOUSE $$

Map p244 (☑617-424-1230; www.commonwealthcourt.com; 284 Commonwealth Ave; r $99-140, per week $400-600; ❋; T Hynes) These 20 rooms with kitchenettes are not super spiffy, but the price is right for this great location. The Euro-style guesthouse is located in a turn-of-the-20th-century brownstone in the heart of Back Bay. Once a private residence, it retains a homey feel and lots of lavish architectural details.

The service is pleasant, but not overly attentive (maid service occurs only twice a week and the office closes in the evenings).

COPLEY INN GUESTHOUSE $$

Map p244 (☑617-236-0300, 617-232-0306; www.copleyinn.com; 19 Garrison St; r $195; T Prudential) This sweet old brownstone is tucked into the residential streets behind Copley Place: it's about as close as you can get to Newbury St while preserving the sense that you're nesting in a slightly quieter neighborhood. Equipped with kitchens and queen-size beds, rooms in this four-story walk-up are relatively roomy, if a bit plain.

463 BEACON STREET
GUEST HOUSE GUESTHOUSE $$

Map p244 (☑617-536-1302; www.463beacon.com; 463 Beacon St; d without/with bathroom from $149/199; P❋☎; T Hynes) This Back Bay brownstone (c 1880) is showing its age, but at least it retains architectural frolics, like a spiral staircase, wrought-iron filigrees and high ceilings. Rooms vary in size and decor, but some of the fancier ones feature hardwood floors and ornamental fireplaces. Daily maid service is not offered. Some bathrooms are cramped – hopefully you won't be spending too much time in there.

MIDTOWN HOTEL MOTEL $$

Map p244 (☑617-262-1000; www.midtownhotel.com; 220 Huntington Ave; r $199-259; P❋☎🏊☎; T Symphony) This low-rise motel looks like it belongs beside a highway instead of in the shadow of the Prudential

Center, but its spacious rooms fill up with families and tour groups because the price is right and the location is unbeatable. The service is friendly and efficient.

INN @ ST BOTOLPH
BOUTIQUE HOTEL $$$

Map p244 (☑617-236-8099; www.innatstbotolph. com; 99 St Botolph St; ste $315-390; P❄☎; T Prudential) Whimsical but wonderful, this delightful brownstone boutique emphasizes affordable luxury. Spacious, light-filled rooms feature bold patterns and contemporary decor, fully equipped kitchens, and all the high-tech bells and whistles. Foreshadowing a coming trend, the hotel keeps prices down by offering 'edited service,' with virtual check-in, keyless entry and 'touch-up' housekeeping, minimizing the need for costly staff. Free continental breakfast.

COLLEGE CLUB
GUESTHOUSE $$$

Map p244 (☑617-536-9510; www.thecollege-clubofboston.com; 44 Commonwealth Ave; s without bathroom from $179, d with bathroom $259-289; ❄☎; T Arlington) Originally a private club for female college graduates, the College Club has 11 spacious rooms with high ceilings, now open to both sexes. Period details – typical of the area's Victorian brownstones – include claw-foot tubs, ornamental fireplaces and bay windows. Local designers have lent their skills to decorate the various rooms, with delightful results. Prices include a continental breakfast.

COLONNADE
HOTEL $$$

Map p244 (☑617-424-7000; www.colonnade-hotel.com; 120 Huntington Ave; r from $329; P❄☎🖥; T Prudential) ✐ There are many reasons to stay at the Colonnade, such as its handsome guest rooms, which are well equipped with both high-tech gadgetry and simple pleasures (like a rubber duck in your bathtub). There's the VIPets program, complete with fluffy beds and walking services. And of course there's the excellent dining and the fabulous location.

But the real reason to stay at the Colonnade is the rooftop pool, or RTP, as it's known. A glamorous place to see and be seen in your bikini, it's also optimal for al fresco dining, sunbathing and even swimming. Open to nonguests weekdays only.

LOEWS HOTEL
HOTEL $$$

Map p244 (☑617-266-7200; www.loewshotels. com; 154 Berkeley St; r from $368; P❄☎🖥; T Back Bay) Perched on the border of Back Bay and the South End, this stunner is housed in the former Boston Police Headquarters. The recent renovation resulted in luxurious rooms done in blues and browns and beiges, furnished with pillow-top beds, high-tech gadgetry and sweet serenity.

LENOX HOTEL
HISTORIC HOTEL $$$

Map p244 (☑617-536-5300; www.lenoxhotel. com; 61 Exeter St; r $315-365; P❄☎; T Copley) ✐ For three generations, the Saunders family has run this gem in Back Bay. And while the atmosphere is a tad old-world, you don't have to forgo modern conveniences to live with that ethos. Guest rooms are comfortably elegant (with chandeliers and crown molding), without being stuffy. If your pockets are deep enough, it's worth splurging for a junior suite, as they boast the best views.The Lenox is a pioneer in green hospitality, implementing hundreds of initiatives to reduce its impact on the environment.

COPLEY SQUARE HOTEL
HOTEL $$$

Map p244 (☑617-225-7062, 617-536-9000; www. copleysquarehotel.com; 47 Huntington Ave; r $269-319; P❄☎; T Copley or Back Bay) The Copley Square Hotel is downright sumptuous, with gorgeous contemporary rooms decorated in muted tones of taupe and gray, with subtle lines and soft fabrics. Flatscreen TVs and iPod docks are de rigueur. The morning coffee bar and afternoon Wine Down are lovely perks.

HOTEL 140
HOTEL $$$

Map p244 (☑617-585-5440; www.hotel140.com; 140 Clarendon St; r from $239; P❄@☎; T Copley or Back Bay) Once a hidden hotel bargain, Hotel 140 has gone upscale with a complete overhaul of its classic brick building. It still feels like a budget hotel in the hallways, but step into the small but stylish rooms, filled with light, and you'll forget about that. Despite all the upgrades, the best thing about this place is still the friendly staff.

🛏 Kenmore Square & Fenway

OASIS GUEST HOUSE & ADAMS B&B
GUESTHOUSE $$

Map p247 (☑617-230-0105, 617-267-2262; www. oasisguesthouse.com; 22 Edgerly Rd; s/d without bathroom $109/149, r with bathroom from $189; P❄☎; T Hynes or Symphony) These homey side-by-side (jointly managed) guesthouses offer a peaceful, pleasant oasis in the midst of Boston's chaotic city streets. Thirty-odd guest rooms occupy four attractive, brick, bow-front town houses on this tree-lined lane. The modest, light-filled rooms are tastefully and traditionally decorated, most with queen beds, floral quilts and nondescript prints. The common living room does not exactly encourage lingering, but outdoor decks and kitchen facilities are nice touches. Free continental breakfast.

HOTEL BUCKMINSTER   HOTEL $$
Map p247 (✆617-727-2825; www.bostonhotel-buckminster.com; 645 Beacon St; r from $220; P❊❋☎❄; ⊤Kenmore) Designed by the architect of the Boston Public Library, the Buckminster is a convergence of Old Boston charm and affordable elegance. It offers nearly 100 rooms and suites of varying shapes and sizes. They're not going to win any design awards, but they have all the tools and toys of comfort and convenience. Pay more for Fenway views.

★VERB HOTEL   BOUTIQUE HOTEL $$$
Map p247 (✆855-695-6678; www.theverbhotel.com; 1271 Boylston St; r from $250; P❊❋☎❄; ⊤Kenmore) The Verb Hotel took a down-and-out HoJo property and turned it into Boston's most radical, retro, rock and roll hotel. The style is mid-century modern; the theme is music. Memorabilia is on display throughout the joint, with a jukebox cranking out tunes in the lobby. Classy, clean-lined rooms face the swimming pool or Fenway Park. A-plus for service and style.

★GRYPHON HOUSE   B&B $$$
Map p247 (✆617-375-9003; www.innboston.com; 9 Bay State Rd; r $225-275; P❊☎; ⊤Kenmore) A premier example of Richardson Romanesque, this beautiful five-story brownstone is a paradigm of artistry and luxury overlooking the picturesque Charles River. Eight spacious suites have different styles, including Victorian, Gothic and Arts and Crafts, but they all have 19th-century period details. And they all have home-away-from-home perks such as entertainment centers, wet bars and gas fireplaces. Prices include a delicious breakfast.

HOTEL COMMONWEALTH   HOTEL $$$
Map p247 (✆617-933-5000, 617-784-4000; www.hotelcommonwealth.com; 500 Commonwealth Ave; r $389-439; P❊☎; ⊤Kenmore) Set amid Commonwealth Ave's brownstones and

just steps away from Fenway Park, this independent luxury hotel enjoys prime real estate. Spacious Commonwealth rooms are more like suites, with king-size beds and two LCD TVs. Fenway rooms are slightly smaller, but they do offer a view into the ballpark. Guests can enjoy the amazing services and amenities, which range from turn-down service to iPods and PlayStations.

ELIOT HOTEL   BOUTIQUE HOTEL $$$
Map p247 (✆617-267-1607; www.eliothotel.com; 370 Commonwealth Ave; r $285-345; P❊❋☎❄; ⊤Hynes) Akin to a small London hotel, the Eliot offers posh quarters, furnished in English chintz and Queen Anne mahogany; bathroom walls are dressed with Italian marble. Other upscale amenities include plush terry robes and down duvets, complimentary shoe-shine service and turn-down service. Two acclaimed restaurants are on the 1st floor.

🛏 Seaport District & South Boston

With the opening of the Boston Convention & Exhibition Center, this district has become a hotbed of hotel development. It's a bit removed from the action unless you are actually attending an event at the convention center, but it's nirvana for seafood eaters and art connoisseurs. Bonus: it's also an easy trip from the airport.

RESIDENCE INN MARRIOTT   BOUTIQUE HOTEL $$$
Map p239 (✆617-478-0840; www.residenceinn.com/bosfp; 370 Congress St; r $349-399; P❊☎; ⊒SL1 or SL2, ⊤South Station) This is not your typical Marriott. Housed in a historic, brick warehouse, this boutique hotel now features an old-style atrium and glass elevators leading up to spectacular, spacious suites. Twelve-foot ceilings and enormous windows are in every room, as is a floor-to-ceiling cityscape mural. King-size beds, fully equipped kitchens and up-to-date gadgetry ensure optimal comfort and convenience.

SEAPORT BOSTON HOTEL   HOTEL $$$
Map p239 (✆617-385-4000; www.seaportboston.com; 1 Seaport Lane; r $239-379; P❊☎❄❋; ⊒SL1 or SL2, ⊤South Station) 🌿 With glorious views of the Boston Harbor, this business hotel is up-to-snuff when it

comes to high-tech amenities (eg automatic motion-sensitive lights so you never have to enter a dark room, and privacy/service lights instead of the old-fashioned 'Do Not Disturb' signs). Soothing tones, plush linens and robes, and a unique no-tipping policy guarantee a relaxing retreat.

🛌 Cambridge

KENDALL HOTEL   BOUTIQUE HOTEL $$
Map p252 (📞617-566-1300; www.kendallhotel. com; 350 Main St; r $198-248; P ❄ 🛜; T Kendall/MIT) Once the Engine 7 Firehouse, this city landmark is now a cool and classy all-American hotel. The 65 guest rooms exhibit a firefighter riff, alongside the requisite creature comforts. The place could use some extra help at the front desk, but at least there's no scrimping at the breakfast table. Indeed, the on-site Black Sheep restaurant is worth visiting for lunch or dinner, too.

IRVING HOUSE   GUESTHOUSE $$
Map p250 (📞617-547-4600; www.irvinghouse. com; 24 Irving St; s/d without bathroom $135/165, r with bathroom from $185; P ❄ @ 🛜; T Harvard) 🏖 Call it a big inn or a homey hotel, this property welcomes the world-weariest of travelers. The 44 rooms range in size, but every bed is covered with a quilt and big windows let in plenty of light. There is a bistro-style atmosphere in the brick-lined basement, where you can browse the books on hand, plan your travels or munch on free continental breakfast.

HARDING HOUSE   INN $$
Map p252 (📞617-876-2888; www.harding-house.com; 288 Harvard St; r without bathroom $155-165, with bathroom $210-260; P ❄ @ 🛜; T Central) This treasure brilliantly blends refinement and comfort, artistry and efficiency. Old wooden floors toss back a warm glow and sport throw rugs. Antique furnishings complete the inviting atmosphere. Noise does travel in this old house, but the place is quite comfortable. Other perks: free parking (!), a thoughtfully designed continental breakfast and complimentary museum passes.

A FRIENDLY INN   GUESTHOUSE $$
Map p250 (📞617-547-7851; www.afinow.com; 1673 Cambridge St; r $97-197; P ❄ 🛜; T Harvard) While this Victorian-era inn gets

mixed reviews, nobody disputes that it is indeed 'a friendly inn.' Service is accommodating and efficient, offering a clean and quiet respite for budget travelers. The old maxim holds true, however: you get what you pay for. Be prepared to sleep in cramped quarters and to forgo the fancypants amenities you may find at an upscale hotel.

A continental breakfast is included, but you may want to head to the cafe down the street for your morning meal.

HOTEL VERITAS   BOUTIQUE HOTEL $$$
Map p250 (📞617-520-5000; www.thehotelveritas.com; 1 Remington St; r from $329; P ❄ 🛜; T Harvard) Most guests agree that the super-chic design and top-notch service more than make up for the small size of the rooms at this Harvard Sq newcomer. Rich fabrics, shimmering textures and local artwork adorn the rooms. Dressed to the nines in Brooks Brothers uniforms, the Veritas team does whatever it takes to ensure a satisfying and truly special experience.

CHARLES HOTEL   HOTEL $$$
Map p250 (📞617-864-1200; www.charleshotel. com; 1 Bennett St; r from $349; P ❄ 🛜 🏊; T Harvard) 'Simple, Stylish, Smart.' Harvard Sq's most illustrious hotel lives up to its motto. Overlooking the Charles River, this institution has hosted the university's most esteemed guests, ranging from Bob Barker to the Dalai Lama. Design at the Charles – including rooms and restaurants – is surprisingly sleek, but the facilities do not lack the luxuries and amenities one would expect from a highly rated hotel.

HARVARD SQUARE HOTEL   HOTEL $$$
Map p250 (📞617-864-5200; www.harvards-quarehotel.com; 110 Mt Auburn St; d $239-319; P ❄ @ 🛜; T Harvard) After a long overdue renovation, the square's namesake hotel is looking fine. Brand new rooms feature bold patterns and warm colors, with oversize photos of local sites adorning the walls. Large windows offer excellent views of the surrounding square. The location – smack dab in the middle of Harvard Sq – is pretty unbeatable

ROYAL SONESTA   HOTEL $$$
Map p252 (📞617-806-4200; www.sonesta.com; 40 Edwin Land Blvd; r $239-359; P ❄ 🛜 🏊; T Science Park) After a recent renovation, the Royal Sonesta now sports smallish

rooms with a sharp black-and-white motif. Those facing the river yield some of the most expansive city views around. Besides the luxurious rooms and up-to-date amenities, there's an incredible contemporary art collection on display throughout the public spaces, including the awesome ArtBar.

The Royal Sonesta overlooks the river in East Cambridge, just around the corner from the Museum of Science.

HOTEL MARLOWE   BOUTIQUE HOTEL **$$$**

Map p252 (☑617-825-7140; www.hotelmarlowe. com; 25 Edwin Land Blvd; d $249-349; ℗※⊕⊛; ⊤Lechmere or Science Park) ✐ The Kimpton Hotel Group's flagship property in the Boston area, just steps from the Charles River, embodies chic and unique, as this organization always tries to do. Perks include down comforters, Sony PlayStations and the *New York Times* delivered to your door – enough to please everyone.

Hotel Marlowe is in East Cambridge, steps from the Museum of Science and just across the bridge from the West End.

Streetcar Suburbs

The streetcar suburbs are a sweet retreat if the city makes you feel claustrophobic. Grand elm trees shade the wide green lawns and gracious mansions, and a short ride on the T brings you into town.

★TAYLOR HOUSE   B&B **$$**

Map p255 (☑617-983-9334; www.taylorhouse. com; 50 Burroughs St; s $165-179, d $189-209, ste $239-369; ℗※⊛; ⊤Green St) Sitting pretty pond-side in Jamaica Plain, this gracious Italianate Victorian mansion has undergone a loving restoration – apparent from the ornamental details throughout the house and the gorgeous gardens outside. The spacious guest rooms have dark polished-wood floors, sleigh beds, bold contemporary art and plenty of sunshine. The suites are in the carriage house behind. Dave is your decorator, designer and amazing host.

BERTRAM INN   B&B **$$**

Map p254 (☑617-295-3822, 617-566-2234; www.bertraminn.com; 92 Sewall Ave; r $189-219; ℗※⊕⊛; ⊤St Paul) Brookline's tree-lined streets shelter this dreamy, Arts and Crafts–style inn, located only a quick jaunt from downtown Boston. A quiet elegance is accented with beautifully carved oak pan-

els, leaded windows and, if you play your cards right, a working fireplace in your room. Amenities and services match those of high-end hotels.

The same owners run the **Samuel Sewall Inn** (☑617-713-0123; www.samuelsewall inn.com; 143 St Paul Ave) across the street – an exquisitely restored Victorian with even more rooms. Both places boast tree-shaded patios, a full gourmet breakfast and a location a heartbeat from the Hub of the Universe.

LONGWOOD INN   GUESTHOUSE **$$**

Map p254 (☑617-566-8615; www.longwood-inn. com; 123 Longwood Ave; r $144-164, ste $174; ℗※⊛; ⊤Coolidge Corner) This big old Victorian mansion is in an odd location midway between Coolidge Corner and Longwood. Affordable rates (including cheaper weekly rates) attract many long-term guests, especially folks working in the nearby medical district. Simple rooms have an old-fashioned charm, with floral bedspreads and antique furniture. The cheapest rooms have detached private bathrooms. Reception closes at 9pm.

BEECH TREE INN   B&B **$$**

Map p254 (☑617-227-1620; www.thebeech-treeinn.com; 83 Longwood Ave; s/d without bathroom $129/159, d with bathroom $189-199; ℗※@⊛; ⊤Longwood) This turn-of-the-20th-century Victorian home contains 10 guest rooms, each individually decorated with period furnishings and wallpaper, ornamental fireplaces with hand-painted screens, floral quilts and lacy curtains. Common areas include a cozy parlor and a patio. It's a romantic return to yesteryear, on a quiet residential street not far from Coolidge Corner and the Back Bay Fens. Breakfast included.

ANTHONY'S TOWN HOUSE   GUESTHOUSE **$$**

Map p254 (☑617-566-3972; www.anthonystown-house.com; 1085 Beacon St; r with shared bathroom from $125; ※⊛; ⊤Hawes St) Halfway between Coolidge Corner and Kenmore Sq, this family-operated guesthouse puts the rolled 'r' in rococo. With more frills and flourishes than should be allowed in one place at one time, the Victorian-era brownstone is downright girly. The 10 rooms are spacious and comfortable and filled with antiques and lacy linens. Affable owners and cheap rates attract plenty of repeat visitors. Cash only!

Understand Boston

Boston Today

Boston is at a turning point. Major urban development projects have been completed, neighborhoods have been transformed, the waterfronts are sparkling and the cityscape looks fantastic. Boston is thriving economically. There's a new mayor at the helm – and he's thinking big. Predictably, the challenges facing Boston are also big. That's okay...we need something to grumble about.

Best on Film

The Verdict (1982) Paul Newman as a Boston lawyer.

Good Will Hunting (1997) Put Southie on the Hollywood map.

Next Stop Wonderland (1997) Heartwarming independent film with a bossa nova soundtrack.

The Departed (2006) Suspense-filled mob movie that won Best Picture.

John Adams (2008) Critically acclaimed TV series chronicling the life and times of the second US president.

Best in Print

The Scarlet Letter (Nathaniel Hawthorne; 1850) Hypocrisy and malice in Puritan New England.

The Given Day (Dennis Lehane; 2008) A suspense-filled historical novel, following two families through the turmoil of post–WWI Boston.

Interpreter of the Maladies (Jhumpa Lahiri; 1999) A Pulitzer Prize–winner that addresses the challenges of migration and multiculturalism.

The Friends of Eddie Coyle (George Higgins, 1972) A crime novel that provides a crash course in the Boston dialect.

Infinite Jest (David Foster Wallace; 1996) A 1000-page tome that is at once philosophical and satirical.

Changing of the Guard

After serving five terms for a total of 20 years, Thomas Menino stepped down as the mayor of Boston in 2014. Menino was Boston's longest-serving mayor, credited with reviving neighborhoods, taking a stand for LGBT rights and greening the city. The 'mayor for life' died later that same year.

The current mayor, Marty Walsh, has big shoes to fill. A Dorchester native and Boston College graduate, Walsh served in the Massachusetts House of Representative for 13 years before being elected mayor. While campaigning, Walsh promised to turn Boston into a 24-hour city. To that end, Bostonians can now ride the T until 2am on weekends. Thanks, Mr Mayor!

Also in 2014, Deval Patrick declined to run for reelection as the Governor of Massachusetts, after two terms in office. The Commonwealth's first African American governor, Patrick's legacy includes improvements in education, an overhaul of the Department of Transportation and the introduction of casino gaming. His successor is Republican Charlie Baker.

Taking a Gamble

In 2011, the Massachusetts legislature passed a law that would allow the establishment of three resort-style casinos and one slot parlor in the Commonwealth. Although casino gaming promises jobs and revenue, it is not without detractors; but a statewide referendum failed to repeal the legislation.

Among the sites selected for the gaming facilities is Everett, an industrial city, largely populated by immigrants, four miles north of Boston. The gambling giant Wynn Resorts has promised to clean up a former industrial wasteland on the Mystic River and transform the site into a casino resort. The development has been mired in controversy, not least because a convicted felon is among its owners (prohibited by the Massachusetts Gaming Commission). More importantly, the development has been condemned by surrounding towns – including Boston – which anticipate sharing the ill effects (if not the benefits) of a large casino resort.

Riding that Train

The winter of 2015 was tough on Bostonians. It wasn't just the 105in of snow that fell – most of it within 30 days. It wasn't only the shortage of street parking, causing neighbors to claim public parking spaces, leave threatening notes and even vandalize others' cars. The kicker was when the T shut down – for days at a time – for snow cleanup and track de-icing.

Shutting down service was perhaps better than the alternative. Delayed service, stranded trains and even forced evacuations were recurring problems for much of the winter. Commuters tweeted their horror stories under #MBTApocalypse. The MBTA's poor performance during 'Snowmageddon' led to the resignation of General Manager Beverly Scott.

The extreme weather highlighted longer-term problems with the century-old transportation system. Aging train cars (some nearly 50 years old) and outdated power and signaling systems are just the beginning of the list of maintenance issues requiring attention. Unfortunately, the underfunded transportation agency does not have the finances to address these problems, partly due to existing debt. Even Scott cited protracted underinvestment in maintenance as a source of the MBTA's performance problems.

With the arrival of spring, the snow melted and the parking spaces reappeared. But the MBTA remains quite broken – and nobody is sure how to fix it. One Charlestown man launched a GoFundMe campaign to raise $30 billion to modernize Boston's transit. That would be a good start.

Bidding on the Future

Boston has been selected as the US candidate-city for the 2024 summer Olympic games (www.boston2024. org). A successful bid would transform the city, with the creation of an Olympic Blvd along the Fort Point Channel, an Olympic Park along the South Boston waterfront and an Athlete's Village further south at Columbia Point. Not surprisingly, Boston 2024 has inspired a vocal and active opposition movement; No Boston Olympics (www.nobostonolympics.org) argues that the city should not divert its resources from more essential priorities like education and transportation.

Whether or not Boston is chosen as an Olympic host – a decision that will be made by the International Olympic Commission in 2017 – the city is likely to see some initial investment and hear lots of heated discussion in the coming years.

if Boston were 100 people

47 would be Non-Hispanic Whites
22 would be Black or African American
18 would be Hispanic or Latino
9 would be Asian
2 would be two or more races
2 would be other

Educational attainment
(% of population)

High school not completed | High school degree | Bachelor's degree

Some college or associate's degree | Graduate or professional degree

population per sq mile

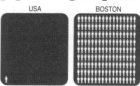

USA   BOSTON

↑ ≈ 87 people

History

In 1614 English explorer Captain John Smith, at the behest of the future King Charles I, set sail to assess the New World's commercial opportunities. Braving the frigid North Atlantic, the plucky explorer reached the rocky coast of present-day Maine and made his way southward to Cape Cod, making contact with the native population, mapping the coastline and dubbing the region 'New England.' Smith noted a tricapped hilly peninsula, connected to the mainland by a narrow neck across a shallow back bay, and with an excellent harbor fed by three rivers. Valued for its freshwater spring, the region was known to the natives as Shawmut.

The Shawmut Peninsula

Prior to the 17th century, there were as many as 100,000 native inhabitants of New England, mostly of the Algonquan nation, organized into small regional tribes that variously cooperated and quarreled with one another.

Before England's religious outcasts (the Puritans) showed up, local natives were already acquainted with Portuguese fishermen, French fur traders, Dutch merchants and Jesuit missionaries. The Europeans were welcomed as a source of valued goods, but they were also feared. In the Great Sadness of 1616–17, a smallpox epidemic devastated the native population, reducing it by three-quarters.

English colonial coastal encampments quickly spread, as seemingly unoccupied lands were claimed for king and commodity. According to John Winthrop, the first governor of the colony, 'God hath hereby cleared our title to this place.'

In 1675 Chief Metacomet, son of the famed Massasoit who befriended the starving Pilgrims, organized a desperate last stand against the ever-encroaching English. Known as King Philip to the settlers, he terrorized the frontier for more than a year before he was finally ambushed and killed. The chief's body was drawn and quartered and his heathen head perched on a pole, while his son was sold into slavery. In less than a hundred years, disease, war and forced migration had reduced the indigenous population by 90%.

TIMELINE	1614	1629	1630
	English explorer Captain John Smith surveys the coast of Maine and Massachusetts. He recounts the journey in his *Description of New England*.	The shareholders of the Massachusetts Bay Colony sign the Cambridge Agreement, which allows the Puritans to govern the colony and to answer only to the king.	Led by Governor John Winthrop, Puritan settlers flee the repressive Church of England and move to the theocratic Massachusetts Bay Colony.

Mission from God

Seventeenth-century England was torn by religious strife. The Puritans, austere Calvinists, wanted to purify the Anglican Church of all vestiges of pomp, pope and privilege. James I, annoyed by these nonconformists, threatened to 'harry them out of the country.'

As the fortunes of the faithful diminished, New England held out hope of renewal. The first trickle of Protestant immigrants came in 1620, when the Pilgrims established a small colony in Plymouth. Ten years later, the flagship *Arbella* led a flotilla of a thousand Puritans on the treacherous transatlantic crossing. In June 1630, their leader, country squire John Winthrop, gazed out on the Shawmut Peninsula and declared, 'we shall be as a City upon a Hill, with the eyes of all people upon us.'

They landed first near Salem and settled further south at present-day Charlestown. Across the river, the Shawmut Peninsula was at this time occupied by the Reverend William Blackstone, who had survived an earlier failed settlement. He invited Winthrop and his scurvy-ridden company to move closer to fresh water. They named their new home Boston, after the town in Lincolnshire where many of the Pilgrims had lived.

Piety, Power & Profits

The new settlement was governed by a spiritual elite – a Puritan theocracy. As such, the Church dominated early colonial life.

Divine Law was above all, and the state was put in service to the Church. The General Court, a select assembly of Church members, became the principal mechanism for lawmaking, while the governor was endowed with extensive powers to enforce the laws. Local affairs were settled at regular meetings, open to the freemen of each town. (Women were allowed to attend if they did not talk.) The tradition of town meetings became a cornerstone of American democracy.

Meanwhile, Boston became a boomtown. The first inhabitants were concentrated near the waterfront, behind the town dock. The back side of the hill served as 'common' lands. Newcomers fanned out along the rivers, looking for farmland and founding new settlements. Fortunes were made in the maritime trades – fishing, shipbuilding, and commerce with the Old World. Well into the 18th century, Boston was the richest city in the American colonies.

But population and prosperity put pressure on Puritan principles. Modesty gave way to display. Red-brick mansions appeared on Beacon Hill, tables were set with fine china and silk linens, and women's shoulders were fashionably exposed.

1635	1636	1638	1675–76
The first public school, now the Boston Latin School, is founded in the Massachusetts Bay Colony, symbolizing the importance of literacy and education in the Puritan philosophy.	Church leaders found a college to train ministers for their role in the theocracy. Three years later, the college is named for its first benefactor, the young minister John Harvard.	Anne Hutchinson is banished from the colony for contesting the ministers. She and her followers establish an outpost near present-day Portsmouth, Rhode Island.	Colonists engage in battle with the Wampanoag and other native tribes over the settlers' expansion. Known as King Philip's War, the conflict devastates the indigenous population.

The Church lost its monopoly on governing when the royal charter was revised to make property-holding the basis for political rights. Life in colonial Boston increasingly felt tension between community and individual, piety and profit.

From Empire to Independence

The demands of empire kept England at war. Colonists were drawn into the fighting in the French–Indian War. Despite their victory, all the colonists got was a tax bill from the king. Covetous of New England's maritime wealth, the Crown pronounced a series of Navigation Acts, restricting colonial trade. Boston merchants conducted business as usual, except now it was on the sly.

The issue of taxation brought the clash between king and colony to a head. In the 1760s, Parliament passed the Stamp Act, the Townsend Acts and the Tea Act – all of which placed greater financial burdens on the colonists. With each new tax and toll, colonial resentment intensified, as exhibited by vocal protests and violent mobs. The acts of defiance were defended by respectable lawyer John Adams, who cited the Magna Carta's principle of 'no taxation without representation.'

To each act of rebellion, the British throne responded with increasingly severe measures, eventually dispatching Redcoat regiments known as 'regulars' to restore order and suspending all local political power.

Under siege on the street, unrepentant Bostonians went underground. The Sons of Liberty, a clandestine network of patriots, stirred up public resistance to British policy and harassed the king's loyalists. They were led by some well-known townsmen, including esteemed surgeon Dr Joseph Warren, upper-class merchant John Hancock, skilled silversmith Paul Revere and bankrupt brewer Sam Adams. Branded as treasonous rebels by the king, the Sons of Liberty became more radical and popular as the imperial grip tightened.

The resented Redcoat presence did not extinguish, but rather inflamed, local passions. In March 1770 a motley street gang provoked British regulars with slurs and snowballs until the troops fired into the crowd, killing five and wounding six. John Adams successfully defended the British troops, who were found to be acting in self-defense. The Sons of Liberty, however, scored a propaganda coup with their depictions of the Boston Massacre, as the incident came to be called.

Shot Heard Round the World

Until now, all but the most pugnacious of patriots would have been satisfied with colonial economic autonomy and political representation.

Anne Hutchinson was a religious free-thinker who was banished from the Massachusetts Bay Colony. Hutchinson insisted on freedom of religion as a founding principle in the charter of Rhode Island, which would later influence the US Constitution.

1689	1700–50	1754–63	1760
The Glorious Revolution overthrows the Stuart Kings. The royal governor – who has angered colonists through his affiliation with the Church of England – is run out of town.	Immigration is spurred by the promise of land and by opportunities in fishing, shipbuilding and trade. By the middle of the century, the population of Boston reaches 15,000.	The British fight over North American territory in the French–Indian War. The war debt causes the Crown to increase colonial taxes.	A devastating fire destroys more than 300 buildings in town and 10 merchant ships in the harbor. The city seeks aid from the Crown, but none is forthcoming.

But the king's coercive tactics aroused indignity and acrimony. Both sides were spoiling for a fight.

British General Gage was sent over with 4000 troops and a fleet of warships. Local townsfolk and yeoman farmers organized themselves into Minutemen groups, citizen militias that could mobilize in a minute. They drilled on town commons and stockpiled weapons in secret stores.

In April 1775 Gage saw the chance to break colonial resistance. Acting on a tip from a local informant, Gage dispatched 700 troops on the road west to arrest fugitives Sam Adams and John Hancock and to seize a hidden stash of gunpowder. Bostonians had their own informants, including Gage's wife, who tipped off Joseph Warren on the troop movement.

Word was then passed to the Old North Church sexton to hang two signal lanterns in the steeple. Paul Revere quietly slipped across the river into Charlestown, where he mounted Brown Beauty and galloped into the night to alert the Minutemen.

At daybreak, the confrontation finally occurred. 'Here once the embattled farmer stood,' Ralph Waldo Emerson later wrote, 'and fired the shot heard round the world.' Imperial troops skirmished with Minutemen on the Old North Bridge in Concord and the Lexington Green. By midmorning, more militia had arrived and chased the bloodied Redcoats back to Boston in ignominious defeat. The inevitable had arrived: the War for Independence.

Boston figured prominently in the early phase of the American Revolution. In June 1775 Bostonians inflicted a hurtful blow on

When royal revenue agents were sent from London to take control of the Boston customs house, they targeted one of the city's richest merchants, John Hancock, impounding his ship, *Liberty,* which was laden with undeclared cargo.

HISTORY SHOT HEARD ROUND THE WORLD

BOSTON TEA PARTY

In May 1773 the British Parliament passed the Tea Act, granting a trade monopoly to the politically influential but financially troubled East India Company. In December three tea-bearing vessels arrived in Boston Harbor, but colonial merchants refused the shipments. When they tried to depart, Governor Hutchinson demanded their cargo be unloaded.

At a meeting in the Old South Church, the Sons of Liberty decided to take matters into their own hands. Disguised as Mohawk Indians, they descended on the waterfront, boarded the ships and dumped 90,000 pounds of taxable tea into the harbor.

The king's retribution was swift. Legislation was rushed through Parliament to punish Boston, 'the center of rebellious commotion in America, the ring leader in every riot.' The port was blockaded and the city placed under military rule. The Sons of Liberty spread the news of this latest outrage down the seaboard. The cause of Boston was becoming the cause of all the colonies – American independence versus British tyranny.

1767-68	1770	1773	1775
The British Parliament passes the Townsend Acts, a series of laws designed to enforce the Crown's right to tax the colonies. British troops are sent to enforce the acts.	Provoked by a local gang throwing snowballs, British troops fire into a crowd and kill five people. The soldiers are later acquitted, but the incident becomes known as the Boston Massacre.	The British Parliament levies a tax on tea, which incites an angry mob to protest by raiding a merchant ship and dumping crates of tea into Boston Harbor.	British troops heed reports that colonists are stockpiling weapons. Warned by Paul Revere and William Dawes, the Minutemen confront the Redcoats in Lexington and Concord.

British morale at the Battle of Bunker Hill. The British took the hill after three tries, but their losses were greater than expected. Fighting on the front line, Dr Warren was killed by a musket shot to the head in the final British charge. A few weeks later, George Washington assumed command of the ragged Continental Army on the Cambridge Common.

Britain's military occupation of the city continued until March 1776, when Washington mounted captured British cannons on Dorchester Heights and trained them on the British fleet in Boston Harbor. Rather than see the king's expensive warships sent to the bottom, the British evacuated, trashing and looting as they went; Boston was liberated.

Athens of America

In the early 19th century, Boston emerged as a center of enlightenment in the young republic. The city's second mayor, Josiah Quincy, led an effort to remake the city's underclass into a group of industrious and responsible citizens. He expanded public education and made the streets safer and cleaner. The 'Great Mayor' revitalized the decaying waterfront with a refurbished Faneuil Hall and the new Greek Revival marketplace, which bears his name.

Influenced by the idealistic legacy of Puritanism and revolution, Boston gave rise to the first uniquely American intellectual movement. Led by Unitarian minister Ralph Waldo Emerson, the transcendentalists shocked and challenged the Christian establishment with their belief in the inherent goodness of human nature and an emphasis on individual self-reliance to achieve spiritual fulfillment. Transcendental influences are exemplified in the romantic literature of Nathaniel Hawthorne and the civil disobedience of Henry David Thoreau. Besides philosophy, the city also became a vibrant cultural center for poetry, painting, architecture, science and scholarship, earning Boston a reputation as the 'Athens of America.'

From Sail to Steam

Boston thrived during the Age of Sail. In the 17th century the infamous 'triangular trade' route was developed, involving sugar, rum and slaves. Merchants who chose not to traffic in human cargo could still make large profits by illicitly undercutting European trade monopolies in the West Indies. In his East Boston shipyard, Donald McKay perfected the design of the clipper ship. The advent of the steam engine in the second half of the 19th century marked the decline of Boston seafaring prominence.

Early on, Boston's industry was related to overseas trading: shipbuilding, fishing and rum. Besides this, the city had small-scale artisan shops. During the war, the disruption of commerce caused acute short-

DECLARATION OF INDEPENDENCE

On July 18, 1776, Bostonians first heard the Declaration of Independence read from the balcony of the Old State House, and there was much rejoicing.

1776	1780	1789–1801	1813
The Continental Army takes Dorchester Heights, giving them a shot at the Royal Navy ships in the harbor. The British evacuate Boston, and the colonies declare independence.	Massachusetts ratifies its constitution, which – written mostly by John Adams – will serve as the model for the US Constitution with its Declaration of Rights and Frame of Government.	John Adams of Quincy, MA, serves two terms as the vice president and one term as the president of the newly independent United States of America.	Merchant Francis Cabot Lowell establishes the Boston Manufacturing Company for the production of cotton textiles, launching the Industrial Revolution in New England.

ages of manufactured goods. In response, some merchants shifted their investments into industry, with revolutionary results.

By the middle of the 19th century, steam power and metal machines were changing the city. Boston became the railroad hub of New England. Leather works and shoe-making factories appeared on the edge of the city. Even Paul Revere abandoned his silversmith shop and set up a rolling copper mill and foundry.

Industrial wealth transformed the landscape. The tops of hills were cropped and used for landfill to expand its size. Back Bay became a French-style neighborhood of elegant boulevards, and the South End, an English-style quarter of intimate courtyards.

Boston's Melting Pot

For nearly two centuries, the city was ruled by a select group of leading families, collectively known as the Boston Brahmins. A reference to the exclusive ruling class in India, the self-deprecating term was coined by Oliver Wendell Holmes Sr, but was readily adopted by the caste-conscious. Their elite status was claimed through lineage to the colonial founders or through wealth from the merchant heyday. They dominated city politics and business, mimicked the style and manners of the European aristocracy, and created exclusive clubs for themselves and cultural institutions for the city.

The rapid rise of industry led to social change. The industrial workforce was initially drawn from the region's young farm women, who lived in dormitories under paternalistic supervision. The 'mill girls' were replaced by cheaper immigrant Irish labor in the 1820s. Although their numbers were still modest, the effect of immigration on local attitudes was great. The world of English-descended Whig Protestants was thrown into turmoil.

Disparaged by 'proper' Bostonians, the Irish were considered an inferior race of moral delinquents, whose spoken brogue was not endearing, but rather suggested a shoe in one's mouth. They undercut workers in the job market; worse yet, the Irish brought the dreaded religion of pomp and popery that the Puritans so detested.

A potato famine back home spurred an upsurge in Irish immigration. Between 1846 and 1856 more than 1000 new immigrants stepped off the boat every month. It was a human flood tide that the city was not prepared to absorb. Anti-immigrant and anti-Catholic sentiments were shrill. The Know Nothing Party sprang up as a political expression of this rabid nativist reaction.

Subsequent groups of Italian, Portuguese and East European Jewish immigrants suffered similar indignities. By the end of the 19th century, the urban landscape resembled a mosaic of clannish ethnic enclaves.

Boston's Original Artistic Institutions

Museum of Fine Arts (Fenway)

Boston Symphony Orchestra (Fenway)

Trinity Church (Back Bay)

Boston Public Library (Back Bay)

1831	1840s	1850s	1851
Cofounder of the American Anti-Slavery Society, abolitionist agitator William Lloyd Garrison publishes the first issue of radical newspaper *The Liberator* from his office on Beacon Hill.	The potato famine spurs Irish immigration to Boston. The influx sparks conflict over religious and cultural differences. By the middle of the century, the Irish population reaches 35,000.	The Fugitive Slave Law requires citizens to return runaway slaves to their owners. Enforcement of this law leads to the arrest of Boston abolitionists in 1850 and 1854.	Built in an East Boston shipyard, Donald McKay's *Flying Cloud* sails from New York to San Francisco with a damaged mast in just 89 days and 21 hours, shattering all previous records.

All Politics is Local

With social change, Brahmin dominance of Boston politics slipped away. By the end of the 19th century, ethnic-based political machines wrested control of local government from the old elite.

While the Democratic Party was initially associated with rural and radical interests, it became the political instrument of the working poor. Irish immigrant neighborhoods provided ready-made voting blocs, which empowered a new type of political boss. These flamboyant populists took an activist approach to government and traded in patronage and graft. No other Boston boss outshone James Michael Curley. He was conniving, corrupt and beloved. The Rascal King had a seemingly endless supply of holiday turkeys and city jobs for constituents, who between 1914 and 1949 elected him mayor four times and governor and congressman once.

After more than 125 years, Massachusetts once again took center stage in national politics with John F Kennedy's election to the presidency in 1960. The youthful JFK was the pride of Boston's Irish Catholics for being the one who finally made it. Kennedy's brief Camelot inspired a new generation of Americans into public service and founded a political family dynasty that rivaled the Adams'.

In 1952, Thomas 'Tip' O'Neill inherited Kennedy's recently vacated congressional seat. O'Neill climbed to the top of the legislative ladder, becoming Speaker of the House in 1977, all the while sticking to the adage that 'All Politics is Local.' Meanwhile, in 1962, JFK's brother Ted was elected to represent Massachusetts in the US Senate – a post he held for 47 years.

In the 1830s, rumors of licentiousness led a Protestant mob to torch the Catholic Ursuline Convent in present-day Somerville. In another incident, an Irish funeral procession met a volunteer fire company along Boston's Broad Street, and a melee ensued, leaving a row of Irish flats burned to the ground.

Reform & Racism

The legacy of race relations in Boston is marred by contradictions. Abolitionists and segregationists, reformers and racists have all left their mark. Massachusetts was the first colony to recognize slavery as a legal institution in 1641, and the first to abolish slavery in 1783.

In the 19th century, Boston emerged as a nucleus of the abolition movement. Newspaper publisher William Lloyd Garrison, Unitarian minister Theodore Parker and aristocratic lawyer Wendell Phillips launched the American Anti-Slavery Society to agitate public sentiment. The city provided safe houses for runaway slaves who took the Underground Railroad to freedom in Canada.

After the Civil War, many blacks rose to prominent positions in Boston society, including John S Rock, who became the first African American to practice in the US Supreme Court; John J Smith, who was elected to the Massachusetts House of Representatives; Lewis Hayden, who was elected to the Massachusetts General Court; and William DuBois, who was the first African American to receive a PhD from Harvard.

1857–1900	1863	1870–76	1881
Boston is transformed when the marshland along Charles River's south shore is filled with landfill from the city's three hills. New neighborhoods, Back Bay, Kenmore and Fenway, are created.	Local boy Robert Gould Shaw is placed in command of the 54th Massachusetts Volunteer Infantry, one of the first all-black regiments in the Union Army.	With a generous donation from the private collection of the Boston Athenaeum, the Museum of Fine Arts is established in a Gothic Revival building on Copley Sq.	Philanthropist Henry Lee Higginson founds the Boston Symphony Orchestra with the aim of 'offering the best music at low prices, such as may be found in all European cities.'

BOSTON STRONG

On Patriots' Day 2013, two bombs exploded near the finish line of the Boston Marathon, killing three and injuring hundreds. Several days later, an MIT police officer was shot dead. The entire city was locked down, as Boston became a battleground for the 'War on Terror.'

The perpetrators were brothers Tamerlan and Dzhokhar Tsarnaev, natives of Chechnya and residents of Cambridge. Tamerlan was killed during a shootout with police. His younger brother Dzhokhar was charged with using and conspiring to use a weapon of mass destruction, resulting in death, as well as malicious destruction of property, resulting in death. In April 2015 he was found guilty on all counts.

The tragedy was devastating, but Boston claimed countless heroes, especially the many victims who inspired others with their courage and fortitude.

In the early 20th century, manufacturing jobs attracted Southern blacks as part of the Great Migration. For newcomers, the north promised refuge from racism and poverty. More than 20,000 strong, Boston's expanding black community relocated to Roxbury and the South End, where a thriving jazz and dance scene enlivened city nights. At one point, Boston was home to both Martin Luther King, a Boston University divinity student, and Malcolm X, a pool-hall-hustling teenager.

Boston did not have Jim Crow laws per se, but it did have its own informal patterns of racial segregation, with African Americans as an underclass. As the city's economy declined, racial antagonism increased. In the 1970s, a judge determined that separate was not equal in the public school system. His court order to desegregate the schools through forced busing violated the sanctity of the city's ethnic neighborhoods and exposed underlying racial tensions. The school year was marked by a series of violent incidents involving students and parents, most infamously in South Boston. The experiment in racial integration was eventually abandoned, and the healing was slow.

Making Boston Modern

In the mid-20th century, the city underwent a remarkable physical transformation. Two of the city's oldest neighborhoods were targeted: Scollay Sq, which was once an area bustling with theaters and music halls, but had since become a rundown red-light district; and the West End, where poor immigrants eked out an existence amid a grubby labyrinth of row houses and alleyways. Urban renewal came in the form of the grim bulldozer, which sent both neighborhoods into oblivion.

Next came the cement mixers that filled the modernist moldings of a new Government Center for Boston's sizable civil-servant sector. The

Black History Sites

African Meeting House (Beacon Hill)

Robert Gold Shaw Memorial (Boston Common)

Black Heritage Trail (Beacon Hill)

Copp's Hill Burying Ground (North End)

1918	1927	1960	1960s
Babe Ruth leads the Boston Red Sox to their fifth World Series victory in 15 years. He is subsequently traded to the New York Yankees, which fans will remember for the rest of the century.	Two Italian anarchists, Nicola Sacco and Bartolomeo Vanzetti, are executed on trumped-up murder charges, revealing the persistence of class and ethnic animosities.	After six years in the House of Representatives and eight years in the Senate, Boston native John F Kennedy is elected president, ushering in the era of Camelot.	In a fit of urban renewal, the city razes Scollay Sq. Over 1000 buildings are destroyed and 20,000 residents are displaced to make way for the new Government Center.

centerpiece was an inverted pyramid, the monumental and cavernous City Hall, which has since become prime evidence in the architectural case against 1960s modernism.

The city's skyline reached upward with luxury condominiums and office buildings. The old customs tower on the waterfront, long the tallest building in town, was overtaken by the proud Prudential Tower and Henry Cobb's elegant John Hancock Tower. Boston was on the rebound.

Past Forward

Boston would not be Boston without a major redevelopment project. The Central Artery Tunnel Project (aka the Big Dig) was an unmatched marvel of civil engineering, urban planning and pork-barrel politics. The project employed the most advanced techniques of urban engineering and environmental science, in order to reroute the Central Artery underground through the center of the city. The project fell far behind schedule and went way over budget. When it finally opened in 2004, the walls leaked and a falling ceiling panel killed a motorist. This bane of Bostonian existence finally materialized as a boon for the city, as residents and visitors alike are now enjoying quicker commutes, easier access to the airport and delightful dallying along the Rose Kennedy Greenway.

Since colonial times, Boston has been a champion of political equality, civil rights and social reform. This tradition has continued in the 21st century, as the city and state have initiated cutting-edge reforms that would eventually be adopted elsewhere in the country. In 2004, Massachusetts became the first state in the union to recognize same-sex marriages, and the first gay marriage took place in Cambridge. In 2006, the Commonwealth enacted a health care reform, resulting in near universal coverage for Massachusetts residents – years before this legislation passed at a federal level. In 2007, Massachusetts elected Deval Patrick, the state's first African American governor (and the country's second), foreshadowing Barack Obama's arrival in the White House.

In the new millennium, nothing has inspired Bostonians' passion and pride more than their local sports teams. After more than eight decades of heartbreaking near-misses, the Boston Red Sox finally won baseball's World Series in 2004 and again in 2007. A 2013 World Series victory was especially sweet, as it occurred at Fenway Park. Moreover, this cathartic event was symbolic of the city's resilience after the horrific tragedy of the Boston Marathon bombings, which had occurred six months earlier.

The Red Sox shared the sports spotlight with local gridiron gladiators, the New England Patriots, who won an amazing three Super Bowls in four years from 2002 to 2005. They repeated one more time in 2015, ensuring the team's dynastic claim. In 2008, the Boston Celtics piled on, winning a historic 17th basketball title. And in 2011, the Boston Bruins brought home the Stanley Cup, completing the city's 'Grand Slam of American Sports.' Now that's something to cheer about.

In 1976, the city organized a triumphant bicentennial celebration, capped with spectacular fireworks and a spirited concert beside the Charles River. Half a million people attended the patriotic party, including Queen Elizabeth II, who showed no hard feelings over past misunderstandings in her salute from the balcony of the Old State House.

1974	1991–2006	2004	2014
The city of Boston institutes a program of mandatory busing in an attempt to desegregate schools. This sparks violence between black and white students in Charlestown and South Boston.	The Central Artery/Tunnel Project keeps all of Boston under construction for 15 years and $15 billion. Behind schedule and over budget, the final product nonetheless transforms the surface of the city.	Massachusetts becomes the first state in the union to legalize same-sex marriage. The city of Cambridge becomes the first municipality to issue marriage licenses to gay and lesbian couples.	Leaving a legacy of revived neighborhoods and bike-friendly streets, Boston's longest-serving mayor, Thomas Menino, declines to run for re-election, after five terms and 20 years in office.

Arts & Architecture

The Puritans were a spiritual people, uninterested in such small-minded pursuits as art or music. It was not until the 19th century that Boston developed as an artistic center, earning its nickname as the 'Athens of America.' Boston can thank the Puritans, however, for founding Harvard College, and thus establishing the Boston area as a center for learning. Attracted by the intellectual atmosphere, other institutions followed suit; not only traditional universities, but also art schools, music colleges, conservatories and more. To this day, the university culture enhances the breadth and depth of cultural offerings.

Literature

By the 19th century, the city's universities had become a magnet for writers, poets and philosophers, as well as publishers and bookstores. The local literati were expounding on social issues such as slavery, women's rights and religious reawakening. Boston, Cambridge and Concord were fertile breeding grounds for ideas, nurturing the seeds of America's literary and philosophical flowering. Ralph Waldo Emerson, Henry David Thoreau, Nathaniel Hawthorne, Louisa May Alcott and Henry Wadsworth Longfellow were born of this era. This was the Golden Age of American literature, and Boston was its nucleus.

In the 20th century, Boston continued to foster authors, poets and playwrights, but the Golden Age was over. The city was no longer the center of the progressive thought and social activism that had so inspired American literature. Moral crusaders and city officials promoted stringent censorship of books, films and plays that they deemed offensive or obscene. Many writers were 'banned in Boston' – a trend that contributed to the city's image as a provincial outpost instead of a cultural capital.

Boston never regained its status as the hub of the literary solar system, but its rich legacy and ever-influential universities ensure that the city continues to contribute to American literature. Many of Boston's most prominent writers are transplants from other cities or countries, drawn to its academic and creative institutions. John Updike, Ha Jin, Jhumpa Lahiri and David Foster Wallace all came to the Boston area to study or teach at local universities.

Boston's 19th-century luminaries congregated one Saturday a month at the old Parker House. Presided over by Oliver Wendell Holmes Sr, the Saturday Club was known for its jovial atmosphere and stimulating discourse, attracting such renowned visitors as Charles Dickens. The prestigious literary magazine *Atlantic Monthly* was born out of these meetings.

Painting & Visual Arts

Boston began supporting a world-class artistic movement in the late 19th century, when new construction and cultural institutions required adornment. Boston's most celebrated artist is John Singer Sargent, whose murals decorate the staircases at the Museum of Fine Arts and the Boston Public Library, both of which were built during this time. Prolific sculptors Daniel Chester French and Augustus Saint-Gaudens also left their marks in parks and public spaces all over town. During this period, Winslow Homer became famous for his paintings of the New England coast, while Childe Hassam used local cityscapes as subjects for his impressionist works.

PORTRAITS

Critics claim that Boston lost pace with the artistic world in the second half of the 20th century. But the visual arts are returning to the forefront of contemporary cultural life in the new millennium. The 2006 opening of the ICA shone the spotlight onto Boston's long-over-shadowed contemporary art scene. Almost in response, the Museum of Fine Arts, the Isabella Steward Gardner Museum and the Harvard Art Museums upgraded their facilities for contemporary art with new and expanded exhibit spaces and programming. Artists are transforming the South End and the Seaport District into vibrant art districts that feed off the growing and changing art institutions.

Architecture

After the American Revolution, Boston set to work repairing and rebuilding the city, now the capital of the new Commonwealth of Massachusetts. Charles Bulfinch took responsibility for much of it, creating Faneuil Hall and the Massachusetts State House, as well as private homes for Boston's most distinguished citizens.

As the city expanded, so did the opportunities for creative art and architecture, especially with the new construction in Back Bay. Frederick Law Olmsted designed the Charles River Esplanade and the Emerald Necklace, two magnificent green spaces that snake around the city. Copley Sq represents the pinnacle of 19th-century architecture, with the Romanesque Trinity Church, designed by Henry Hobson Richardson, and the Renaissance Revival Boston Public Library, designed by McKim, Mead and White.

Boston artist John Singleton Copley is considered the first great American portrait painter: you can see a huge collection of his works at the Museum of Fine Arts.

The 20th century witnessed plenty of noteworthy additions. IM Pei is responsible for the much-hated City Hall Plaza and the much-beloved John F Kennedy Library. His partner James Cobb designed the stunning John Hancock Tower. Reflecting Trinity Church in its facade, this prominent modern tower takes its design cues from Boston's past, a recurring trope in the city.

The century closed with a remarkable project in urban planning – not building, but un-building – as parts of the Central Artery were re-routed underground and replaced by the Rose Kennedy Greenway, a network of green parks and plazas. And where the Central Artery is not hidden, it is on display, as it soars over the Charles River on the new Zakim Bunker Hill Bridge, one of the widest cable-stayed bridges in the world.

Several new buildings on the MIT campus – particularly Frank Gehry's Stata Center – have made industrial Kendall Sq a daring neighborhood for architecture. Across town, the Harvard campus now boasts a striking Renzo Piano design, housing the new Harvard Art Museum. Meanwhile, the dramatic space for the Institute for Contemporary Art has kicked off a spate of construction along the South Boston waterfront. All around Boston, there is a burgeoning interest in design as an art form that affects us all: the Design Museum Boston explores these questions with exhibits and presentations all over town.

Music

Contemporary Music

Boston has a tradition of grooving to great music. Classic rockers remember Aerosmith, the Cars and the J Geils Band. (Peter Wolf, lead singer of the J Geils Band, is frequently sighted at celebrity events around Boston.)

The pinnacle of the Boston music scene, however, is reserved for the punk rockers of the 1990s. Bostonians still pine for the Mighty Mighty

Bosstones and the Pixies, the most influential of many B-town bands from this era. Nowadays, no one makes more real, honest hardcore punk than the wildly popular Dropkick Murphys, a bunch of blue-collar Irish boys from Quincy.

Boston is also home to a thriving folk tradition, thanks to the venerable nonprofit Club Passim, while the Berklee College of Music sustains a lively jazz and blues scene.

Classical Music

Possibly Boston's most venerated cultural institution, the Boston Symphony Orchestra was founded in 1881 and is rated among the world's best orchestras, thanks to the leadership of several talented conductors. It was under Serge Koussevitzky's reign that the BSO gained its world-renowned reputation, due to its radio broadcasts and its noteworthy world premieres. Seiji Ozawa, the BSO's longest-tenured maestro (1973–2002), was beloved in Boston for his passionate style. James Levine (2004-2011) was known for challenging Boston audiences with a less traditional repertoire, though he suffered from ill health throughout his tenure. In 2014, Boston proudly welcomed Andris Nelsons, a dynamic young maestro from Latvia, who brings unbridled emotion and energy to his conducting.

The Boston Pops was founded as an effort to offer audiences lighter fare, such as popular classics, marches and show tunes. Arthur Fiedler, who took the helm of the Pops in 1930, was responsible for realizing its goal of attracting more diverse audiences, thanks to free concerts on the Charles River Esplanade. The Pops' current conductor is the young, charismatic Keith Lockhart, who has reached out to audiences in new ways – namely by bringing in pop and rock singers to perform with the orchestra.

Theater

Boston's strong Puritan roots have always exercised a stranglehold over its desire to become a world-class city, and this clash is most apparent in the city's stunted theater tradition. Only in recent years has the city developed as a destination for interesting alternative or cutting-edge theatrical productions. Nowadays, there are several excellent professional drama theater companies – namely the Huntington Theatre Company and the American Repertory Theater – that perform outside the Theater District. The Boston Center for the Arts in the South End hosts a slew of smaller companies that stage engaging and unconventional shows.

Dance

Boston's preeminent dance company is the Boston Ballet, founded by E Virginia Williams in 1965. The current director is Mikko Nissinen, veteran of the Finnish National Ballet and the Kirov Ballet in St Petersburg, Russia. The season usually includes timeless pieces by choreographers such as Rudolph Nureyev and George Balanchine, as well as more daring work by choreographers-in-residence. And it always includes the classic performance of *The Nutcracker* at Christmas. The Boston Ballet performs at the Opera House.

The Carpenter Center on the Harvard campus is the only Le Corbusier building in the country, and across town, MIT boasts buildings by Eero Saarinen and Alvar Aalto – emblematic of how these academic institutions have enabled design prowess.

Universities & Colleges

No single element has influenced the city so profoundly as its educational institutions. Aside from the big ones mentioned here, dozens of smaller schools are located in Fenway. The residential areas west of the center (Brighton and Allston) have been dubbed the 'student ghetto.' Academic suburban sprawl means there are also excellent schools in Medford, Waltham and Wellesley, north and west of Boston.

The Big Boys

Harvard University

A slew of superlatives accompany the name of this venerable institution in Cambridge. It is America's oldest university, founded in 1636. It still has the largest endowment, numbering $36 billion in 2014, despite losing almost a third of it playing the market in previous years. It is often first in the list of national universities, according to *US News & World Report*. Harvard is actually comprised of 10 independent schools dedicated to the study of medicine, dentistry, law, business, divinity, design, education, public health and public policy, in addition to the traditional Faculty of Arts & Sciences.

Harvard Yard is the heart and soul of the university campus, with buildings dating back to its founding. But the university continues to expand in all directions. Most recently, Harvard acquired extensive land across the river in Allston, with the intention of converting this working-class residential area into a satellite campus with commercial, residential and academic facilities.

Boston is a funny place, and we mean funny ha-ha. Many of Boston's famous jokesters are graduates of Emerson College, which offers scholarships and workshops specifically devoted to comedy.

Massachusetts Institute of Technology

At the opposite end of Mass Ave, the Massachusetts Institute of Technology (MIT) offers an interesting contrast (and complement) to Harvard. Excelling in sciences and engineering – pretty serious stuff, by most standards – MIT nonetheless does not take itself too seriously. The campus is dotted with whimsical sculptures and offbeat art, not to mention some of Boston's most daring and dumbfounding contemporary architecture. MIT students are notorious practical jokers, and their pranks usually leave the bemused public wondering 'How did they do that?'

Despite the atmosphere of fun and funniness, these smarty-pants are hard at work. The school has claimed some 81 Nobel Laureates and 56 recipients of the National Medal of Science since its founding in 1861. Some recent accomplishments include artificially duplicating the process of photosynthesis to store solar energy, developing computer programs to decipher ancient languages, and creating an acrobatic robotic bird.

The MIT campus stretches out for about a mile along the Charles River. The university has a few museums, but it's really the art, architecture and atmosphere of innovation that make the place unique.

The Best of Boston

Boston University

Boston University (BU) is a massive urban campus sprawling west of Kenmore Sq. BU enrolls about 30,000 undergraduate and graduate students in all fields of study. The special collections of BU's Mugar Memorial Library include an outstanding 20th-century archive. Public exhibits showcase the holdings, which include the papers of Isaac Asimov, Bette Davis, Martin Luther King Jr and more. The BU Terriers excel at ice hockey, with frequent appearances in the national college championships, the Frozen Four, as well as victories in the local Beanpot tournament.

Boston College

Not to be confused with BU, Boston College (BC) could not be more different. BC is situated between Brighton in Boston and Chestnut Hill in the swanky suburb of Newton; the attractive campus is recognizable by its neo-Gothic towers. It is home to the nation's largest Jesuit community. Its Catholic influence makes it more socially conservative and more social-service oriented than other universities. Visitors to the campus will find a good art museum and excellent Irish and Catholic ephemera collections in the library. Aside from the vibrant undergraduate population, it has a strong education program and an excellent law school. Its basketball and football teams – the BC Eagles – are usually high in national rankings.

MIT computer scientist Joseph Carl Robnett Licklider first conceived of a 'galactic network' in the early 1960s, which would later spawn the internet.

A WALK ACROSS THE HARVARD BRIDGE

The Harvard Bridge – from Back Bay in Boston to MIT in Cambridge – is the longest bridge across the Charles River. It is not too long to walk, but it is long enough to do some wondering while you walk. You might wonder, for example, why the bridge that leads into the heart of MIT is named the Harvard Bridge.

According to legend, the state offered to name the bridge after Cambridge's second university. But the brainiac engineers at MIT analyzed the plans for construction and found the bridge was structurally unsound. Not wanting the MIT moniker associated with a faulty feat of engineering, it was suggested that the bridge better be named for the neighboring university up the river. That the bridge was subsequently rebuilt validated the superior brainpower of MIT.

That is only a legend, however (one invented by an MIT student, no doubt). The fact is that the Harvard Bridge was first constructed in 1891, and MIT moved to its current location only in 1916. The bridge was rebuilt in the 1980s to modernize and expand it, but the original name has stuck, at least officially. Most Bostonians actually refer to the bridge as the 'Mass Ave bridge' because, frankly, it makes more sense.

By now, walking across the bridge, you will perhaps have noticed the graffiti reading: '50 smoots... 69 smoots... 100 smoots... Halfway to Hell...' and you are probably wondering, 'What is a smoot?'

A smoot is an obscure unit of measurement that was used to measure the distance of the Harvard Bridge, first in 1958 and every year since. One smoot is approximately 5ft 7in, the height of Oliver R Smoot, who was a pledge of the MIT fraternity Lambda Chi Alpha in '58. He was the shortest pledge that year. And yes, his physical person was actually used for all the measurements.

And now that you have reached the other side of the river, surely you are wondering exactly how long the bridge is. We can't say about the Harvard students, but certainly every MIT student knows that the Harvard Bridge is 364.4 smoots plus one ear.

Northeastern University

Located in the midst of student central, aka Fenway, Northeastern is a private regional university with programs emphasizing health, security and sustainability. Northeastern University (NU) boasts one of the country's largest work-study cooperative programs, whereby most students complete two or three semesters of full-time employment in addition to their eight semesters of studies. This integration of classroom learning with real-world experience is the university's strongest feature.

Art & Music Schools

Massachusetts College of Art & Design

The country's first and only four-year independent public art college was founded along with MIT and the Museum of Fine Arts in the late 19th century, when local leaders wanted to influence the state's development by promoting fine arts and technology. It seems safe to say that their long-term goal was successfully met. Nowadays, Massachusetts College of Art and Design (MassArt) offers a highly ranked art program, with specializations in industrial design, fashion design, illustration and animation, as well as the more traditional fine arts.

Berklee College of Music

Housed in and around Back Bay in Boston, Berklee is an internationally renowned school for contemporary music, especially jazz. The school was founded in 1945 by Lawrence Berk (the Lee came from his son's first name). Created as an alternative to the classical agenda and stuffy attitude of traditional music schools, Berk taught courses in composition and arrangement for popular music. Not big on musical theory, Berk emphasized learning by playing. His system was a big success and the school flourished. Berklee's Grammy-laden alumni include jazz musicians Gary Burton, Al Di Meola, Keith Jarrett and Diana Krall; pop/rock artists Quincy Jones, Donald Fagen and John Mayer; and filmmaker Howard Shore.

BEANPOT

Held annually since 1952, one of Boston's biggest annual sporting events is the Beanpot, a local hockey tournament between Harvard, BU, BC and Northeastern. It takes place on the first two Mondays (men) and Tuesdays (women) in February.

Emerson College

Founded in 1880, Emerson is a liberal arts college that specializes in communications and the performing arts. Located in the Boston theater district, the college operates the Cutler Majestic Theatre and the Paramount Center, and its students run Boston's coolest radio station, WERS. Emerson celebs include Norman Lear, Jay Leno, Denis Leary and Henry Winkler, aka 'the Fonz.'

Survival Guide

Transportation

ARRIVING IN BOSTON

Most travelers arrive in Boston by plane, with many national and international flights in and out of Logan International Airport. Two smaller regional airports – Manchester Airport in New Hampshire and TF Green Airport near Providence, Rhode Island – offer alternatives that are also accessible to Boston and are sometimes less expensive.

Most trains operated by **Amtrak** (☑800-872-7245; www.amtrak.com; South Station) go in and out of South Station. Boston is the northern terminus of the Northeast Corridor, which sends frequent trains to New York (4½ hours), Philadelphia (six hours) and Washington DC (eight hours). The Lakeshore Express goes daily to Buffalo (12 hours) and Chicago (23 hours), while the Downeaster goes from North Station to Portland, Maine (2½ hours).

Buses are most useful for regional destinations, although **Greyhound** (☑617-526-1800, 800-231-2222; www.greyhound.com) operates services around the country. In recent years, there has been a spate of new companies offering cheap and efficient service to New York City (four to five hours).

Flights, tours and rail tickets can be booked online at www.lonelyplanet.com.

Logan International Airport

On Massachusetts Route 1A in East Boston, **Logan International Airport** (☑800-235-6426; www.massport.com/logan) has five separate terminals that are connected by the frequent shuttle bus 11. Downtown Boston is just a few miles from the airport and is accessible by bus, subway, water shuttle and taxi.

Silver Line Bus

The silver line is the MBTA's 'bus rapid transit service.' It travels between Logan International Airport and South Station, with stops in the Seaport District. Silver line buses pick up at the airport terminals and connect directly to the subway station, so you don't have to buy another ticket for the T.

This is the most convenient way to get into the city if you are staying in the Seaport District or anywhere along the red line (Downtown, Beacon Hill, Cambridge). Prices and hours are the same as the T.

Subway

The **MBTA subway** (☑617-222-3200; www.mbta.com; per ride $2.10-2.65; ☺5:30am-12:30am Sun-Thu, to 2am Fri & Sat), known as the T, is another fast and cheap way to reach the city from the airport. From any terminal, take a free, well-marked shuttle bus (22 or 33) to the blue-line T station called Airport and you'll be downtown within 30 minutes.

Boat

Several water shuttles operate between Logan and the Boston waterfront. In both cases, fares to the North End and Charlestown are twice as much as fares to downtown. Take the free water transportation shuttle bus no 66 from the airport terminal to the ferry dock.

Boston Harbor Cruises Water Taxi (Map p236; ☑617-227-4320; www.bostonharborcruises.com; Long Wharf; ☺7am-10pm Mon-Sat, to 8pm Sun) Service to Long Wharf and other waterfront destinations.

Rowes Wharf Water Taxi (Map p236; ☑617-406-8584; www.roweswharfwatertaxi.com; Rowes Wharf; one-way/round-trip $12/20; ☺7am-10pm Mon-Sat, to 8pm Sun Apr-Nov, 7am-7pm daily Dec-Mar) Serves Rowes Wharf near the Boston Harbor Hotel, the Moakley Federal Courthouse on the Fort Point Channel and the World Trade Center in the Seaport District. Taxis also go to the North End and Charlestown for a higher fare.

Car

If you're driving from the airport into Boston or to points north of the city, the Sumner Tunnel ($3.50 toll) will lead you to Storrow Dr or over the Zakim Bridge to I-93 North. To points south of Boston, use the Ted Williams Tunnel ($3.50) to I-93 South. To or from points west, the Mass Pike connects directly with the Ted Williams Tunnel. When you're heading to the airport from downtown Boston, take the Callahan Tunnel. All three tunnels are off I-93 and free when heading inbound.

Taxi

Taxi fares from Logan are approximately $25 to Downtown Boston, $30 to Kenmore Sq and $35 to Harvard Sq.

Manchester-Boston Regional Airport

Manchester-Boston Regional Airport (603-624-6556; www.flymanchester.com) A quiet alternative to Logan, Manchester Airport is just 55 miles north of Boston in New Hampshire.

Flight Line Inc (800-245-2525; www.flightlineinc.com; 9am-11pm) This shuttle runs every 30 to 60 minutes between Manchester Airport and Boston Logan. There is also a shared van service that drops off and picks up directly at your hotel. Reservations required.

TF Green Airport

TF Green Airport (www.pvdairport.com) Just outside the city of Providence, RI, TF Green Airport is serviced by major carriers. Southwest Airlines, in particular, offers very competitively priced tickets. The airport is one hour south of Boston.

The **MBTA commuter rail** (800-392-6100, 617-222-3200; www.mbta.com) travels between TF Green Airport and South Station ($11, 90 minutes, 10 daily), with stops at Ruggles and Back Bay stations along the way.

South Station

Located in downtown Boston, South Station is a stop on the red line of the T. It is also the junction where the silver line buses connect to the subway system.

From New York to Boston by Bus

The infamous 'Chinatown Buses' originated in the late 1990s as a cheap way for Chinese workers to travel to and from jobs. They offered super-cheap tickets between Boston and New York, traveling from Chinatown to Chinatown. Young, savvy travelers caught wind of the bargain transportation, and the phenomenon began to spread. It was crowded and confusing and probably not that safe, but it sure was cheap.

In recent years, more and more companies are running buses on this route. With competition has come improved service and better safety records. They don't always start and end in Chinatown. Many offer free wireless service on board. But the prices remain blissfully low.

Lucky Star Bus (www.luckystarbus.com; South Station; one-way $20) Twelve daily departures. Tickets must be purchased at least one hour before departure time.

Megabus (www.megabus.com; South Station; one-way $10-30) Rates vary depending on the time of day of travel

and how far in advance they are purchased.

Go Bus (www.gobuses.com; Alewife Brook Pkwy; one-way $18-34; TAlewife) Departs from Alewife station in Cambridge.

GETTING AROUND BOSTON

Boston is geographically small and logistically manageable. The sights and activities of principal interest to travelers are contained within an area that's only about 1 mile wide by 3 miles long.

This makes Boston a wonderful walking or cycling city. Otherwise, most of the main attractions are accessible by subway. Some outlying sites require a bus ride. And a few – namely the Boston Harbor Islands – require a boat ride or two.

Incidentally, Boston is a waterside city, and riding in boats is part of the fun. Water shuttles are a convenient transportation option for a few harborside destinations, including the airport.

Bicycle

In recent years, Boston has made vast improvements in its infrastructure for cyclists, including painting miles of bicycle lanes, upgrading bike facilities on and around public transportation and implementing an excellent bike-share program. Boston drivers are used to sharing the roads with their two-wheeled friends (and they are used to arriving *after* their two-wheeled friends, who are less impeded by traffic snarls). Cyclists should always obey traffic rules and ride defensively.

The Hubway

Hubway (www.thehubway.com; 24/72hr membership

$6/12, 30/60/90min free/$2/4; ☉24hr) Boston's bike-share program is the Hubway. There are 140 Hubway stations around Boston, Cambridge, Brookline and Somerville, stocked with 1300 bikes that are available for short-term loan. Purchase a temporary membership at any bicycle kiosk, then pay by the half-hour for the use of the bikes (free under 30 minutes). Return the bike to any station in the vicinity of your destination.

The Hubway pricing is designed so a bike ride can substitute for a cab ride (eg to make a one-way trip or run an errand), not for leisurely riding or long trips, which would be expensive. Check the website for a map of Hubway stations. Helmets are not legally required – except for children aged under 17 – but they are recommended and available for purchase at reduced rates at the vendors listed on the Hubway website.

Bikes on the MBTA

You can bring bikes on the T, the bus and the commuter rail for no additional fare. Bikes are not allowed on green-line trains or silver-line buses, nor are they allowed on any trains during rush hour (7am to 10am and 4pm to 7pm, Monday to Friday). Bikes are not permitted inside buses, but most MBTA buses have bicycle racks on the outside.

Bicycle Rental

Urban AdvenTours (www.urbanadventours.com; 103 Atlantic Ave; rental per day $35; ☉9am-6pm Mon-Sat; TA-quarium) Bikes available for rental include road bikes and mountain bikes, in addition to the standard hybrids. For an extra fee these eco-friendly guys will bring your bike to

your doorstep in a BioBus powered by vegetable oil.

Cambridge Bicycle (www.cambridgebicycle.com; 259 Massachusetts Ave; rental per day $30; ☉10am-7pm Mon-Sat, noon-6pm Sun; TCentral) Convenient for cycling along the Charles River. Rentals are three-speed commuter bikes – nothing fancy, but solid for city riding.

Back Bay Bicycles (www.papa-wheelies.com; 362 Commonwealth Ave; city/road bike per day $35/65; ☉11am-6pm Mon-Sat, noon-5pm Sun; THynes) Convenient for riding along the Charles River. City bike rentals are Cannondale Daytrippers; lock and helmet also included.

Bicycle Exchange (www.cambridgebicycleexchange.com; 2067 Massachusetts Ave; rental 1 day $25, additional days $10; ☉9am-6pm Tue-Sat, noon-5pm Sun; TPorter) This bike shop is located just north of Porter Sq, convenient to the Minuteman Bikeway.

Boat

While boats will likely not be your primary means of transportation, they are useful for a few destinations, primarily the Boston Harbor Islands and Charlestown. Ferries to Provincetown and Salem provide a pleasant transportation alternative for day trips out of the city. There is also a water-shuttle service to the airport and water taxis that make stops at destinations along the waterfront.

Bus

MBTA (☎617-222-5215; www.mbta.com; rides $2.10-2.65) The MBTA operates bus routes within the city. These can be difficult to figure out for the short-term visitor, but

schedules are posted on its website and at some bus stops along the routes. The standard bus fare is $2.10, or $1.60 with a Charlie Card. If you're transferring from the T on a Charlie Card the bus fare is free.

The silver line, a so-called 'rapid' bus, starts at Downtown Crossing and runs along Washington St in the South End to Roxbury's Dudley Sq. Another route goes from South Station to the Seaport District, then under the harbor to Logan International Airport. This waterfront route costs $2.65 ($2.10 with a Charlie Card), instead of the normal bus fare.

The silver line is different from the regular MBTA buses because it drives in a designated lane (supposedly reducing travel time). More importantly, the silver line starts/terminates inside the South Station or Downtown Crossing subway terminal, so you can transfer to/from the T without purchasing an additional ticket.

Subway (The T)

MBTA Subway (☎617-222-3200; www.mbta.com; rides $2.10-2.65; ☉5:30am-12:30am Sun-Thu, to 2am Fri & Sat) The MBTA operates the USA's oldest subway, built in 1897 and known locally as the 'T.' There are four lines – red, blue, green and orange – that radiate from the principal downtown stations: Downtown Crossing, Government Center, Park St and State. When traveling away from any of these stations, you are heading 'outbound.'

Although the MBTA might like you to believe otherwise, the silver line is a bus line with a dedicated traffic lane – not a subway line. Tourist passes with unlimited travel (on subway, bus or water shuttle) are available for periods of one day ($12) or one week ($19). Kids under 11 ride for free. Passes may be purchased at the Boston Welcome Center on Tremont St and at the following T stations: Park St, Government Center, Back Bay, Alewife, Copley, Quincy Adams, Harvard, North Station, South Station, Hynes and Airport. For longer stays, you can buy a monthly pass allowing unlimited use of the subway and local bus ($75). Otherwise, buy a paper fare card ($2.65 per ride) or a Charlie Card ($2.10 per ride) at all stations.

Of an evening, the last red-line trains pass through Park St around closing time (depending on the direction), but all T stations and lines are different: check the posting at the station.

Taxi

Cabs are plentiful but expensive. Rates are determined by the meter, which calculates miles. Expect to pay about $12 to $18 between most tourist points within the city limits, without much traffic. If you have any

trouble hailing a cab, head to any nearby hotel, where they congregate. Recommended taxi companies include:

Chill Out First Class Cab (617-212-3763; www.chilloutfirstclasstransportation-services.com; airport $30-45) Offers flat-fee airport transfers from Cambridge.

Cabbie's Cab (617-547-2222; www.cabbiescab.com; airport $35) Offers flat-rate airport transfers from all parts of Boston and Cambridge.

Train

MBTA Commuter Rail (800-392-6100, 617-222-3200; www.mbta.com) The MBTA commuter rail services destinations in the metropolitan Boston area. Trains heading west and north of the city, including to Concord and Salem, leave from bustling North Station on Causeway St. Trains heading south, including to Plymouth and TF Green Airport in Providence, leave from South Station.

TOURS

Bicycle Tours

Urban AdvenTours (Map p232; 617-379-3590; www.urbanadventours.com; 103 Atlantic Ave; tours $55; T Aquarium) Founded by avid cyclists who believe the best views of Boston are from a bicycle. The City View Ride provides a great overview of how to get around by bike, but there are other specialty tours such as Bikes at Night and the Emerald Necklace tour.

Boat Tours

Boston Green Cruises (Map p236; www.bostongreen-cruises.com; 60 Rowes Wharf; adult/child from $28/24; T Aquarium or South Station) See the sights and hear the sounds of the city from Boston's first super quiet, zero-emissions electric boat. Spend an hour floating in the Boston Harbor or cruising on the River Charles (or upgrade to a 90-minute combo trip for $39/35 per adult/child).

Boston Duck Tours (Map p244; 617-267-3825; www.bostonducktours.com; adult/child $36/25; T Aquarium, Science Park or Prudential) These ridiculously popular tours use WWII amphibious vehicles that cruise the downtown streets before splashing into the Charles River. The 80-minute tours depart from the Museum of Science, the Prudential Center or the New England Aquarium. Advance reservations recommended.

Boston Harbor Cruises (Map p236; www.boston-harborcruises.com; 1 Long Wharf; adult/child $25/21; T Aquarium) Boston Harbor Cruises offers a slew of options for those who want to get out on the water, such as a Historic Sightseeing Tour around the Inner Harbor. The Charles River & Locks Tour is a 90-minute loop around the whole of the Shawmut Peninsula. Other special events include a Mother's Day brunch cruise and summer fireworks cruises (prices vary).

Trolley Tours

Overheard on a Duck Tour: 'Trolleys can go in the water, too...once.' Nonetheless, trolley tours offer great flexibility because you can hop off at sites along the route and hop on the next trolley that comes along. All trolleys offer discounts for online purchase.

Upper Deck Trolley Tours (Map p236; www.bostonsupertours.com; basic adult/child $29/14, premium $39/20; 🖭; 🚇Aquarium) Super-tall trolleys give passengers a view over the traffic. This is the only trolley tour that goes to Cambridge. The premium ticket – which is good for three days – includes a ride on the Super Duck Splash, admission to a few museums, plus the Hahvahd Tour.

Old Town Trolley Tours (Map p236; www.historictours. com; Long Wharf; adult/child $41/20; 🖭; 🚇Aquarium) Save 10% when you book online. From November to March,

this ticket will get you into the Boston Tea Party Museum free of charge.

Ghosts & Gravestones (Map p236; www.ghost-sandgravestones.com; Long Wharf; adult/child $36/23; 🖭; 🚇Aquarium) A hair-raising tour telling tales of Boston's darker side, hosted by a cursed gravedigger.

Walking Tours

The granddaddy of walking tours in Boston is the Freedom Trail, a 2½-mile trail that traverses the city from the Boston Common to Charlestown. Most of the companies listed here lead tours of the Freedom Trail, as does the **National Park Service** (www.nps.gov/bost). Tours that focus on a particular neighborhood are covered in their respective neighborhood sections.

Boston by Foot (www.bostonbyfoot.com; adult/child $15/10; 🖭) This fantastic nonprofit offers 90-minute walking tours, with neighborhood-specific walks and specialty theme tours like Literary Landmarks, the Dark Side of Boston and Boston for Little Feet – a kid-friendly version of the Freedom Trail.

Photo Walks (☎617-851-2273; www.photowalks.com; adult/youth $40/20; 🖭) A

walking tour combined with a photography lesson. Different routes cover Boston's most photogenic neighborhoods.

Freedom Trail Foundation (Map p234; www. thefreedomtrail.org; adult/child $14/8; 🖭; 🚇Park) This educational nonprofit group leads excellent tours of the Freedom Trail, broken up into bite-size portions (eg Boston Common to Faneuil Hall, North End). Frequent departures from Faneuil Hall and Boston Common make this a convenient option. Tour guides are in period costume, for whatever that's worth.

On Location Tours (www. screentours.com; tours $23) It's not Hollywood, but Boston has hosted its share of famous movie scenes. More than 30 films were shot along Boston's Movie Mile, which you will see on this 90-minute walking tour. For even more movie madness, the company offers a three-hour bus tour that visits 40-plus sites.

Boston Chocolate Tours (www.bostonchocolatetours. com; tours $48) If you believe that 'the best things in life are chocolate,' then pick a neighborhood and let the experts show you where you can sate your craving.

Directory A–Z

Customs Regulations

For up-to-date information, see www.cbp.gov.

➡ **Personal Exemptions** Each traveler is permitted to bring up to $800 worth of merchandise into the US without incurring any duty, assuming they have been out of the country for at least 48 hours.

➡ **Alcohol & Tobacco** Each visitor is allowed to bring 1L of liquor and 200 cigarettes duty-free into the US, but you must be at least 21 and 18 years of age, respectively.

Discount Cards

Thanks to its student-heavy population, Boston is one of the few US cities that usually offers students discounted admission, so bring your student ID and always inquire. Other programs that offer discounted admission to area museums and attractions:

Go Select Boston Pass (www.smartdestinations.com) Pick a package or design your own, choosing two or more sites from the 46 included options. You have 30 days to use your pass, which usually guarantees a savings of 20%.

Boston City Pass (www.citypass.com; adult/child $54/39) Includes admission to five popular spots: Museum of Fine Arts, Museum of Science, New England Aquarium and Skywalk Observatory, and either the Old State House or the Harvard Museum of Natural History. You have nine days to use your tickets. It makes for a busy week, but if you use them all, you'll save $47.

Go Boston Card (www.smartdestinations.com; pass adult/child 1-day $48/32, 3-day $88/72, 7-day $148/112) This card allows unlimited admission to 49 Boston-area attractions, including most museums, tours and historic sites. Also offers discounts at local restaurants and shops. The card is good for any number of days (from one to seven, depending on what you pay), so squeeze in as much as you can to get your money's worth. In reality, you would need a pretty ambitious itinerary to make this worthwhile.

Emergency

Ambulance, Fire & Police (☑911)

PRACTICALITIES

➡ **Currency** The US dollar ($) is divided into 100 cents. Coins come in denominations of 1¢ (penny), 5¢ (nickel), 10¢ (dime), 25¢ (quarter) and the rare 50¢ piece (half-dollar). Banknotes come in $1, $2, $5, $10, $20, $50 and $100 denominations.

➡ **Radio** Boston is blessed with two public radio stations – WGBH (89.7FM) and WBUR (90.9FM) – broadcasting news, classical music and radio shows. For sports talk radio all the time, tune into 850AM. Out of Emerson College, WERS plays 'music for independent minds' at 88.9FM.

➡ **Smoking** No smoking in Boston hotels, restaurants or bars.

➡ **Weights & Measures** US customary units are based on imperial units, measuring distance by mile, weight by pound and volume by pint, quart or gallon.

Electricity

120V/60Hz

Gay & Lesbian Travelers

Out and active gay communities are visible all around Boston, especially in the South End and Jamaica Plain. Stop by **Calamus Bookstore** (Map p242; www.calamusbooks.com; 92 South St; ⊙9am-7pm Mon-Sat, noon-6pm Sun; ⊤South Station), which is an excellent source of information about community events and organizations.

There is no shortage of entertainment options catering to LGBT travelers. From drag shows to dyke nights, this sexually diverse community has something for everybody.

The biggest event of the year for the Boston gay and lesbian community is June's **Boston Pride** (⊘617-262-9405; www.bostonpride.org), a week of parades, parties, festivals and flag-raisings.

Other excellent sources of information for the gay and lesbian community:

Bay Windows (www.baywindows.com) A weekly newspaper

for LGBTQ readers. The print edition is distributed throughout New England, but the website is also an excellent source of news and information.

EDGE Boston (www.edgeboston.com) The Boston branch of the nationwide network of publications offering news and entertainment for LGBT readers. Includes a nightlife section with culture and club reviews.

Internet Access

Most hotels and hostels offer internet access in one way or another. Usually that means wireless access, though some hotels also have an on-site business center or internet corner that provides computers. Aside from hotels, wi-fi is common in cafes, on buses and even in public spaces like shopping malls and airports.

Boston Public Library (www.bpl.org; 700 Boylston St; ⊙9am-9pm Mon-Thu, to 5pm Fri & Sat year-round, 1-5pm Sun Oct-May; 🛜; ⊤Copley) Internet access free for 15-minute intervals. Or get a visitor courtesy card at the circulation desk and sign up for one hour of free terminal time. Arrive first thing in the morning to avoid long waits.

Cambridge Public Library (www.cambridgema.gov/cpl; 449 Broadway; ⊙9am-9pm Mon-Thu, to 5pm Fri & Sat; 🛜; ⊤Harvard) The sparkling new glass library has dozens of zippy computers that are free to the public. It's busy, so you may have to wait your turn.

Wired Puppy (www.wiredpuppy.com; 250 Newbury St; ⊙6:30am-7:30pm; 🛜; ⊤Hynes) Free wireless access and free computer use in case you don't have your own. This is also a comfortable, cozy place to just come and drink coffee.

Money

ATMs

Automatic teller machines (ATMs) are great for quick cash and can negate the need for traveler's checks entirely, but watch out for ATM surcharges. Most banks in Boston charge at least $2.50 per withdrawal. Look for ATMs outside banks and in large grocery stores, shopping centers and gas stations.

Changing Money

If you are carrying foreign currency, it can be exchanged for US dollars at Logan International Airport. Bank outlets around the city are not so reliable about offering currency exchange, but this service is provided at any full-service branch of the **Bank of America** (www.bankofamerica.com).

Credit Cards

Major credit cards are accepted at hotels, restaurants, gas stations, shops and car-rental agencies. In fact, you'll find it hard to perform certain transactions, such as renting cars or purchasing concert tickets, without one. Some small B&Bs and family-owned shops and restaurants may not accept credit cards. Visa and MasterCard are the most widely accepted.

Tipping

Many members of the service industry depend on tips to earn a living. Servers and bartenders, in particular, get paid less than minimum wage in the US, so tips constitute their wages. Use the following guidelines for tipping your service providers:

➡ **Baggage carriers** $1 to $2 per bag.

➡ **Bar & restaurant staff** 20% for good service, 15% for adequate service; any less than 15% indicates dissatisfaction with the service.

➡ **Housekeeping** $3 to $5 for one or two nights, more for longer stays.

➡ **Taxi drivers** 10% to 15% of the fare.

Traveler's Checks

Traveler's checks offer protection from theft and loss. Most companies now offer a convenient Traveler's Check Card, a prepaid card that is not linked to a bank account. For refunds on lost or stolen traveler's checks or cards, call **American Express** (☑800-221-7282; www.americanexpress.com) or **Thomas Cook** (☑01733-224-800; www.thomascook.com). Keeping a record of check numbers and those you have used is vital for replacing lost checks, so keep your records separate from the checks themselves. Traveler's checks are as good as cash in the US, but only if they are in US dollars.

Newspapers & Magazines

Boston Globe (www.boston.com) One of two major daily newspapers, the *Globe* publishes an extensive Calendar section every Thursday and the daily Sidekick, both of which include entertainment options.

Boston Herald (www.bostonherald.com) The more right-wing daily, competing with the *Globe;* has its own entertainment section on Friday.

Boston Magazine (www.bostonmagazine.com) The city's monthly glossy magazine.

Improper Bostonian (www.improper.com) A sassy biweekly distributed free from sidewalk dispenser boxes.

Opening Hours

➡ **Banks** 8:30am to 4pm Monday to Friday; sometimes to 6pm on Friday and/or 9am to noon on Saturday.

➡ **Bars & Clubs** Open to midnight daily, and often stay open to 1am or 2am on Friday and Saturday nights.

➡ **Businesses** 9am to 5pm Monday to Friday.

➡ **Restaurants** 11am or 11:30am to 9pm or 10pm; restaurants serving breakfast open from 7am; some places close from 2:30pm to 5:30pm.

➡ **Shops** From 10am or 11am until 7pm Monday to Saturday; sometimes noon to 5pm Sunday. Major shopping areas and malls keep extended hours.

Public Holidays

New Year's Day January 1

Martin Luther King Jr's Birthday Third Monday in January

Washington's Birthday Third Monday in February

Evacuation Day March 17

Patriot's Day Third Monday in April

Memorial Day Last Monday in May

Bunker Hill Day June 17

Independence Day July 4

Labor Day First Monday in September

Columbus Day Second Monday in October

Veterans Day November 11

Thanksgiving Day Fourth Thursday in November

Christmas Day December 25

Safe Travel

As with most big US cities, there are run-down sections of Boston in which crime is a problem. These are primarily in Roxbury, Mattapan and Dorchester (where tourist attractions are limited). Parts of the South End border Roxbury, as does Jamaica Plain.

➡ In the South End, avoid areas southeast of Harrison Ave and southwest of Massachusetts Ave after dark.

➡ In Jamaica Plain, stay on the west side of Hyde Park Ave, Washington St and Columbus Ave at night.

➡ Avoid parks such as Franklin Park and the Back Bay Fens after dark. The same goes for streets and subway stations that are otherwise empty of people.

Taxes & Refunds

The state of Massachusetts charges a 6.5% sales tax on all items that are not considered necessities. Foodies and fashionistas will be happy to hear that food (purchased from a store, not a restaurant) and clothing (up to $175) are indeed considered necessities!

In addition to the 6.5% sales tax, hotel rooms are subject to a 14.45% tax in Boston and Cambridge (which includes a city and state hotel tax, as well as a convention center tax). B&Bs with three rooms or fewer are exempt from this tax.

Telephone
Cell Phones

The US uses a variety of cell-phone systems, most of which are incompatible with the GSM 900/1800 standard used throughout Europe and Asia. The main cell-phone companies that have extensive coverage in Boston and around New England are AT&T, Sprint and Verizon, which have outlets around Boston.

Phone Codes

All US phone numbers consist of a three-digit area code followed by a seven-digit local number. Even if you are calling locally, you must dial all 10 digits. If you are calling long distance, dial ☑1 + area code + seven-digit number.

➡ **Area codes** Boston 🖉617; suburban Boston 🖉781; North Shore 🖉978; South Shore 🖉508

➡ **Country code** 🖉1 for USA

➡ **International dialing code** 🖉011

Time

Boston is on Eastern Standard Time, five hours behind Greenwich Mean Time. When it's noon in Boston, it's:

➡ 9am in San Francisco

➡ 5pm in London

➡ 9pm in Moscow

➡ 2am in Tokyo

➡ 4am in Melbourne

This region observes daylight saving time from the second Sunday in March until the first Sunday in November.

Tourist Information

Boston Common Information Kiosk (GBCVB Visitors Center; Map p234; www.bostonusa.com; Boston Common; ⊙8:30am-5pm; Ⓣ Park St) Starting point for the Freedom Trail and many other walking tours.

Boston Harbor Islands Pavilion (Map p236; www.bostonharborislands.org; Rose Kennedy Greenway; ⊙9am-5pm May-Oct; 🕾; Ⓣ Aquarium) Ideally located on the Rose Kennedy Greenway, this information center will tell you everything you need to know to plan your visit to the Boston Harbor Islands. Don't miss the nearby Harbor Fog Sculpture, which immerses passers-by in the sounds and sensations of the harbor.

Cambridge Visitor Information Kiosk (Map p250; www.cambridge-usa.org; Harvard Sq; ⊙9am-5pm Mon-Fri, 1-5pm Sat & Sun; Ⓣ Harvard) Detailed information on current Cambridge happenings and self-guided walking tours.

Massachusetts Office of Travel & Tourism (🖉617-973-8500; www.massvacation.com) Information about events and activities throughout the state, including an excellent guide to green tourism and resources especially for gay and lesbian travelers.

National Park Service Visitors Center (NPS; Map p236; www.nps.gov/bost; Faneuil Hall; ⊙9am-6pm; Ⓣ State) The brand new NPS Visitors Center has loads of information about the Freedom Trail sights. This is also the starting point for the free **NPS Freedom Trail Tour** (⊙10am & 2pm Apr-Oct; Ⓣ State). There is an additional NPS Visitors Center at the Charlestown Navy Yard.

Travelers with Disabilities

Boston attempts to cater to residents and visitors with disabilities by providing cut curbs, accessible restrooms and ramps on public buildings; but old streets, sidewalks and buildings mean that facilities are not always up to snuff.

➡ **Sights** Most major museums are accessible by wheelchair, while the Isabella Stewart Gardner Museum, the Museum of Fine Arts and the Museum of Science offer special programs and tours for travelers with disabilities.

➡ **Activities** Many tours use vehicles that are wheelchair accessible, including Boston Duck Tours and New England Aquarium Whale Watch. Walking tours like the Freedom Trail and the student tour of Harvard Yard are also accessible, though the historic buildings may not be.

➡ **Transportation** MBTA buses and commuter trains are accessible, although not all subway trains and stations are. See MBTA Accessibility (www.mbta.com/accessibility) for more information. Ferries to the Boston Harbor Islands, Provincetown and Salem are all accessible.

Visas

➡ Check with the US State Dept for updates and details on entry requirements.

➡ The Visa Waiver Program (VWP) allows nationals from 36 countries (including most EU countries, Japan, Australia and New Zealand) to enter the US without a visa for up to 90 days.

➡ VWP visitors require a machine-readable passport and approval under the Electronic System for Travel Authorization (ESTA) at least three days before arrival. There is a $14 fee for processing and authorization (payable online). Once approved, the registration is valid for two years.

➡ In essence, ESTA requires that you register specific information online (name, address, passport info etc). You will receive one of three responses: 'Authorization Approved' (this usually comes within minutes; most applicants can expect to receive this response); 'Authorization Pending' (you'll need to check the status within the next 72 hours); or 'Travel not Authorized.' If this is the case, it means you will need to apply for a visa.

➡ Those who need a visa – ie anyone staying longer than 90 days, or from a non-VWP country – should apply at the US consulate in their home country.

➡ Canadians are exempt from the process. They do not need visas, though they do need a passport or document approved by the Western Hemisphere Travel Initiative.

Behind the Scenes

SEND US YOUR FEEDBACK

We love to hear from travelers – your comments keep us on our toes and help make our books better. Our well-traveled team reads every word on what you loved or loathed about this book. Although we cannot reply individually to your submissions, we always guarantee that your feedback goes straight to the appropriate authors, in time for the next edition. Each person who sends us information is thanked in the next edition – and the most useful submissions are rewarded with a selection of digital PDF chapters.

Visit **lonelyplanet.com/contact** to submit your updates and suggestions or to ask for help. Our award-winning website also features inspirational travel stories, news and discussions.

Note: We may edit, reproduce and incorporate your comments in Lonely Planet products such as guidebooks, websites and digital products, so let us know if you don't want your comments reproduced or your name acknowledged. For a copy of our privacy policy visit lonelyplanet.com/privacy.

OUR READERS

Many thanks to the travelers who used the last edition and wrote to us with helpful hints, useful advice and interesting anecdotes:

Anna Cartier, Damien Vacheron, David Price, Friederike Haberstroh, Katja Daniel, Kersten Heineke, Peter Watkins, Steve Gustus.

AUTHOR THANKS
Mara Vorhees

Thanks, weather gods, for the unprecedented snowfall while I was researching and writing this book (105 inches and counting). Thanks also to the Somerville school system, for closing schools at every possible opportunity. And thanks (for real) to our neighbor Kenny for fixing our heater when the professionals could not. Despite the challenges, it's always a treat to write about my adopted home town... even in winter.

ACKNOWLEDGMENTS

Cover photograph: Rose Kennedy Greenway with view of the Custom House tower; Mark Hunt/Corbis.

THIS BOOK

This 6th edition of Lonely Planet's *Boston* guidebook was researched and written by Mara Vorhees, who also wrote the previous two editions. This guidebook was produced at Lonely Planet by the following:

Destination Editor Dora Whitaker
Product Editors Paul Harding, Briohny Hooper
Senior Cartographer Alison Lyall
Book Designer Mazzy Prinsep
Assisting Editors Victoria Harrison, Jodie Martire, Saralinda Turner

Cover Researcher Naomi Parker

Thanks to Imogen Bannister, Sarah Billington, Carolyn Boicos, Wayne Murphy, Catherine Naghten, Martine Power, Alison Ridgway, Ellie Simpson, Luna Soo, Angela Tinson, Lauren Wellicome, Tony Wheeler

NOTES

see also separate subindexes for:

✗ **EATING P223**

🍷 **DRINKING & NIGHTLIFE P224**

☆ **ENTERTAINMENT P224**

🛍 **SHOPPING P225**

🏃 **SPORTS & ACTIVITIES P226**

🛏 **SLEEPING P226**

Index

Boston Maps

Sights

- Beach
- Bird Sanctuary
- Buddhist
- Castle/Palace
- Christian
- Confucian
- Hindu
- Islamic
- Jain
- Jewish
- Monument
- Museum/Gallery/Historic Building
- Ruin
- Shinto
- Sikh
- Taoist
- Winery/Vineyard
- Zoo/Wildlife Sanctuary
- Other Sight

Activities, Courses & Tours

- Bodysurfing
- Diving
- Canoeing/Kayaking
- Course/Tour
- Sento Hot Baths/Onsen
- Skiing
- Snorkeling
- Surfing
- Swimming/Pool
- Walking
- Windsurfing
- Other Activity

Sleeping

- Sleeping
- Camping

Eating

- Eating

Drinking & Nightlife

- Drinking & Nightlife
- Cafe

Entertainment

- Entertainment

Shopping

- Shopping

Information

- Bank
- Embassy/Consulate
- Hospital/Medical
- Internet
- Police
- Post Office
- Telephone
- Toilet
- Tourist Information
- Other Information

Geographic

- Beach
- Hut/Shelter
- Lighthouse
- Lookout
- Mountain/Volcano
- Oasis
- Park
- Pass
- Picnic Area
- Waterfall

Population

- Capital (National)
- Capital (State/Province)
- City/Large Town
- Town/Village

Transport

- Airport
- BART station
- Border crossing
- Boston T station
- Bus
- Cable car/Funicular
- Cycling
- Ferry
- Metro/Muni station
- Monorail
- Parking
- Petrol station
- Subway/SkyTrain station
- Taxi
- Train station/Railway
- Tram
- Underground station
- Other Transport

Note: Not all symbols displayed above appear on the maps in this book

Routes

- Tollway
- Freeway
- Primary
- Secondary
- Tertiary
- Lane
- Unsealed road
- Road under construction
- Plaza/Mall
- Steps
- Tunnel
- Pedestrian overpass
- Walking Tour
- Walking Tour detour
- Path/Walking Trail

Boundaries

- International
- State/Province
- Disputed
- Regional/Suburb
- Marine Park
- Cliff
- Wall

Hydrography

- River, Creek
- Intermittent River
- Canal
- Water
- Dry/Salt/Intermittent Lake
- Reef

Areas

- Airport/Runway
- Beach/Desert
- Cemetery (Christian)
- Cemetery (Other)
- Glacier
- Mudflat
- Park/Forest
- Sight (Building)
- Sportsground
- Swamp/Mangrove

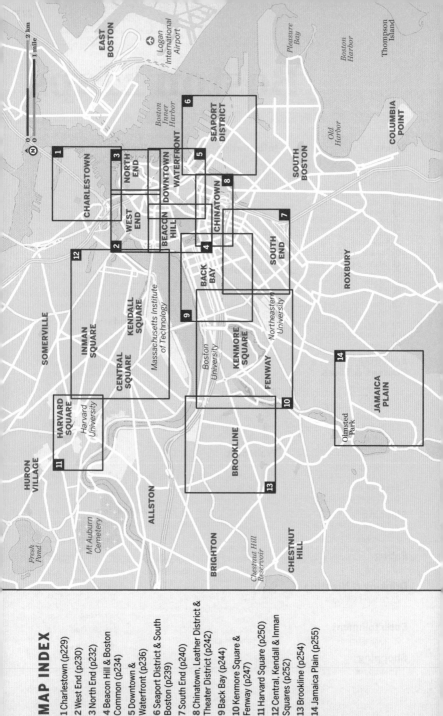

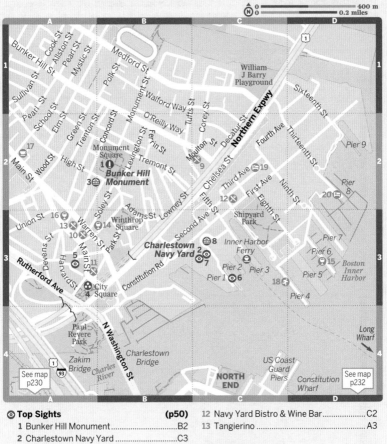

WEST END

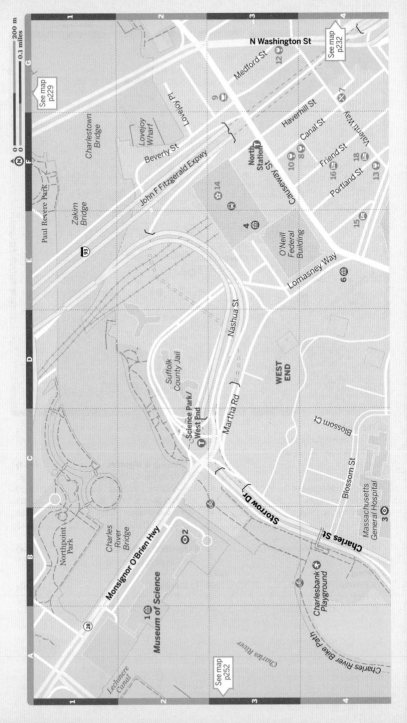

See map p229

See map p232

See map p252

N Washington St

Medford St

Lovejoy Pl

Beverly St

John F Fitzgerald Expwy

Haverhill St

Canal St

Causeway St

Valenti Way

Friend St

Portland St

North Station

O'Neill Federal Building

Lomasney Way

Nashua St

Suffolk County Jail

Science Park/ West End

Martha Rd

WEST END

Storrow Dr

Blossom Ct

Blossom St

Charles St

Massachusetts General Hospital

Charlesbank Playground

Charles River Bike Path

Monsignor O'Brien Hwy

Museum of Science

Charles River Bridge

Northpoint Park

Paul Revere Park

Charlestown Bridge

Zakim Bridge

Lovejoy Wharf

Lechmere Canal

Charles River

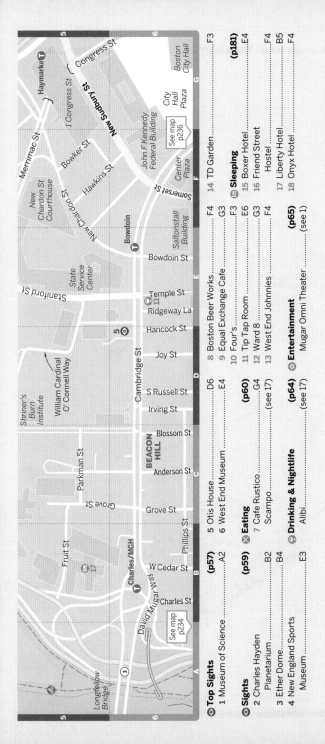

Top Sights	(p57)	14 TD Garden	F3
1 Museum of Science	A2		
		● Sleeping	(p181)
● Sights	(p59)	15 Boxer Hotel	E4
2 Charles Hayden		16 Friend Street	
Planetarium	B2	Hostel	F4
3 Ether Dome	B4	17 Liberty Hotel	B5
4 New England Sports		18 Onyx Hotel	F4
Museum	E3		

● Top Sights	(p57)	8 Boston Beer Works	F4
5 Otis House	D6	9 Equal Exchange Cafe	G3
6 West End Museum	E4	10 Four's	F3
		11 Tip Tap Room	E6
● Eating	(p60)	12 Ward 8	G3
7 Cafe Rustico	G4	13 West End Johnnies	F4
Scampo	(see 17)		
		● Entertainment	(p65)
● Drinking & Nightlife	(p64)	Mugar Omni Theater	(see 1)
Alibi	(see 17)		
Alibi	E3		

NORTH END

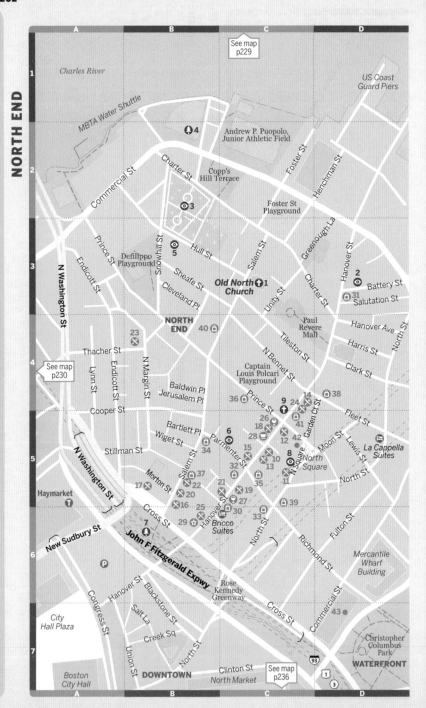

See map p229

Charles River

US Coast Guard Piers

MBTA Water Shuttle

4

Andrew P. Puopolo, Junior Athletic Field

Commercial St

Charter St

Copp's Hill Terrace

Foster St

Henchman St

3

Foster St Playground

Greenough La

Hanover St

2 Battery St

Prince St

Endicott St

N Washington St

Defilippo Playground

Snowhill St

5

Hull St

Sheafe St

Cleveland Pl

Old North Church 1

Salem St

Unity St

Charter St

Salutation St

31

Hanover Ave

Paul Revere Mall

Harris St

North St

NORTH END

40

Thacher St

23

Tileston St

Clark St

Lynn St

Endicott St

N Margin St

Baldwin Pl

Jerusalem Pl

Cooper St

Captain Louis Polcari Playground

N Bennet St

36

Prince St

14

38

9 24

Fleet St

Bartlett Pl

Parmenter St

6

26

18

41

Garden Ct St

Moon St

La Cappella Suites

Wiget St

34

28

12

42

Lewis St

Stillman St

Salem St

15

32

10

8

North Square

North St

N Washington St

Morton St

37

22

13

N Square

11

Haymarket

17

20

21

19

35

27

39

16

25

Hanover St

30

North St

Fulton St

New Sudbury St

John F Fitzgerald Expwy

29

Cross St

7

Bricco Suites

33

Richmond St

Mercantile Wharf Building

P

Hanover St

Salt La

Blackstone St

Rose Kennedy Greenway

Commercial St

43

City Hall Plaza

Congress St

Creek Sq

North St

Cross St

Christopher Columbus Park

Union St

Clinton St

North Market

WATERFRONT

Boston City Hall

DOWNTOWN

See map p236

93

1

3

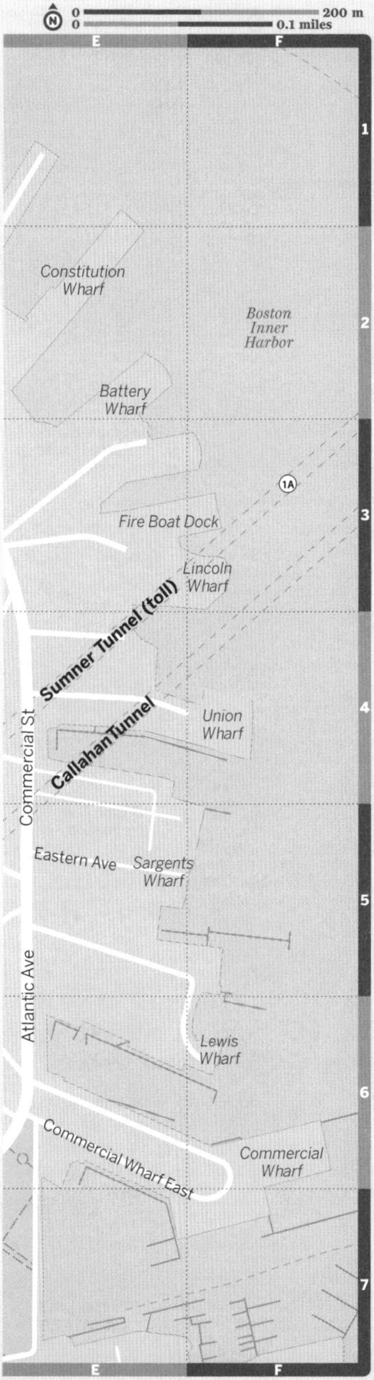

0
200 m
0
0.1 miles
E
F
1
2
3
4
5
6
7
Constitution Wharf
Boston Inner Harbor
Battery Wharf
1A
Fire Boat Dock
Lincoln Wharf
Sumner Tunnel (toll)
Union Wharf
Callahan Tunnel
Commercial St
Eastern Ave
Sargents Wharf
Atlantic Ave
Lewis Wharf
Commercial Wharf East
Commercial Wharf

Top Sights (p58)
1 Old North Church........C3

Sights (p60)
2 All Saints Way........D3
3 Copp's Hill Burying Ground........B2
4 Langone Park........B2
5 Narrowest House........B3
6 North End Branch Library........C5
7 North End Park........B6
8 Paul Revere House........C5
9 St Leonard's Church........C4

Eating (p61)
10 Carmelina's........C5
11 Carmen Trattoria........C5
12 Daily Catch........C5
13 Galleria Umberto........C5
14 Giacomo's Ristorante........C4
15 Gigi Gelateria........C5
16 Lulu's Sweet Shoppe........B5
17 Maria's Pastry........B5
18 Mike's Pastry........C5
19 Modern Pastry Shop........C5
20 Neptune Oyster........B5
21 Parla........C5
22 Pauli's........B5
23 Pizzeria Regina........B4
24 Pomodoro........C4
25 Taranta........B6

Drinking & Nightlife (p65)
26 Caffé Dello Sport........C5
27 Caffé Paradiso........C5
28 Caffé Vittoria........C5

Entertainment (p65)
29 Improv Asylum........B6

Shopping (p65)
30 Bricco Salumeria........C6
31 In-Jean-ius........D3
32 LIT Boutique........C5
33 North Bennet Street School........C6
34 Polcari's Coffee........B5
35 Salumeria Italiana........C5
36 Sedurre........C4
37 Shake the Tree........B5
38 Twilight........D4
39 V Cirace & Son, Inc........C5
40 William Carlton Workshop........B4
41 Wine Bottega........C5

Sports & Activities (p66)
42 Old Boston Tours........C5
43 Urban AdvenTours........D7

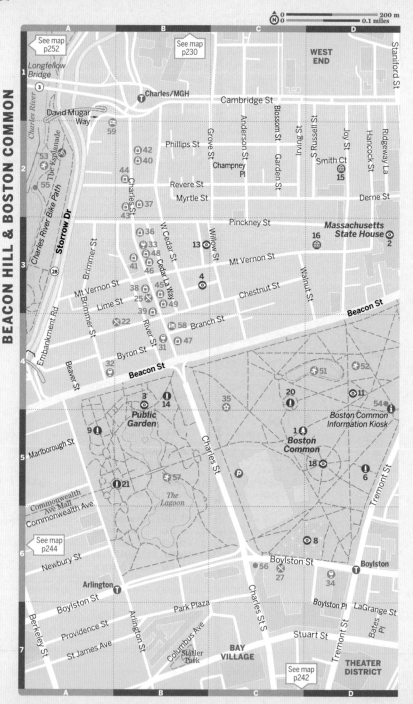

0 200 m
0 0.1 miles

See map p252

See map p230

WEST END

Staniford St

Longfellow Bridge

Charles River

Charles/MGH

Cambridge St

David Mugar Way

59

Phillips St

42
40

Grove St

Anderson St

Blossom St

Irving St

S Russell St

Joy St

Hancock St

Ridgeway La

Smith Ct

15

The Esplanade

53

55

44

Charles St

Champney Pl

Garden St

Derne St

Revere St

Myrtle St

37

43

Pinckney St

Massachusetts State House

Charles River Bike Path

Storrow Dr

36

33

48

46

41

W Cedar St

Cedar St

13

Willow St

Mt Vernon St

16

2

Brimmer St

Mt Vernon St

38

25

45

La Way

4

Chestnut St

Walnut St

Embankment Rd

Lime St

39

49

Beacon St

Brimmer St

22

River St

58

Branch St

Byron St

31

47

Beacon St

32

Beaver St

3

14

51

52

Public Garden

20

11

54

9

35

Boston Common Information Kiosk

Marlborough St

1

Boston Common

18

6

Charles St

21

57

The Lagoon

Commonwealth Ave Mall

Commonwealth Ave

See map p244

Newbury St

8

Boylston St

Boylston

56

27

34

Arlington

Boylston St

Boylston Pl

LaGrange St

Berkeley St

Providence St

St James Ave

Park Plaza

Columbus Ave

Arlington St

Statler Park

BAY VILLAGE

Charles St S

Stuart St

Tremont St

Bates Pl

THEATER DISTRICT

See map p242

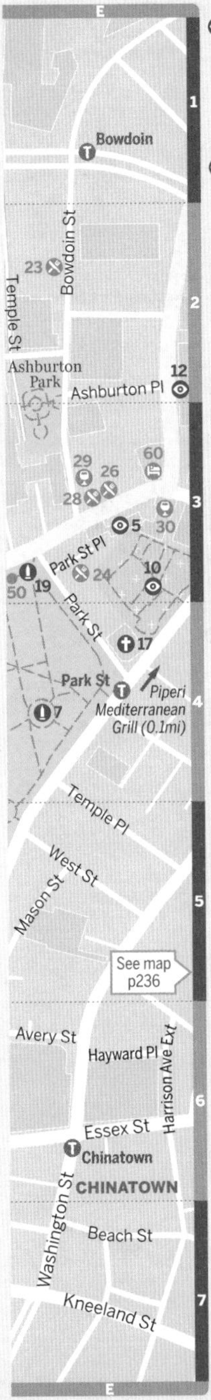

BEACON HILL & BOSTON COMMON

Bowdoin

Bowdoin St

Temple St

Ashburton
Park

Ashburton Pl

Park St Pl

Park St

Park St

Piperi
Mediterranean
Grill (0.1mi)

Temple Pl

West St

Mason St

See map
p236

Avery St

Hayward Pl

Harrison Ave Ext

Essex St

Chinatown

CHINATOWN

Washington St

Beach St

Kneeland St

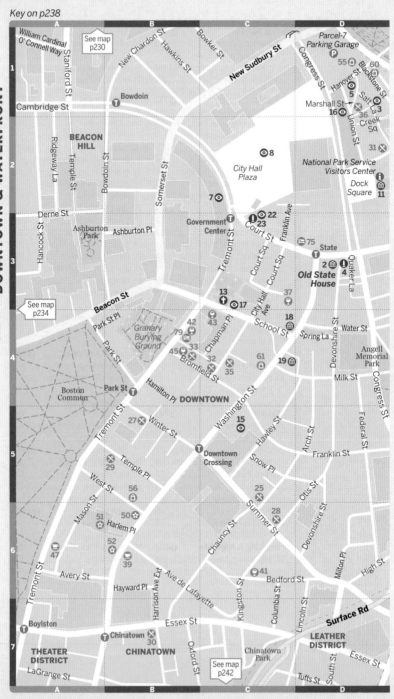

Key on p238

See map p230

William Cardinal O' Connell Way

New Chardon St

Hawkins St

Bowker St

New Sudbury St

Congress St

Parcel-7 Parking Garage

55

60

Blackstone St

Hanover St

5

Salt

Stanford St

Bowdoin

Cambridge St

Marshall St

16

36

Union St

3

Creek Sq

31

BEACON HILL

Ridgeway La

Temple St

Bowdoin St

Somerset St

City Hall Plaza

8

National Park Service Visitors Center

Dock Square

11

Derne St

Hancock St

Ashburton Park

Ashburton Pl

7

Government Center

Court St

22

23

Franklin Ave

State

75

Tremont St

Court Sq

Court Sq

Old State House

2

4

Quaker La

13

17

City Hall Ave

37

18

School St

Spring La

Water St

Devonshire St

Angell Memorial Park

Beacon St

See map p234

Park St Pl

Granary Burying Ground

42

43

Chapman Pl

79

33

45

32

35

Bromfield St

61

19

Milk St

Congress St

Boston Common

Park St

Hamilton Pl

DOWNTOWN

Washington St

Tremont St

27

Winter St

15

Hawley St

Arch St

Franklin St

Federal St

Downtown Crossing

Snow Pl

Temple Pl

29

West St

56

Mason St

50

51

Harlem Pl

52

39

25

Summer St

28

Otis St

Devonshire St

Milton Pl

High St

47

Avery St

Chauncy St

41

Bedford St

Kingston St

Columbia St

Lincoln St

Surface Rd

Hayward Pl

Ave de Lafayette

Harrison Ave Ext

Essex St

LEATHER DISTRICT

Boylston

Chinatown

30

Tremont St

THEATER DISTRICT

CHINATOWN

Oxford St

See map p242

Chinatown Park

South St

Essex St

LaGrange St

Tufts St

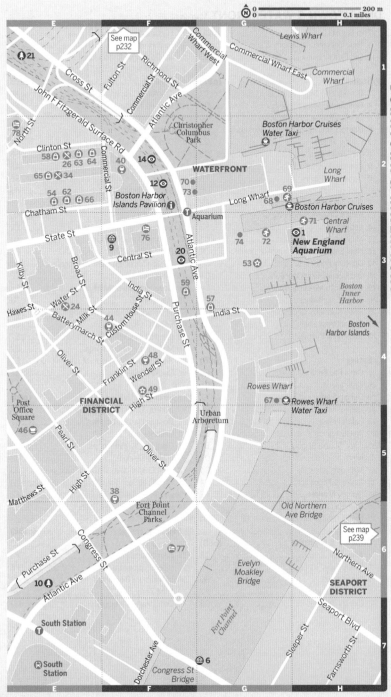

200 m
0.1 miles

See map p232

21

Lewis Wharf

Commercial Wharf West
Commercial Wharf East
Commercial Wharf

Cross St
Fulton St
Richmond St
Commercial St
Atlantic Ave

John F Fitzgerald Surface Rd

North St

78

Clinton St
58
26 63 64
40

65 34

54 62
66

Commercial St

Chatham St

Christopher Columbus Park

Boston Harbor Cruises
Water Taxi

14

WATERFRONT

Long Wharf

12

70
73

Long Wharf

69
68

Boston Harbor Cruises

Boston Harbor
Islands Pavilion

State St

Aquarium

71 Central Wharf

9

76

Central St

74

72

New England Aquarium

20

53

Boston Inner Harbor

Kilby St

Broad St

Water St

24

59

57

India St

Boston Harbor Islands

Hawes St

Batterymarch St
Milk St

India St

Custom House St

44

Oliver St

Franklin St
Wendell St

48

Rowes Wharf

High St

49

67 Rowes Wharf
Water Taxi

Post Office Square

FINANCIAL DISTRICT

Urban Arboretum

46

Pearl St

Oliver St

Matthews St

High St

38

Old Northern Ave Bridge

See map p239

Purchase St

Congress St

77

Atlantic Ave

Fort Point Channel Parks

Evelyn Moakley Bridge

Northern Ave

SEAPORT DISTRICT

10

Seaport Blvd

South Station

Fort Point Channel

Sleeper St

Farnsworth St

Dorchester Ave

South Station

6

Congress St Bridge

DOWNTOWN & WATERFRONT *Map on p236*

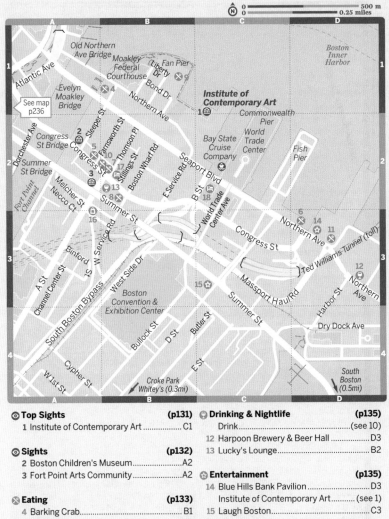

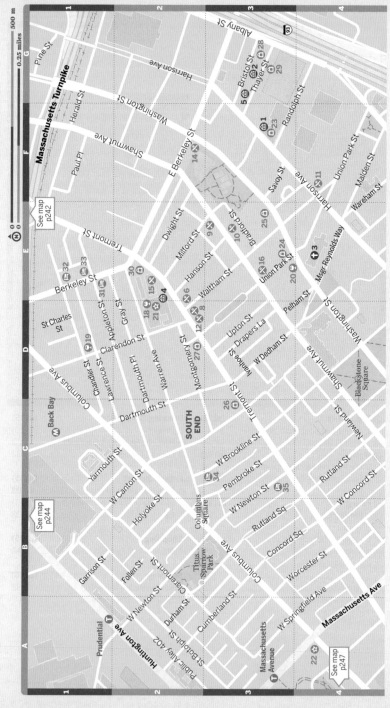

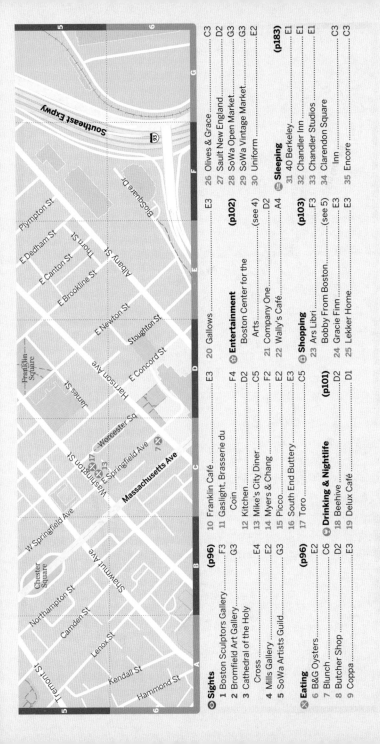

SOUTH END

◎ Sights   (p96)
1 Boston Sculptors Gallery	F3
2 Bromfield Art Gallery	G3
3 Cathedral of the Holy Cross	E4
4 Mills Gallery	E2
5 SoWa Artists Guild	G3

✕ Eating   (p96)
6 B&G Oysters	C6
7 Blunch	D2
8 Butcher Shop	E3
9 Coppa	D1
10 Franklin Café	E3
11 Gaslight, Brasserie du Coin	D2
12 Kitchen	C5
13 Mike's City Diner	F2
14 Myers & Chang	E2
15 Picco	E3
16 South End Buttery	C5
17 Toro	E2

◐ Drinking & Nightlife   (p101)
18 Beehive	D2
19 Delux Café	E3
20 Gallows	E3

✪ Entertainment   (p102)
Boston Center for the Arts	(see 4)
21 Company One	D2
22 Wally's Café	A4

⊕ Shopping   (p103)
23 Ars Libri	F3
Bobby From Boston	(see 5)
24 Gracie Finn	E3
25 Lekker Home	E3
26 Olives & Grace	C3
27 Sault New England	D2
28 SoWa Open Market	G3
29 SoWa Vintage Market	G3
30 Uniform	E2

⊘ Sleeping   (p83)
31 40 Berkeley	E1
32 Chandler Inn	E1
33 Chandler Studios	E1
34 Clarendon Square Inn	C3
35 Encore	C3

CHINATOWN, LEATHER DISTRICT & THEATER DISTRICT

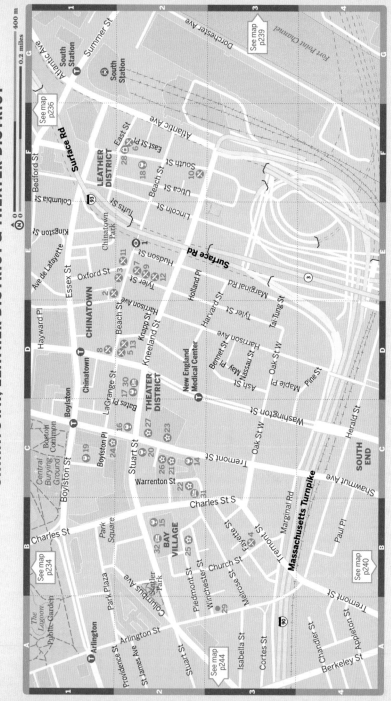

CHINATOWN, LEATHER DISTRICT & THEATER DISTRICT

BACK BAY

Key on p246

A B C D

1

Charles River

Storrow Dr

Harvard
Bridge

Charles River Bike Path

Back St

65

Storrow Dr

Beacon St

Marlborough St

Exeter St

2

Fairfield St

8

66

Hereford St

Gloucester St

Commonwealth Ave

Massachusetts Ave

Commonwealth Ave-Mall

2

50 52

41

38

23

70

54 79 Newbury St

30

BACK
BAY

20 51 42

17

53

62

36

76

48

44 40

Boylston St

27

33 56

47

Newbury St

Massachusetts Turnpike

Ring Rd

See map
p247

Hynes

Cambria St

57

Massachusetts Turnpike

16

35 63

Scotia St

43

60

Belvidere St

Dalton St

9

St Germain St

Prudential

72

Haviland St

Clearway St

69

Hemenway St

Norway St

14

75

Edgerly Rd

Burbank St

7

Reflecting Pool

71

Follen St

W Newton St

Westland Ave

Public Alley 402

St Botolph St

Durham St

Titus
Sparrow
Park

Massachusetts Ave

Huntington Ave

78

Cumberland St

Symphony Rd

St Stephens St

Symphony

Blackwood
St

Claremont St

Hemenway St

Gainsborough St

Albemarle
St

7

A B C D

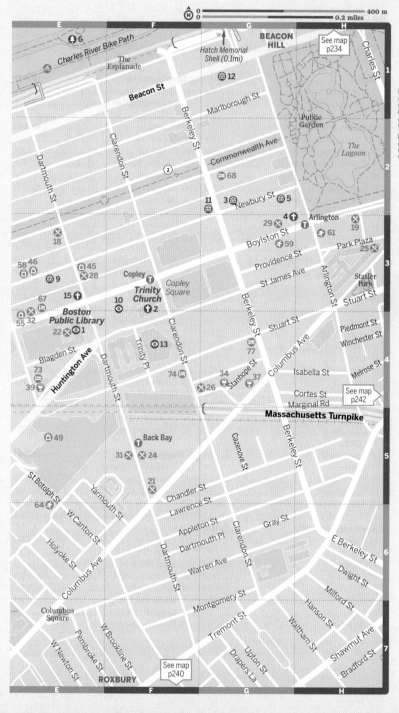

BACK BAY

See map p234

See map p242

See map p240

BEACON HILL

Charles River Bike Path

The Esplanade

Hatch Memorial Shell (0.1mi)

Beacon St

Marlborough St

Public Garden

The Lagoon

Commonwealth Ave

Newbury St

Clarendon St

Berkeley St

Dartmouth St

Arlington

Boylston St

Providence St

St James Ave

Park Plaza

Statler Park

Stuart St

Copley

Trinity Church

Copley Square

Boston Public Library

Clarendon St

Berkeley St

Stuart St

Columbus Ave

Piedmont St

Winchester St

Isabella St

Melrose St

Blagden St

Huntington Ave

Dartmouth St

Trinity Pl

Cortes St

Marginal Rd

Massachusetts Turnpike

Back Bay

St Botolph St

Yarmouth St

Cazenove Ave

Berkeley St

Chandler St

Lawrence St

W Canton St

Appleton St

Gray St

E Berkeley St

Holyoke St

Columbus Ave

Dartmouth Pl

Dartmouth St

Clarendon St

Warren Ave

Dwight St

Milford St

Hanson St

Columbus Square

W Brookline St

Montgomery St

Tremont St

Waltham St

Shawmut Ave

W Newton St

Pembroke St

Drapers La

Upton St

Bradford St

ROXBURY

BACK BAY *Map on p244*

KENMORE SQUARE & FENWAY *Map on p248*

KENMORE SQUARE & FENWAY

Key on p247

KENMORE SQUARE & FENWAY

Charles River

Soldier's Field Playground

Essex St

Soldiers Field Rd

Storrow Dr

7

Commonwealth Ave

Boston University

Grandy St

Sherborn St

Bay State Rd

Dummer St

BU Central

Babbit St

BU East

Blandford

Commonwealth Ave

Lenox St

90

Cummington St

Beacon St

Mason St

Prescott St

Euston St

St Mary's St

Mountfort St

Massachusetts Turnpike

2

See map p254

Chilton St

Ivy St

Arundel St

9

Overland St

21

Armory Playground

Churchill St

St Mary's

Keswick St

Aberdeen St

Miner St

Munson St

Burlington Ave

Brookline Ave

Yawkey Way

St Mary's

Fenway

Beacon St

St Mary's St

Monmouth St

Fullerton St

Carlton St

16

Borland St

Hawes St

Park Dr

Kilmarnock St

10

Chatham St

Muddy River

12

11

Beech Rd

Pilgrim Rd

28

Colchester St

Back Bay Fens

Queensberry St

Short St

The Fenway

Longwood

Deaconess Rd

Brookline Ave

Binney St

Blackfan Circle

Ave Louis Pasteur

Isabella Stewart Gardner Museum 2

Riverway

Netherlands Rd

Binney St

Longwood Ave

Palace Rd

Evans Way

LONGWOOD

6

Parkway Rd

Shattuck St

Longwood Medical Area

Vining St

Francis St

Fenwood Rd

Huntington Ave

McGreevey Way

Vancouver St

Tremont St

Alphonsus St

Smith St

Horadan Way

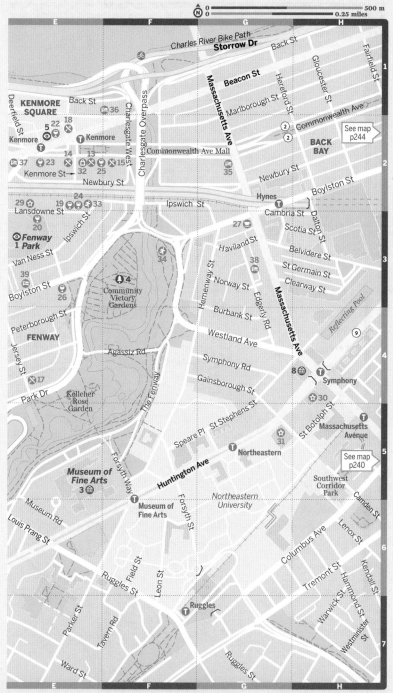

0   500 m
0   0.25 miles

Charles River Bike Path
Storrow Dr
Back St

KENMORE
SQUARE
Back St
Kenmore
Beacon St
Massachusetts Ave
Marlborough St
Hereford St
Gloucester St
Fairfield St
Commonwealth Ave
See map
p244
BACK
BAY
Kenmore
Commonwealth Ave Mall
Newbury St
Boylston St
Kenmore St
Newbury St
Charlesgate Overpass
Charlesgate West
Hynes
Ipswich St
Cambria St
Scotia St
Dalton St
Lansdowne St
Ipswich St
Haviland St
Belvidere St
St Germain St
Clearway St
⊙ **Fenway**
Park
Van Ness St
Hemenway St
Norway St
Edgerly Rd
Reflecting Pool
Boylston St
Community
Victory
Gardens
Burbank St
Westland Ave
Peterborough St
FENWAY
Agassiz Rd
Symphony Rd
Gainsborough St
Symphony
Jersey St
Park Dr
Kelleher
Rose
Garden
The Fenway
Speare Pl
St Stephens St
St Botolph St
**Massachusetts
Avenue**
Northeastern
See map
p240
Forsyth Way
**Museum of
Fine Arts**
Huntington Ave
Museum of
Fine Arts
Forsyth St
Northeastern
University
Southwest
Corridor
Park
Camden St
Museum Rd
Louis Prang St
Ruggles St
Field St
Leon St
Columbus Ave
Lenox St
Tremont St
Hammond St
Kendall St
Parker St
Tavern Rd
Ruggles
Warwick St
Westminster
Ward St
Ruggles St

HARVARD SQUARE

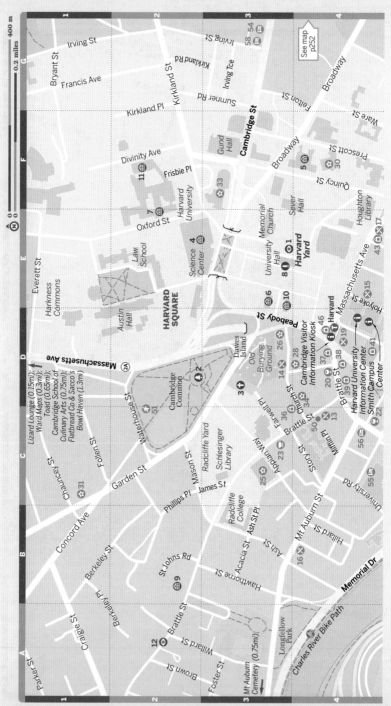

CENTRAL, KENDALL & INMAN SQUARES

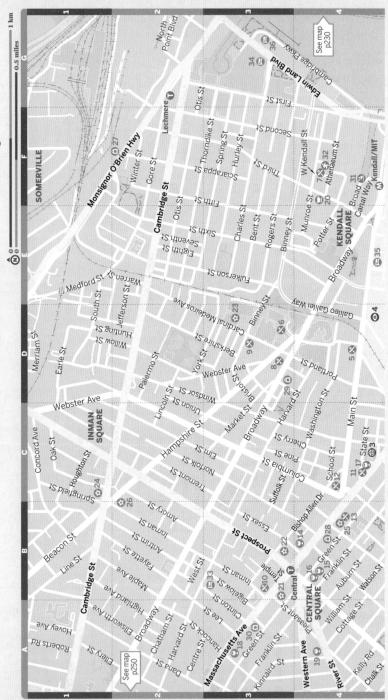

CENTRAL, KENDALL & INMAN SQUARES

BROOKLINE

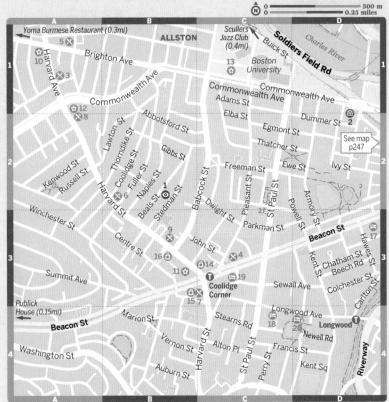

JAMAICA PLAIN

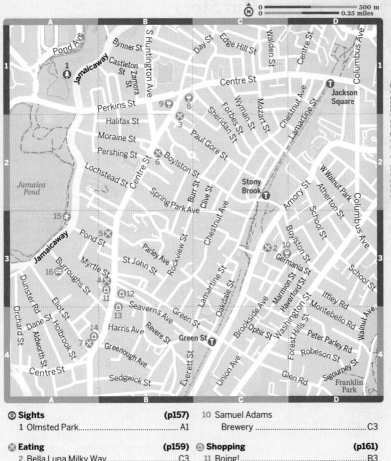

Our Story

A beat-up old car, a few dollars in the pocket and a sense of adventure. In 1972 that's all Tony and Maureen Wheeler needed for the trip of a lifetime – across Europe and Asia overland to Australia. It took several months, and at the end – broke but inspired – they sat at their kitchen table writing and stapling together their first travel guide, *Across Asia on the Cheap*. Within a week they'd sold 1500 copies. Lonely Planet was born.

Today, Lonely Planet has offices in Franklin, London, Melbourne, Oakland, Beijing and Delhi, with more than 600 staff and writers. We share Tony's belief that 'a great guidebook should do three things: inform, educate and amuse'.

Our Writer

Mara Vorhees

Born and raised in St Clair Shores, Michigan, Mara traveled the world (if not the universe) before finally settling in the Hub. She spent several years pushing papers and tapping keys at Harvard University, but has since embraced the life of a full-time travel writer, covering destinations as diverse as Russia and Belize. She lives in a pink house in Somerville, Massachusetts, with her husband, two kiddies and two kitties. She is often seen eating doughnuts in Union Square and pedaling her bike along the Charles River. The pen-wielding traveler is the author of Lonely Planet's *New England* and *New England's Best Trips*, among other titles. Follow her adventures online at www.havetwinswilltravel.com.

Read more about Mara at:
https://auth.lonelyplanet.com/profiles/mvorhees

Published by Lonely Planet Publications Pty Ltd
ABN 36 005 607 983
6th edition – Nov 2015
ISBN 978 1 74321 006 2
© Lonely Planet 2015   Photographs © as indicated 2015
10 9 8 7 6 5 4 3 2 1
Printed in China